Apr. 2, 2017

So Long for Now

For Diane Albert
With deepest Thanks.

[signature]

So Long for Now

A SAILOR'S LETTERS FROM
THE USS *FRANKLIN*

Jerry L. Rogers

Foreword by Robert M. Utley

University of Oklahoma Press : Norman

Poem excerpts in chapters 4, 10, and 12 were published in Bishop D. McKendree, *Barbed Wire and Rice: Poems and Songs from Japanese Prisoner-of-War Camps* (Ithaca, NY: Cornell University, East Asia Program, 1995), and are quoted here with permission.

Library of Congress Cataloging-in-Publication Data

Names: Rogers, Elden Duane, 1926–1945, author. | Rogers, Jerry L., 1938– editor.
Title: So long for now : a sailor's letters from the USS Franklin / Jerry L. Rogers.
Other titles: Sailor's letters from the USS Franklin
Description: Norman, OK : University of Oklahoma Press, [2017] | Includes bibliographical references and index.
Identifiers: LCCN 2016035947 | ISBN 9780806156323 (hardcover : alk. paper)
Subjects: LCSH: Rogers, Elden, 1926–1945. | Franklin (Aircraft carrier) | Sailors—United States—Correspondence. | World War, 1939–1945—Campaigns—Pacific Ocean. | World War, 1939–1945—Naval operations, American. | Sailors—United States—Biography. | Rogers family. | World War, 1939–1945—Personal narratives, American. | Vega (Tex.)—Biography.
Classification: LCC D774.F7 R65 2017 | DDC 940.54/5973092 [B] —dc23
LC record available at https://lccn.loc.gov/2016035947

To those who work for peace

THE VETERAN AND THE HISTORIAN

I wonder what he thinks, the old Vet
Whom I have troubled for an interview
And asked so little.

Burbling, bumbling, indirect, I look
Into eyes that have seen what I long to know
And go silent.

Does he see a fool, or hear my silence
Whisper humility,
Shout respect?

—JERRY L. ROGERS
October 11, 2011

CONTENTS

ILLUSTRATIONS

FOREWORD

ROBERT M. UTLEY

I have known Jerry Rogers, both personally and professionally, for more than half a century. From the first, I have also known of his deep feeling for his older brother Elden, a sailor killed in World War II. Jerry had the letters his brother wrote home, as well as those his parents wrote Elden. Elden's letters, however, told nothing of where he was or what he was doing. Strict navy censorship reduced his letters to so little that about the only information they communicated was that he was still alive. He was permitted to let his parents know he served on the aircraft carrier USS *Franklin*, a sister ship of the *Yorktown*. Newspaper accounts sometimes referred to the *Franklin*, so they knew he was somewhere in the Pacific theater. When within sight of the Japanese home islands in 1945, a Japanese dive-bomber damaged the ship so badly she almost sank. Elden's fate remained unknown until the dreaded telegram from the Navy Department reached his home in little Vega, Texas, in the Panhandle near Amarillo.

During all those years, I knew that Jerry longed to learn the whole story, both of the *Franklin* and of life in his hometown during the war. The latter consisted mainly of what his parents wrote to Elden and his own memory as a youth entering first grade when Elden was killed.

I was only dimly aware that Jerry was applying his skill as a historian to the task of researching the matter, but I did not know how thorough—and how personal—was the quest, both in official records in the National Archives and through interviews with veterans of the war and older residents of Vega who could tell him about life there during the war and relate stories about many of the residents. How he achieved such success while pursuing his distinguished career in the National Park Service is a story in itself. As a historian myself, and as an author who reconciled my own research and writing with a career in the National Park Service, I know it was a daunting task.

I suspect that Jerry pursued this decades-long project mainly for his own understanding of his brother's life after enlisting in the navy in 1944. I doubt that he thought much about sharing it with any but family and close personal friends. When finally finished, however, he surely recognized that it had the potential to contribute significantly not only to family history but also to the history of the war. A few inquiries caught the attention of editors at the University of Oklahoma Press, an appropriate venue. The result is this book, the title drawn from the parting line of many of Elden's letters.

Jerry's thorough research into the history of the Pacific War and his day-by-day record of what was happening to and aboard the *Franklin* allows him to speculate plausibly on where and what Elden was doing. This exhaustive account of a *Franklin* sailor is an important contribution to the history of the naval war in the Pacific.

Likewise, his recounting of wartime life in small-town Vega reaches beyond just the citizens to tell of the many wartime sacrifices the people back home endured. I lived a similar wartime boyhood in a small Indiana town like Vega. The chapters devoted to this subject brought back many memories, and doubtless older readers of this book will enjoy the same experience.

In short, *So Long for Now* is a significant contribution to the history both of the war overseas and of the people back home. Besides, it is an eminently readable narrative.

PREFACE

I have waited too long to do this work. My parents, who would have gotten the most from it, are gone. Others who would best understand it because they participated in the war or lived in a small town in the 1940s are rapidly going. Yet kinship and a residue of grief require that it be done.

Seaman Second Class Elden Duane Rogers was in the U.S. Navy for a year and two days, from March 17, 1944, until his death on his nineteenth birthday, March 19, 1945. The navy told him to write to friends and family as often as he could. It would keep them from worrying so much, and it would help stave off the homesickness that could interfere with a sailor's focus upon his work. So write the folks often, the navy said; just don't say where you are, where you have been, or where you are going. Don't tell what you are doing, or what has been happening in your daily life—don't even write about the weather. The enemy was believed to have an extensive spy network, and in the wrong hands a letter containing any of these details could put mighty ships and even fleets at risk.

Elden's family, which grew after his death to include another brother, Elvin D. Rogers, has long possessed a body of correspondence (now in the possession of Barbara Rogers of Lubbock, Texas, and the author) that resulted from the navy's encouragement. A reader who with great anticipation extracts such letters from the envelopes that have enclosed them for seven decades, thinking of the poignant and intensely human dramas contained in similar letters from soldiers in the Civil War, is doomed to disappointment. Because of the rules of censorship, they consist almost entirely of small talk, gossipy and repetitive small talk at that. From the historian's point of view of trying to extract information about the past, the letters tell far more of what was happening in sleepy little Vega, Texas, than of the new experiences, thrills, terrors, premonitions—and in the end tragic fulfillment—that Elden was experiencing.

There is, however, an enabling aspect in the fact that the people who would have gotten the most from the story, specifically our mother and father, are gone. Some parts of the story are not pretty, and in fact are horrible. It is important to me to write those parts as accurately and as graphically as I can bear to do. The task has sometimes been emotionally wrenching, and I do not believe I could have done it had our parents been alive to read it.

There are other people, whom I know and about whom I care, who for their own well-being should not read this book. Some who paid the price of service while the war was raging are still paying internally. Some have developed ways to shut away memories and to stifle thoughts that when confronted only revive pain. If you are one of these people, I believe you will recognize yourself in this paragraph, and I urge you to read no further. I am required by filial duty to write this, but you are not required to read it.

It is not my purpose to add to the store of knowledge about how and where World War II was fought. On the contrary, I wish to draw upon the excellent work of other researchers, oral historians, and writers as well as original sources to learn as much as I can of what Elden saw, heard, felt, tasted, and otherwise experienced on a daily basis. My purpose is to tell the story that one young sailor who lost his life in battle was not allowed to tell, and I must tell it now if only because I know he wanted to tell it.

He was my brother, and I do it for him.

So Long for Now

Prologue

NAZI Germany's repeated aggression in one place after another in the late 1930s gradually stiffened the resolve of other nations, particularly Great Britain and France, to resist. When Hitler invaded Poland in 1939, the terms of Poland's mutual defense alliance with Britain and France were triggered and soon virtually all of Europe was at war. Across the Atlantic a few clear thinkers, most notably President Franklin D. Roosevelt, could see that the United States could not avoid the conflict, and they began to make preparations as rapidly as the peace-focused American public would permit.

Japan depended on the sea for food and on other nations for oil, steel, rubber, and similar matériel necessary to a modern economy. The nation harbored an ancient tradition that exalted personal sacrifice in warfare, and its citizenry willingly believed that their emperor was literally divine and allowed the professional military to make him a figurehead and to rule in his name. This mix led Japan to join the cadre of other nations that sought empire as the twentieth century began. Thus that nation set upon a collision course with the United States of America, which, although just beginning to repent of its own imperialism, still had sovereign presence in several Pacific islands or island groups, most notably Hawaii, the Philippines, Guam, Wake, Midway, and the Aleutians. Throughout the first three decades of the twentieth century, the United States and Japan maintained contingency plans for war with one another. Despite these similarities, the difference between them was profound. In a naive and bumbling way the United States struggled to stay out of war, while Japan planned for it intently and grew ever more focused until contingency faded and plan became intention.

Japanese planners saw that Roosevelt's preparations meant U.S. power in the Pacific would increase with each passing month. War, Japan decided, was inevitable, and therefore the rational course was to act before the enemy became stronger—to destroy the United States Pacific Fleet in its headquarters at Pearl Harbor, Honolulu, Hawaii Territory. Admiral Isoroku Yamamoto, who understood American industrial power better than his colleagues did, advised against war but believed that if war came, it must begin with a decisive first strike.[1] Consequently, on December 7, 1941, Japanese carrier planes attacked Pearl Harbor with devastating effect. Fighters went after American aircraft on the ground, and torpedo planes targeted ships moored at dockside. Japanese navigator Takeshi Maeda, whose seat faced backward in his torpedo plane, had a clear view of several torpedo trails, including the one his plane had just dropped, heading for the USS *West Virginia,* and was confident this piece of American power would soon be no more.[2]

The Japanese officials who made this decision for war inadequately considered at least two vital factors, one political and one strategic. They were blind to the political effect of their preemptive action, which a visibly and audibly furious Roosevelt characterized as infamous and cowardly, a sneak attack. They shook the American public from its torpor and created a popular energy against which the Japanese regime could not possibly prevail. Strategically, they erred in a way so common as to be cliché—planning too much to fight the last war and too little to fight the technologically different war they had ignited. In previous wars, the determinant power of navies had been big guns on big battleships; airpower, such as it was, had resided mostly in land-based aircraft. The Pearl Harbor strike, which destroyed or damaged eight battleships, three cruisers, and several support vessels, might have been decisive in an earlier war, but it did no harm at all to the emerging power of U.S.

aircraft carriers, all of which were at sea away from Pearl Harbor on that fateful day.

World War II would rage on, eventually to consume the lives of an estimated 62 to 78 million human beings, including Elden Rogers. His loss became the single most important event in an entire generation of one family. He left behind a stack of letters written to his family at home, as well as letters he received from a girlfriend named Virginia, dated from September 6, 1943, to February 21, 1945, that survived in his locker and were sent to his parents. Elden wrote to Virginia from September 13, 1943, until at least March 8, 1945. He mentioned her in his last letter home, saying he had not heard from her in quite a while. But mail posted four months earlier was only then catching up with him, and it is not possible to know when she might last have written. Any letters posted by Virginia at about that time were probably returned to her undelivered. We do not have Elden's letters to Virginia and can only infer from her letters what he was saying, thinking, and doing. There are also letters from Elden's mother to him, several of which were returned undelivered. Other than a very few minor changes for clarity and my withholding the surnames of Virginia and a few others out of respect for privacy, the letters are presented verbatim, including occasional use of certain terms that were common when the letters were written but are now considered derogatory, and without correction or acknowledgment of errors.

Letters from fighting men of past wars have been wonderful sources for historical research, not only telling what an army or a fleet or a ship was doing, but adding personal touches that enable historians to extract graphic details and underlying human realities from them. During World War II, however, strict censorship was put into effect to prevent useful information from falling into enemy hands. Elden tried hard to obey these rules, and as a result his family knew next to nothing of what was happening to him.

Telling what was happening to him, on as nearly a daily basis as possible and in as personal a way as can now be done, is the purpose of this undertaking. By filling in around and between the letters exchanged by Elden, his mother, and his girlfriend, I hope to explain what was happening at home, but I especially seek to tell what he wanted to write but could not—the story that he was living but was forbidden to tell. This is Elden's story, and I write on his behalf.

People have always been careful how they behave and what they say at partings. It was Elden's grandmother Julia Tegarden's habit to wave to loved ones as they departed from her but always to turn away before they went beyond some obstacle or horizon. "Watching a person out of sight" was bad luck, she thought. Hanging on too long to the sight of a disappearing loved one was a form of selfishness, tempting fate to deny a chance ever to see him or her again; and turning away was a small sacrifice to mollify cruel fate. I sustain this habit myself to this day, rationalizing it as tradition rather than superstition. With untimely death so common in wartime and its potential so genuine, many people avoided the word "goodbye," attributing to it a dreadful finality. Sailors and soldiers especially tended to use parting words like "so long," meaning "until we meet again." Elden was no different.

Once during World War II, so says a story that is surely apocryphal, a low-ranking sailor unexpectedly found himself face to face and alone with Fleet Admiral William F. Halsey. Reacting to the seaman's visible nervousness, the admiral asked what was wrong. The boy confessed to being a bit rattled in the presence of such a great man. Halsey replied, in a line for all times: "There are no great men. There are only great jobs, and ordinary men must do them."

This is the story of one of the ordinary men who was one of a crew of 3,000 on one of dozens of warships under Halsey's command. He was doing a great job. They all were.

1   The Telegram

"WELL, here comes Iva, and something is wrong!" said Grace Rogers on the morning of April 13, 1945. My older brother Gerald and I joined our mother in looking through the pane in the front door, past the red, white, and blue banner with the blue star in the center that told the world our family had a son in the war. Almost no one ever entered the house through the front door, but now a car was there, and our neighbor and Grace's longtime best friend was getting out of it, along with Dr. O. H. Lloyd and John Van Meter. Inside, one of them said, "We have some bad news," and handed Grace a small yellow paper. Our blue star was about to change to gold.

Telegrams in those days came to the Western Union agent, who also staffed the local depot of the Rock Island Railroad. Telegrams were costly. Good news could be conveyed in an inexpensive letter, so news urgent enough to be sent by wire was almost invariably bad. This was *the* telegram that wartime families dreaded, and depot agent Cap Shelton was wise enough to know it had to be delivered by someone close to the recipient. In Iva Mathes he had chosen the right person, perhaps the *only* person, to bring the news. Van Meter presumably came along as a representative of the local draft board, and Doc Lloyd because the shock of bad news might be accompanied by a need for medical attention.

Telegram, Washington, D.C.
April 13, 1945

Mr & Mrs Ancell Rogers

The navy department deply regrets to inform you that your son Eldon Duane Rogers seaman second class USNR is missing following action while in the service of his country The department appreciates your great anxiety but details not now available and delay in receipt thereof must nessarilly be expected To prevent possible aid to our enemies please don not divulge the name of his ship or station

    Vice Admiral Randall Jacobs

    Chief of Naval Personnel

    829 AM

It was the most important moment in the history of this generation of our family. We would never afterward be the same. Knowing the words almost before she read them, Grace glanced at the paper and said, "Elden's missing. Go get Ancell."

Our father, Ancell, was tending to our four milch cows and a few other animals before he left for his job at the Texas Highway Department. Gerald ran out the back door toward the cow lot and, not seeing his father, shouted the alarm, "Dad! Come in the house! Elden's missing!" Ancell did not come immediately. In all probability he had inferred an ill meaning in the car at the front of his house, and he may have taken three or four minutes to prepare himself while finishing his chores. Then, in the small, dim living room, lighted by a single window in the front and a glass in the door, he confronted the news.

"You'd better go on to school," Grace said to Gerald.

Gerald had a major part in a class play less than thirty-six hours afterward, with dress rehearsals that very day. Before the arrival of television, school plays were annual entertainment highlights attended by most of the community. President Franklin D. Roosevelt, so revered in this family that his photograph hung on their wall, had died only the day before, already casting a pall over the fun people anticipated from a comedy called *This Night Beware.*

In small, close Vega, Texas, the pain of tragedy for one family was felt throughout the community, and soon visitors began to arrive, bringing the comfort of friendship, prayer, and an abundance of covered dishes that would keep the family from having to worry about cooking. We had joined a select few other local families, among them the McKendrees and Baleses, who were comforted in the collective arms of the community because we had suffered acute loss for the benefit of the country.

2 The "Westerers"

GOING down slowly and straining to stay erect, the slumping walls of the story-and-a-half frame house where Elden Rogers entered this world survived into the twenty-first century amid the aromatic lilacs and purple flags that his grandmother had nurtured early in the twentieth. It was March 19, 1926, at four o'clock in the afternoon, and the house stood smartly then. It had a bedroom on the south end, a living room in the middle, and a lean-to kitchen and dining room to the north. Above the main section were two attic rooms big enough to contain beds, and under it was a small unlined dirt cellar. Gutters channeled into a cistern rainwater that was raised by a hand pump for drinking and the household uses for which gypwater would not work. The house was too small to be proud, but with its white exterior and green trim it compared favorably with the sod house it had replaced and in which Elden's mother had been born, and especially with the dugout that had preceded the soddy. The Coin homestead was in the rural community of Cora, sixteen miles northwest of Alva, Oklahoma. Turkey Creek trickled past in a deep ravine, and a high hill just to the northwest was capped with a layer of alabaster—the source of the dissolved gypsum particles that made both the creek's water and the aquifer undrinkable.

Elden was the firstborn of Ancell Robert Rogers and Grace Evalena Coin, neighbors who had married eighteen months before. Twenty-seven-year-old Ancell and Grace, not quite twenty-one, were living on a rented farm two miles to the east. Both had sprung from families that had been in America for two hundred years, with long traditions of frontier hardship, risk, work, and potential. In the duality of the frontier, they were accustomed to getting along with little but were also ingrained with the optimism that had led nearly every generation of their American ancestors to pull up stakes and move farther west. When Elden was three years old, he had pulled an April Fool's joke on his uncle Charlie Coin. The uncle had played along, pretending to be fooled, and the tot botched his "April Fool!" punch line by exclaiming "Apricot!" Fondly remembered by his parents and that generation of adults, this little story was repeated for the next half century. Two months and ten days after this vignette, in the same house, Elden's brother Gerald Blane was born. Photographs of the two as children always show them together. Perhaps this simply reflects prudent use of expensive Kodak film, but they played together and shared the same formative experiences.

But something else was in the wind by the time Gerald was born. Ancell and Grace would soon imitate their ancestors in the westward movement. Several families of the Cora community, perhaps in response to a passing land salesman, had purchased unplowed virgin or newly broken prairie 240 miles southwest near Vega, Texas. Among the group was the extended family of Charles L. "Grandpa" Steward, who had employed Grace at the age of sixteen as a clerk in his general store. Ancell had followed the tradition of frontierspeople by buying a quarter section—160 acres. He also bought a two-cylinder John Deere "D" tractor with lug wheels, a nine-foot one-way plow, and a drill for wheat planting. The mules and nineteenth-century farming methods he had used in Oklahoma were left behind, and both the move and the mechanical equipment symbolized this couple's new beginning. For the first year or two, with Grace's brothers Carl and Ernest Coin, Ancell would drive a Model T Ford down to Vega, plow the land, plant a crop, and then return to Oklahoma until harvest time. Once he even rode to Texas on a freight train to check on his crop, leading his children years later to declare with questionable pride: "My Dad was a hobo!"

The virgin land, as it almost always does at first, produced abundantly. Things looked good, and the young couple must have felt they were doing a great and daring thing when, in 1930, they moved their household to Vega. Their first home was in a small black shed just north of the MacDonald house on South 12th Street. It was covered with tar paper on the exterior and had actually been used before as a chicken house, but they bravely moved their little family and few possessions into it and set about making a go of things.[1]

Vega was a new town. Although Grace and Ancell perceived a sense of being newcomers, in fact almost everyone had arrived fairly recently. A short three decades earlier the town site had been an empty part of the great Llano Estacado, named four hundred years earlier by the expedition of Spanish conquistador Francisco Vásquez de Coronado. In 1849 U.S. Army captain Randolph B. Marcy, passing nearby, had called it the "Great Zaraha" of North America that had always been and must forever remain uninhabited. He was wrong about past, present, and future. Native Americans had been in the area for millennia, the powerful Comanche tribe lived very well there at the time, and in 1874 to 1875 the U.S. Army would remove them and make way for cattle ranchers. When the Rock Island Railroad arrived in 1909, it brought a wave of farmers to replace the ranchers. Grace and Ancell arrived toward the conclusion of that wave.

⚓

The oil for which Texas was legendary never amounted to much in the Vega area, but there was a big, booming industry only fifty-five miles to the northeast, and like mineral booms everywhere it was rough and tough—a mixed blessing if a blessing at all. Founded in 1926, the city of Borger, Texas, within a year had 45,000 residents of less than sterling character and was run by a "lawman" who was actually a member of an Oklahoma crime syndicate. From time to time, the Texas Rangers would raid the town, arrest a core bunch of bad men, and tell everyone else who did not have a job to get out of town. They did exactly this in April 1927.[2]

Billy Williams was no fool—he read the papers and had figured out that Borger's expatriates would become some other town's immigrants. He reckoned himself a good judge of character, he knew trouble when he saw it, and there it stood right in front of him. The very next day after the Rangers had begun their cleanout of Borger, three rawboned toughs were in his Vega Drug Store, asking questions about the town, peering out the windows and looking here and there, obviously casing the place. Their Ford roadster out front had Oklahoma tags. Billy could put two and two together. As soon as they left, he went straight to the sheriff's office in the Oldham County Courthouse across the street to report what he had seen. Soon everyone knew, and as the day ended businessmen were dragging canvas cots out of closets and assembling them in their stores. Forsaking the comfort and companionship of their wives to snuggle instead with their shotguns, they slept little that night or not at all.

Ancell had left Grace and the year-old Elden at home in Oklahoma, and with Ernie and Carl made the two-day drive in a 1925 Ford to complete purchase of a piece of land north of Vega. The three of them noticed being treated with particular respect, as Vega people stepped off the sidewalk to let them pass. Small knots of townspeople gathered here and there in apparent conversation, but instead of looking at fellow conversants they seemed to be looking at the new arrivals. The next day, as the three drove a few miles north to visit with an acquaintance from home who was drilling a well in hope of finding oil, a big touring car followed at a discreet distance. When they headed back toward town by the same route, the car dodged off the road and waited behind a mesquite tree until they passed, then whirled around and followed.

As the boys ate bowls of chili in a café near the northwest corner of the courthouse square, men outside were peering through the plate-glass window. A town drunk, seemingly the only person unafraid of them, sat down and asked what was going on. When they asked what he meant by the question, he said, "The law is watching either you or me, and I don't think it's me."

The men at the window were the same ones who had been in the touring car—the sheriff, his regular deputy, the city marshal, and others who had been quickly deputized and armed as an old-fashioned posse. Eventually the lawmen took the three strangers into a form of custody just short of arrest and escorted them to the courthouse, followed by a crowd of somber onlookers. There a diminutive deputy wearing an undiminutive six-shooter demanded, "We know you three are up to something, and you had better tell us about it." Ancell replied that he had just bought land and "planned to make this town my home, but if this is how you treat everyone I believe I'll change my mind." Flinty faces sagged, and the crowd evaporated faster than it had condensed. Soon all had slunk away, leaving only City Marshal Frank Smith to apologize and to offer reparations in the form of fountain drinks at the Vega Drug Store. Carl Coin observed, "I thought Texans were tough, but three Okies came down here and scared the hell out of a whole town of Texans."[3]

Ancell never had another brush with the law in his almost eighty-eight years, not even a parking ticket, but if he had decided to take a walk that night from his room in the Vega Hotel, he might never have grown older than twenty-nine.

⚓

Young Vega and most of the region in which it was located were still in a stage of initial self-definition. The cattlemen had arrived after 1875 virtually in the dust of the Comanches reluctantly moving to reservations in Oklahoma. Afterward, and for not much more than a quarter century, the region was dominated entirely by cattle ranches—not small independent spreads but mostly huge outfits run by corporations, many of which were foreign. Cowhands came there from everywhere to work. They were Confederate veterans, former slaves, northern adventurers, and recent immigrants from overseas—more nearly wage slaves than the self-reliant individuals of mythology. They called themselves "hands," but the terminology that eventually evolved was meaningful: cow*boys* who owned little more than their horses and saddles worked for cow-*men* who owned the land and the cattle. They were not great in number because ranching did not require many people, and many of them only stuck with the work or the ranch for a few years before moving on in search of something better, or to elude someone in search of them. The ranching industry had sown the seeds of a national myth, but it had not jelled into a culture by the time farmers arrived with Ukrainian hard winter wheat that could be grown in this harsh land. Although some cowboys and small ranchers took up farming, a large percentage of the farmers arrived from wheat-growing states to the north and east, lands that had themselves been populated only recently from elsewhere. The 1940 census found in Vega 113 adults born in Texas, 150 born in other states, and 4 born in other countries. Of these adults, 65 had come from states outside the Confederacy. Like Ancell, 11 had been born in Kansas; and like Grace, 35 had been born in Oklahoma. Today, more than a century having passed, the non-Hispanic population of Vega has become more homogeneous, speaking with a more nearly uniform twang derived from Texas and the upper South. Indeed, even among families who have traditionally spoken Spanish, the twang has begun to replace the melodic lilt of Spanish-accented English. In the Vega of 1927, and even 1945, one heard a greater variety of accents and experienced the customs and mannerisms of a greater number of cultural backgrounds.

Building a new life on 160 acres had worked well enough in rainier lands to the east, but rainfall diminished with every mile westward, and Oklahoma itself was on the margin of where nature allowed for successful farming on such limited acreage without irrigation. Tens of thousands of small farmers carried the tradition too far west onto land that was too dry, and Ancell was one of them. Beyond the 100th meridian, and especially on the Staked Plains of Texas, four or five—even ten—times that acreage was necessary for so-called dry farming during good times. And good times were about to disappear under the triple apocalypse of depression, drought, and dust. All too soon Ancell was no longer a landowner in an area where "steady" jobs were few, and he had to find what work he could day by day. Internally driven by his own ethics to give full measure or better for his wages, Ancell's motto and lifelong advice to his sons was "Make a hand," meaning "Earn your pay." But almost all workers were forced into idleness much of the time. Some were comfortable with loafing, but most took pride in work and found its unavailability humiliating.

The family moved to another rental house, and then another. They planted vegetable gardens; kept cows, chickens, and pigs; and scraped by. The boys helped out by caring for the animals and doing such "chores" as staking the cows on grassy vacant town lots each morning and bringing them in every evening. Grace and Ancell bought food in bulk directly from farmers when they could, and Grace canned fruits and vegetables, baked her own bread, churned butter, made clothes from flour and feed sacks, and pieced quilts from scraps of worn-out clothes to save money. To bring in a little cash, she took in ironing from women who could afford to pay for it, and she sometimes washed towels for barber Wallace Moore. Grace explained later that they were able to "hang on" only because almost everyone was "in the same boat," and people helped one another. This was especially true among the network of people who had moved to Vega from the Cora community—several families of Stewards, and Cal and Iva Mathes, in addition to the Rogerses. When one of these families harvested corn or potatoes, or slaughtered a pig or calf, they shared the bounty with others. Grace, unable very often to afford transportation back to Oklahoma, grew homesick for her mother, who spent bits of her small pension to send postage stamps to her faraway daughter, but returning in defeat to Oklahoma and being a burden on relatives there was not an option. Ancell and

Grace were determinedly, and eventually contentedly, at home in Vega. They are buried there now.

But life was never easy. Grace recalled that there were a few times when all she had to feed Gerald and Elden was home-churned butter on homemade bread sprinkled with a little sugar. She boiled wheat as though it were rice, and served it as hot cereal with cream and sugar. There came one time—happily one—when there was no food in the house at all. Ancell said he would go to the S&W grocery store, across the street and at the east end of the same block, for some food. Grace, concerned that Ancell had long been out of work and that their tab at the store was already high, worried, "What if they won't charge anymore?" The same Billy Williams who had sparked panic when Ancell had arrived in Vega had refused credit for medicine for Elden and Gerald when the penniless family had been quarantined with scarlet fever, and the grocer might also have a limit. Ancell, near the end of his tether, said, "I'll get it anyway." The sympathetic storeowners, less pecuniary than the druggist, did charge it, so we never had to learn what this shy and impeccably honest man might have done. Elden and Gerald knew times were hard, and they went without many things they wanted, but Ancell's stoic silence spared them awareness of the anguish of a hardworking man denied the chance to earn his keep and close to his inner limit of forbearance.

In the early 1930s, dust storms of a type and severity no American had ever imagined, let alone seen, compounded the economic hardship. They rolled in, puffy like cumulus clouds but brown and on the ground rather than high in the sky, so darkening things that people turned lights on midday, so dirtying the little rented duplex that afterward Ancell had to shovel dust out of the house with a wheat scoop before Grace could sweep it clean with a broom. As late as 1939, Grace placed dampened sheets over the crib of her infant third son to catch the dust, and I presume it helped to protect me.

3 "The Past Is a Foreign Country"

"THE past is a foreign country; they do things differently there," novelist L. P. Hartley famously wrote. Elden and Gerald grew up in a small-town culture that even as late as 1945 was so drastically different from the present that it is now difficult to understand fully. Trying to do so is like discovering the differences between one English-speaking country and another; there are similarities, but each has a distinctly individual culture. That difference is a significant part of this story.

You could tell you were accepted if people called you something other than your given name. In the Vega, Texas, of the early 1940s, almost every boy, some girls, a few women, and a good many men were known by nicknames. So nearly universal was this characteristic that it is one of the most conspicuous points these letters reveal about how small-town West Texas during the war years differed from the world we experience seven decades later. Elden so successfully mimicked the voice of a popular radio sitcom character called the Great Gildersleeve that his nickname became Gildersleeve, soon shortened to "Sleeves." As "Rog," Gerald took on an abbreviation of his family name, as did Ed "Murph" Murphy. Some, like Carlton "Half Dozen" Six, endured puns on their names. Many nicknames originated in specific events or were based on physical characteristics. Odell "Eggs" Brents had once as a child refused to share his candy Easter eggs, and his brother Leon "Beans" Brents had taken a dare to eat locust tree beans that all kids knew with erroneous certainty to be deadly. Charles "Bugeye" or "Bugs" Steward had prominent eyes. Leon "Speck" Price had freckles. Wilburn "Wig" Price and Edith "Mop" Boydstun both had curly hair. Because Mop's brother Glenn once worked as a "pumper" on a railroad crew, everyone including his wife ever after called him "Pumper," and the two of them named their son Ted but called him "Butch." Aubrey McKendree's wife called her husband by his given name, but everyone else called him "Hot Dog." George "Elephant" Miller was a large man with large ears, but we can only guess at the origin of Howard "Snails" Blasingame and C. E. "Smoky" Roark. Buford "Boots" Montgomery was a cowman. Howard "Shaky" Hill, Robert "Sleepy" McCombs (whose wife was "Babe"), "Fat" Jackson, and his obviously fraternal twin "Slim" all must have been named for physical characteristics. Everett "Stalkanall" Wiseman had repeated too many times a story about cattle that had eaten their feed "stalk and all." Of the bachelor Ruhl brothers, "Hank" was shortened from Henry, and Ralph was called "Dutch." O. H. Lloyd, the only physician who had ever lived in Vega, was, of course, "Doc," and "Widow" McGowan had long ago lost her husband and ran a farm by herself. Nicknames were so nearly ubiquitous that if this story were lighthearted instead of tragic it might have been titled from a letter in which Elden inquired about the military status of Charles Steward and Howard Blasingame Jr. with the question "What's the dope on Bugs and Snails?"[1]

In big cities people may see the drama of social life on stage or screen, in movies, plays, opera, or ballet, but in little Vega it was to be seen in a handful of places that most everyone contacted or visited from time to time. One, contacted by remote means, was the telephone exchange; two others visited in person were the drugstore and the barbershop.

"Pop" and "Coogie" Landrum operated the local telephone company like an extended conversation. Many families, including ours, did not have telephones until after the war had ended, but those who did could find out how a sick person was doing, or where a fire was when the alarm sounded, by turning the crank on their phone, waiting for Pop or Coogie to say "number please," and asking their question. Pop irritated some women and flattered others by addressing any female voice as "Hon," but both Landrums were focal points of the community.[2]

By the forties Joe Montgomery owned the Vega Drug Store, and it became a primary center for the exchange of news. If you wanted to know whose wheat crop had been hailed out, or whose vegetable garden had been rooted up by a neighbor's pig, who had done something wonderful and who had misbehaved, that was the place to find out. Through the distorted lens of hindsight, we tend to disapprove such talk as gossip, and gossip it was, but it was not quite what we think. Every life was a human drama validly equal to every other life, and the crises and accomplishments of each one were both interesting and important. People needed to know about others, and, with some exceptions, needed others to know about them. Naturally some of the gossip carried a due amount of negativity and disapproval, but it was rarely malicious and in fact was usually based on a humane concern. It not only spread the news; it also helped to discipline behavior in a disparate group of people who were gradually coalescing into a community.

Wallace Moore's barbershop was a center for information one level beyond gossip. In a world before television, people amused one another by telling stories, and it was expected that the limited subject matter of small-town life would be enhanced with each retelling. The barbershop was the place where this happened most and best. From such stories grow myths, and upon myths grow cultures. Thus some local individuals came to be "characters" in oft-repeated stories, some authentic and some invented—some willing, some not, and some unwitting. Hank Ruhl, whose choice of words was consistently never quite right, became famous for his malapropisms. Red Marshall, one barbershop story said, while serving a short jail sentence for drunkenness, had been allowed to relieve his boredom by repainting the courthouse interior. Knowing more about the chemistry of paint thinner than his captors knew, Red drank the ethanol-based product and had a high old time at taxpayer expense. Moore himself was fond of drink, and in this dry county where liquor was scarce he was said occasionally to resort to a swig of Lucky Tiger hair tonic from the shelves behind his barber chair. The barber also created and cultivated his own image as the nemesis of kids. Preteen boys learned to stay on the alert when walking past the shop behind the candy-striped pole, lest they feel the snap of a wet towel on their rear ends. Gullible lads were sent to the lumberyard to borrow board stretchers or to the hardware store for a gallon of striped (pronounced stripe-ed) paint to refinish the barber pole. Others had their vocabularies tested with exclamations like "My God, you have garments all over your back!" or, in a confidential tone, "I want to warn you that I saw you hesitating on the street the other day, and you need to be careful doing that in public."

One popular story told of bachelor cowboy Hank Ruhl, who could read and write nothing more than his own name, coming in from his lonely cabin at Ysabel Camp on the Mansfield Ranch for a haircut. On this particular day, the barber's attractive wife, Orbis, childless and with little to do in their tiny home, was herself passing the time by sitting in the barbershop and chatting with customers. Bored even doing that, as Hank got into the barber chair Orbis offered to give him a manicure—no charge. "What's a manicure?" Hank wondered. "You just sit still and I will show you." As the woman took Hank's crusty hand in her own soft one and moved it to where his nails could soak in a pan of warm water, the bachelor cowboy who rarely even saw a woman and absolutely never touched one, became physically aroused. The barber finished the haircut before the wife finished the manicure, and Hank fished in his pocket for the fifty cent fee, standing in an awkwardly sidelong posture to keep from revealing the effect she had produced. Orbis said, "Wait just a minute, Hank, I will get a hot towel and push your cuticle down." Hank, flushing a deep red, said, "That's alright, Ma'am, it'll go down after I walk off a little way."

Adult stories of this sort had a tendency to revolve around the alcohol-fueled antics of one or another of the several "town drunks." They frequently originated on election night, when a crowd would gather on the courthouse lawn to socialize and to watch the vote count be posted from time to time on a large chalkboard just outside the west door of the courthouse. The Republican Party was not a factor in Texas in those days, so the Democratic primary in the warm weather of June was at least as important as the general election in November. Oldham County was dry, and the thirty-five-mile distance west to legal alcohol in Glenrio, New Mexico, or east to Amarillo was not enough to support the risk of bootlegging, but it was far enough during times of gasoline rationing to be a problem for friends of John Barleycorn. The drinkers pooled their ration coupons, toughed it out through figurative dry spells, and found interim relief by swigging imitation vanilla extract, which was legally available at the grocery store even though, had it been considered a beverage, it would have been labeled 36 proof. These "town drunks" were not really all that bad nor all that drunk that often, but there was not a lot else to be talked about. Three Protestant churches, mostly associating alcohol with Satan, indirectly encouraged the talk by their disapproval. There was also a Catholic church where sacramental wine was drunk weekly and whose members generally took a less restrictive view.

As adults created their own word-of-mouth news services and carefully cultivated minor incidents into folklore, kids created their own amusements. Our family of boys paid little mind to the "sissy" ways in which girls occupied their time. Playing "house" seemed an endless sequence of making mud pies that could not be eaten, sweeping imaginary rooms, changing diapers on dolls, and bossing other people around. This imitation of what little girls observed their mothers doing tells much about the lives of the mothers—an endless sequence of cooking, cleaning, caring for infants, and supervising older children.

Boys did not so faithfully imitate their fathers, but rather patterned themselves after mythological heroes like Tom Sawyer or Buffalo Bill. Movies were just beginning to influence the fantasy lives of boys, but radio dramas such as *Jack Armstrong, the All-American Boy,* aimed at preteens and early adolescents, were already a powerful factor.

Boys were supposed to have adventures. With small-town life providing little of interest, let alone excitement, the adventures had to be first invented and then made to happen. And with danger not yet the exaggerated concern it nowadays has come to be, boys of school age were generally free to go where they wanted and to do what they dared. This led to such antics as young Gerald tying ropes to the four corners of a bedsheet, looping the ropes under his arms, and jumping off a building behind the Vega Hotel in the expectation of drifting pleasantly to earth in his homemade parachute (it did not work out that way).

More characteristically, it led to creation of a club called the Rinky Dinks. Members of this elite bunch of approximately ten-year-old boys brought picks, shovels, and spades from home to the west end of town, dug a network of holes and connecting trenches, covered them with scrap lumber, and covered the lumber with the dirt from the holes. The result was a series of multiroom "caves" connected by tunnels. The rooms had fireplaces with flues to take smoke away, and yes, the boys built fires in them. Parents were not unduly concerned if a son asked for a potato, acknowledging that a group of boys were going to meet after dark, build a fire, and roast and eat potatoes. At one point, this enterprising club actually built something they called a "clubhouse" on top of an eight-foot-high sign beside the yet-to-be-paved Highway 66. The sign read VEGA CITY LIMIT and was probably the only city limit sign in the United States with a penthouse.[3]

4 War

WHEN war came to the United States on December 7, 1941, Elden Rogers was nearly sixteen years old. His brother Gerald was thirteen and a half, and his baby brother, Jerry, was two weeks shy of his third birthday. Our mother was thirty-six, and our father had just turned forty-three. Grace and Ancell Rogers, who had been worried that the war already raging in "the old country" for a year and a quarter might someday take their teenage sons, were doubly worried now. President Roosevelt's furious eloquence and the "infamy" of the "sneak attack" made war the talk of the town and of the nation, and patriotic anger ran rampant. Many young men went immediately to volunteer for the fight. As usual in the beginning stage of a war, its length, cost, and horror were underestimated, and as usual the eagerness to serve would fade as these things became clear.

For little Vega, Texas, the war had begun by taking two of its boys prisoner and confining them in remote camps where abuse and malnutrition were the norm. The whole town, barely half a thousand souls, joined the boys' parents in worry and fear, and clung with hope to the scraps of information that on rare occasions came through about Jimmy Bales and Bish McKendree.

Bishop Davis McKendree, a brother of Aubrey "Hot Dog" McKendree, whose wife, Marie Steward McKendree, was very close to Grace and Ancell Rogers, turned twenty-one in December 1940. At that age Bish, as he was locally known, became subject to the draft. James E. Bales, son of Emory and Effie Bales, was two years younger, but these two pals did things together, and if they enlisted they had choices not available to draftees. The Walcott brothers from Vega, J. C. and Tubby, had joined the Field Artillery together five months before and had signed up for duty in the Philippines, and that sounded exciting. McKendree and Bales inquired with the marine corps, but wound up volunteering for the army on February 12, 1941, choosing the 60th Coast Artillery, an antiaircraft regiment on Corregidor in the Philippine Islands.[1]

McKendree later wrote that Jim underwent an uncharacteristic and tragically prophetic change before the two arrived at Manila on April 22, 1941. Normally funny, he became moody and seemed to believe they might never see home again.[2]

Japan, in its hope to prevail in one bold stroke, made its attack on the core of American strength—the Pacific Fleet based at Pearl Harbor—on the morning of December 7, 1941. Over 350 Japanese fighters, bombers, and torpedo planes, launched from six aircraft carriers, reached the fleet in total surprise and easily sank or seriously damaged eight American battleships, three cruisers, and three destroyers and destroyed 188 aircraft, mostly on the ground. They killed 2,400 fighting men and wounded almost 1,300 others. The United States declared war on the Empire of Japan the following day. Alliances began to kick in, and war with Germany and Italy came three days later.

"Fool me once," the saying goes, "shame on you; fool me twice, shame on me." Five thousand miles west of Hawaii in the Philippines, where General Douglas MacArthur was in command, the United States was fooled a second time when Japanese forces destroyed virtually all American airpower on the ground. No airplanes meant no ability to fight offensively, and this single stroke converted the Philippines into a trap—under siege and unsustainable.[3]

Concentrated into the Bataan Peninsula and the nearby island fortress of Corregidor, commonly called "the Rock," beyond reinforcement or resupply, the only thing the American garrison could do in defense was to delay the Japanese advance by holding out as long as possible. It was a duty of doom; even on minimal rations their food would eventually be gone and they would have to surrender. MacArthur's troops saw him so rarely that the appellation "Dugout Doug" appeared in a song to the tune of "The Battle Hymn of the Republic." It would plague the general for the rest of his life.[4]

> *Dugout Doug MacArthur lies shaking in "The Rock,"*
> *Safe from all the bombers and from any sudden shock.*
> *Dugout Doug is eating from the best there is in stock,*
> *And his troops go starving on.*
>
> *Dugout Doug, come out from hiding.*
> *Dugout Doug, come out from hiding.*
> *Send to Franklin the glad tidings*
> *That his troops go starving on.*[5]

Under orders from the president—the "Franklin" in this song—who correctly considered him too valuable to lose, MacArthur left General Jonathan Wainwright in charge and escaped by PT boat on the night of March 11. He went first to the southern Philippine island of Mindanao and then to Australia, from whence he would plan and conduct the southern approach to eventual victory. The Bataan garrison, "battling" by starving themselves, held out for another month, and the Corregidor garrison lasted for two. As men came to realize that promises of reinforcements would not—could not—be kept, they expressed their despair in rhyme, such as this one that later became well known.

> *We're the battling bastards of Bataan:*
> *No mama, no papa, no Uncle Sam,*
> *No aunts, no uncles, no nephews, no nieces,*
> *No pills, no planes, or artillery pieces.*
> *And nobody gives a damn.*[6]

The inevitable surrender of Corregidor came on May 7, 1942. Bish McKendree and Jimmy Bales became prisoners of war.[7] Bish scavenged a mess kit and Jimmy found two canteens and gave one to Bish; the water it carried saved his life then and many times afterward. As they moved toward their place of imprisonment, the column slogged past an American soldier who had died at his machine gun days before, with one hand in the air.[8] His image inspired the poem "The Unknown Soldier," which is featured prominently among poems McKendree collected, preserved at great risk, and later published. In part, it says:

> *The weary eyes of the men that morn*
> *Saw a sight not soon forgot*
> *Of broken guns, and broken men*
> *Whose bodies were left to rot.*
>
> *I saw the corpse of a youngster;*
> *Just a lad, too young to die.*
> *One blackened arm was raised*
> *And pointed to the sky.*
>
> *Where are you pointing, soldier?*
> *What message would you give?*
> *What are you trying to tell us,*
> *The ones who are left to live?*
>
> *. . . Well, we must march on and leave you,*
> *Just a pile of flesh and bone.*
> *You may be better off than we,*
> *For our fate is yet unknown.*[9]

As the American press reported these losses, the people of Vega felt hurt and fear in their hearts and wondered whether Bish and Jimmy had survived. The *Oldham County News* reported on May 14 that the McKendrees had received a letter written by Bish sometime in February and that it was hoped he had evaded the enemy.[10]

The two Vega boys managed to make it, as did most of the prisoners, to Cabanatuan Camp No. 3, where quarters were primitive but where at least they could rest. The "battling bastards" had "fought" from December until May by forgoing half the calories required for life, and the march to prison had weakened them further. Now their daily diet became one rice ball and one cup of onion soup; malnutrition progressed to starvation.[11] Disease and death were everywhere every day. McKendree contracted cerebral malaria and experienced hallucinations, but somehow recovered.

At the end of October 1942, some prisoners, including Jimmy Bales, were shipped to Main Camp Chikko at Osaka, Japan.[12] One day the next January Jim found himself unguarded in a food storage facility. Helpless to resist, he ate more than his fragile system could handle. In terrible irony, after six months of half rations and seven months of even more severe prison diet, Jimmy Bales died from overeating.

Bish was better off, as bad as Cabanatuan was, to have been left behind. Shortly after Jim had left, the Japanese began to provide prison kitchens a few carabao, commonly called water buffalo. This only meant that a cup of soup might contain two or three tiny bits of meat, but at least there was food three times daily and the increment of protein and fat slowed the process of starvation. The situation changed significantly only when canned food began to arrive from the South African Red Cross, and soon afterward from the American Red Cross. Eventually, in February 1943, a day came when no one died—the first such day in nine months.[13]

Like U.S. Navy censors, Japanese prison officers were concerned about the flow of information. They wanted no information going out of the camp, coming into the camp, or even going around within the camp. To prevent this, they prohibited on pain of death possession by prisoners of paper, pencils, pens, or any other accoutrement of writing. It seems almost universal, however, that oppressed people will find ways to do what their oppressors try to prevent, and soon a few daring kitchen workers were soaking the paper labels off food cans and drying them out. The back sides of these labels made fine stationery for the few pencils that could be filched here or there.

And to what high purpose, might we suppose, would writing materials gathered at the risk of life itself be used? Would prisoners sneak messages to Filipino guerrillas for relay to MacArthur in Australia? They knew little that would be of value to MacArthur, and they had higher and better intentions.

They wrote poems!

They poured the anger and pain and despair and bitterness of their abandonment, and the bits of hope they sometimes could muster, into words on paper. They published their works by passing them hand to hand in secret. It was a strange and touching act of defiance by spirits that refused to break, and a heartening assertion of one of the better human instincts in contravention of some of the worst. Some of the poetry was quite good, and all of it full of important information about their experiences. McKendree recognized the importance of the writings and, to his great credit, collected them and hid them away through a succession of ever-worsening horrors.[14]

Despite Roosevelt's efforts to prepare his reluctant country for a war he had known would come, the public had been almost completely unready. Japanese leaders, although optimistic before launching war, were astonished by their success at Pearl Harbor and Manila, and then at how quickly and easily they had been able to gain control over the western Pacific. Debate among War Department leaders over whether remaining U.S. naval power should be employed for defense rather than offense produced an initial timidity that left the path wide open for Japanese expansion. The president, however, insisted upon some expression of offense, and on March 10, 1942, just short of Elden's sixteenth birthday, U.S. carrier-based planes sank three Japanese ships near New Guinea. Six weeks later, American bombs fell on Tokyo itself from the famous carrier-launched one-way raid by a squadron of B-25 bombers led by Jimmy Doolittle.[15]

By April 1942 order was taking shape. MacArthur had the lead in the part of the Pacific that lay south of the equator and west of meridian 160°, and Nimitz had the lead in the rest of that vast ocean.[16] In competition with one another and simultaneously in cooperation, MacArthur would attack Japanese holdings from the south and Nimitz would hit them from the east.[17] Japan's opening attack at Pearl Harbor, devastating though it appeared to be, had serious strategic shortcomings. It had focused primarily upon "charismatic" vessel types that many military planners were only beginning to realize were past their peak in importance. It had sunk ships in shallow waters and in port, while leaving adjacent dry docks intact, thus allowing many vessels to be raised, repaired, and readied for combat. Japanese targeters had overlooked all-important fuel supplies, and, most significantly, the attack had not even touched the American aircraft carriers, which were on duty elsewhere that day.

The days of naval battles in which big ships with big guns would slug it out were almost over, and this new war would be fought substantially by aircraft—fighters, bombers, and torpedo planes—from ships that never came within sight of one another. Soon the admirals figured this out, and began using carriers on the offensive and protecting the carriers with task groups made up of myriad other kinds of ships. In particular, they learned to use the speed of new "fast" carriers that could keep the enemy guessing about the location of American power and where it might strike next. New carriers could also outdistance older battleships and cruisers to such an extent as to make the latter sometimes difficult to use together.

On June 4, 1942, six days before Gerald Rogers turned fourteen, the American victory at the Battle of Midway was won by carrier planes. The news was celebrated, though few could see then what many now see in hindsight—that the course of the war turned with this success. Although the American war effort had only begun, after Midway Nimitz was confident that the United States would win. Experts were predicting the task might take until 1949; Nimitz believed it would take less time, though he did not know how much less.

Japanese weapons industries had been at peak production for a substantial time before Pearl Harbor, perhaps long enough to have lost just a bit of their creative edge. American counterpart industries, in contrast, had been dormant as a result of an isolationist reaction to World War I and in consequence of the Great Depression. The Pearl Harbor attack had produced anger, which had released a kind of economic adrenaline, and American industry had everywhere and overnight gone into high-energy action.

By the first anniversary of the Pacific War, December 7, 1942, the United States had turned the tide in both the northern and southern Pacific and had begun to consider the "island-hopping" approach that would win the war earlier and with fewer casualties than either Americans or Japanese had expected.[18] A heavy price had been paid in loss of the *Wasp* (CV-7), *Yorktown* (CV-5), *Hornet* (CV-8), *Lexington* (CV-2), and even the original 1920 American carrier *Langley* (CV-1). On that all-important anniversary, in the Norfolk Navy Yard, the keel was laid for the USS *Franklin*. With fast work the *Franklin* would be launched October 14, 1943, commissioned January 31, 1944, as CV-13, and assigned Air Group 13.[19]

In the navy's system for identifying vessels, *C* meant carrier and *V* stood for flying craft that were, unlike blimps and dirigibles, heavier than air, so an aircraft carrier was a CV. Ships were numbered sequentially as they were commissioned for service, and the *Franklin* became CV-13 because she was commissioned two months after the second

Hornet (CV-12) and three months before the *Ticonderoga* (CV-14). The U.S. Navy had eight CVs when the nation entered the war, some of which were pretty primitive. The USS *Langley* (CV-1), for example, had been a collier, a floating bucket of coal to power other ships, before a flight deck was nailed to her top. After *Langley,* carriers rapidly became larger and better, but the USS *Essex* (CV-9), launched in July 1942, was very large and entirely modern. It became the prototype for big U.S. carriers in World War II, and American industry averaged launching one each month for the duration of the war. The convention of naming fleet carriers for battles has led many to guess that the *Franklin* was named for the Civil War Battle of Franklin, Tennessee, but it was not so. Instead, she was *Franklin* the fifth, named as a successor to four previous U.S. warships named *Franklin,* the first of which had been named for Benjamin Franklin. Soon she was nicknamed "Big Ben."[20]

5   What's the Matter with
Kids Today?

B_{ACK} in Vega, Texas, the teenaged Elden Rogers, an excellent singer, was perfecting his imitation of deep-voiced country crooner Ernest Tubb. Popular among his peers, Elden was always the joker in the crowd. On one occasion he and another boy halted their car in front of Auzie Taylor's café on Highway 66, letting other kids nearby know they had just returned from a "hootch" run to Amarillo. Playing the scene for all of the misguided admiration they could squeeze from their gullible audience, they announced they needed to ferry the booze indoors before the law happened by. With a touch of drama they retrieved something from the trunk of the car and walked past the boys, each holding one end of a two-ounce single-drink bottle of bourbon.[1]

Elden's peers recall him having a clever wit, citing an example of a time when several boys were in Amarillo and one of them was in urgent need of a restroom. They were outside a nightclub called the Mayfair but did not want to pay the cover charge that would get them inside where they could access the needed facility. As they wondered whether it might be possible to sneak past the bouncers, Elden suggested that the troubled friend might "creep in, crap, and creep out."[2]

He also showed a too assertive streak of too much independence at too early an age. Although remembered by Bob Walcott as a good student, Elden dropped out of high school to the extreme displeasure of his parents. At some point Elden worked briefly at night for the Walcotts, who then ran the Conoco service station on Route 66, and on one very busy shift he sold $100 worth of gasoline.[3]

In May 1943, he traveled by bus as far as Carlsbad, New Mexico. We do not know why, but economic realities make it unlikely that he was traveling only for pleasure. One might presume he was looking for work, and he was most likely was accompanied by Carlton Six and Bugeye Steward, who was not yet sixteen. A month later they were in southeastern Colorado, apparently having more fun than success finding or keeping jobs. There Elden met a girl. He was just over seventeen years old, and Virginia was one month shy of that age. He wanted to dress to impress.

June 30, 1943

Dear Folks,

How is everyone in Texas? We are working hard as usual. Met some good looking girls. Please send my sport coat to me. The weather is pretty cool here.

Your Son,
Elden[4]

He was in a city park with Carlton Six; Virginia was with her friend Maureen. The girls flirtatiously dropped some letters, feigning an accident in order to get the boys' attention. It worked, and their earliest acquaintance seems to have progressed through subsequent meetings in the park. The girls thought the boys did not show much interest in them, but the historical record shows otherwise. Elden was soon engaged in an active correspondence with Virginia.

Aside from these letters, we know little about Virginia. The things we do know reveal a girl who had several things in common with Elden. She was almost the same age, and she dropped out of high school by not beginning the fall term in 1943, perhaps indicating that Elden might have been a bad influence on her. We know that she worked, that she changed jobs fairly frequently, that she repeatedly expressed an intention to leave her hometown and parents to live and work somewhere else, that she frequented an apparent nightclub called the Cape, and that she expressed serious feelings for Elden but freely told him of flirtations and dates with other boys, especially one who had a nice car and money. She found her hometown boring, and she enjoyed going to fun places away from the routine. She had two older brothers in the service and two younger ones still at home. Her parents had jobs, and she looked after her little brothers, sometimes making them supper. They were a respectable family and lived in a rented house in the town of Las Animas.

Elden returned to Texas after the summer was over but visited Colorado from time to time and spent several weeks there during the fall. He led Virginia to believe that he had a car, which at best suggests that he had stretched the truth, perhaps referring to a Model A Ford that Ancell bought for its tires. Elden and several other Vega boys (Bugeye Steward, who wanted the girls to call him Chuck; Sheets, whose other names are unknown; Carlton Six; and a Jimmy whose last name is unknown) had established a special connection with a number of the girls who lived there. By the highway network of 1943, these girls lived a long day's drive from Vega, for which gasoline rationing coupons were probably pooled among several passengers in a car. Elden's dad was always short of coupons, and he never exceeded the "patriotic" gas-saving 35 mile-per-hour highway speed. It is a safe assumption that young boys drove much faster.

Altogether, the image of Virginia is one of a teenager trying to be grown up and wanting to be in love, remarkably open in what she wrote to Elden as a boyfriend or fiancé, adventuresome, and a bit "wilder" and less serious than Elden's mother would have preferred. Of course, the image of Elden is one of a boy who himself was wilder than his mother would have preferred as well. The liberating force of the automobile combined with at least some spending money and the terrible uncertainty that war created about the future made a great many young people more than a bit wild during that time. Perhaps the most telling points are that Virginia seems to have written Elden more or less faithfully throughout his time in the navy and that her letters and his relationship with her seem to have been very important to him.

We cannot escape assuming that Elden may have been troubled by the transparent ambivalence in many of Virginia's letters. Yet as time passed, he seems to have increasingly valued the relationship and at times clearly felt he was in love with her. Most likely his feelings were much affected by the fact that the navy had uprooted him from familiar territory, put him on a ship with an all-male crew larger than the population of whole counties in the Texas Panhandle, and taken him half a world away into the midst of a terrible war. Was this relationship as serious as the letters sometimes make it sound, or did it reflect the desire of virtually all unmarried sailors to hear from girls back stateside and the girls' romanticized willingness, even sense of duty, to write to young men in the service? This was not an uncommon situation, as evidenced by the numerous early and impromptu marriages, and by less common "Dear John" experiences and infrequent divorces. Virginia herself wrote of friends who eloped and then split only days later, and of married women openly dating men while their husbands were away in the war. It was not an easy time to know who you were, what you wanted in life, or what was right and what was wrong.

September 6, 1943

Dear Tex,

Well I got out of going to school. I think I have anyway. This is the first day and it is 9:00 so I guess I'm not going. My dad is really angry with me.

I work at the Trojan now from 2:00 P.M. till 10:00 P.M. I don't know whether you know where it is or not but it is across the street from the

Park Hotel & next to the theater. When you come home I mean when you come back to Las Animas You can order your meals there. We really serve the good ones. Maureen washes dishes & I'm a waitress. Say, I haven't heard from you for a long time, have you forgotten all about me? I don't blame you if you have, but this is the first time anyone has completely forgotten me. I must be losing something. When you come back to old Las Animas we'll get acquainted all over again.

I have hay fever, I guess you knew that. It sure has been cold here, just like winter. That makes my hay fever worse. The cold weather I mean.

A bunch of us kids went to Rocky Ford the other night to the water melon day fair. The boy that had the truck lost his keys and we had to sit up in the Rocky Ford depot all night. We couldn't catch a bus until 7:00 A.M. the next morning. I had to go to work right after I got back and boy, I was sure sleepy. If anyone ever mentions going to Rocky Ford again I'll croak them.

How is Sheets getting along. I think I owe him a letter & I <u>know</u> you owe me one. Well, I have to write some more letters so goodby for now.

Virginia

Sandy soil and Arkansas River water make the Rocky Ford area famous for melons even today, and the watermelon day fair must have been a big event. Getting stranded out-of-town overnight cannot have been a good way to impress the boss in Virginia's new job as a waitress, nor her parents, who were unhappy with her decision to quit school. Perhaps because of this incident, Virginia had apparently lost this job in less than two weeks.

It is unlikely that Elden or anyone in Vega or Las Animas would have known that after ten months of riveting, welding, wiring, and painting, the *Franklin* was launched on October 14. She began test cruises in Chesapeake Bay and the Caribbean Sea.

Sometime between September 17 and October 16, Elden was in Las Animas, where he discovered Virginia on a movie date with another boy. Perhaps hurt, he mailed a card to her from her own hometown and returned to Texas.

October 16, 1943

Dearest Tex,

I received a card from you that you mailed from Las Animas, so I don't know where you are now. You could have gotten a job here and made enough money if "Bug Eyes" and "half dozen" hadn't spent all their money on beer and stuff. They will probably read this so I won't say anything else about them. I sure like them though, they are swell kids, but who likes kids? <u>Ha</u> Tell them hello and don't let them read this.

Honey, don't be mad at me for being with that kid in the show. I'm really sorry. I got bawled out for it from all sides I guess. He is only a friend. I don't like him in the same way I like you. He is a sissy. (Six said he was anyway) I don't care for sissies so you won't have to worry about him any more.

I hope you can come up here again some time. I will be waiting for you but you can't expect me to stay home until you come back can you? I know you will understand how it is. I won't tell you I love you yet because I'm not sure. All I know is I like you better than any boy I know.

Love,
Virginia

Four significant things may be understood from Virginia's next letter: Elden may be planning to visit her again soon; there is the first in what will become a long string of negatives about Bugeye (whom she calls Chuck); Elden seems to have told Virginia that his fifteen-year-old brother is seventeen, whereby we may guess he had told her he is older; and, although friendly, Virginia uses a deliberately cooler tone than in the two earlier letters.

November 4, 1943

Dear Tex,

I'm sorry it has taken me so long to answer but I have really been busy, believe it or not. I'm glad you are coming back up here. I haven't seen you for so long.

Do you believe everything Chuck tells you? He said he wrote to you and said that he was out all night with me. That is a lie. You shouldn't believe anything that guy tells you because I don't think he ever tells the truth. (Don't let Chuck read this).

There isn't much to write about. Tell Six Janet still loves him. Maureen moved yesterday so tell Jimmy he will have to hunt her up by himself if he likes her as much as Chuck said.

I will have to put Chucks letter in with yours because I have only one stamp.

Do you really have a brother 17 years old? If you have why don't you bring him up here. I would like to see him if he looks anything like you.

Well, I hope I will see you soon.

A friend,

Virginia

Virginia's receipt of a card from Elden three days later—apparently promising to visit her the following Sunday—immediately revives the previous affection. She reveals another interesting clue about Bugeye, but the clue joins other negative remarks that suggest much about the times and perhaps about Elden and Virginia and the crowd they ran with. Steward, four months past sixteen years of age, has been seeing the wife of a man who was away in the service.

November 7, 1943

Dearest Tex,

That sure was a cute card I got from you this morning. My kisses don't last 7 days though.

I hope you hurry up and come back to Las Animas. I haven't gone any place for 4 weeks. I've had plenty of chances but I'm waiting for you. I have something very important to tell you. Say, why don't you bring your car back with you. We could have a lot of fun then.

Its really getting cold here. It has snowed once.

I'm really sorry I've been so long in writing to you. I have been pretty busy though. I have finally made up my mind between two people. I will tell you about it when you come back up here.

Tell Chuck Bernice's husband is home so he better wait awhile before he comes back here. I seen them at the show Friday night.

Well, I am looking forward to Sunday. You had better be sure and be here.

Loads of Love,

Virginia

Elden seems to be preparing to visit Colorado again as Virginia writes about the uncertain things that preoccupied young girls during wartime, as she considers joining the Women's Army Auxiliary Corps. It is in some way significant that Elden has sent her a special delivery letter that cost more and also provided proof that Virginia had received it. In the meantime, since Bugs cannot date Bernice because her soldier husband is at home and ready to fight, he is moving in on Carlton Six's girlfriend Janet.

November 12, 1943

Dearest Tex,

I received a special delivery letter from you this morning so I had better answer before you get up here.

Yes, I guess Chuck is beating Six'es time with Janet. She likes Chuck an awfully lot. Say, I know a boy up here that would like to fight Chuck. He is a soldier and he leaves Monday, so if he wants to fight him he had better hurry up here.

I guess I will join the W.A.A.C.s. There isn't anything to do here. Do you like women soldiers?

If you don't I won't join them. There isn't anything to do here. I don't see how you kids can stand to come to Las Animas, its so dead. Amarillo sounds like it is bursting with excitement.

Tell Chuck that Janet sure misses him. She has to sit all by herself in the show since he went away. Tell him I'll try and answer his letter too.

Love,

Virginia

Wandering boys are worrisome to mothers, and Elden had wandered back to Colorado by November 28 when Grace addressed a letter to him there. Meanwhile, as she frets about how he is spending time that could have been spent writing her, other American boys not much older—but very different because they had become United States Marines—were finishing up their victory at Tarawa, capturing the last island of the atoll after eight days of fighting.[5]

Twenty years later, Grace would be one of the last women in Vega who baked bread regularly, but in 1943 many did so. Women cultivated a bit of live yeast rather than buy it at a store, and if their yeast was used up or had been allowed to expire, they simply borrowed new starter from a friend. Mary Steward, Bugeye's mother, who refers to him as Bud, has come to get some yeast and has indirectly brought a bit of news about Elden. The Tom mentioned in this letter is also Mary's son, who apparently did not like his given name of Irwin and had adopted the shorter name.

November 28, 1943

Dear Son Elden,

Im going to try writing a few lines again to see if I can hear from you. Why don't you write? Ive been looking for a letter for a week. I got your card you wrote just after you got there & I answered it with a card.

What are you doing? Mary was up here one evening to get some yeast and she had a letter from Bud & he said you guys was going out to shuck some Corn the next day. What about your job on that road?

I seen Letha yesterday at the store & she said Toms wife & Baby was at Marys Thursday.

What did you do Thanksgiving & did you have a good dinner?

We had a pretty nice dinner as we butchered that white pig we got from Stewart & had liver for dinner. Sure was good as we had Cranberries Celery & pumpkin pie to go with it.

We have had a little winter. It snowed Thursday Night & Friday. Was pretty Cold too. We never went to Sunday school this morning. I made an Angel food Cake as tomarrow is Dads Birthday, So we celebrated today, too bad you wasn't here to help us.

I forgot to tell you that we got Jerry some Cow boy boots that night after we left you. Got them at Stubblefields They are black. He sure likes them & I ordered his Cow boy hat & got it & his plaid shirt. He sure looks cute in his hat but he hasn't got to wear it yet.

We never got our picture proofs till yesterday. I don't like them much. I don't like the way he had you & Gerald to lean over. If you was here I would make them take them over. The ones of you alone are good But we like the one Where you are not smiling so Much the best.

The old red sow had 15 pigs last night. She still has 12 don't know how shes going to do with them With 9 tits.

Well its 10:30 and Dad may go to Amarillo in the Morning if he Can get a ride so guess Id better sign off & go to bed. Now if you don't have a letter on the way to me you get busy and write me a letter. I am always uneasy when I don't hear from you. & let us know what you are doing.

From a Loving Mother.

[in Ancell Rogers's handwriting:] Mon-29 got your cards today Will ans Tues Am in Amarillo today.

From dad

Pork liver for Thanksgiving dinner! Turkey was not commonly available at that time and place, and roast chicken was our normal Thanksgiving meal until the early 1950s, but cranberries, celery dressing, and pumpkin pie were part of the tradition. We could have chicken almost any time, and usually did when an old hen had passed her productive time and stopped laying eggs. Liver, however, was a particularly special treat to be enjoyed when it was available. In those days before frozen food was common and when even the block of ice to cool our small icebox was almost a luxury, liver was neither purchased in a store nor kept for later use. It was eaten with great delight on the fall day when the butchering had been done, and that day was determined by factors such as whether one had to work elsewhere, whether frost had killed the flies for the season, and whether the weather was cold enough to keep the meat fresh during the process. Most families who produced their own meat ate all the fresh liver they could immediately and offered some of it to friends and neighbors. Today, when we are inclined to think of the carbon footprint of food raised, processed, packaged, frozen, and transported long distances before being eaten, it is worth noting that, aside from the cranberries that came from faraway New England, the carbon footprint of that 1943 Thanksgiving was very small.

Elden had written three cards in sixteen days, not a very bad record for a seventeen-year-old boy who is off exploring the world, but it was not good enough for Grace, for whom a prompt answer to a card or letter was an expected courtesy. More was being expressed than frequency of correspondence, however—she clearly was displeased and worried about what Elden was up to. The question about a job on a road suggests that Elden had probably talked up job prospects before but had not gotten the job. Her letter of November 29 presses harder, asking about what seems to have been a job prospect with a construction company, clucking at the boys' decision to rent an apartment, questioning its cost, and admonishing him to save money. Times at home are still very hard. Ancell does not have a steady job and has not worked at all for two weeks. Rationing has a significant impact on what people can buy and what they can do. With gasoline severely rationed, Ancell did not drive to Amarillo but rather caught a ride with someone taking a dog to the veterinarian and then rode a bus back to Vega. Grace's interjection of "ha" is all she needs to write to reveal that our family would not have considered spending scarce money on medical treatment for a sick dog.

November 29, 1943

Dear Son,

Ill try writing again tonight. We got your 2 Cards today written Nov 26. But I hadn't got but one Card from you before & it was the one you wrote Just after you got there So if you wrote any more we never got it. And I answered that card right back So I have been wondering why we didn't hear from you.

Dad went to Amarillo today and took the picture proofs back. They are supposed to have them finished by Dec 10.

How come you kids rented an Apartment? Looks like a Cabin would suit you better. No we haven't moved yet. Don't know yet where we are going.

We seen in the Amarillo paper the other day where Jack Williams got married. Had a Church wedding in Amarillo & Bro Godwin was the minister.

Gerald went to scout meeting & Jerry is in bed asleep.

Dad came out on the bus. He rode in with Mrs. Fosters Brother. He was taking his dog to the Dr. <u>ha</u>. It had got hold of some rat poison.

Well if you don't need your sugar stamp Ill keep it & send the books on. But be sure & don't loose them. The Next sugar stamp wont be good till Jan 15.

(Tuesday A.M.) There is a shoe stamp in one of these Books so I wont send the one with No 18 in it as you wont be apt to buy more than one pair. I can send it if you want it.

What happened to the road after that Construction Co. left? I wouldn't think they could leave till it was finished.

What do you have to pay for the Apartment You better be trying to save some Money As we could use what we got coming to pay on the pictures.

Dad hasn't worked any since you left.

Well I will sign off so Dad Can take this & get it Mailed. And I will get at my ironing.

So we will be looking to hear from you.

Love. Mother

Grace and Ancell were thinking of moving from the house on the cemetery road rented from Bose McNabb, but had no definite plans and had not yet bought the place at 504 East Main Street in town, to which they would move in 1944. The McNabb house had several disadvantages. There was no well, and water for household use and for animals had to be hauled from Louis Linger's well in a trailer tank and in a steel barrel on the front bumper of the Model A. A plot for a vegetable garden had to be borrowed from either the Linger family or the Funk family, who lived not far away.

Elden has written at least one more card and has asked to borrow another $10, a pretty brazen request after his mother had questioned his judgment in renting an apartment, admonished him to be saving money to repay what he already owed, and told him that his father was out of work. That these thrifty parents went ahead and loaned Elden the equivalent of several days' pay even though Ancell had no job signifies that they were more indulgent than their bluster about thrift and repayment would suggest. More importantly, it indicates that Grace and Ancell had money in the bank—surely not much, but they carefully managed what little they did have. A few months later they bought two city blocks in Vega for $100 per block and bought a little house from Iva and Cal Mathes. Grace told me shortly before her death that they never went into debt to buy anything, but always saved first and then bought with cash, probably a lesson learned from their experience buying the little farm in 1927. Even when Ancell's work was intermittent, they were saving to buy the house and land in town. Elden may or may not have known that, but this underscores another reason why they were not happy about having to send him money for his adventures while he could have been living at home for virtually no additional expense to the family.

But there was enough money for me to have a new shirt, a cowboy hat, and cowboy boots from Stubblefield's department store in Amarillo.

On December 6, 1943, Ancell went to "the sale" in Amarillo. In local parlance, that automatically meant the livestock auction. More nearly to save gasoline ration coupons than money, Ancell got a ride with Robert Hobbs. He was evaluating his assets, which existed primarily in the form of livestock, and probably trying to choose the best time to sell and to estimate how much he might net from the proceeds.

Seven of fifteen piglets surviving, and a hen with her tail bitten off—these were the things that mattered most. Without a regular income, the food we raised was more important than the food we bought; the difference between seven pigs and fifteen pigs was enormous, and eating an injured laying hen was a matter of salvage. Hens were stewed in a big pot with homemade noodles after they became too old to produce eggs, but never during their productive time.

⚓

Four hooks in the ceiling; whatever else might be found in the living rooms of most of Grace's friends, you could count on four hooks in the ceiling. These were the insignia of a quilting circle that allowed an occasional break from the daily routine of hard work at home. Women who belonged to the group brought covered dishes and their young children to one member's home, worked together for several hours hand-stitching a quilt, and enjoyed a good meal and gossip while the kids played outdoors. From the hooks a quilting frame could be suspended by cords. The frame held the quilt that was being created, and the apparatus could be lowered to a level where women sitting in chairs could easily work on it. Then the whole thing could be raised back to just below ceiling level when work was not being done.[6] This was a very important and highly productive way of making needed, often beautiful, and always durable items from scraps of old clothing while sharing news, enjoying companionship, and reinforcing the bonds of community. Today's economy has made this practice obsolete. Communities would be stronger today if more houses had four hooks in their ceilings.

In the letter below, Pauline was the wife of Howard Blasingame Sr., and Mrs. Voiles was the mother of Jay Voyles. By my memory, other members of this group of a dozen probably included Loretta Fergerson, Iva Mathes, Linda (always pronounced Lindy) and Mary Steward, Marie McKendree (Hot Dog's wife), and the wife of George "Elephant" Miller.[7] This group was close enough that they exchanged small Christmas presents and drew names to determine who gave a present to whom.

Dear Son,

I will write a few lines tonight. We got your card this morning.

Dad went to Amarillo today. To the sale. He went with Robert Hobbs. He wanted to see how cattle was selling.

I washed today. Sure was chilly hanging out the Clothes. Got them all dry. I had the quilting last Thursday. Got the Quilt done. Sure had a good dinner & a good time. There was about a dozen women here. We will have our Christmas quilting at Paulines Dec 16. I got Mrs. Voiles Name and Jerry got Cecil Blasingames.

I may get to go to Amarillo one day this week as Mrs. Landrum wants me to drive for her.

Dad said he would send you $10. But he is going to expect you to send it back & that other $10 too when you get your Check So we can have it to pay for the pictures when they are finished.

Is the weather fit for you to work? If you are not getting in any time & not making enough to keep going you had better be at home. You can find something around here to do.

We are going to have Chicken tomarrow. Dads old red sow bit a hen's tail off this evening so I killed her. She was a laying hen too. I sure hated it. His sow only saved 7 pigs out of the 15. But it was Bad weather when they came.

Did I tell you Jerry has his Cow boy hat Boots & plaid shirt. He really thinks hes big.

Well I don't know any news for now so guess Id better Close & go to bed. So write soon & we'll be seeing you before Christmas.

Love.

Mother

The letter above was sent by registered mail, requiring a return receipt signed by Elden, indicating that the envelope contained a check or money order for ten dollars.

Two weeks later, we can infer from Virginia's next letter, Elden has been to Las Animas only shortly before, has returned to Vega, apparently having survived an automobile accident en route, and has written to Virginia. More importantly, he has proposed marriage. The seriousness of the proposal seems uncertain, however, from the sometimes lighthearted ways she writes of it in this and other letters. He is still three months short of age eighteen, but is very much aware that he must soon enlist or be drafted. Millions of young people during the war years found themselves in situations similar to that of Elden and Virginia, and large numbers of them were propelled into marriage at ages much younger than would have been normal. Many decisions made under this pressure were ill-considered and unfortunate, but the feeling of pressure was appropriate.

Having been spotted honky-tonking with a boy, Virginia hastens a preemptive confession before Chuck Steward can tell Elden. She further reveals that she has harbored a strong attraction to Chuck and that he has been among the other boys she has dated. She has resolved her ambivalence in favor of Elden after Chuck did something too terrible to put in writing, and she no longer speaks to him. Perhaps for this reason she seems unaware that Chuck, although barely sixteen and a half years old, has sworn to the navy that he is older and enlisted on December 14 and is probably already at boot camp.

As for the war itself, in faraway Honolulu, Fleet Admiral Chester Nimitz was contemplating war strategy and deciding that his next target would be Kwajalein, 2,000 miles southwest of Hawaii.[8]

December 20, 1943

Dearest Tex,

I was sort of surprised to hear from you. I didn't think you would be there yet. You just about didn't get there I guess. You all could have gotten killed when that car turned over. It would have scared me to death.

Saturday night I went with that kid from La Junta. Chuck saw us so I suppose he will write and tell you. He brought his guitar down and a soldier came with him in a 1942 convertible coupe. I guess it was 1942, and another girl & us went to the cape. There wasn't very many out there though. I really don't like this kid very well but he has money and usually has a car. I can hardly stand him though.

No Chuck hasn't been down since you left. I have seen him a lot but never talked to him. When I said I had made up my mind between two people it was between you and Chuck. When you kids first came down here I thought Chuck was cute and I really didn't know whether I liked him or you the best but I found out not long ago. I guess he has a way with the girls until they see his true colors. He thinks he can get a date with any girl he wants to but I would like for him to ask me to go with him again. I believe I would slap his face. Why don't you bet him some money that he can't get me to go with him. He thinks anyone will. You will make some money that way and then you can come back up here and see me.

Yes, I went to La Junta but forgot to get that negative. I went to get it once and they were closed until 3 o clock and then I forgot all about it. I didn't get a job either. I guess I will have to take you up on that proposal but I don't think you really like me well enough to marry me. If I married you would I have to get a job? Where would we live? I like you awfully well but I don't know whether I love you or not. You don't give me a chance to fall in love, because I don't see you enough. If we went together steady about three times a week maybe I would. It takes time, for me anyway because I fell for a boy once before and he jilted me and I hate him now.

I hope you can read this. I am writing pretty fast because I want to get ready and go to the show tonight.

Those kids that got married haven't come back from Kansas yet. I guess they are working in defense at Wichita.

Well, I will close this now and write again after you do.

Lots of Love,

Virginia.

By the New Year the passage of time, perhaps the mellowing of the Christmas season, and almost certainly the approach of military service and forced separation have produced a significant increase in Virginia's expressed affection. Still, the ambivalence seems juvenile, as in one sentence she says she will wait to decide about marriage until she sees him again and in another she calls herself engaged to be married. She also needles Elden about not having an engagement ring and says she is still spending time with the guy from La Junta. She has not joined the WAAC as mentioned earlier, but now plans to move to join the Nurses Aid in Pueblo, which will get her away from her hometown and out of her parents' house.

January 4, 1944

Dearest Darling,

I am sitting here thinking about you and copying songs. Maureen is teaching me how to sing "Pins and Needles In My Heart." It is sure pretty don't you think. Do you still want the words to "The End of the World." I have them all I think.

I think it would be nice to marry you honey, but I won't promise until I see you again and I hope that will be soon.

Did I tell you Maureen and I were going to Pueblo and join the Nurses Aid? We get 40 cents per hour. I guess we will have to find a room. I don't know whether we'll make enough to live on or not but we can try. I will send you my new address as soon as we get up there. When you get your car fixed you & Six can drive up there and see us and I'll cook you a big dinner all by myself. It would probably kill you. Ha You can bring someone else besides Six tho because Maureen & Him don't get along so well.

The Cape is closed for two weeks. They are re-decorating it into a horse-shoe bar, then they'll serve cock-tails. I'll have to stay home on Saturday nights now since I'm engaged to be married to you. The trouble is I don't have anything to prove it.

Mickey (from La Junta) came down last night and played his guitar until I was asleep (almost). He brought a soldier with him for Maureen. He was sure cute too.

Well, I have to write some more letters now so keep thinking of me once in a while.

Sending you all my love & kisses
Forever Yours,
Virginia

By January 11 Virginia withdraws the needle about not having a ring, speaks firmly of intent to marry, and reveals that she has broken up with the guy from La Junta. She has heard from Elden, who apparently has kidded her about a hidden meaning in putting the stamp upside down on the envelope.

January 11, 1943

Dearest Tex,

I am sending the song "To The End of the World." I hope you can read it. I heard you were a real good singer but I never heard you sing. Maybe you will sing to me after we are married. Will you?

That kid from La Junta, (Mickey) and I broke up. I finally told him off. I just couldn't stand him any longer. I sure wish you would come up here with a car. We could have lots of fun. If a person doesn't have a car there isn't much to do.

Forget what I said about a ring. Maureen dared me to write that to you. I can still love you just as much without one.

We haven't gotten any money to get to Pueblo with yet. I guess we will get there some day though.

It is getting pretty warm here. The snow isn't all melted yet but its real warm. I bet you are about frozen down there in Texas. You should come back to warm Colorado and go in the Main Café and play the Music Box. They have some swell records on it by Ernest Tubb.

Tell Carl Six "hello" for me. Does he know we are going to get married? What does he think about it. I don't think he likes me very well. He or Chuck either one did.

I'm glad that Ferguson kid got to come home.[9] He was too young to be in the Navy anyway. I think it will do Chuck good though.

I didn't know when stamps were on upside down that it meant don't answer. I'm sorry I put it on that way. I want you to write as often as you can.

All My Love,
Virginia

Bob Walcott's family has moved from Vega to Alamogordo, New Mexico. The teenage banter in his postcard refers to five individuals in Vega, only one by a given name and four by nicknames.

January 20, 1944

Dear Sleeves,
Well old boy how is every thing running up at Vega? I guess Bump is still around. I wrote Murph and Slim a letter but they haven't ans. Yet.

Say could you send me some gas stamps. I sure could use them. Is there any snow up there now. Damn it is sure warm here. The women are thick as hair on a dogs back.

Boy we have our choice here about the dances, we can go to one with an ocrestra or a foot and fiddle. What happened to Louie Brents. Tell Murph & Slim hello & ans soon.

A Pal,
Bob

Soon we learn that Elden has told Virginia that Chuck Steward already dislikes the navy. Elden has a new job that apparently will require his moving from Vega for a while. Concerning the matter of both Virginia and Elden running with the wrong crowds, it is surely significant that Virginia's parents would allow her to move to Pueblo, but not with Maureen, who seems to be her best friend.

January 20, 1944

Dearest Tex,

It is sure getting warm here but I guess its just getting ready to snow again. That's the way it does, when it gets nice and warm for a day or two and brings our hopes up it snows again.

I'm sorry to hear Chuck doesn't like the Navy, but I think it will do him a lot of good to take something he doesn't like for once.

I guess you are wondering why I haven't gotten to Pueblo yet, but my folks had different ideas about it. They won't let me go. If I went with someone besides Maureen she would tho. She doesn't like her very well.

My ears are sure burning, someone must be talking about me. My nose itches too, so maybe someone is coming. I hope they do, because I'm getting tired of sitting at home all the time. I had a swell time Monday night. I haven't went any place with Maureen for about a month. She has to stay out on a ranch with her Uncle and Aunt. Her Aunt is going to have a baby.

Did I tell you about the murder we had up here? Well I'll tell you again in case I didn't. Lawrence Kennedy (I don't know whether you know him or not, but he has lived here all his life and is only 17 years old). He went to Mr. Hudnell's house here in Las Animas and said "This is a hold up and I'm serious" Mrs. Hudnell came to the door and Mr Hudnell was behind her. Lawrence said he wanted $100.00 so Mr Hudnell went and got his bill fold and handed it to him & he took it with the same hand he had the gun in & Mr. Hudnell knocked it out of his hand & reached down to pick it up & Lawrence stabbed him with a hunting knife in the back two or three times. They say he will get the electric chair but I think he is too young for that. Colorado is getting about as bad as Texas isn't it. A man out at the fort [Fort Lyons State Hospital] hung himself the other day. I guess he was a patient though.

I guess I will mail this now so you will get it before you leave for that other job you have. I hope I can see you real soon.

Love,

Virginia

Japan had long expected and prepared for an American attack in the southern Marianas, but they had not expected Nimitz to hit the atoll of Kwajalein in the Marshall Islands far to the east on January 31. It had been lightly defended and was quickly conquered.

Never one to lose time, two weeks after securing Kwajalein Nimitz went after Eniwetok, which was within reach of land-based air support from the powerful base Japan had maintained at Truk since 1939. How to capture Truk, Japan's counterpart to Pearl Harbor as the center of its naval power in the Pacific, had been a source of worry in the navy and of much speculation in the press. Instead of attempting to capture it, Nimitz chose to hit it hard in order to prevent Truk-based aircraft from resisting the Eniwetok landing. Planes from U.S. carriers on February 16 and 17 conducted a fierce surprise attack of 1,250 combat sorties, dropping five hundred tons of bombs and torpedoes on installations and ships in the lagoon. The attack knocked out 200,000 tons of shipping and destroyed two hundred planes, and was so successful that Truk was effectively neutralized and required little attention thereafter.[10] The episode demonstrated, to the surprise and chagrin of Japanese military leaders and to the delight of their American counterparts, that the Japanese occupation of the Pacific could be overcome without capturing every Japanese-held island in the region—even the strongest and most important ones. The strategy later called "island hopping," which concentrated on capturing only the key islands and leaving others isolated and beyond reinforcement, has generally been attributed to MacArthur, but in fact it grew out of the experiences of both MacArthur and Nimitz.

The United States established control of Eniwetok by February 23 and began immediately to convert it into an enormous base for carriers and their supporting fleets as well as a rest and relaxation area for their crews. The inner defenses of the Japanese empire had been breached and a pattern set of aggressive operations based on overwhelming carrier-based airpower.[11]

Neither Elden nor Virginia can know that he will be at this faraway atoll in barely more than four months, but they know his civilian time is short, and they can no longer avoid talking of it.

February 16, 1944

My Dearest Tex,

I will send you the picture as soon as the man in La Junta sends it to me. He said he would send it C.O.D. so I'll have to stay pretty close to home.

It sure is cold here. There isn't any snow but frost is on the trees and they look so pretty. It seems like spring is coming. There are a lot of birds anyway.

I'm glad you are going to join the Navy instead of the Army. I think you will look swell in a sailor uniform. You are right when you said we should wait until after the war to get married. I think it would be best, and I'll wait for you until the war is over even if it lasts for 10 years, because I really like you an awfully lot, even if I do go with other boys I like you the best of all. I hope you can come up here and see me before you leave. If you don't I'll be very angry with you. Is Carl going to join the Navy too?

It sure surprised me to hear Carl quit drinking. I didn't know whether you ever drank or not. Oh yes, I remember now you were drunk in the theater one night. I knew you didn't drink as much as Chuck & Carl though.

Cyle, Charles, and Herman and all those boys are still here. I don't know why they don't go to the Army. I know they are old enough. Maybe they have flat feet or something.

I went to the show last night with Mom. It wasn't very good. Tomorrow night is "Pistol Packin Mama." I sure want to see it.

I'm going to a party tonite I guess. I went to one last Sunday nite and it was sure a failure. I didn't have a bit of fun.

Well, I hope you can get up here pretty soon. You can get on out at the Fort. Dad said they were hiring men out there now. Your salary would be $100 a month and you wouldn't be drafted. Well, I hope you don't get tired reading this book.

I'll be looking for you honey, so don't disappoint me by not coming. Because I'm awfully lonesome for you.

All My Love,
Virginia

The once-universally understood "C.O.D." may not be familiar to everyone today. "Collect on delivery" (or "cash on delivery") was a service offered by the Post Office in which the letter carrier would collect payment from a customer for an item upon delivery and then send the money to the person or business who had mailed the item.

The movie *Pistol Packin' Mama,* recommended by Elden and mentioned by Virginia, is a 1943 "crime musical," of limited quality starring Ruth Terry, Robert Livingston, and Wally Vernon. Probably the best thing about it was the fact that it included Nat King Cole and his King Cole Trio. The title had been expropriated from the most popular song in the nation at the moment and pasted onto a plot that resembled the song lyrics only in that both included women and pistols. One suspects that Elden liked the movie mostly for its association with the song, about which we will hear more.

The next letter reveals that Chuck Steward is back in Las Animas, presumably on leave after completing basic training. Elden's eighteenth birthday, when he will become subject to the draft, is less than one month away and both he and Virginia are becoming acutely conscious of time.

February 24, 1944

Dearest Tex,

I received the pictures today so will send you one. I got two of them reprinted as my sister wanted one too. They don't look like the other ones and I told him to make them exactly like the first ones but he made them smaller. I would like to pull his hair out. My mouth looks too big. I know its big but I didn't want it to show in the picture. Don't show it to anyone.

Oh, gee honey, I miss you so much. I wish you would hurry and come up here. If you don't I'm liable to come down there, how would you like that? I think I have fallen in love with you finally. "Absence Makes the Heart Grow Fonder" you know. Don't think I'm just telling you this because I'm not. I mean I never tell anyone I love them unless I really do, and you are the first boy I ever really loved I think. If what I feel for you is love, I'll wait for you until the war is over if it lasts for ten years.

Excuse the paper. I got this when I was up in the mountains on a trip.

My mother is working today so I have to get dinner for my little brothers when they get home from school.

Are you going to bring Carl with you when you come up here? Oh, I saw Chuck last night at the show. We looked right at each other and I never spoke to him because I hate the very ground he walks on. You can tell him if you want too, then he'll know I don't like him. Tell Carl hello for me and tell him I wouldn't let Chuck take Janet away from me if I was him. I think she likes Carl the best anyway. I don't see how she can stand old Chuck. Write soon.

With All My Love,
Virginia

Virginia has developed an intention to move to Kansas, where she says she hopes to work and expects to live with her aunt, whom she calls "sister" in this letter. She seems not to have done so until August, but the anticipation of a move and the certainty of Elden's impending departure cause her to plead with him to visit her again soon. Typically, however, it does not prevent her writing to him about being with cute boys.

March 9, 1944

My Dearest Tex,

I think its your time to write but its very important for you to hurry up here. I'm leaving for sure now. I already have the money to go on and everything. I just want to see you before I leave. I'm going to Fort Scott Kansas to visit my sister & work in some plant there.

It has been real warm here, just like spring. I kind of hate to leave on that account, because its probably pretty cold in Kansas.

I don't know whether you are in Texas or not, but I hope I see you real soon and hope you had a nice time visiting your relations & friends.

You will have to excuse the scribbling but I'm in an awfully big hurry.

I went to Hasty last night. They sure have some cute boys there. Earl went with us and a bunch of Hasty girls & boys. I sure hate to leave all my friends here but I guess I can make more only it takes me pretty long. Maybe I'm just not the friendly type.

Well, I have some work to do so will quit for now and hope I see you in a few days. If you can't come tell me and I won't be so disappointed. We would just have to say goodbye anyway & I hate goodbyes.

All my Love,
Virginia

Elden made a farewell tour, visiting relatives and friends in several places prior to enlisting, including a visit to Virginia in Las Animas.

Hitchhiking, in those days of limited money and rationed gasoline, was a respectable way of getting around, and he used it. By extraordinary coincidence a truck that stopped to pick him up turned out to be driven by his first cousin Lyle Roberts, the son of Ancell's sister Cloria.

Many people in those days and in that part of the country delighted in paying surprise visits to distant friends and relatives without notice. Usually the surprised party was equally delighted to put a few more potatoes in the pot, add a little milk and flour to the gravy, put kids to sleep on the floor so grown guests could have a bed, and to play host on the spur of the moment.

Elden has saved the best of his tour for last, no doubt anticipating a thrilled welcome from Virginia when he appears unexpectedly. A last date before committing one's life to war would be *the* date—the most important of his life—when all that mattered to two people was being together. Unimaginable things might happen.

They did. On the night he arrived unannounced, Virginia had a date with the older guy with the nice car and money and farms enough to exempt him from the draft. Quickly improvising the fiction that Elden was her cousin, she paired him with Maureen and went double-dating to the Cape nightclub. Capping disappointment with humiliation, at some point she and the older guy left Elden and Maureen stranded at the Cape while they went to yet another joint called the Alpine. Confronted with the unanticipated choice of a farewell evening with "Dearest Tex," and having future dates while Tex was away, Virginia had hedged her bets.

Elden had falsely told Virginia he had a car, and that he was older than he really was. Now they were even, and apart, and unhappy.

"Selective" was an apt word in the Selective Service law that would make Elden subject to the draft when he reached age eighteen on March 19, 1944. The obligation of young men to register for the draft was universal in this great democracy, but after the registration step little about it was either universal or democratic. Many factors came into play as local draft boards *selected* who among the registered would go into ships, planes, tanks, and foxholes. The same decisions by omission determined who would remain at home, dating the girls with reduced competition, selling crops at war-boosted prices, and even accumulating land and wealth while under the protection of those who had been selected. A married man was slightly less likely to be drafted than one who was single, and a married father less likely than a childless married man. A married man with two or more children was in most places unlikely to be drafted. Age was a factor, with younger men more vulnerable than older ones. The most troublesome factor was one that took into account the importance to the war effort of the kind of work a man did. Some jobs were undeniably vital to the war effort, and men who owned land or had money were far more likely to be doing something vital while men with lesser means were more likely to be sent before the guns. Food production was among the most vital home front functions, and the sons of locals who owned and farmed land were lower on the draft priority list than those who did not.

Hard times produce many losers and a few winners. Had Ancell been able as some had been during the Dust Bowl to increase his holdings by double, quadruple, or more, his sons might have been engaged in vital home front work. But bad markets and dry winds had taken his farm from him and he could not shelter his footloose, unschooled, and intermittently employed boy. The draft was lawful and rational, perhaps even right, but no power on earth could make it fair. Beneath the surface of the united America so fondly remembered today lay this almost-forgotten divisive unfairness that everyone knew about and that almost everyone accepted. Elden knew it, he felt it, and he accepted it.

6 Hang Up Your Flags and Put On Your Pins

ELDEN'S choice was to be drafted the day after Sunday, March 19, and most likely to be assigned to the U.S. Army or the Marine Corps, or to volunteer before that date for the service of his choice. He had thought at length about the branches of the armed forces, and he knew the differences. The "Dogfaces" of the army and the "Leathernecks" of the marine corps faced danger in personal and individual ways, slogged through and slept in dust and mud, and often ate packaged rations when and where they could. Sailors faced danger as members of crews, unable to duck or dodge or jump into a foxhole, but they slept in clean and sheltered bunks and for most meals sat at tables to eat freshly cooked food. With that difference uppermost in mind, he took a train on March 16, 1944, from Amarillo to the induction station in Lubbock, Texas, and joined the United States Navy on Friday, March 17, becoming serial number 357-53-50. Five slots ahead of him in the enlistment process was a tall strapping lad from the town of Miles, near San Angelo, Texas. Roy Treadaway soon became his best buddy.[1]

March 17, 1944

Dear folks,

Well hang up your service flags & put on your navy pin as I am now a Sailor. Well Chopear just as well quit licking his chops as I was sworn in about 5 P.M. I passed the test I was perfect on everything. Mental and all. Had five inch chest expansion the Best out of 48 men. Well I leave for San Diego at 1 P.M. tomorrow. I will write more when I get there.

Elden

"Chopear!" Now there was a nickname that did not convey acceptance into a peer group. It was surreptitiously applied to Raymond L. Thompson, president and chairman of the board of the First State Bank of Vega. Just short of forty years old, married, a father, and a substantial farmer, he was sheltered from the draft, and as a leading citizen of the county he was head of the draft board. Many years before, Thompson had part of an ear bitten off during a fight and was sometimes behind his back called names that referred to the slight disfigurement. Early in the century Thompson's father had been "depot" agent for the Rock Island Railroad in Wildorado, Texas, and then in Vega and in nearby Adrian. Raymond had graduated from college when few others did and was a self-made man who had earned his place of respect in the community; but there are signs here of a divide between the haves and the have-nots.[2]

When Elden left to join the navy, Gerald had mumps, a very contagious glandular inflammation endured without much harm by most people in childhood but potentially dangerous to adults. Elden and the family he left behind were concerned that he, too, might come down with the mumps at a critical moment in travel or during the physical rigors of training.

As Elden rode westward across New Mexico and Arizona on this critical birthday, under-aged and unhappy Bugeye Steward boarded the troop transport USS *General J. R. Brooke* (AP-132) bound for New Caledonia, and the brand-new *Franklin* sailed from her Norfolk, Virginia, birthplace for test runs in Chesapeake Bay.[3]

In Washington, D.C., Nimitz and Fleet Admiral Ernest J. King met for a significant update in planning. Rapid success in the Marshall Islands operation had strengthened their strategic concept of using

Eniwetok as a major base from which U.S. forces would move westward through the central Pacific to the Marianas and eventually invade Japan. They worried about MacArthur's press for a strategy of moving northward from Australia until he could return as promised to the Philippines and only then move toward Japan. While stateside, Nimitz took a brief moment to participate in his daughter's wedding, and then by March 21 he was again on duty at Pearl Harbor.[4]

Waiting eagerly for MacArthur in the Philippines, Vega boy, army man, and prisoner of war Bish McKendree received his first letters and a box of "luxuries" from home. After almost two years in prison camps, the letters from home were wonderful, but they brought news that Jimmy Bales was dead.[5] As Bish was dealing with conflicting emotions, Vega boy, navy man, and raw recruit Elden Rogers was learning his new reality in boot camp near San Diego, California.

March 22, 1944

Dear Folks,

Well I have about ten minutes so I'll write a few lines. I am O.K. They are working me pretty hard but I can take that. I got two shots & 1 vactination yesterday so my arm is pretty sore. I will get a leave in about Six weeks. I'll get five days besides traveling time, in other words five days at home. It sure is hot here now. I'll get a liberty in three weeks to go to town. Saw Krahn [E. L. Krahn from Vega] and bob Walcott last nite. Buchanan [Don Buchanan from Vega] is in the hospital with Scarlet fever.

Well So Long
Elden

The wandering Elden, having prematurely broken the bonds of adolescence and having spent so much of the past year away from home, may not have experienced homesickness in the navy. His letters do not convey that feeling, but now that home is beyond reach at his volition they do begin to show a strong interest in connecting with friends and family that will continue to the very end. These first two letters from boot camp mention four other Vega boys who are in the same camp, and they ask about three more who are not. He also related an attempt to speak with his uncle Lloyd Rogers, Ancell's older brother, who lives in California.

March 26, 1944

Dear Folks,

Well this is Sunday and I don't have anything to do so I'll send my Birth Certificate. Put the other junk in my collection. I Saw E.L., Bob Walcott, & Carlton Buck last night we was at the Canteen for awhile then we went to the U.S.O. show they had a bunch of actors from Hollywood here It sure was a good show. My company is about 90% Texans. When is Pumper [Boydstun from Vega] comeing out. Get Bug-Eyes and Louie Brents addresses and send them to me. I had a 3 ½ hour layover in Los Angeles. I found Loyds [Elden's paternal uncle] Tellephone no. in the directory but there didn't get an answer when I tried to call. Well I don't know much news so I'll close. I'll write evertime I get any Spare time.

Love
Elden

The navy is interviewing Elden's group of recruits, probing haphazardly for a sense of how best to use their skills, and sowing false hope that they might get safe and easy duty stateside rather than being assigned to warships. Elden has been asked his preferences for service and led to believe that he might be sent to school in Virginia or Connecticut to learn diesel mechanics. Later in the training period he will briefly "study" other things. Eventually many recruits would come to believe that this had all been meaningless, and that actual duty assignments were made virtually at random.[6]

March 28, 1944

Dear Mom, Dad, & Bros,

Well I received a letter from you yesterday & one today was glad to hear from you. I just got off guard duty I was on from Six to Eight tonight. Sure was glad I wasn't on in the middle of the night again. Well I get another haircut and two more shots tomorrow. I was interviewed today and I got Basic engeneering Specialising in Desil. And Second choice was Fireman on a merchant Ship. Armed Guard as the navy calls it. Well I had to go through an Obsticle cource today It was pretty rough. We had to climb up a rope ladder on the side of a wall 18 feet high and jump off the other side and swing over a hole of water about three feet deep. I really like the navy especially since I found out I was going to school. I will probably go to scool in Virginnia, or conn. Krahn & Walcott signed up for Submarine Duty they will be Sent to Connecticut for Schooling. I better close as I have to help swab the deck (floor) tonight.

Love
Elden

Bobby Walcott was born at Dexter, New Mexico, October 25, 1925. Later his family had lived north of Vega on the "Rafter-O" ranch and then in town in a house near the lumberyard. Bobby had joined the navy on January 29, 1944.[7] His mother was an enrolled member of the Choctaw nation, and his older brother Vincent, known as Tubby not because he was corpulent but because Tubbi was a pet name derived from the Choctaw language that their mother applied to her beloved child, had enlisted earlier and was serving in the Pacific.[8] Either Elden was mistaken about Krahn and Walcott signing up for submarine duty or they did not get it. Elden, new to the navy, appears a bit more credulous than he should have been about possible duties being mentioned to him.

March 31, 1944

Dear Mom, Dad & Bros,

Well I just finished another Day. I got my washing done so I thought I'd send this Insurance Policy home and write a few lines.

Well I had two teeth filled yesterday. They are going to put a corner on that front tooth that is broken. I don't know whether it will be gold or silver. They filled the teeth with silver they sure did do a good job of it. Well I get a liberty to go to town a week from Monday. I'll get some pictures taken and send you some. Say How about sending me about three Dollars as I am about broke. I have 65 cents to be exact.

Well Krahn was over last night he thinks he'll be shipped out any time he don't know for sure. He said he thought that Walcott had been shipped out as he hadn't seen him in about a week. I talked to Carlton buck on the phone last nite and decided to get a pass and go over to camp Paul Jones and go to the show with him Sunday. I am in camp Decater. I move to camp Farragut Monday but my address will be the same. Well the first bugle blowed just now so I have five minutes before taps. So Long For now.

Your Son

Elden

P.S. Haven't taken the mumps yet.

If Elden was keeping up with the navy's own news on this Sunday of April 2, as one might presume "boots" were encouraged to do, he probably read that Truk and other islands in its atoll had been bombed and strafed during the past few days. He might also have read that Nimitz was reviewing an investigation into the accidental shelling of two American landing craft by an American destroyer during the attack on Eniwetok six weeks earlier. Thirteen men had been killed and forty-six wounded. With or without the news, however, cookies from home during this time of heavily rationed sugar were a special treat, and Grace had cut short her home baking in order to pamper her absent son. The bunkmate from Lubbock, who also benefited, has yet to be identified.

April 2, 1944

Dear Folks,

Well I guess Krahn has been shipped as I haven't seen him for three or four days. Well fifteen of our company will get a leave in about two weeks then fifteen more when they get back and so on. So I don't know which bunch I'll be in. I got the letter yesterday morning and the cookies last nite. They sure was good. My bunkmate and I hid out and ate on them. He is a Kid from Lubock.

Yes I like the navy fine so far. They feed me pretty good & I've had beans for breakfast they aren't so bad.

I am on serving detail today so I have to work from 11:00 to 1:00 then I'll be off long enough to wash my clothes and go to the show this afternoon. Did they pay for the clothes. (express bill). Well Carlton Buck just called me up and made a date with me for the show at 2:30 this evening. He said he hadn't seen Krahn either I get to go to town in about a week so I'll have some pictures made and send some. They say to fall in so I've got to go.

Your Son
Elden
[Back of the envelope says: "Sailors Mail Rush Like <u>Hell</u>"]

Where you stand depends on where you sit, so they say, and the maxim seems to apply here. A mere twenty days past his own time of wishing he did not have to serve, Elden is beginning to define himself as a sailor, evidenced in part by negative references to people whom he now believes should be in the service but are not. Presumably these people are well within their legal rights, but a few—Ed Murphy in particular—may not have behaved ideally. From this time on, expressions of resentment about those he, Virginia, and Grace perceive not to be doing their part will grow steadily.

Among those who remember one of the more unusual characters ever to live in Vega, the name "Ed Murphy" may conjure a chuckle. The son of farmer and onetime barber Harry (Pat) and his first wife, Rena Bell Murphy, who was herself a landmark personality, Ed started a newspaper when he was a small boy. He sold advertisements for a few pennies each, filled four pages with aphorisms but not with news, printed a few issues on an irregular schedule, and hawked them on the sidewalks. This probably netted him as much as a buck or two in Depression times, and caused some to regard him as a "boy genius," to use a cliché of the era. In his early teens he sometimes donned a cape and, as "The Whispering Shadow," leaped out of dark corners to terrorize younger boys who were on the streets after sundown. He had more than one fistfight with his father and bragged to other boys about stealing small amounts of wheat from the old man.

In the late 1940s Ed became locally famous, after enjoying the intoxicating delights of Amarillo bars, for visiting an undertaker's showroom to try coffins on like suits in a haberdashery. To top the day off, the story goes, he then hired the undertaker's ambulance in lieu of a taxi to drive him home to Vega. As the ambulance sped into the sleepy little town, people came out of their houses to see what occasioned the rare wailing of a "sy-reen." At the town's primary intersection, the ambulance screeched off the asphalt of Highway 66, raced northward on the unpaved South Main Street, raised a cloud of dust as it slid around the corner between the courthouse and the bank, then stopped at Murph's little shack on West Main. With a flair worthy of W. C. Fields, Murph exited the ambulance, bowed slightly and tipped his hat to a small gawking audience, and tacked with unsteady dignity to his door.

He became the subject of much speculation after another man—supposedly passed out from drinking, missing his bankroll, and in a car stopped at night on a railroad crossing—was killed by a train. In middle age he had his own close call when he was kidnapped by two men who robbed the service station where he worked a night shift, and afterward would recount to available listeners details of the debate between the thugs about whether and when to kill him. He invented a good many unflattering nicknames that stuck to their unfortunate targets, and he graced the little barn behind his house with a circled pentagram, taking delight in the town's uncertain suspicion that it meant something different and dark. Different was his trademark, and he seemed happy to let "dark" enhance it. As late as his sixties he occasionally printed issues of the *Oldham County News,* still newsless and containing only ads, editorials, and sayings from *Poor Richard's Almanac,* in episodic resurgences of a still boyhood-level genius. He lived a reasonably long life and is buried beneath one of the two tombstones, three miles apart, that he erected for himself a dozen years before his death.

A natural magnet for gossip even as early as 1944, Murphy, then twenty-two years old and single, had either volunteered for or been drafted into the service. He had been sent to the navy's Camp Farragut training center in Idaho, but was soon back in Vega with what one veteran described as a "self-induced" discharge. For some reason he was in the Oldham County Jail.

Vega boys in the navy were looking for one another and were exchanging letters to facilitate their searches. Elden has learned from Wilburn "Wig" Price that Price's ship, the USS *Copahee* (CVE-12), is nearby and he plans to visit Price during his first liberty five days hence. The *Copahee,* named for Copahee Sound on the South Carolina coast, was a *Bogue*-class carrier escort. These small, short, and flimsily constructed carriers were being built and launched even faster than the larger *Essex*-class carriers. They provided replacement planes to their bigger sister ships, and also engaged in combat. With all of the negative characteristics of the big ships and fewer of the positives, when they got into the fighting they were dangerous places to be. Their crews joked that CVE stood for "combustible, vulnerable, expendable."[9] In April 1944, the *Copahee* had just returned from delivering planes to Pearl Harbor.

April 6, 1944

Dear Mom, Dad & Bros,

got your letter today so thought I'd write a little. Well the worst of boot camp is over now. I get liberty Tuesday so I guess I'll have a big time in San Diego. I don't guess I'll find me a girl as they all say there are 90 Sailors to every girl. I got a letter yesterday from Wig Price the other day he is in Port at Diego so I guess I'll look him up Tuesday. Did you get the Insurance Policy yet? When Pumper gets here you get his address from Berneice and send it to me as I'll be in a different camp than him. I'd like to see him.

Is Edd [Murphy] still in jail? I hope they keep him there as that is where he belongs.

I got an easter card from Grand-Ma she wrote a few lines so I guess I'll answer it with a few lines. I don't have much to write about but I guess they'd like to hear from me. I guess Krahn and Wallcott is already gone. Carlton Buck is still here as I saw him last Sunday.

I've been pretty lucky so far between you, Six & Virginia I get a letter or two every day. I am writing this in the Recreation hall I'ts so noisy I can hardly think. I don't know wheither I'll get a leave before I go to school or not. If I do I't be in two or three weeks. I'll get five days besides traveling time. So I may see you pretty soon. I'll let you know when it will be when I find out.

So Long for now,

Your Son,

Elden

Given the comment about a letter or two every day, we may be missing some of Virginia's letters, as almost a month has passed since the one dated March 9. If she made the anticipated visit to Kansas, she did not remain there. The April 7 letter contains a reference to yet another rather distinctive nickname, "Bulb Nose," whose unfortunate possessor is unidentified. This letter's reference to "yellow boys" is her first open expression of the resentment about some people not serving while others did.

April 7, 1944

Dearest Tex,

Well, how do you like those California girls? I hear they have something us Colorado girls don't have. I guess the most beautiful girls in the world live in California. When you get your first furlough I'll try to meet you in Vega. If I can't maybe we'll see each other after the war. That isn't going to be very long I hope.

Maureen got on down at the laundry again. I had my name in there but they won't hire me. Maybe I look lazy or something.

They had that boys trial yesterday, you know, the one that stabbed a man in the back. Well he got life. I think I would rather get hung than have to stay in prison for life.

About 20 more boys are leaving next week for the army & navy. This place is really dead. Alvin is still here tho & has a nice car. You know him don't you? He took us to the Cape that nite. He can't go to the army because he owns too many farms. Merlan works for him now so he won't have to go. There are more yellow boys around here. I won't go with boys that are yellow & most of the ones left here are.

Well, I have to go to bed now. I'm sure sleepy. I haven't seen old "Bulb Nose" for a long time.

All my Love,
Virginia

If we are seeking to know Elden's daily experiences, we know that on Monday, April 10 the navy, not wasting money on frills like trucks, had him carry his bed, his uniform, and all his possessions to a new camp. The letters begin to be repetitive as he again says he intends to visit Wig Price, mentions Pumper Boydstun and Don Buchanan, and tells that he has seen E. L. Krahn. Elden notes that seeing people from home helps Krahn, who seems to have been homesick, but this entire body of correspondence shows that the contacts were very important to Elden as well.

April 10, 1944

Dear Mom, Dad & Bros,

Well we moved to another camp today. I sure got tired as I had to walk about a mile with my materess, Hamock, Pillow, Blankets and all my clothes on my shoulder. I sure was heavy but I made it. I get to go to town tomarrow so I'll have a big time I guess. Wig Price is in San Diego so I'll try to look him up.

You might as well write Virginia and ask her to come down. In case I get to come. I wont know untill about a day before I get to go. The most of them are getting leaves now so I'll get one too.

If I go to school I may not get to come before I get through with my schooling which will be about two or three months. I may be transferred somewhere else. I hope so as it sure is hot here. I saw Krahn last night he said he wasn't going to get to go home. I would like to see him get to go as he comes to see me and he's pretty home sick he claims he's not but I can tell. He sure does look downhearted when I first see him but when he leaves he's feeling better I guess it does him good to see someone from home.

I got an easter card from grandma & answered it. I wrote to about everybody in Oklahoma yesterday. I'll send the easter card to you and you can put it with my junk. I guess Pumper left today send me his address In case I dont run on to him. Get Don Buchanans address from Six or have him to get it for me I haven't seen him yet. My address is United States Naval Training Center.

I better close and go to bed.

Your Son

Elden

In the present millennium, when methods of accessing music are myriad and wonderful, it may be useful to recall that in the 1940s music enjoyed at home was most often from large black 78 rpm vinyl recordings played on phonographs. Virginia's new phonograph is *electric,* and the adjective reminds us that spring-powered phonographs that did not use electricity were still common until the early 1950s.

Cousin stunts? Elden has asked her a question, and we have to combine her answer with her April 7 letter in order to understand that disappointing farewell night when she treated him as a cousin, took him to the Cape, and deserted him there. In all likelihood it is this episode that has brought their relationship to a low enough point that he has given her address to a boot camp buddy and welcomed him to write to her. "That other boy" has sent her a photograph.

April 12, 1944

Dearest Tex,

I received a letter from you and that other boy too. That picture was really awful of me wasn't it? You always take a good picture. What did the other ones look like? I never did use the rest of my film up. When I do Ill send you some of them.

Tex, I never did get me a job yet so I don't suppose I can come down to Vega to see you. I sure wish I could but it doesn't look like I'm going to get to. Maybe I won't see you again until after the war. I hope not because the war may last a long time.

I got me an electric phonograph last nite. My mother bought it for me. I have some good records too. "Born to Lose," "No Letters Today," and some of "Roy Acuffs." I can't find any Ernest Tubb records.

I'm sorry to hear that Chuck Steward was shipped out. He will come back okay tho. Hes to mean to get killed.

Earl is still fooling around town. I don't know why he can't get in the army. Maybe he is dodging the draft.

Don't forget to send me a picture of you in your uniform when you get it taken in San Diego. Boy, I bet you make a handsome sailor.

No, I haven't pulled any of those cousin stunts anymore. No one believes them. I'll have to think up something different. Alvin doesn't interest me very much. Its just his car that I like. He's a pretty good guy tho, but he's pretty old for me.

I've stayed home every night this week, don't you think I'm getting good? I'm going to the show tonite. I think its going to be pretty good.

Tell that boy that sent me the picture thanks and if you'll send me the negatives I'll get me some made off if they are any good.

Well, write when you can and don't go with too many of thoes San Diego girls.

Loads of Love,
Virginia

The physical rigors of training clearly agree with Elden, as he enjoys sailing and rowing after a six-mile hike and other exercises. He is pleased that he has built up to 178 pounds, which, on his six-foot height, meant he had a pretty wiry build. He got his anticipated liberty two days before and had taken in a burlesque show and heard music by country swing star Bob Wills, but he did not get together with Wig Price. Elden's information about the Walcott brothers is not quite correct. In an interview of July 15, 2005, Bob Walcott said that he had almost met his brother Tub at Pearl Harbor, but had narrowly missed him.

April 13, 1944

Dear Mom, Dad & Bros,

Well I have tonight off so I'll write a few lines. Well I made a six mile hike this morning and jumped off a 18 foot tower into the water it sure was a drop. We came back and went sailing in a sailboat then we got in row boats. I sure enjoyed it. I got a letter from Mac and Eva [cousin Mac Rogers and his mother, aunt Eva Rogers] wrote a few lines. It sure is a lot easier since I mooved to camp Faragut. I got liberty last Tuesday I had a pretty good time. San Diego is the trashiest and dirtiest town I ever saw. I had some pictures made. I'll send you one even if I't isnt very good.

Well I don't know whether or when I'll get a leave or not. If I go to sea I'll get one I know. They Draft you for Schools or Sea duty and you don't know which you get until they call your number. Krahn is still here I guess I haven't saw him for about a week though. Do you know Pumper's address yet? I guess they still have Edd Murphy in jail don't they? What are they going to do with him? I haven't heard from Six lately. Got a letter from Virginia yesterday.

They sure had a good burlesque show in Diego Tuesday. I saw Bob Wills at another one. I am at the library they have a piano in hear and I can't think for listening to it.

Bob, Charles, & Tub Walcott met up together in Pearl Harbor The other day. I'll bet they sure was glad to see each other.

Some of the company will probably get their leaves in about I don't have any idea when I get one but I hope to see you soon. Well I have gained 12 pounds since I got in the navy I weigh 178 now. It sure is building me up. I've hardened a lot. Well I better close as this place closes in five minutes.

Your Son
Elden

A piano in a library—now there is an interesting idea!

Grace has managed to save up enough sugar to make a batch of candy and send it to Elden. The five-inch guns he has enjoyed learning to fire appear to have been the size of the artillery with which an aircraft carrier defended itself.[10]

On the other side of the country, the *Franklin* has finished her shakedown cruise and is approaching Norfolk, where she will dock the next day.

April 14, 1944

Dearest Mom, Dad & Bros,

Well I got the candy at noon it sure is good. My bunk mate and I have been eating on it. I was afraid to eat much of it as I took my last shot today and they say that candy will make you sick after taking shots. It was the tetnus shot.

Well we had a drill with some five inch .38 caliber guns today It sure was a lot of fun.

I haven't heard from Six lately I guess he's still there. Do you know Pumper's address yet? I went to a bunch of new companys hopeing to find him but couldn't locate him. The navy sure has some funny rules You cant whistle or chew gum. You cant chew gum because every body will step in it. & you cant whistle because everything is run by whistles here a certain kind of a whistle means a certain thing.

Has Dad ever got the car fixed yet? I don't imagine since he is working. I got my Second Class seamans rateing a few days ago. I get $54 dollars a month. I get a payday the twentieth of this month. I put in for Six Dollars & twenty five cents worth of Defence stamps a month. So $6.40 for Insurance and $6.25 for that will leave me about $42.35 per month I guess I'll get by on that.

I guess Murphy is still in jail Isn't he. I hope they keep him there.

Has any body left for the army? I guess McNabb and Everett and them guys are still dodging aren't they. Well I better sign off and write Virginia.

Your Son
Elden

On April 17 Virginia received the invitation Elden had asked Grace to extend, to come to Vega during his anticipated leave. She shared with Elden yet another reason, very likely the principal one, why she will not accept: she is simply reluctant to meet his mother. In the same letter she also reveals her deep negative feelings about Chuck Steward but leaves us to wonder, as she left Elden, what was the cause.

April 17, 1944

Dearest Tex,

I received a letter from your mother today. She wants me to come down to Vega when you get your furlough, but I'm afraid it is impossible. I would love to go but I have a lot of reasons for not going. I'm pretty bashful when it comes to visiting with someones folks. Your mother sounds like she is a real nice person and I would love to meet her. Maybe after the war everything will turn out alright. I hope so anyway.

I got a V-mail letter from Chuck today. He sounded awfully friendly but I'll never forgive him for the dirty way he treated me once. Someday I'll tell you all about it.

For the present I'll just tell you I hate him, even if he is one of your best friends.

It snowed today and now it is just about all melted. That's the way Colorado is, it snows & melts all in one day. I think I'll take some pictures today so I can get thoes pictures we took when you were here developed. Don't forget to send me the films of the pictures we took with your camera so I can get me some made off of them.

I guess I'll go to the show with Maureen & her boy-friend. He really thinks a lot of her and she don't even care for him at all. I think he's pretty cute. He's younger than me tho.

Maureen just came over & said to tell you "hello"! She still works at the laundry. I think they will call me next week, so that's another reason why I can't go to Vega. I hope you don't feel to badly about me not coming. This old world is full of disappointment & heartache.

Well, I must quit for now. I hope you can read this scribbling.

Honey, I'll be thinking about you every minute of the day. I sure do miss you and hope the war is over before long so we can go on from where we left off.

Loads of Love,
Virginia

This April 22 telegram was surely sent and received with great excitement.

Please wire $20 get leave tomorrow see you soon.
Elden Rogers

And the letter of the next day must have been written and received with great disappointment. For a significant insight into life during wartime, note the comment about four to six hours being required to get a line for a long-distance telephone call. This reflects both the limitations of the phone system and the drastic increase in both civilian and military demand placed upon it by the war. At least for the time being, Elden has not been pining away for Virginia. He had said earlier that there were ninety sailors to every one girl in San Diego, so the day he had spent at the beach with a good-looking girl was a special treat. He must have been pretty conscientious, however, as he used part of his second liberty to visit a battleship, a destroyer, a carrier, a submarine, and an aircraft factory.

April 23, 1944

Dearest Mom, Dad, & Bros,

Well I got up this morning to get ready to leave for home tonite and they had postponed our leaves I will have to go before the request mast and ask for a leave. By going there I think I can get 14 days. My company commander likes me better than anyone else in the company at least he acts like it. He said he would help me get a leave. He offered me a third class gunners rateing which pays $76 a month but I turned it down as I didn't want to be a gunner.

I haven't done anything since I've been here in Paul Jones but lay around. The trouble with it here is there isn't any tables in these barracks to write on so I'm sitting on my bunk trying to write. Well Krahn & Carlton Buck was right across the street when I first moved to P.J. but they left yesterday for San Francisco for a submarine school.

I got liberty Tuesday I went to town and caught a ferry to Mare Island and went abord a Battleship, Destroyer, carrier and in a submarine and looked around it was pretty interesting.

I haven't ever called Lloyd as you can't use a telephone when on the station and when you get to town it takes from 4 to 6 hours to get connections as it sure is Buisy here on the west coast.

I went to Consolidated aircraft company Tuesday and saw them making P.B.Y. Catelena Flying Boats. It was kinda a educational trip. The coast guard has a bunch of P.B.Y planes here. There is one over here nearly all the time.

Well one of my buddies here has got a cousin in Diego. So I got acquainted with her. She is pretty good looking She and I went swimming in the Pacific. Hopeing to see you soon.

Your Son
Elden

On the opposite side of the United States on this disappointing day, the *Franklin* was loading cargo in Norfolk, preparing to head for the Pacific.[11]

The next day, in the Cherokee national capital of Tahlehquah, Oklahoma, Peggy Sifford, who will marry Jerry Rogers and become mother to Elden's niece Tiana and nephews Houston and Jeffrey, is being born.

Meanwhile, Virginia writes to Grace declining the invitation to come to Vega on grounds that her job made it impossible. Twelve days earlier she had told Elden that she did not have a job, and seven days earlier she had told him she was too shy to accept and also that she thought the laundry might call her for a job soon. Apparently it had done so.

April 24, 1944

Dear Mrs. Rogers,

I received your nice letter and invitation to visit you last week. I am sorry I won't be able to come down as I am working now. I do hope you will understand and Elden too.

I would like very much to meet you and your family and hope I may have that privilege some time soon.

I got a large group picture from Tex Saturday. It was sure nice. It wasn't hard to find him in it, even if he does look different with his hair cut off because he looks like the youngest one in the bunch & the best looking. I would sure like to see him in his uniform.

We are certainly having our share of rain this spring. Hardly a day passes without a little rain. I guess everyone is tho.

Well, I have to write some more letters and hope you will understand why I can't come down at this time and do hope you will write again sometime.

With Love,
Virginia

Virginia seems to have learned very quickly that Elden's leave had been canceled, but her letter reflects his apparent belief that he still was likely to get leave before being shipped out. Her explanation that she continues to date one person because "He has a car and plenty of gas" highlights another significant point about who bore the burdens of war, for many people who had cars were unable to get more than small amounts of the severely rationed fuel to make them run. Ration coupons for this vital commodity were allocated to people according to whether they could get along without them and according to the importance of their mobility to the war effort. Elden did not have a car, and had he been near Virginia and only intermittently employed as before, he would have been allocated very few gasoline coupons. The other fellow, who "can't go to the army because he owns too many farms," for that very same reason *does* have a car and *can* get all the gasoline he needs. The circumstance and the system enabled him not only to produce his portion of the needed agricultural products but also to drive sixty miles round trip to take a sailor's girlfriend to a dance.

April 28, 1944

Hello Honey,

How is the mail you get from me? Do I write too much or not enough? I have a job now down at the laundry, I work in the dry cleaning dept. as cashier. I take in the money & keep the books. It sure is a lot of fun. I get to meet so many people. Everyone that wants something cleaned comes to me & I check the clothes in so you see I couldn't possibly come to Vega when you get your leave. I would sure like to but I'm afraid I can't. We will have to wait until after the war I guess if you aren't too mad at me.

I got the picture you sent me of your out-fit. You sure look different in your uniform. I just about couldn't find you. You look like the youngest & best looking in the bunch. I want a big picture of you tho. You remember Delmers picture don't you? That big one in the frame that I have my big one in? well, I want one that big so I can throw his picture away and put yours in it.

I guess I told you I got a letter from Chuck. I wrote back to him and said the meanest things. I'm really ashamed of myself but I hate him so bad I couldn't help telling him what I thought of him.

Have you ever been to Holbrook Lake up by Rocky Ford? They have kind of a carnival & dance hall & swimming & boats & nearly everything up there in the summer time. Its going to open up the Saturday after this one and I sure want to go. I guess theres only one way to go & that's with Alvin. Do you remember him? He has a car & plenty of gas. I wish you were here to go with us & we would make Maureen go with him.

Well, I guess your eye sight will give out after reading all this scribbling so I better close for now.

The size of picture I want is 8 by 10, don't forget.

I hope your next leave won't be canceled even if I won't get to see you. Maybe you could buy your ticket to Las Animas & see me for a minute then take a bus to Vega.

Well "bye now" & don't forget me.

All my Love,
Virginia

On May 1 Elden informed the folks at home that his duty now is cooking and that he likes it because the workload is light. The letter reveals that farm workers at Vega are paid four dollars per day and possibly more, in sharp contrast to the time only a few years before when Ancell had worked for as little as seventy-five cents per day with room and board.[12] A decade later, I would do the same kind of work for eight dollars per day. Elden has applied through a different channel for a leave and still hopes to get it. His reassuring postscript soon proves to be wrong, however, because the RTU on his address meant what it implied.

May 1, 1944

Dear mom, Dad & bros,
Well this finds me O.K. still out here I went to town nite before last. I had some pictures made they are pretty good.

I went to a stage show at the U.S.O. auditorium and saw a bunch of movie stars they sure were good.

I don't know yet when I'll get a leave yet. I made out an application for a leave and the Barracks C.P.O. Signed it. I'll have to wait till I'm called now then I go before Comander Curley and if he Signs it I'll see you. It will be a week probably before my number comes up.

I may have told you before but I'm a cook now I only have to work four or five hours a day now. And get every other nite off so I Kinda like it.

I put thirty dollars in the bank so I'll have it if I get a leave. Tomorrow is pay day I only get 19 dollars tho I don't need much money now. I only spend fifty or seventy five cents in town for a show.

Tell Jerry I enjoyed his letter and to write again. What is Bose doing now? Does he ever say anything about you moving any more?

I think I told you about getting a letter from Wig Price. Well I wrote back and ask him how I could find him and he never answered I guess he was shipped out again.

Today is Sixes birthday so I guess the draft will catch him pretty soon but he will get 21 days after he takes his examination so it probably will be in six weeks before he gets out here if he gets the navy.

When is school out? About the twentyeth wont it? It won't be long. Odell Price will have to go then so I guess Verda Mae's [Mathes] heart will be broken. I will Probably get to see him out here. I guess I'll write to him and tell him to write me when he gets here and I will come to see him.

I wrote to bug-Eye when I first got his address but haven't heard from him yet. I don't guess I've hardly had time.

Virginia said she got your letter and you sounded real nice. She said she would like to meet you but she didn't think she could. Maybe she will get to anyway.

I guess It will break Gerald's heart when school is out. He can get at least four dollars [a day for farm work] this summer and he ought to ask for five, he could get it.

I guess I'll write to Grandma and send her a picture. I wrote to Frances and Rowena and sent them a picture last nite. The pictures cost 20¢ each but I guess they are worth it.

I notice the flag is flying at half mast I guess it's because the secretary of the navy died.

I have to close for now as news is scarce here.

Love,

Your Son

Elden

P.S. My address has a R.T.U. on it now which means Recruit Transfer Unit but don't let that scare you as I will be in the states for at least six weeks after I'm transferred from here.

Elden has sent Virginia a pin, most likely a navy pin identical to the one now in his wallet. After all the preenlistment talk of engagement and marriage, one presumes this pin was a token of more than casual affection.

Elden may not have found anything worrisome in Virginia's admission that she has twice been caught by the police in violation of what was probably a local curfew ordinance applicable to people under a certain age. And he may not have been concerned when she mentioned having seen a person with whom she and Elden were acquainted who has been banished from the county for stealing gasoline. We can be sure that Grace would have found plenty of concern in both statements.

Virginia notes that one young man she considers a draft dodger is always with two or three girls. This was exactly the sort of thing that caused resentment among men who were in the service and who yearned for the company of girls, and Elden may have felt that effect. The sensitivity of such subjects probably never occurred to Virginia.

My Dearest Tex,

I got the pin you sent today, its really swell. I'm awfully proud of it, and you are too sweet to me I think. I really don't deserve anything that nice. Thanks a whole lot.

I hope you can read this. I'm in bed, writing on my stationary box so its kind of lumpy.

I saw Herman Sunday. He stole some gas and some other things and is supposed to stay out of the county but he was in town Sunday dodging the cops.

Earl is still here. He is always with 2 or 3 girls. I think he should be in the army or something.

Say, ask that boy you met from La Junta if he knows Bob Mickey or George Snider or Ray Harnsworth from La Junta. I don't know him myself.

I sent thoes films off about two weeks ago & they have never come yet. I will send you some as soon as they do.

The cops caught me Saturday night sitting in a car in front of the Trojan after curfew time. Then, Sunday night Maureen & I were sitting in front of my house in the car & they caught us again. I guess I'll get fined this time.

I sure wish I could see you when you get your furlough. You will never know how bad I feel about not being able to see you until after the war because I really think a lot of you. You are one of the nicest boys I've ever gone with. I only wish we had spent more time together before you went to the Navy.

Well, I guess I will go to sleep now. I'm just about there now. Working doesn't agree with me. I'm so tired in the evenings that I don't get to go any place, only to bed.

Well, "bye-now." I'll dream of my "sailor boy" tonite. I hope.

All my Love,
Virginia

Birthdays were not major occasions in the Rogers family, but they were observed. Grace must have felt at least a slight disappointment that Elden did not express wishes for happiness in this card, written on her thirty-ninth birthday. Nor would she have been thrilled that the reverse side of the card bore a photograph of him and a buddy in a prop representing the Owl Bar. She would, however, have been happy to hear from her son. The Owl Bar prop seems to have been one used by a lot of boots.

May 2, 1944

Dear Folks,

I went to town last nite and had some pictures made. This is one of them. Don't get excited as it's not a real bar. I have to go to work and its trying to rain.

Elden

Elden's short letter the following day says that the sailor with Elden in the Owl Bar photo is from Big Spring, Texas, and is related to the Glenn family in Vega. Roy Treadaway said in 2005 that he believed his name may have been Rice.[13]

May 3, 1944

Dear Mom, Dad, & Bros,

Well; I'm at the library this morning and don't have anything to do. I think I wrote you yesterday but It won't hurt anything to write again.

I get liberty tonight so I think I'll go to Mission Beach as Tex Ritter is putting on a show there tonight.

I guess you have got the card with me and another kid behind the bar. The other kid is from big spring his mother is some relation to V. T. Glenn at Vega.

I haven't heard from Krahn since he left. He said he will write. I don't know. I wrote to Bug-Eye but he hasn't answered it yet.

I got a letter from Virginia she is working at the laundry she is casheer now.

I've been thinking about having an 8x10 enlargement made for you as I may never get the chance after I leave here. I think I'll let my hair grow out first.

Love,

Elden

Elden's first cousin La Veta Roberts, sister of the Lyle Roberts who had picked Elden up hitchhiking two months before, is among the many people with whom he corresponds. He encloses with this letter a pin that he has had for a month, almost certainly the navy pin he had kept in his wallet and identical to the one he has sent to Virginia. He is working on airplanes and he can tell by now that he will soon be assigned to an aircraft carrier. The island where he was assigned at the time was probably North Island Naval Station. The *Franklin* left the Norfolk Navy Yard on May 5, and will tie up at North Island about two weeks later.[14]

May 7, 1944

Dear Mom, Dad & Bros,

Well Ive got two letters from you since Ive wrote so I'll write a few lines.

How many head of cattle do you have now since you bought some?

I don't imagine I'll get the desil school now they told me that when I put in three or four weeks of sea duty. I can ask for what I want and will probably get it. I'm pretty well satisfied with the Armed Guard.

I ask at the personell office about getting in the coast guard and they said that it didn't come under the navy Dept they said that I could get transferred into the marines and I told them I was well enough satisfied with the navy. That I didn't want the marines.

That kid said you had to swim fifty yards before you get to go home well that's right. I never made it until the nite before my leave was canceled.

I don't imagine Mrs. C. would come down as she works at fort Lyon.

Well there are some boys in my barracks that just got out of the stockade for going over the hill and they just now took off again said they were going over the hill again. Im never going to do that if I never get to go home.

Well I go up for a special Pay in the morning and I'm on the Prospective transfer list so I may leave any time now. Most of these guys are going to Norman, Okla I sure hope I'm that lucky as I could come home on a thirty six hour leave.

Well I've been figuring on sending this pin for a month so I'll send it in this letter.

I got a letter from La Veta the other day she said that as far as she could find out that I was the first one in the family in the navy.

Well I may not be here over a week but write me as it will follow.

I have to shut my mouth and go to work now.

Love

Your Son

Elden

Well I fooled around and didn't get this letter mailed and so I was transferred. I am at an island out of San Diego I work on airplanes here. From the looks of things I'll be [on] an aircraft carrier I don't know how long it will be before I get shipped out but don't worry about me.

Don't give up hopes of me getting a leave as I may get one yet. I'll keep trying anyhow.

I have to get a ferry to San Diego when I go to town. It's lots of fun.

Well my company is all split up they are all over the world I guess. There is one of them with me he's from San Angelo Texas.

I sure like it here I don't have to do anything much but lay around on the beach in my bathing suit.

My mail goes through San Francisco but these guys said that it wasn't censored. The C.A.S.U. means Carrier Aircraft Service Unit.

This is my day off so I can go to town or anything I want to.

I better close and go to dinner.

Love, Your Son,
Elden

Virginia now revives an intention to visit Elden in Vega when he gets leave, which one would presume gave him renewed hope.

May 9, 1944

My Dearest Sailor,

I'm sorry I haven't written sooner but I've really been busy. I owe so many people letters but I'll write to you first because you're really the only one I care about. I've been thinking about you a lot lately and about coming to Vega when you get your furlough. I can ask my boss if he'll let me off for about a week. I'd hate to lose my job. I'll try anyway because I want to see you awful bad.

I'm sending those pictures we took. You can have them if you want them because I have some just like them. They are good of you but I look awful in them. They look too much like me. If this letter don't make sense don't blame me because my little brother is trying out some new records on the phonograph and I'm trying to write & listen too.

It sure has been rainy here. It rains every other day. I'm beginning to feel like a duck.

I can't think of anything to write. I'll finish it after supper.

Here it is Friday, already & I haven't finished this. I have to go to work in about 10 minutes so will mail this now & try to write you a nice long letter tonite. Bye now,

With all my Love & Kisses,

Virginia

On May 16 the *Franklin,* whose width like that of other *Essex*-class carriers had been designed to do so, squeezed through the Panama Canal. By the day Elden wrote his next letter she was approaching or perhaps already at Pier F at the Naval Air Station, where she would be resupplied and have her planes put into the best possible order.[15] Elden still hopes for a leave and now he specifically mentions the possibility that he might fly to Amarillo in a short five hours—certainly an adventure far beyond the experience of any member of the Rogers family.

Gerald, nurturing an interest in aircraft, knows very well the SNJ fighters and SDB dive-bombers on which Elden has been working, and envies the fact that Elden has flown in them. From a piece of soft wood, Gerald has carved with his pocket knife an excellent five-inch-long facsimile of an F2A Brewster Buffalo. Elden is very pleased with the food he gets in the navy, and indeed it sounds quite good. The reality of war creeps in, however, when he is distracted from his writing by loud gunfire from nearby army and marine training exercises. The Verda Mae Elden mentions is the red-haired daughter of Grace's dear friend Iva Mathes and husband Cal Mathes; and Verda Mae's husband, Odell Price, is the son of Mamie and Alonzo Price. When the Rogers family moved from the cemetery road into Vega, they would be virtually next-door neighbors of both the Mathes and Price families.

The birthday Elden mentions will be Gerald's sixteenth, and the hint that Gerald could get into the merchant marine at sixteen cannot have been a comfort to Ancell and Grace.

May 16, 1944

Dear Mom, Dad & Bros,

Well, I'll start writeing with ink but I'm afraid It will run out any minute so if I finish in Pensil you'll know what happened.

I realy do like it here as I don't have to do anything. I am an airplane mechenic I guess I am pretty lucky to get that. Tomorrow is pay day and I sure do need it. I have enough in the bank to come home on if I get a chance. I can catch a plane to Amarillo any time and be there in five hours.

I haven't got but two letters since I've been here One from you and one from Grandma.

I get 36 hours liberty every week so I think I'll go see Loyd next week. Well Al Dexter is going to be at mission beach Sunday so I guess I'll go hear him sing Pistol Packin Mama.

There are some guys here that's been here for three years so I think I'll be here quite a while.

I notice that you have been sending my letters air mail. If you are going to send them that way it only takes six cents to mail them here.

I guess Verda Mae is greiveing her head off as Odell only has ten days left to stay. I told him to write me when he got here and I'd come to see him.

I have about six suits of dirty clothes to wash and I sure am dreading it. I think I'll wash them and go down to the beach for a swim when I get this letter wrote.

We sure have good chow here. We have all we want and it is usually steak or pork chops.

The army and marines are having maneuvers here They came in landing barges and they have guns banging until I cant think.

I had my uniform cut down it sure fits good now.

I just got back from chow I had Roast beef, mashed Potatoes & gravy & English Peas, Cake & Coffee. Sure was good since I didn't get up in time for breakfast.

Tell Gerald I'm working on SNJ and SBD Planes SNJ is a fighter and SBD is a dive bomber. He probably has a picture of them. I get to go for a hop every day if I want. Another thing I like about it here you can take your clothes to the laundry and you can let your hair grow out they don't give G.I.s any more.

Well Gerald has a birthday in a few days I guess he'll be fifteen or Sixteen wont he I forgot.

I saw in the paper where boys between Sixteen and seventeen and a half could get in the merchant marines I wish I had got in that.

Well I cant think of anything else to write so I better close pretty soon. Have you got a garden yet? These guys that just got back from overseas says that Germany will quit the next ninety days.

Love,
Your son
Elden

⚓

"Honky-tonk" was a nearly phonetic descriptor for a certain genre of music. It was applied as well to the cheap but not always sleazy establishments in which it was played, and "honky-tonking" became the very active verb to describe enjoying such places. Around the fundamental core of a bar and a dance floor, a honky-tonk featured a band that cranked out western swing music from perhaps a honking cornet, trumpet, or trombone; a tonking piano; and the usual guitar, fiddle, bass, and drums. Lonely men and lonelier women found comfort there, and just to enter one was a declaration of something, even though the declarer may have not quite figured out what. Unsurprisingly, joints of this type were scenes of frequent conflict. In the rough, tough oil fields of East Texas, Al Dexter had owned, operated, and performed in his own honky-tonk.

Pistol Packin' Mama! Those three words convey as clear and concise an image as any three in the vernacular. One of Dexter's married male customers had been carrying on a bit too much with one of his barmaids. Word got back to the wife, who armed herself with a pistol and went after the floozy who ran through a barbed wire fence in her haste to escape. Showing that art imitates life, the episode had inspired Dexter to write a song that, with a catchy verse and fast country swing rhythm, became the most popular song in the nation in early 1944. It made Dexter a touring "star," and was even recorded by Bing Crosby and by the Andrews Sisters, who were among the most popular singers in the country. Seeing Al Dexter live was a big deal for Elden, and he was not going to miss the chance.

⚓

Virginia's May 21 letter reveals that she has not heard from Elden for some time, and seems to convey anxiety that he may not be happy with her. Perhaps he was not, after she had declined the invitation to come to Vega and the mixed series of explanations that preceded it. Yet even this letter contains a reference to seeing other boys, news that probably did not make Elden particularly happy. On the day she wrote, five LST (landing ship, tank) vessels loaded with ammunition blew up in Pearl Harbor in a chain of enormous explosions.[16] This was not due to enemy action, but it was a frightening reminder to military and civilian alike that war was real and present.

May 21, 1944

My Dearest Tex,

Why don't you write? It seems like ages since I last heard from you. I miss your letters so terribly much. Did you ever get thoes pictures I sent? They were awful of me weren't they.

I sure hope you get a furlough before you go across, even tho I won't get to see you, your folks will and they miss you a whole lot too.

Did you ever hear from Chuck: I did once & I'm ashamed of what I wrote back to him. It wasn't very nice. I hope he doesn't ever let you read it. You might not like me any more if you like me at all now, which I doubt very much.

Do you still write to Janet? How are her & Carl Six getting along. They sure have their ups and downs don't they.

They shipped in 32 soldiers to work at Fort Lyon to help take care of the patients. They are sure good-looking to. There is always soldiers every where you look any more. Sailors are for me though. They have always been my favorite.

A boy from Garden City Kansas was supposed to come & see me tonite. I knew him when he lived in La Junta. It looks like he isn't coming tho. Its about 9:00 P.M. already. I don't care very much.

I'm sure sleepy. I can't even write in a straight line.

Well, I guess I'll go to bed. I hope you will write to me real soon & think about me real often. Maybe someday I will see you again. I sure hope so. Well "keep em sailin" sailor boy & don't forget the little gal who is waiting back here for you after you've sailed the seven seas & won the war.

All my Love,

Virginia

7 The World in Seven Decks under an Airfield

"Myers," "Rogers," "Treadaway," the officer called out to break the silence that morning in May after he had asked who among the group of ten men from Carrier Aircraft Service Unit 5 wanted to volunteer. The whole purpose of the unit had been to assemble men for service aboard aircraft carriers, but these men had internalized the maxim never to volunteer for anything. Perhaps at random and perhaps because he knew they were buddies from similar West Texas small-town backgrounds, the officer "volunteered" Nelson Myers from Richland Springs, Elden Rogers from Vega, and Roy Treadaway from Miles for service aboard the USS *Franklin*. On Saturday May 20, at the Naval Air Station Pier F, the three made a long, steep climb up the gangplank from terra firma to their new home on water.[1]

The bigger change happened in the early morning hours four days later when the ship cast off. Moving slowly at first to get through the nets that defended San Diego Harbor against enemy torpedoes, and accompanied by the destroyers *Leary*, *Cushing*, and *Twiggs*, the giant ship passed two miles south of the Point Loma Light and on May 24 the three boys from the prairie plains were at sea. Almost immediately they heard the signal for general quarters, and learned what it was to run to their battle stations. With a discernible burst of speed that must have impressed the novices, the *Franklin* was far enough out by 1012 to begin gunnery practice, firing at a towed raft target.[2] Elden had heard artillery before, but it was altogether different to hear it from on board or inside the ship doing the firing. A little after midday they turned into the wind and Elden heard the ship roar and felt it shudder as it came up to speed, putting additional lift under the wings of the planes that began launching at 1255. A similar maneuver followed when they recovered the planes an hour later. The experience taught the young sailors that things happening aboard a carrier made a lot of noise, created vibrations, and happened quickly. Just so they didn't get too comfortable after evening chow at 1924, they went into torpedo defense mode, which involved rapid turns and changes in speed.[3]

Chow and comfort may not have been compatible concepts at that point, as Elden was seasick. The sea gives no mercy to those who venture onto it, and nothing was to be done but tough it out. Eventually Elden overcame the nausea and discovered within himself the stable, quiet, and private center that enabled him to live with an outside world of unending pitch, yaw, people, and sound.

Three days later they were back at San Diego, and Elden found time to write.

May 27, 1944

Dear Mom Dad & Bros,

Well Sorry I haven't wrote sooner but I've been to sea. I am on the U.S.S. Franklin. I am going to leave for Pearl Harbor in a few days we was out about 1000 miles on a test run the other day. I really was sea sick the first nite. We are going to take some planes to Pearl Harbor and then we will be back to San Francisco for about one month. So I know I won't see any action for two or three months. I get sea pay now which makes me about $70 a month. This ship is 1086 feet long carries 90 Planes has a crew of 3000 men.[4] It travels with a bunch of destroyers so it is as safe as anything so you don't need to worry about me.

I might get a leave when I get to Frisco as they are going to Put a new Catapult on it and will take thirty five days at least. I get cigarettes for 5 cents a package, all my laundry done free, candy 2 for 5¢ & free shows every nite.

My address is:

E.D. Rogers S 2/c U. S. N. R.

U.S.S. Franklin V-1

c/o Fleet Post Office

San Francisco

California

Love

Your Son

Elden

This information proved as wrong as nearly everything else the navy had told Elden. Not only did information about location and destination get through the censors, but so much was wrong that one wonders whether it might have been deliberate—what we now call disinformation—to keep the unseasoned boots from revealing actual facts, and perhaps a matter of training to get the men used to change and uncertainty. And, of course, perhaps it was scuttlebutt generated by the crew and not "provided" by anyone official.

May 28, 1944

Dear Mom, Dad & Bros,

Well my ship is just like this one [picture postcard shows USS *Wasp*] only it's a little bigger. I had quite a lot of fun today. I ran on to some guys I knew here. Will write more later.

Elden

No ship was exactly like the USS *Wasp* (CV-7), which was the only carrier of her class. The *Franklin* (CV-13) was of the USS *Essex* (CV-9) class and was, as Elden wrote, larger.[5]

Virginia's question as to whether Elden is at Pearl Harbor reveals that he has written to her. The real significance of her May 26 letter is that it reveals to us what she had done back in March on her last opportunity to be with her supposed fiancé before he went to war. She had shunted him off to another girl in order to keep her date with the guy who had farms, a nice car, and plenty of gas coupons.

May 26, 1944

Hello Sailor,

Are you at Pearl Harbor yet? I heard a lot of sailors got killed in an explosion there, Sunday. I sure hope you wasn't in it. How do you like your ship. I've never heard of it, but probably will before long.

Is Carl Six in the service yet? He's about 18 isn't he? Maybe he will wait till he's drafted or something. Say did you ever get thoes pictures I sent. You never did say anything about them. They were pretty corny weren't they.

Did you have a very good time that night Maureen & I took you to the Cape in Alvin's car. I just did that to show you a good time before you had to leave. I still feel like you don't think very much of me for going with him when you came all the way from Texas to see me. I'm really sorry. I won't do that if you come back again sometime. Maureen told you I would come back drunk after I left & went to the Alpine. I still can't figure out why she told you that unless she wanted to make you not like me. Maybe she thought you would like her if you knew I drank. I've never been drunk in my life & never hope to get that way. I just hate to see drunk women, they act so silly. I guess I go to pretty rough places but I just go for the excitement & to dance, so please still like me. I'm really a nice girl underneath.

I sure hope the war is over pretty soon so you can come back & see me. No matter how long it lasts tho, I'll wait for you if it takes 10 years to whip the Japs.

I guess you'll need glasses after you read this book I wrote. This is about the longest letter I ever wrote so better quit before I break my record. O, I got a raise this week. I get 35 cents an hour now. I did get 30 cents. Pretty good isn't it Maureen & Wanda got on up at the air base in La Junta. Maybe I'll go up there & try to get on if they make a lot at it.

Well, bye for now. I'll be thinking about you every spare minute.

Loads of Love,

Virginia

Elden must have felt somewhat reassured by word that the *Franklin* would soon spend some time at San Francisco rather than immediately go into combat. It was not to be so, for when she sailed again on June 1 she was outward bound. A mere thirty-three days later Elden would be on the far side of the vast Pacific, seeing places unlike any he had ever seen with names he had barely heard if at all, and under fire from an enemy who wanted to destroy his ship and him with it.

The *Franklin* stretched for nearly three city blocks, or three football fields, with a flat top 109 feet wide and 867 feet long. A thin sheet of steel was covered with Douglas fir or white pine planking to produce a flight deck with better traction for both men and planes.[6] From the edge of that flat expanse it was seventy feet straight down to the water. Her ninety planes included Grumman Avenger torpedo planes, F6F Hellcat fighters, and Helldiver bombers, about two-thirds of which were normally firmly tied down with wings folded on the deck. A tall tower called the island was squeezed onto the starboard (right) side to accommodate the bridge and functions most immediately vital to the captain and his top subordinates. Forward and aft of the island were rotating turrets with five-inch guns capable of sinking enemy ships, should one somehow come within range. At the top of the island were the rotating radar antennas that could spot enemies far away and dispatch fighter planes of the combat air patrol to destroy them long before they could be seen with the naked eye or hit with gunfire. Around the edges of the flight deck were 40 mm "quads," doubled pairs of rapid-firing antiaircraft guns to hit enemy planes that came within range.[7]

When planes were being launched, every plane to go up had its engines warming up, making the whole flight deck aft of the island and the catapult one big forest of choppers waiting to reduce a man to fragments. Elden would have noticed, and perhaps found it novel at first, that the tips of the propellers would sometimes create small vapor trails that would move backward in the prop wash, enveloping the fuselage in a white spiral of mist (see fig. 9).

Among the busiest parts of a carrier was the hangar deck, a large thirty-foot vertical space that ran side to side and almost end to end of the ship immediately beneath the flight deck. It consisted of large bays with wide doors between them that could be closed, but when the doors were open the deck was one big area. Steel curtains on the sides could be raised during daytime for ventilation, creating the impression of a pavilion with a roof but without walls; and the curtains could be closed to shut out weather or to provide the plane captains and their crews a lighted space to work on planes at night without the light being visible to an enemy. Made of heavy-plate steel, the hangar deck carried the weight of planes and some very substantial machinery and also held the ship together structurally.[8] The men were warned, and Elden could see for himself, that the hangar deck was a place prone to explosion, whether from enemy bombs that could penetrate the thin flight deck or from internal sources such as spilled gasoline. The bulkheads were designed to contain explosions and fires, whereas the relatively weak overhead and sides gave explosive force somewhere to go without destroying the entire ship. Although the flight deck was above it, the hangar deck was called the "first deck" in a numerical order that went all the way down to a seventh deck far below the waterline.[9]

Planes not on the flight deck were in the hangar deck, at times just riding there when outside the war zone, but most of the time being repaired, maintained, or fueled and armed before flying. Elaborately designed patterns of movement plus three elevators enabled rapid transfer of numerous planes between all parts of the flight deck and all parts of the hangar deck. The number 1 elevator was in the middle and well forward on the flight deck and at the extreme forward end of the hangar deck. The number 2 elevator, usually called the deck-edge elevator, extended partially off the flight deck on port side directly opposite the island. The number 3 elevator was in the middle of the hangar deck and topside just sternward from the gun turrets.[10]

At the very back of the hangar deck was a separate balcony-like open space called the fantail. Sheltered above by the end of the flight deck and defined by a railing, it was a pleasant space where men often relaxed when not on duty.[11]

Elden and members of his division slept in a designated section of bunks stacked three and even four high in crowded, cramped, and poorly ventilated compartments on the second deck, immediately below the hangar deck (see fig. 8). They ate, usually together, in a mess hall amidships one deck farther down. This was another place that was almost always very busy, as the galleys and a bakery provided as many as 9,000 meals each day and under certain conditions had serving lines open continuously. There was little the navy could do to keep weevils out of its stores of flour, and men who were initially disgusted at finding tiny bugs baked into the bread gradually learned to think of them as adding texture and protein. Food was served directly onto partitioned aluminum trays, which eliminated the need for plates. Boys who had yet to outgrow adolescent appetites, from places that had yet to become particular about the culinary arts, found the chow good. More importantly, it was plentiful. Elden was told to take all he wanted but to eat all he took. Shipboard space was too precious for even a small part of it to be used for food that would not be eaten. That, of course, was not a problem for this child of the Great Depression who had grown up in a household that viewed wasting food as a moral transgression.[12]

Yet this floating city, self-contained between occasional days for refueling and resupplying, was almost a speedboat. Her top speed of thirty-three knots was, by land reckoning, faster than the 35 mph "patriotic" speed limit most Americans observed in their automobiles and could move her and all of her enormous power 900 miles in a day and night, and her planes could easily add 800 miles to that.[13] In an era when the locations of enemy ships and even fleets at sea were generally discerned by visual reconnaissance, this speed made the fast carriers difficult to track. The *Franklin* could carry two million gallons of fuel and consumed 14,000 gallons a day. This meant she could operate for weeks without refueling and could also serve as a fueling source for other ships.[14]

The captain, James M. Shoemaker, respected his men, kept them informed, and was well liked. He had recognized the need to counteract superstitious jitters caused by the ship's numerical designation and the big 13 painted on the flight deck near the bow, and had declared thirteen to be his lucky number.[15] It appeared to be so.

The new world of shipboard life gave Elden plenty to think about besides Virginia. For a boy from a town of five hundred who had never before been more than two hundred miles from home, riding a train to California, going through boot camp, seeing movie stars and honky-tonk legends, and flying in airplanes had all amounted to a great new adventure. Boarding an *Essex*-class carrier with 3,000 men mostly from the East and many from big cities was like having that newly discovered larger world condensed, compressed, and canned. Suddenly he was among twice the number of people who lived in his entire home county, all squeezed into a single structure three blocks long, a third of a block wide, and seven decks deep with a landing strip for a roof. There was no such thing as privacy, anywhere, ever. None of the 3,000 was female, and although in a way they were almost all having the same new experience, most of them came from very different backgrounds than Elden and spoke with very different accents. Although Elden may have had a shy side, he seems to have overcome it with his sense of humor and soon came to be regarded by shipmates as "the most jolly fellow in the division," keeping everyone in hysterics.[16]

We have no information on exactly what uniform and supply items Elden had when he boarded the *Franklin,* but below is the order for what was required for a "full bag" on August 9, 1945, after she was back at the New York Navy Yard.[17] In all likelihood, this is approximately what Elden possessed.

1 belt, woven (black and white)	3 jumper, white
1 pair blankets	1 jersey
1 cap, complete	1 pair leggings
1 cap, watch	2 mattress covers
4 pairs drawers, light or med.	1 neckerchief
4 pairs dungarees trowsers	1 pea coat
12 handkerchiefs	4 shirts, chambray
4 hats, white	2 pairs shoes
1 jumper, dress blue	6 pairs cotton socks
2 jumper, undress blue	1 outfit toilet articles
2 towels, large and small	3 pairs white trowsers
2 pairs blue trowsers	4 undershirts, light or med.

Elden was issued a pocket-sized Personal Information Booklet with blanks in which he could write down basic things that he needed to remember. Although he regrettably left blank nearly all of the pages that might have told us about his daily life, the book tells us that his laundry was done on Thursdays.

From the moment Elden boarded the *Franklin* until his death, his return addresses indicate that he was in V-1 Division. The six V divisions worked with the aircraft, enabling them to operate and actually operating them, and because of this association were nicknamed Airedales by the rest of the ship's crew.

As flight deck sailors Elden and his buddies in V-1 worked directly with the aircraft at times when the planes were alive with energy, movement, and noise; and this made their jobs among the most dangerous of any in the navy. In groups of eight, the men manhandled the big craft, removing the tie-downs and wheel chocks, unfolding and securing wings, pushing the planes into position, and getting them onto the catapult and into the air. They learned to do this as quickly as possible, aware that each minute of idling engine meant less flying time for a plane that might exhaust its fuel and be just as lost as if shot down. When enemy aircraft approached, every second a *Franklin* fighter spent being readied for launch was an increment of increased danger to themselves and their ship. It was the men of V-1 who had to avoid being lifted off their feet by the prop wash of one revving plane and sent tumbling into another propeller behind. A man thus destabilized had to save himself by grabbing on to anything handy, sometimes the small indentations in the deck to which planes were securely tied when not operating.[18]

Planes launched had to be recovered later, and this presented a whole different array of dangers. Elden's division readied and operated the cables that caught a returning plane's tailhook and quickly brought it from flying speed to a stop, and they saw to the barrier nets that stopped or tried to stop the planes that sometimes missed the cables. On occasion a bomb or external fuel tank would detach from landing aircraft and spread potential destruction or actual fire down the deck (see fig. 13). Sailors dodged the hurtling tons of uncontrolled metal that a landing airplane became when cables and barriers failed, and even the broken cable itself, the whipping ends of which could take a man's head off.[19]

Colleagues in other V divisions had specialties of their own. V-2 was made up of metalworkers and mechanics who worked in the hangar deck below, patching holes that had been shot into planes and repairing frequently damaged parts such as propellers and landing gear. V-3 served as staff to the air officer, seeing that his commands were executed and handling the paperwork. The men of V-4 operated the radars, lookouts, and radios of the vital "CIC," the Combat Information Center, and were responsible for knowing where both friendly and enemy planes and ships were located, and for guiding the *Franklin's* planes to their quarry and back. V-5 fueled the planes; affixed the bombs, rockets, and torpedoes; and saw that each plane's guns had ammunition. V-6 members were the pilots and crews of the planes that went after the enemy and represented the purpose of the whole enormous ship.[20]

Without doubt Elden heard, and probably shuddered at the thought, of the additional hazard of working on the unlighted flight deck at night. It was not uncommon for a man to lose track of his surroundings in extreme darkness and to walk off the edge, unnoticed until too late. It would happen to Lou Casserino's buddy Felix Cerra in the early morning hours of October 22, 1944, and anyone could just as easily find himself alone in the middle of the world's largest ocean, watching his ship sail away unaware of his absence. If he was not miraculously found by another ship, his best hope was to drown or die of hypothermia *before* being found by sharks.[21]

Shipboard life was not totally without amenities; Elden has already written home about buying candy for pennies, and Steve Nowak later recalled that "there was a big mess hall on the third deck. It had what we called the Poggy Bait station, a place where you could go down and buy a box of candy for a couple of bucks, and candy bars were ten cents. Cigarettes were six cents a pack."[22]

The business end of an aircraft carrier was its airplanes, and the *Franklin* in 1944 carried ninety of them. One way of understanding just how important aircraft were is to note that these largest American warships and each of the 3,000 men aboard existed almost exclusively to put armed and fueled airplanes into places where they could be effective; and that literally dozens of battleships, cruisers, destroyers, destroyer escorts, and submarines sailed with the carriers to protect and support them. Each carrier the size of the *Franklin* had an air group consisting of "a fighter squadron designated VF for fighter, a dive-bomber squadron designated VB for bomber, and a torpedo bomber squadron designated VT for torpedo." "The air group that was specifically created to serve aboard *Franklin* was designated Carrier Air Group 13 (CAG-13)"; "two large white numbers on the tail of each aircraft identified Air Group 13."[23] A diamond-shaped symbol also identified planes from the *Franklin* (see fig. 11).

June 1, 1944

Dear Tex,

How is the Navy treating you now? I'm sure glad you are on a good ship. That was really a pretty one on the post card you sent. If yours is larger than that it must be awfully big.

Say did you ever get thoes pictures I sent? I would like to know if you got them or not. I know they were awful of me.

I had a long distance phone call a little while ago from a kid in Garden City Kansas. He is a nice kid but too young for me. He is even younger than me. That's the way it is anymore. Either too young or too old.

Maureen & some girls work up at the base now. I guess I will try to get on up there. You get a bunch of money there.

Well I'm getting pretty sleepy & can't think of very much to write, except that I miss you very much. Do you miss me any? I guess the girls out there have what it takes. I will close now & write more next time.

Bye now.

Lots of Love,

Virginia

Once far enough from San Diego and well into the empty Pacific the *Franklin*'s gun crews began to practice their art. This was also a form of aural training for new sailors like Elden who learned to recognize the roar of the five-inch turret guns and the rhythmic pom-pom of the twelve dual pairs of 40 mm antiaircraft quads.[24] The sounds, heard and felt throughout the ship, became the basis for a rudimentary understanding of what sort of action was taking place. On a carrier these weapons were used for defense, and so their sounds—when gunnery practice was not scheduled in the Plan for the Day—would come to mean that the ship was under attack.

By the time the air group took off and flew to the Kahululi air station on the Hawaiian island of Maui,[25] Elden knew his hope for leave had been misplaced. His letter dated June 4 may have been written over a two- or three-day period, as it seems to reflect having been in port long enough to receive mail.

June 4, 1944

Dear Mom & Dad & Bros,

Well I hate to tell you this but I guess I wont get a leave for quite a spell as I have left the states. It will probably be at least 18 months before I get leave but I am like thousands of others who didn't get to come home. If they can stand it I can too. Don't worry about me as I am alright I am on the newest and one of the safest ships in the fleet. I'll be O.K. & besides it does no good to worry anyhow.

I wont get a leave for 18 months but this old war will probably be over by then and I can come home with an honorable discharge. At least they cant say I was a slacker like Edd Murphy. I can say I done my part and be Prowd of it.

I got a letter from Bug Eye the other day he didn't have much to say as usual.

Did Odell go to San Diego? I sure would have liked to got to see him. I sure was glad to get the school paper. That did a lot of good to read about the kids at home.

I guess I must not have told you but I bought me a navy ring about a month ago it cost six dollars. I sure do like it. You won't have to get me one. Thanks a lot anyhow. Say figure up and see how much I owe you and I'll send it to you as I can save money out here and I'll send it to you. Cigarettes is all I have to buy. They cost 50 cents a carton & I get 70 dollars a month now.

It sure don't take long to get your letters when I'm in port I got one in 3 days and it went through C.A.S.U. so it gets them over the road.

Will you get me E.L. Krahns address and Bob Walcotts and any of the boys from Vega as I might run on to some of them sometime.

If I ever see Wig I think I'll mop up on him for not comeing to see me when he was at Diego.

Did Jack Dewees get a leave I sure hope he did as I know how to feel for him as He & I are in the same shoes.

I got a letter from Six and I told him to stay on the ground as long as he could as I did. They came out where I was working one morning and wanted three Volunteers for this ship and nobody steeped up so they came back and picked out three of us out of a group of ten.

I was glad that the other two were my buddies I have been running around with since I've been in the navy. I better sign off for now. I am still gaining weight but I wont get like S.C. as I am getting hard instead of fat.

Lots of Love
Your Son
Elden

The peak of towering Haleakala on Maui hove into view sixty miles to the southwest on the morning of June 6, then a few hours later Diamond Head appeared directly westward.[26] As evening fell, all hands were on flight deck and at attention in salute as they passed the USS *Arizona,* which served then and now as a tomb for almost 1,200 men of her crew who had died on December 7, 1941.[27] They tied up at pier F-13, just across the end of Ford Island from the grave of the honored battleship.[28]

Exotic Hawaii! Verdant, mountainous, rainy, and beautiful; with sandy beaches on a blue ocean, a distinctive music, girls who danced in grass skirts, tropical fruits—Hawaii had everything that dry, flat, little Vega did not. It may be impossible for the children of today's interconnected world to imagine what "exotic" meant at that time. And here, for a little while, Elden was up to his neck in it at the world-famous Pearl Harbor, sleeping each night close enough to the hallowed *Arizona* to hear her ghosts demanding redemption. During each of the next ten days the *Franklin* sailed out a short distance for training, her crew rehearsing virtually everything that needed to happen on a carrier or in its planes. With liberty on June 10 and perhaps some other evenings, Elden piled into a taxicab with five or six or more other sailors and rode to the Waikiki area of Honolulu, experiencing things unlike anything he had ever known in Vega, Amarillo, Las Animas, or even San Diego.

Jack "Red" Dewees, the Vega boy of whom Elden wrote, served aboard the USS *Pensacola* (CA-24), the namesake of a class of two light cruisers. An old ship by 1944, the *Pensacola* had been built at the New York Navy Yard in 1930, and she would survive many perils only to meet an ignominious end as a practice target for navy artillery in 1948. As we will see in later correspondence, Dewees was in a great many battles.

The "other war" was the source of the big news during this brief period in Hawaii, and Elden and his buddies, like Americans everywhere, would have been talking about it. The long-awaited invasion of mainland Europe had begun on the day the *Franklin* arrived. By the time she left Hawaii, 300,000 Allied soldiers were ashore at Normandy.

8　The Home Front

SIXTEEN-YEAR-OLD Gerald heard a sound he had never heard before and, with five-year-old Jerry at his heels, ran outside to see what it was. Twin-piston-driven aircraft engines with big propellers had distinctive "voices," and some aircraft types could be recognized aurally. Gerald was a serious plane spotter—a hobby a bit like bird-watching but with distinctly grave implications during wartime. He had diagrams showing the shapes of virtually every kind of American, Allied, and enemy aircraft. Whenever he heard the sound of an airplane, he would grab his diagrams, run outside, spot the plane, identify it, and log it in a list made for that purpose. Because Vega was located on the original 1930 Trans World Airlines route, on which planes had found their way across the continent visually by following beacon lights twelve miles apart (one such light was one mile south of our house and was very much in use), a good many planes came over, and Gerald was able to log them. The sound he heard for the first time on this particular day announced a pair of twin-engine, twin-fuselage P-38 Lockheed Lightning fighters. Seeing them was a rare thrill, and logging them seemed a significant accomplishment.

Everyone, including those safe at home and far from combat, had a stake in the outcome of the war, and government policies constantly reminded them of their responsibility to contribute to the war effort. A "front" in warfare is the dividing line between opposing forces—the place where the actual fighting and dying takes place. To make the war seem real to everyone and to emphasize the important role each person could play, President Roosevelt used the term "home front" to create a sense among ordinary citizens of personal commitment to the men who were fighting on the actual front. Americans of every age could "fight" by the ways they lived, the things they did, and the things they did without, and those who seemed not to be doing their part became the subject of gossip and scorn. With Elden in the navy, the Rogers family became more conscious than ever of specific things they could do on the home front. Plane spotting was something a teenager could do. The data about planes were never reported to anyone beyond a scoutmaster, but it felt important nonetheless.

Although far inland and militarily valuable only for its few agricultural products and for the personnel it could provide, Oldham County complied with requests for nationwide preparedness and developed a plan for a blackout system to ensure that enemy aircraft would not be able to navigate at night by streetlights or the lights in windows. Blackout wardens were appointed to oversee the effectiveness of the system.[1]

H. H. Weimhold, publisher, editor, reporter, and general staff of the weekly *Oldham County News,* urged readers to save burlap, a previously cheap and almost ubiquitous fabric used to make bags that we called "gunny sacks" for a wide range of products but now suddenly scarce because the war interrupted its production and transport. Farmers were urged to be sparing in their use of steel wire for tying bales of hay, and to save and reuse wire, bolts, nuts, screws, and machine parts. If a farmer could not himself use those items, he was urged to sell or give them to someone who could.[2]

In order to prevent inflation, profiteering, hoarding, and inefficient use of products needed by the military, the federal government established systems of wage and price controls and rationing of many vital things. Among rationed items were butter, soap, sugar, shoes, gasoline, tires, and many personal items. The Rogers family felt the resulting scarcity with regard to manufactured goods, but the rural and small-town semisubsistence economic practices that had brought us through the Great Depression allowed us to produce for ourselves a good many of the things that people in other parts of the country had to do without. In the spirit of the time, editor Weimhold in 1942 offered a year-long subscription to his newspaper for "one setting hen, four dozen eggs, one-hundred pounds of maize, four guinea fowl, two ducks, or one big dollar."[3] Unfortunately for Weimhold, the scarcity of paper, more than any shortage of ducks or dollars, would put his little paper out of circulation within a matter of weeks.

Butter was not a problem for the Rogers family, who usually had one or more milk cows. Grace skimmed the cream off the milk, allowed it to become sour, and then made butter and its by-product buttermilk in her big three-gallon churn. Rarely, but at least once, the family bought oleomargarine, the butter substitute that families who were more store-dependent than we had to use. The influence of the dairy industry was such that this product was legally required to be sold uncolored, as a white substance that resembled lard. A yellow powder came in a separate packet, and when it was mixed in, the white stuff at least looked like butter.[4]

If food production was so important to the war effort that a farmer could be spared military service, it made sense to encourage people to produce additional food on a small scale as well. People everywhere responded to government encouragement to plant "victory gardens" on whatever plots of soil could be so used. Many suburban backyards, flower beds, and even front lawns lost their ornamental plantings for the sake of vegetables. City dwellers cultivated food on vacant lots or in window boxes and in planters atop buildings. In places like Vega, where vegetable gardens were normal, they became even more common and were made larger.

The emphasis on frugality showed up in clothing styles, as the long flowing dresses of the 1930s were replaced by skirts above the knee that required less cotton or wool. Male office workers postponed buying new suits, and a slightly shabby look became common. Factory and farm workers wore their clothes out, and then wore them with patches, as they had done through the Depression years, but now the look reflected patriotism rather than just poverty. Grace Rogers took scissors to a red felt hat that had become unstylish, and by cutting a scalloped border around its edges made it a "new" hat.

A lot of food was fried in those days, and the grease left over in the frying pan was poured into a large container and taken to a collection station for use, it was said, in making ammunition.

Grace also used her leftover grease more directly to make her own soap. When four or five gallons of grease had been accumulated, she would melt it in a large pot on her kitchen stove and then stir in lye (caustic soda). After a few minutes of stirring, the mixture would congeal into a brownish-yellow soap. Children were made to stay well away, and the whole operation was conducted with great caution, as the bubbles from the boiling oil could splash painfully burning drops onto a person's skin, and a small amount spilled into the flame below could result in a conflagration. The lye itself was dangerous and capable of dissolving skin or the flesh beneath. When all of this had been done and the substance had cooled, the soap was cut with a knife into four-inch by six-inch blocks, which could be used for cleaning and for laundry. It was a little too harsh for use on human skin, however, so the family occasionally used ration coupons to buy Palmolive, Lifebuoy, Camay, or Lava soap.

Sugar was acutely rationed and was used very sparingly. Grace once told her family, "When this war is over I am going to make cakes and pies until you guys get enough." She did, but that is another story. In the meantime, as we have already seen, she used a substantial percentage of her sugar allotment to make cookies that were sent to Elden.

Shoes were limited by the rationing system to two pairs per person per year. This was not a problem because shoes in those days were well made and durable, and even without rationing, people in the Rogers family normally made do with a single pair, usually purchased in late August just before school began. For the first year the new shoes would be reserved for special occasions, like Sunday school and church, last year's "good" shoes would become this year's everyday shoes, and shoes entering their third year of use might finally be thrown away after all possible use had been extracted from them. For this to work, kids' shoes had to be bought one or more sizes too large in order to allow room for growing feet. New shoes, therefore, meant loose-fitting shoes, and because they had not yet become flexible from use, new shoes meant friction that would produce painful blisters on heels. Because of this, Grace had little trouble getting her boys to cooperate in conserving their "good" shoes, as their newness did not compensate for the pain involved in wearing them.

Grandpa Boydstun's shoe repair shop was a magical place. Located on the west side of the courthouse square between the Red and White food store and the Cotton Hotel, it was a big dark room filled with strange machines, the unforgettable smell of leather and polish, and a nice old man and woman who dipped snuff. We went there once a year. At about the time when shoes were old enough to become "everyday," a hole would finally wear through the heavy leather soles. The hole would be temporarily blocked with a piece of cardboard until the sole of the companion shoe also wore through, after which the pair would go to Grandpa Boydstun's shop for a half-sole and a new heel cap. Small children, especially boys, went barefoot during summer, thus saving three months' wear on shoes. Huckleberry Finn had nothing on us.

Japan's capture of rubber-producing areas in Southeast Asia and the war's interruption of transportation and trade made it difficult for Americans to get tires. Rubber-tired farm tractors and other vehicles when not in use were jacked up and rested on blocks to keep their weight off their tires, and wheels were covered to shelter the tires from the deteriorating effects of the sun's rays.[5] Tires were used until no trace of a tread remained, and if they were pierced by something, a "boot" or "reliner" was inserted between tire and tube at the point of the hole and the tires continued in use. On one occasion Ancell bought a Model A Ford Tudor sedan for the sole reason that it had, in his parlance, "good rubber." The tires were actually more important than the car itself and were promptly transferred to the Town Sedan that he preferred. (Elden may have had the Tudor in mind when he told Virginia that he had a car.)

Gasoline stations paid two cents a pound for scrap rubber, which they then sold to companies that could recycle it. Reasoning that scraps of rubber might be found where the greatest number of automobiles came and went, and motivated both by patriotism and profit, Gerald and his friend Robert "Windy" Ballard secured gunny sacks and scoured the roadsides of Route 66 between Vega and Everett Switch, five miles to the east. Their surmise proved correct, and between the two of them they collected thirty pounds of tire fragments. After selling it all they took their sixty cents to the soda fountain at the Vega Drug Store, where they squandered a dime on two root beers and went home with a quarter each.

The country had begun to become automobile-dependent back in the 1920s, and gasoline rationing had perhaps the greatest effect of all wartime limitations. We have earlier noted that gasoline coupons were allotted to families due not only to how dependent they were on automobiles and trucks, but especially to the perceived importance of their work to the war effort. A farmer could get coupons because he needed to reach his fields, power his tractors, and haul his produce to the grain elevator. Ancell, who at first did day labor and later worked steadily with the Texas Highway Department, could get only a few coupons. When he drove into a gasoline station, he never asked the attendant to fill the tank, but rather he ordered the number of gallons—usually five—for which he had coupons. Ancell walked to work, and Grace walked the half mile to the grocery store, often pulling her boys' little red wagon with several dozen eggs to sell to the store, and then using it to haul home her purchases—things like coffee, flour, baking powder, salt, and pepper that could not be produced at home.

Any time Grace was "in town," meaning near the courthouse square, she did all her other business that required going to that area. She might pay the light bill, get something from the drugstore, and pick up mail from the post office. A portion of any change she might have while at the post office would be spent on "savings stamps" at ten cents each. The stamps were pasted into booklets, and when a booklet was full it was redeemed for a twenty-five-dollar "war bond." Almost every kid had such a booklet, and reluctantly became accustomed to being favored with a stamp in lieu of two candy bars (which were rarely available anyway).

Scrap metal became precious because it could quickly be melted and reshaped into war matériel. Although our family bought few things that came in metal cans, we saved those cans we did use and also walked along roads gathering cans that had been carelessly thrown away. We soaked the labels off the cans, cut out tops and bottoms, smashed them flat, and turned them in at collection points. Kids peeled the thin layer of aluminum foil from chewing gum wrappers and cigarette packages to save the metal for recycling. Boy Scouts and Girl Scouts collected paper for recycling and books to be sent to soldiers who were in hospitals and other places that allowed them the opportunity to read.[6] Vega school students conducted a scrap drive and filled a half-block space with old car bodies, motors, nuts, bolts, and anything that would attract a magnet. School officials made arrangements for a convoy of army trucks to come from Amarillo to pick up the scrap. Gerald and others his age were thrilled to talk with the uniformed soldiers and to help load the trucks. A few of the hardest-working kids were rewarded by being allowed by school officials to ride in the truck cabs with the soldiers to Amarillo. Even though the trucks were so loud that conversation with the soldiers amounted to shouting, most of the boys decided right then that they would join the army as soon as they were old enough.[7]

Local women organized a chapter of the Red Cross to collect donations of medical supplies and to knit sweaters for soldiers. The government provided the yarn, and the women provided the knitting needles and the labor. Grace and her friends participated in this, sometimes together in a social setting and sometimes in spare moments at home. A local committee of "United China Relief" collected money and matériel to provide food, clothing, and medicine for the people of China.[8]

The activities and sacrifices of the home front did much to unite the country in support of the war effort and, perhaps more importantly, allowed people to feel less helpless about their inability to protect from harm their loved ones who were far away and on the real fronts.

9   Farewell, Fibber McGee

Don't open that door, McGee!" was a line shouted in alarm by Molly in almost every episode of the popular weekly radio comedy *Fibber McGee and Molly*. Listeners knew in advance that McGee would forget that his hall closet was crammed to the top with a disorderly array and that after he opened the door we would hear several long seconds of sound effects that created a mental image of things cascading down. It was a laugh line, always a surprise to McGee but never to the audience, and it was always funny.

Hearing that program on his eighth day at Pearl Harbor brought Elden thoughts of home and what he would be doing if he were there. The chores he mentions—feeding and watering cows, pigs, and chickens; milking the cows; gathering the eggs and shutting the chickens safely in the henhouse—once annoying obligations, were remembered almost fondly now. His statement that it was hard to write because of restrictions on what he could write about is a strong precursor, as letters after this become so uninformative and repetitive as to communicate frustration more than anything else. It also points up why we are doing this work seven decades later, to tell what he was experiencing and would have liked to have communicated, but because of censorship could not.

June 14, 1944

Dear Mom, Dad, & Bros,

Well I just finished listening to "Fibber Magee" I was thinking about if I was home we would be hurrying around to get the chores done in time to hear him. I haven't got any mail for a week & a half we should get some mail tonight if it gets here before bedtime. I'll gladly wait up if the Bugler blows mail Call. He just blew chow call so I'll "Knock off" [a navy expression for quit] until after Supper.

I never got to see E.L. the other time. I am hopeing for a letter from you tonight with his address in it. So I can go see him in a day or two. I haven't heard from Virginia since I left the states She must not have sen't my letters air mail If not they haven't had time to catch up with me yet.

Well I never Realized what the red Cross meant when I was a civilian. They passed out Red Cross Packages on here yesterday there was soap, a book, paper, Envelopes, Pensil, Shoe Strings, Razor blades, Sewing Kit and candy in them. Every man on the ship got one. We sure was glad to get them. I have to wear my white uniforms here. I sure do hate them as they get dirty in about two or three hours.

I never hardly even heard Earnest Tubbs music on the juke boxes in San Diego but there is more of his records than anyone Else here.

It sure is hard for me to write a letter anymore as I always wrote about what I was doing or going to do all my life untill now.

I can't tell you where I am what I am doing or anything about the weather. I better close for this time will write more tomorrow nite.

Lots of Love

Elden

P.S. I see the mail man comeing I have my fingers crossed but I know I'll hear from you & Probably Virginia. You wanted to know what the U.S.N.R. was. Well it is United States Naval Reserve.

As the *Franklin* put out to sea two days later, Elden surely joined in cheers at word that American B-29s had made the first bombing raids on a Japanese home island since Doolittle's famous raid more than two years before. They had hit Kyushu, which would later become very important in this story. The big ship's importance was underscored by a growing escort that now included the cruiser USS *Denver* and the destroyers *Cushing, Leary, Rowe,* and *Twiggs*. But the group took a westward course; no shred of hope remained in the near future for leave at home or a safe and happy time in San Francisco. On the same day, Elden heard that U.S. marines had hit the beach at Saipan after a preinvasion bombardment by planes and artillery that seemed to leave no possibility of remaining Japanese defenders. By evening, however, he may have heard that the appearance had been illusory, as the Japanese defense was among the fiercest in history and Americans paid a high price just getting ashore and establishing a beachhead.[1] He probably wondered how many Vega friends were in this fight, as indeed Tub Walcott was.

Also happening as the *Franklin* moved westward by southwestward through day and night was the Battle of the Philippine Sea. Japan lost two more carriers, and her planes, now piloted by young and hastily trained men, were shot down with ease in great numbers. Even as Radio Tokyo told a gullible Japanese public that eleven American carriers and most American planes had been destroyed, Elden and his shipmates may have heard the battle more accurately described as the Great Marianas Turkey Shoot.[2]

Six days steady going covered the 2,400 miles to Eniwetok in the Marshall Islands group. Entirely unlike mountainous Oahu, this low coral atoll had been converted in the four months since conquest into a forward staging area for Nimitz's whole fleet.[3] Anchored at berth 413, "Big Ben" topped up fuel tanks and crammed every available space with supplies and ammunition as the men had a very different kind of "liberty." No overloaded taxicabs to the honky-tonk district and no hula girls—just two beers with hundreds of other men on the beach. No Fibber McGee either; Tokyo Rose was the evening radio entertainment, and the crew was astonished to hear her declare that their very own ship had been sunk. One sailor, with a wit so similar to Elden's that it might even have been he, jumped up and said, "Hell, I'm going up topside to see for myself."[4] It was another great laugh line, but it only partially masked the new experience of hearing their ship's name pronounced in an enemy broadcast—the Japanese knew there was a carrier called the *Franklin* and that it was in the Pacific. This seemed to be evidence that the warnings about spies had been serious, and hearing it for himself may have made Elden even more conscientious about adhering to censorship rules.[5]

Great numbers of flies made it hard to enjoy even the beach time at Eniwetok. Word went around that the flies had hatched and matured in unburied bodies of Japanese who had died in the recent fighting, and the thought made each touch of a fly more unpleasant than usual. Worse, an outbreak of impetigo was rumored to have been carried by the flies from the dead to the living, and this added revulsion to the normal concern about a very contagious infection.[6]

June 24 brought Elden a dramatic demonstration of how quickly things would happen in his future. The victorious fleet from the "turkey shoot" returned and now jammed the lagoon from one side to the other.[7] What must a new sailor have felt! Did he, like many others, talk about how they wished the *Franklin* had been on time to be in on it, or did he recognize the distinction between bravado and the quieter nature of genuine bravery? It was another distinct step in his gradually escalating experience. If berthing near the *Arizona* back at Pearl had invoked somber recognition of a very real war, and if heading west from Hawaii meant home was unimaginably far behind, greeting the returning victors at Eniwetok must have brought an anticipatory shot of the adrenaline rush of danger and victory combined.

This was Task Force 58 in Vice Admiral Raymond Spruance's Fifth Fleet. The task force itself was divided into four task groups, each with two or more carriers at its heart. As they left Eniwetok at the end of June, the brand-new *Franklin* carried Admiral Ralph Davison and served as the flagship from which he would direct Task Group 58.2. Elsewhere in the task force sailed the carriers *Hornet*, *Yorktown II*, *Wasp II*, *Monterey*, and *Cabot*; cruisers *Baltimore*, *Boston*, *San Diego*, *San Juan*, *Vincennes*, and sixteen more; plus about twenty destroyers, including

The Sullivans, famously named for five brothers killed in combat eighteen months earlier.[8]

$$\text{⚓}$$

Back at home, Tom Steward's eyes had a faintly hard look even when he tried to smile. He also had round patches of scar tissue under his shirt where Nazi bullets had entered and exited his body. He was Bugeye's older and heroic brother, at home on recovery leave after being wounded in the landing at Anzio five months before. He was connected by marriage to Virginia's family, and she wrote of him while Elden was at Eniwetok.[9]

June 24, 1944

Dearest Tex,

I was sure glad to hear from you. I thought maybe you had forgotten all about poor little me.

I'm sure sorry you didn't get a furlough. I guess you just weren't lucky. Maybe some day we can make up for all the disappointment we've had.

Things have certainly been dead around here. A few boys are left. The ones that live on farms.

I sure wish you could get your furlough now, because I have the money to go down to Vega on. I'll keep it until you do get one if I can.

Herman & Earl are still around & Charlie. I sure wish they would go to the army & bring back some boys I like.

I guess Chuck's brother, Tom, came back on a leave from Italy. Helen was down at Vega when he came up here. I guess he didn't know she was down there.

There has been a carnival in town for the last two weeks now. It sure is a small one but its some place to go.

Did Carl Six go to the army yet? Maybe he won't have to go if hes working on a farm. Do you remember that girl Chuck said he married? Well, she is married for sure now to a soldier from La Junta. I bet he feels funny to think his wife got married.

Well I guess I'll quit now & mail this. Hope you can find time to write again real soon.

All my Love & kisses,

Virginia

Time, distance, and unavailability of alternatives—to Elden altogether and to Virginia at least up to a point—appear to be rekindling romance. Elden has grown sentimental as the first anniversary approaches of his meeting Virginia in a park, and he has asked her if she remembers it. Virginia's response, in a very short letter, tells us more about Elden in a personal way than most other sources.

June 30, 1944

Dear Tex,

I received a letter from you today. It's the first one for a long time. I guess it has been quite a while since I last wrote, tho.

I'm glad you sent me your picture. Its pretty good, I think. I'm sure proud of my big handsome sailor. I hope I get to see him real soon now.

Yes, I remember the day we first met. In fact I remember every time I was ever with you. Those were the good old days weren't they. You was about as bashful as me, but I really liked you even from the very first. I didn't think you cared any thing about me. You acted like girls bored you or something. I hope you still act that way around girls, all except me.

I sure miss you. It seems like you are about the only boy I ever really cared anything about. I'll be waiting for you to come back & I'll count the days even tho it may seem like years, if you want me to wait for you. Do you remember the plans we made that we said we'd do after the war was over?

Well, goodnite honey. All my Love,
Virginia

Shipboard life began in earnest for Elden on that same day as the fleet sailed from Eniwetok. For the next six weeks he would walk on decks of steel and wood rather than on land. His life, as in war zones everywhere, would be routine to the point of boredom but subject to sudden action, adrenaline, and even terror.

The seemingly universal tendency of humans to separate into groups of "us" and "them" found expression in rivalry among members of various branches of the armed services. This had been most extreme back in San Diego and Honolulu where alcohol had lubricated bar brawls between marines, soldiers, and sailors for no reason other than their different uniforms. Aboard ship, where small fights were common but major brawling unacceptable, the rivalries were manifested in good-natured teasing and name-calling, softened with a grin. There were marine contingents aboard many navy ships, particularly those like the *Franklin* that carried an admiral, whose personal bodyguard was made up of marines. Everyone of every rank on a carrier suffered the danger of being bombed or torpedoed, but a shipboard admiral was in virtually no danger that could have been warded off by guards. This meant that much of the marines' duty consisted of standing outside the admiral's compartment and of being assigned to menial errands for the admiral and his aides. Because of this, the *Franklin*'s sailors called these marines "bellhops."[10] Where admirals were not to be found, this nickname was probably not dared.

One other separation of "us" and "them" was so natural as to be almost unavoidable. The majority of the men aboard a carrier were devoted to running the ship itself, and a substantial but smaller number, in divisions designated "V" followed by a numeral, were devoted specifically to the aircraft and were nicknamed the "Airedales." Robert Ladewig recalled that this distinction aboard the *Franklin* was not acute, although negative references by either group about the other might be heard in conversation. According to him, what most annoyed the ship's crew was that flight operations sometimes required that flight deck personnel be fed first before the rest of the ship's crew. "The Master at Arms would be stationed at the head of the chow line, and if you weren't wearing a colored T-shirt you were not allowed to go through the line."[11] Elden was in V-1 Division, flight deck personnel, and must have been able to partake of this privilege. Also, he apparently wore a colored T-shirt.

Ensign Byron Robinson, V-2 Division, recalled that it was very hot when the ship was in the low latitudes. Ventilation was minimal and there was nothing like air-conditioning. Most of Elden's duty was on the flight deck and the hangar deck, and Robinson's words convey what Elden would have experienced.

> We always worked on the hangar with the curtains open to get a little air during daylight hours, but in the late afternoon they would pipe down to "darken the ship." Then we had just thirty minutes to close all hatches and the hangar deck curtains. There were something like 114 separate switches, all of which had to close before the hangar deck lights would come on so all the crew could go to work, because during the night hours everything had to be completely dark so the ship wouldn't be visible. Then the men would strip down to their skivvies and work all night long with sweat rolling off of them. It was only when reveille was sounded could we open the curtains to get air. The way it was—heat or no heat—it was nonstop work. The men were just exhausted all the time. It was constant misery.[12]

Heat, humidity, sweat, and limited fresh water for bathing were a combination sure to produce more than mere discomfort. Men swallowed salt tablets with the extra water they had to drink in order to avoid dehydration. Fungal infections commonly called prickly heat or jock itch that "felt like five hundred mosquito bites simultaneously itching" were pretty nearly constant and universal.[13] They were no respecters of rank, and sometimes became so bad as to keep a man from duty.

Discomfort shortened tempers and generated fights. The chow line, perhaps because it was a break from serious work, seems to have been a place for conflict as well as for laughing, joking, and talking. Elden's best buddy, the boot camp cohort and fellow West Texan Roy Treadaway, was one of the three biggest men on the ship. (The other two were Jumbo, the tuba player in the band, and Milkshake, who ran the "gedunk" stand).[14] Paul Dalton and Ernest Scott were in line for chow with Roy one time when a tough little guy grubbed the line—sailor slang for cutting in—two or three spots ahead. The big Texan reached over the heads of a couple of men in front of him, tapped the tough on the shoulder, and, pointing to the rear, told him the line begins back there. The tappee responded belligerently, "Who's gonna make me go?" Treadaway pointed to himself, and the line grubber said, "Oh yeah, well where I come from we say, 'The bigger they are, the harder they fall.'" Treadaway, again reaching over two or three guys in front of him, simply brought his fist down like a hammer on top of the guy's head, knocking him unconscious, and said, "Where I come from we say, 'The smaller they are, the higher they bounce.'"[15]

Two chaplains, Reverend Clarence A. Chamberlin Jr. and Father Edward J. Harkin, provided guidance and comfort and counseled the men to get along with one another[16]; Electrician's Mate Second Class George Shapiro served as rabbi to approximately sixty Jewish crewmen, one of whom was Elden's buddy Bob Bamburg.[17] Although the music of Saxie Dowell's orchestra at services surely provided extra reasons to attend, in all of his letters Elden made only three references to "church." The New Testament issued to him at the beginning of boot camp shows no sign of wear, so we do not know how large or small a role religion played in his navy life. Most likely he paid more attention to religion now than he had before enlisting, both to find an emotional connection with his faraway home and as reassurance in the heightened recognition of his own mortality. In everyday behavior, however, he was almost certainly a normal sailor who without the civilizing influence of females used notoriously profane language. Admiral Davison clucked that sailors in general were bad about cursing, and that *Franklin* crew members were worse than most.[18]

"There is nothing like a dame," went a song in a postwar movie, and nothing makes a young man more aware of that than being totally away from female company. Free movies every night and big-band swing concerts on the hangar deck by Saxie Dowell's orchestra probably did a great deal of good for Elden's morale, even with his preference for Ernest Tubb's country crooning. Movies, music, or not, nighttime meant blackout, for no light at all was allowed to escape. Hatches from outside onto the hangar deck were equipped with automatic switches, and whenever anyone opened such a hatch, all lights on the hangar deck went out until the hatch was secured. This sometimes interrupted concerts, but Bob St. Peters told Joseph Springer that it caused a roar of unholy hell from men who were engaged in poker games.[19]

Among the cursing, scratching, rash-bedeviled crew that sailed from Eniwetok, Elden drew enviable duty. His job at this point was in the cold-storage locker, which was located on the starboard side, aft, on the third and fourth deck directly beneath the number 2 elevator.[20] His thoughts are of home, and the mere sight of the Cudahay meatpacking company's brand on a ham sets him yearning for the home-cured stuff and invokes musing about whether this very hunk of pork might have come from his dad's own pigpen. He even longs to be working the hard, dirty, and extended hours of the wheat harvest, which in West Texas happens in early July. Evading the censors, he indirectly shares information about the *Franklin* by recommending an article in *Popular Mechanics* magazine. As he writes on July 1, the *Franklin* has been under way for a day, and Elden probably feels pride that she flies the flag of an admiral.

By now Elden almost certainly knows the *Franklin* and the task group that surrounds her on every side are headed for combat near the Bonin Islands.[21] Vital links in the line through which Japan supplied her holdings to the south, these islands with compound names the second word of which was "Jima," were still virtually unknown to Americans. Any strike in the Bonins would accomplish more than the direct damage it might inflict—it also meant less fuel and ammunition, or maybe meals skipped, for Japanese fighting men farther down the line.[22] A new routine of taking battle stations at each dawn and sunset—when Japanese flyers could attack with the sun in the eyes of shipboard gunners—was reminder enough that danger was growing.[23] His postscript telling folks at home not to worry seems written to himself as well.

Tell Gerald that Hopalong Casidy is on at the show tonite. Come and see it.

July 1, 1944

Dear Mom Dad & Bros,

Well I am off of work so I'll write a few lines. I have been working in the Cold Storage Locker this week. We all get one week of that and three months mess cook each year. I don't know when they will put me on mess cooking. I was handleing meat and I noticed it was cuddahays brand. I just wondered if any of our hogs were in that batch. I Knew Dad had sold to them quite a lot. I sure would like to eat some ham from some of your hogs only I had rather that they were home cured. Maybe I'll get to before too much longer. If I ever get a leave I'm not going to waste any time getting home I'll tell you for sure.

Has Six ever left for the navy yet? I guess he has.

Say did you get the June Issue of Popular Mechenics? It has about four or five pages telling about aircraft carriers & has pictures of them. It sure looks real. I cant tell you much about it but that explains it all. If Joe hasn't got one at the Drug store I think henry Steward takes them and you could borrow his. I sure do want you to read it as it would tell a lot about it that you don't know.

How is the harvest comeing by now? Good I hope. Well I can remember Dad telling me that I would see the day when I would be glad to work in the harvest. Well In a way I would like to be there. But this is the place for Guy of my age or older. I don't mind it so bad out here as everything I do is Interesting.

With Love

Elden

P.S. Don't worry about me. I'll be O.K.

10   Not a Holiday

AMERICANS have come to think of the fireworks with which we celebrate Independence Day as things of beauty and even works of art, but
in fact they symbolize the unlovely sights and terrifying sounds of war.
Elden's Fourth of July in 1944 featured the real thing. He was awak-
ened early and as an air crew member had an early breakfast, then the
big new *Franklin* turned into the wind and at 0408 launched her first
combat strike. Her planes hit Iwo Jima, while identical planes from the
Hornet, Yorktown, and *Bataan* struck Chichi Jima. To enable sailors like
Elden to understand the relevance of their work to actual battle action,
Captain Shoemaker piped the radio transmissions of the air crews
throughout the *Franklin* on the speaker system. The men, accustomed
in civilian life to intense radio dramas whose listeners created visual
images in their own minds, listened to the real-life sounds of airborne
shipmates bombing targets, dodging return fire, knocking down defending fighters, evaluating the damage they had done—and reporting
comrades lost. This was so effective that it became the normal practice
when the *Franklin* had planes in combat within radio range[1]; the practice motivated the crew to peak performance, launching, for example,
planes as little as twenty-eight seconds apart.[2] Elden and his shipmates
knew they were thirty-five miles off Iwo Jima, and four hundred miles
from Tokyo[3]; when they heard one pilot report being able to see Japan,
it was almost as though they could see it themselves.[4]

The real fireworks of war involve more than just bombing, shooting, and torpedoing, and there was much to do aboard the *Franklin* that day in addition to listening to radio transmissions. The twenty-four planes that flew predawn missions had been loaded with rockets the night before under a three-quarter moon, but after that the loading went on throughout the day. Six crews of four men each from V-5 Division loaded the rockets onto the planes only after all other preparations had been made and the wings were leveled and locked for flight. The morning was still young when at 0737 the tailhook of a returning plane missed the cable. Without that restraint it then ripped through the barrier net and careened sideways into a tug tractor, killing Elden's division mate Electrician's Mate Second Class James E. Mulligan and seriously injuring the pilot. That horror was still fresh in the minds of flight deck sailors when, barely two hours later, another plane crashed into the barrier. Almost at that instant the ship went into torpedo defense as she experienced or perceived her first hostile attack.[5] Education by experience came quickly and emphatically in the war zone.

In the early afternoon of that bright, clear, and sunny day, they held a brief funeral for poor Mulligan—who as a V-1 Division member was someone with whom Elden worked, ate, bunked, and shot the bull when off duty—and committed his body to the deep. If Elden did not know it before, this loss taught him that his emotional mind, where feelings like sorrow, sympathy, revulsion, and fear resided, could be—had to be—kept under control by the rational mind.

Elden and his buddies knew on that Independence Day that the purpose of their work was to prevent Japanese planes based on these islands from helping to defend Guam and Saipan.[6] Utilizing the fast carrier's ability to keep an enemy guessing about its location, the *Franklin*'s Task Group 58.2 swung around and sped southeastward toward Saipan and Guam.

Every sailor had been warned against keeping diaries that might fall into enemy hands and provide information dangerous to the American cause. The navy was serious enough about this rule that one *Franklin* sailor, Radarman Third Class Elmer Fry, was tried, convicted, and punished for having one. A number of men disobeyed the rule, however, and at least one, Machinist's Mate First Class Peter Brady, got away with it. Brady's diary is an important source of information today, although it sometimes records events that normally would have been in the ship's deck logs but are not. Such an event was an attack upon the *Franklin* by two torpedo bombers, which Brady says happened at 1930 on the evening of July 5, and which he says kept the men at general quarters for half an hour. He also says that at 2030 a fire discovered in the number 3 elevator was quickly extinguished with negligible damage.[7] Elden's personal lesson for the day was that although danger could appear suddenly, it also could pass quickly.

⚓

Back in the wheat belt, on the plains of southeastern Colorado and western Kansas, as elsewhere in the United States, the social disruption of war was prompting hurried and ill-considered marriages among children who were nowhere near ready.

July 5, 1944

Dearest Tex,

I guess I'll drop you a few lines tonight before I go to bed. How do you like my new stationery [features a girl slipping on ice and the words "Snow foolin, I fell pretty hard"]. Its about all I could find around here.

I got the snapshot you sent. You really make a handsome sailor, no kidding. I'm really proud of you. I only wish you were here so I could show you off to all my friends.

My oldest brother is in France now. I guess he's in the very middle of it. My other brother came home on a furlough yesterday. He gets 10 days. I get to run around with him & his girl friends & really have lots of fun.

Wanda got married last Friday. Do you remember her? She used to run around with Maureen & I sometimes. Maureen went down to Kansas with them & got to be there bridesmaid. She is pretty young to be married. Only 16 years old.

I bet you had a big time the 4th. I sure didn't. I slept most all day.

Well, I guess I'll quit now & go to bed. Did you know Chucks brother, tom is back. I saw him today. It's really nice that he got to come home.

Well, goodnite darling,

All my Love,

Virginia

P.S. Write soon.

⚓

The small Micronesian island of Guam mattered a lot to the United States. Together with Saipan, it was key to control of the Mariana Islands, which itself was key to reaching the Japanese homeland. Beyond that, however, it had been an American territory for almost half a century since the end of the Spanish-American War. Lightly defended in December 1941, Guam had been easily captured by Japan, and together with the loss of the Philippines and the attack on Hawaii, the loss had been a wound to national pride. Two days after the attacks on the "Jimas," Admiral Davison had the *Franklin* and his task group east of Rota and northeast of Guam, off Pati Point, which sharply defines the northeasternmost point of the northeast-to-southwest island. From there the carrier planes went after targets on both islands, preparing for the invasion that was to begin two weeks later.[8]

As the afternoon of July 6 waned, at 1650 Elden heard the captain say that the previous two days of American raids on Chichi Jima, Ha Ha Jima, and Iwo Jima had sunk two destroyers, three destroyer escorts, two medium tankers, two small tankers, two small freighters, and one tanker escort, and destroyed eighty-nine planes, including fifty-seven on the ground. One might assume that this word brought cheers. Somber and respectful silence likely followed the recitation of U.S. losses: twenty-two planes, twelve pilots, and seven crew members. The day was not over yet; at 1800 the *Franklin* thwarted a torpedo attack through evasive action, and at 2000 planes shot down a Japanese bomber.[9]

Elden knew all of this before going to sleep that Thursday night. He did not know that on that same day, which was yet to arrive in the United States, a circus tent fire would kill 168 people in Hartford, Connecticut, and a troop train wreck in East Tennessee would kill seventeen, and he did not know what was happening to a Vega friend not far away.

On Saipan, which was probably just out of view of the *Franklin* on the evening of July 6, Japanese general Yoshitsugu Saito came to a point of desperation. He was defeated and he knew it, but the culture in which he lived would not permit him to save either himself or his men by such a rational act as surrender. With death for all the only honorable end, he gave orders for his men to sacrifice themselves in one last fanatical banzai attack, after which he would ritually disembowel himself. In the predawn darkness of 3:00 A.M., the men carried out the order, charging through a gap between two American battalions and throwing their living bodies against fire, steel, and lead. Reaching the artillery battalions of the 10th Marines, where Vince Walcott fought, the attackers came on in such numbers that the gunners lowered the muzzles of their 105 mm howitzers and fired point-blank into the hordes as one might fire a pistol. Just before being overrun, the last living defenders removed the firing locks to disable the guns and fell back to fight as infantry until the last force of the Japanese surge played itself out in hand-to-hand struggles. The human loss was beyond description, but an insanely militaristic honor had been upheld. Amid this trampling, blasting, grinding, screaming force driven by the worst aspects of patriotic devotion, some men simply disappeared. The body of Vincent Walcott, lovingly called Tubbi by his mother, was never identified.[10]

The senselessly bloody end of the battle for Saipan calls to mind a poem that speaks to all sides in all wars. "The Call of War" was written by prisoner of war Martin F. Owens and squirreled away by Bish McKendree.

Send me your youth, the best of your youth,
The courageous, clean, and strong,
From city, hamlet, and countryside,
Where life is a careless song.
Have him forget his house of dreams,
With ivy 'round his door.
I have a job for his eager feet;
Wallowing deep in gore.

Send me your youth, the pick of your youth,
You can keep the other kind.
I'll tear the smile from his careless lips,
The dreams from his boyish mind.
I'll send him where the cannon roar
And rend him limb from limb,
And when I'm through you can have him back;
Or all that's left of him.

In a mind that is free from brutality,
I'll sow the seeds of hate
'Till he rushes forth with a lust to kill
Like a crazed inebriate.
I'll twist his soul with shameful lies
As he carries my banners high,
And prate to him of a noble cause
As he stumbles out to die.

You've sent me your youth, the best of your youth,
A thousand times or more.
I've left their bones in a shallow grave
On some beleaguered shore.
I've plundered the world and laid it waste
With youth as my helpless tools.
Each time I call you send them all;
For you are such hopeless fools.[11]

With all the task group protection that surrounded the big and important carriers, the American admirals must have felt very confident in order to use one as a decoy, for that is exactly what they did on July 9 and 10. Davison sent and Shoemaker took the *Franklin* close in to Guam hoping to goad Japanese artillery commanders into firing. The guns might easily have hit the ship, but by the time they had fired a few shots to determine the range, they would themselves have been hit by American planes and guns. The Japanese did not take the bait, but it did not require a military genius for the men on the *Franklin* to recognize that they were under guns and within range. The fact that Davison was aboard the *Hornet* during this exercise rather than in his normal place on the *Franklin* would have been a subject of conversation by Elden and his crewmates.[12]

Underscoring sailors' need to keep the rules always in mind, on July 9 a seaman was tried, convicted, and punished for smoking within ten feet of an airplane.[13] Elden would have heard this news.

Decoy duty did not mean light duty. On Monday July 10 the men were at battle stations at 0445, and seventy-five minutes later they were launching planes carrying two-thousand-pound bombs to blast Orote airfield. Seventy-four minutes after that there would have been cheering throughout the ship as the men heard that Saipan had been taken. As though to counteract any tendency to lighten up, in midmorning a plane crashed into the barrier, tore off its tailhook, and damaged its propeller. By day's end, however, things were sufficiently less intense that the captain invited such crewmen as could do so to take a moment to look at Guam, which was visible just six miles off the port bow, and we can safely guess that Elden did so.[14]

Much had happened to the *Franklin* and everyone aboard her in the past week—the first enemy attacks received, first aggressive strikes launched, Saipan conquered, an enemy-held American island halfway around the world from home seen close up, planes crashing on the flight deck and killing sailors, and more. Elden could communicate exactly none of it, and his July 10 letter drips with frustration. The letter includes a strange speculation that he might possibly even be home in a month, and one wonders whether that conveys a recognition that his ship might be hit and required to return stateside for repair. He seems to be writing in late morning or around noon.

July 10, 1944

Dear Mom, Dad, & Bros,

Well we don't have anything to do until three this afternoon so I'm writeing letters and catching up on lost sleep. I guess Gerald is working in the harvest or has been I guess its about finished up by now tho. Well I have been working pretty hard I cant say what I'm doing but I work about 16 or 18 hours a day. Well I drew most of my money the 4th and bought bonds with it. I had them made out to you as I'm getting more money than I need. That is the only way I can draw all my money. By the time the war is over I'll have all the bonds I need. I't wont hurt me to help you a little instead of you always helping me.

I'll send the money for the watch if I ever get back to the states. I cant draw but five dollars each pay-day. (every two weeks).

I like the Idea as I don't have anything to buy and if I had a lot of money it would probably get stolen.

I sure would like to tell you what we've been doing but I can't. You have probably read some of it in the paper. But just don't know who Done it.

I guess Jerry is getting bigger every day. Tell Him that before long he will be big enough to drive a tractor like Gerald does.

I sure would like to be home for Christmas, I doubt it. I'ts not impossible for something might turn up and I'd be home a month from now. Don't look for me till you see me comeing tho.

Well I know this is not much of a letter. I cant tell anything hardly. Only that I am O.K. & don't worry about me. So long for now.

With Lots of Love
Elden

The next day the crew went to general quarters at 0440, at 0830 they were refueling destroyers, and at 1400 their planes bombed Rota with no American losses.[15] Still full of excitement, eager to tell what could not be told, and perhaps having time on his hands compared to the previous week of eighteen-hour workdays, Elden wrote again. The increasingly frequent reassurances, "Don't worry about me," were probably sincere, but also were probably a sublimated way of saying that he had been experiencing danger. The censored word beginning with C near the end of the letter almost certainly was China.

July 11, 1944

Dear Mom, Dad & Bros,

Well I'll try writeing a few lines today to let you know I'm still O.K. & hope you are the same.

They haven't sent mail off the ship for about three weeks so I guess you will get all these in one bunch.

I am pretty close to where I think "Bug Eye" is. I don't know where he is but if my guess is right I ain't too far. I might see him some of these days. I sure would like to run on to him.

I imagine that everyone has finished cutting their wheat but Bose. I might know he won't be through until Christmas at least he never is. Has Charles ever went to the service yet or is he still dodgeing.

I guess Gerald has been working all this summer and making Plenty of money as Bose says.

Have you ever found a place to live yet or you still at the same old Place?

We just got the news yesterday of us captureing Sipan. We sure were glad to here it. It will help a lot in the war in the southwest Pacific. I look for them to [censored] then go to the [censored]. That is my guess. If they get C[censored] back we can whip them in just a little while.

Well I still say don't worry about me I'm still allright and will be till I get home. Which wont be too long I hope. I'm still hopeing to be there for Christmas.

With Love,

Your Son,

Elden

Elden has guessed that he is pretty close to Bugeye and might "run on to him." This is the first of many attempts to tell his family approximately where he is without violating censorship rules, by referring to another Vega boy whose parents might have some idea of his location. Elden knew that his own parents would promptly compare notes with Bugeye's parents, and that both families might decipher hidden information by doing so. In the enormousness of the Pacific Ocean, however, and perhaps aboard a fast carrier, "pretty close" takes on a whole new meaning, for Bugeye was then aboard the USS *Hoel* probably about 2,500 miles to the south-southeast of Elden.

July 12 was a day of surprises, morning, noon, and night. Almost immediately after the *Franklin*'s crew had gone to general quarters at 0445, the catapult malfunctioned during a launch and a fighter went into the water close by. The destroyer *Hancock*, trailing just behind the *Franklin* precisely to deal with such accidents, quickly picked up the unhurt pilot and had him back on the *Franklin* by 0752. The accident was an exception, however, and U.S. fighters and bombers pounded Guam throughout the morning, then at 1240 the combat air patrol shot down a Mitsubishi bomber that seemed to have been trying to hit the *Franklin*. The attacks on Guam continued into the evening darkness, when night fighter crews saw flashlight signals from the shore. The destroyer *The Sullivans* went in close through Japanese artillery fire and picked up George R. Tweed, an American naval radioman who had been on Guam since 1939 and had eluded capture.[16] This amazing news would have gone quickly through the fleet.

The declaration of victory at Saipan on July 10 did not mean that all fighting there was over. Small scattered groups of the enemy fought to the death. The backbone of Saipan runs from south to north, culminating in a high point from which a precipice now known as Suicide Cliff drops several hundred feet to a plateau where Japan had a fighter base, and from the plateau's end a second drop, now known as Banzai Cliff, falls into the churning surf. Motion pictures survive of Japanese soldiers, indoctrinated with values like those of General Saito, guzzling the last of their beer when hope was gone and then one after another taking running jumps off Suicide Cliff.[17]

In the midst of the great overarching drama, thousands of individual life-and-death scenes played out. We can safely guess that Elden was deeply affected by a horrible accident that occurred on July 16. The *Franklin* was launching planes against Guam early on this Sunday morning, when at 0530 a Baltimore boy named James R. Smiley—another member of Elden's V-1 Division who worked with planes on the flight deck every day—momentarily allowed his concentration to lapse. As Smiley bent forward to perform some task, his head went into a spinning propeller and instantly disappeared. We do not know where Elden was at this moment, but we know that division members bunked together, ate together, and worked together. Smiley was a close crewmate, perhaps a buddy, and in all likelihood it fell to V-1 sailors to clean up the splatters. When poor Smiley's headless body was buried at sea in early afternoon in services led by Chaplain Chamberlin, every man in the crew and especially Elden and others in Smiley's division must have been shocked, saddened, sickened, and reminded that not all dangers came from the enemy. Nothing in the correspondence even hints at this tragedy, but its emotional effects must have been difficult to suppress.[18]

The strikes went on, as they had to, and the very next day the air group set a new record in recovering planes, averaging less than two minutes between landings. Seven fighters had landed at an impressive average of thirty-six seconds apart.[19] This was largely the accomplishment of the V-1 Division, and the intense focus on getting the job done probably helped take the men's minds off Smiley and his fate.

The Japanese who defended Guam endured the most thorough pre-assault bombardment of the Pacific War up to that time. For thirteen days the island was pounded by American battleships and by almost constant daytime strikes by planes from the *Franklin* and other carriers. Roads, bridges, runways, and facilities of all types that might be useful to the defenders were destroyed, as well as aircraft and such guns as could be located. Enemy personnel were targeted when possible, and a Japanese bivouac was firebombed just south of the Guamanian capital of Agana. The V divisions scarcely rested as planes were fueled, armed, launched, and recovered; then refueled, rearmed, re-launched, and recovered again and again. By July 21, D-Day for the invasion, the Americans believed that everything of military advantage to the Japanese had been destroyed. Only ten American aircraft had been lost, less than one each day, and all but one of their crews had been rescued.[20]

Flight deck sailors were not the only ones who could lose their lives in an instant of inattention—it could even happen to medical officers who normally worked below. Dr. James Moy, topside for some reason and perhaps less attuned to the need to maintain awareness of where the deck ended, took a step into empty air. A second later and seventy feet down, he survived the first hazard of hitting the water at high speed. Of 3,000 pairs of eyes on the *Franklin*, not one had seen him disappear. One pair of ears heard a faint cry for help and a tweet from a whistle, so it was reported that someone may have gone overboard. The *Franklin* continued on course, however, and the doctor was alone in the ocean. Never having imagined he might find himself in such a spot, he had no life jacket. He did, however belatedly, have his wits about him. He got rid of shoes, pocket contents, and anything else that added weight, then removed his pants, tied the ends of the legs, and captured air inside them to keep himself afloat. This worked for a short while until the air seeped through the warp and woof, then he had to tread water with foot action while he lifted the pants above his head to refill them with air and swung them down upon the water. He repeated this action every few minutes for thirteen long hours until finally, with great good luck, he was spotted by someone on a destroyer.[21] When the destroyer transferred the lucky surgeon back to the *Franklin* on a cable chair mechanism called a breeches buoy, the captain ordered all hands on the flight deck as a welcoming party.[22] Shoemaker knew that this public ribbing of an officer would provide badly needed comic relief and at the same time teach a lesson. Danger was everywhere, always, and from caution there could be no liberty.

July 19 must have been the high point of carrier-based activity against Guam. Five hundred strikes hit the island that day. Announcing this on the speaker system, the captain joked that the crew had done so well that they were going to get better chow as a reward.[23] For Elden and others this must have produced a chuckle.

Other days were hardly less active or exciting. At 0912 on July 20 a fighter with half its tail shot off and barely controllable made its way back to the *Franklin* and safely landed. Almost immediately afterward another fighter crashed into the sea to starboard next to the destroyer *Phelps*. Both pilots survived.[24]

Guam could not be once again American, however, until American forces occupied and controlled the island, and with planes from the *Franklin* and other carriers laying fire ahead the landing began at 0800 on July 21. As in most other landings in the Pacific War, those who thought there was nothing left to bomb were wrong. Fighting men, guns, and even tanks popped up as from nowhere and resisted with powerful determination. A group of four tanks fired at a close-in destroyer, which promptly blew them to bits with a volley of five-inch shells.[25]

At midday July 22, as the crew savored news that Hitler had almost been assassinated by some of his own generals, the *Franklin* swung rapidly northward and by late afternoon was launching planes against Tinian, where troops were to land the next day. Obviously unworried, probably because Americans had almost total control of the air, the captain had his ship virtually at water's edge, a mile and a half offshore. That evening she anchored in Saipan Harbor, where the National Park Service now manages the American Memorial Park, and replenished her supply of bombs and food.[26] World War II was as much a war of logistics as of combat, and the existence of this supply center in a spot that had been in enemy hands only days before is a mark of the navy's amazing logistical capability.

With ground fighting still raging on Guam, Admiral Davison put the speed of his fast carriers to work and took his task group, centered upon the *Franklin*, *Wasp*, *Monterey*, and *Cabot*, rapidly southwestward toward the Caroline Islands[27]; back in Colorado, Virginia is trying with no semblance of success to imagine what Elden's life in the navy is like. Wanda, the sixteen-year-old whose wedding was mentioned in Virginia's last letter, is already separated from her husband, but that doesn't keep Virginia from wishing she were married.

[Stationery shows a girl bouncing on hearts, and the words "My love grows by leaps and bounds"]

July 24, 1944

Dear Tex,

I guess you owe me a letter. It seems like I haven't heard from you in ages, but maybe I'm the one that owes one.

Yes, I remember last year this time. It was swell wasn't it. Maureen & I would go over to the park just to see you & Carl Six. If you kids weren't there, we would be so disappointed. You kids didn't act like you liked us very well tho.

I went swimming Sunday & really got sun-burned. I'll be glad when you come home, maybe you can teach me how to swim. Boy, we could have a lot of fun if you were here, just you & I, nobody else.

I was in a car wreck Sunday. It just turned over on its side & no-one got hurt. I was really scared tho.

It sure has been hot here. How is it out there? Do you ride on ships all the time from Pearl Harbor to San Francisco? Do you ever get sea-sick? I guess you have a girl in every port like all sailors. I don't care as long as you don't forget about me sitting back here waiting for her sailor-boy to come home.

I've been staying home a lot lately. Oh, did you hear about Wanda getting married? Her & her husband lived together 18 days & they are separated now & Wanda is in Denver. Andy & Barbara & Florence & Pat are still together & happy I guess.

I sure wish I was married. I guess it's a fever going around or something, because every girl I see says the same thing. They are really getting married fast too.

My Uncle & Aunt are here from Kansas & want me to go back with them. I don't know what to do. I would probably die of homesickness.

Well, honey, I think I'll go to bed. My eyes won't stay open.

Goodnite Darling,

Virginia

11 Fair Weather and Foul

The thousands of tiny islands in the Palauan group resemble a fantasy world of green mushrooms rising from blue water and curving out over the waves that splash against their stems. Babeldaob, Peleliu, and Anguar are the large islands with normal shapes, and on Peleliu the Japanese had built an airfield from which their planes could reach the Philippines. MacArthur, having left Jimmy Bales, Bish McKendree, and the other American and Filipino troops to be captured on Bataan and Corregidor, had vowed to return. He was on his way back now from Australia, taking one island, skipping some, and taking another, and soon would be ready to fulfill his promise. If the Philippines were to be recaptured, it was believed that Japanese power in Palau had to be neutralized, and to that end an invasion was scheduled for September.

The first step was to find out what was there, and two of the *Franklin*'s Hellcat fighters carried cameras for just that purpose. The planners wanted more than just pictures; they wanted to assemble thousands of individual photographs into a map. Creating a usable array of pictures required the planes to fly back and forth in orderly patterns. The observable regularity of such flights would have made them easy to anticipate and certain to be shot down, so just to get the map the navy had to create the impression that much more was happening. For two days, American bombers would create the impression that an invasion was imminent, and so fighters and bombers would accompany the reconnaissance planes to keep Japanese ground troops dodging bullets rather than focusing on them. At 0600 on July 26 the *Franklin* launched her first wave of thirty-six bombers to begin this distraction.[1]

Babeldaob could be seen thirty-eight miles ahead from the *Franklin* by 1651.

The law of gravity came into conflict with Murphy's law that day and Murphy won. "What can go wrong, will go wrong," and when one bomber tried to release its load, a one-hundred-pound bomb resisted the urge to fall to earth and instead became jammed in the open bomb bay. When the plane returned to the *Franklin,* the normal sudden stop was enough to break the jam, and a fully fused and very dangerous explosive went skittering forward along the flight deck as members of Elden's V-1 Division jumped out of its way. When it finally stopped without detonating, boys from V-1 pushed it overboard. Was Elden on deck to see this, or even to dodge the bomb? Did he help get rid of it? Maybe. If he did not, crewmates close to him did, and we can be certain that as part of the nervously animated joking at chow and in the bunks that evening he said or heard others say that thirteen seemed to be serving well as the captain's lucky number.[2]

The *Franklin* had moved to a position ninety miles south-southwest of Babeldaob at 0600 on July 27 when she launched forty planes to hit the island. One plane was lost, and as the strike returned another could be seen in its own struggle with gravity. It was badly damaged and was barely above the margin that separated flying from floating or sinking. Rather than put the ship again at risk for the sake of a single plane, this one was sent into the water about a hundred yards away. The pilot was quickly rescued. As the day went on the ship came closer to the island, and by 1500 shore was only eleven miles away. Japanese airpower at Palau was no more, and Elden probably saw the tall column of smoke with a firelight glow at its base and knew it represented a good day's work.[3]

By Friday, July 28, the *Franklin* appeared to be finished with her disguised reconnaissance mission. The big ship carried a lot of fuel, and during the morning it shared some with the destroyers *The Sullivans* and *Tingey*. At 1100, as the destroyer *Hancock* was alongside returning pilots rescued from the previous day's action, a Japanese submarine was detected only a half mile ahead—much closer than expected to the heavily defended carrier. Cruisers and destroyers went after it with depth charges—sinkable bombs with fuses set to detonate at the depth where an enemy submarine was calculated to be. The sub was believed to have been destroyed, but another one discovered later off the port beam invoked ten more minutes of depth-charge booms and splashes.[4] Elden doubtless was at his battle station, wherever that was, and he may have heard or seen or felt this battle action. Certainly he knew it was happening.

Another Rogers made the surname questionably famous throughout the ship on July 31. Seaman First Class John Rogers was tried, convicted, and sentenced to twenty-five extra hours of police duty for urinating over the side of the ship. Not to windward, one hopes for the sake of the clan.[5]

On the day when Elden or his V-1 buddies had dodged the skittering bomb on the flight deck, President Roosevelt himself flew to Honolulu. The differing strategic intentions of Nimitz and MacArthur were of concern, and Roosevelt knew better than anyone that the whole thing was his responsibility. Besides, it was an election year, and one month earlier the Republicans had nominated New York Governor Thomas E. Dewey for president. Flying out into the Pacific was a good way of campaigning without actually campaigning.

MacArthur, mentioned only weeks before as a possible Republican nominee for vice president, displayed the characteristics that in the next war would get him sacked by a different president and would cause a biographer to dub him the American Caesar. The general was too busy, he said, to come all the way to Hawaii for a mere meeting with the commander in chief of the armed forces. He came, though, in response to a direct order from Army Chief of Staff George C. Marshall.[6] The meeting was a great concentration of rank, and during one luncheon an aide counted 136 stars on the collars of the generals and admirals present. It was no easier for Roosevelt to decide then than it is for us now which of his two great Pacific champions was right. The question was not even clear, much less the answer, but the navy's strategic plan for 1944 seemed still to be in effect. Nimitz would move his headquarters to Guam, where he would proceed with his drive.[7]

July 31, 1944

Dear Tex,

I guess I'll write a few lines to let you know that I'm still thinking about you and wish you were here so we could go swimming or some thing. It's really hot today. I'm just about roasted.

No, I'm not having very much fun either. I work all day & am to tired to go any place at night. I guess you are pretty bored not having anything to do but work, but after the war we will really make up for lost time. We might be pretty old by then but we'll have fun any way.

The landlady just came in & said she was going to re-decorate our house tomorrow. It sure needs some thing done to it.

A bunch of us kids went swimming last Thursday up at Holbrook. I still can't swim. We got a boat & rode around in it most of the day. I got a nice sun-burn too.

Gee, I wish you could get a furlough & come to Las Animas. I sure would love to see you again. It seems like ages since that night you stayed all night with me. That doesn't sound so good does it? If any one gets nosy we'll tell them we sat up all night & listened to the radio, if they don't believe that we'll say my mother was right in the next room. I guess she remembers it. We had the radio on loud enough & was making plenty of noise.

Earl has to leave for the army with the next group. I heard he got married the other day. I don't know if its true or not.

My mother is canning cherries today. Shes canning me some too for when I get married, she said. Do you like cherry pie? If you do I'll make you one when you come back here.

I guess Maureen is going to get married Saturday night. I had a chance but I thought about you & decided I would rather marry you than any one in the world if you will have me.

I have to write some more letters so will quit & write more later.

Be good & write.

All my Love,

Virginia

On this day when Virginia complains about boredom, opines that Elden must be bored too, writes that everyone is getting married as well as drafted, remembers a time when she and Elden had stayed all night together, and reveals that she has received but declined an offer of marriage, Bish McKendree, in the prison camp at Cabanatuan, received a letter from his parents.[8] One among the very few he would receive over four years, it made July 31 an extraordinary day for him. For Elden it was probably a relaxed day, as the *Franklin* cruised northeastward at moderate speed.

In the twenty-five days since the *Franklin*'s first combat action, her green crew had matured into veterans, and they knew it. Boys like Elden thought of themselves differently now. They had experienced danger and loss and had seen enough to test any man's sense of reality, but in general things had gone very well. Even the pilots, the ones everyone knew faced danger almost routinely, had come through without many losses. The 3,000 men, floating together on the gigantic mass of steel, were not the same at the end of July as they had been at the end of June. With fuel tanks, food lockers, and magazines all getting low, the *Franklin* headed back toward Saipan, where Garapan Harbor had already been converted into a supply center. Less hurried now, they arrived there August 1 in late afternoon.[9]

When Elden writes on that day, he says he has received no mail for over four weeks. In this muffled and muted way he is telling us that his ship has been moving too fast, doing too many things, in places that were too dangerous for mail to be a priority. Similarly, his stated expectation that mail would go off that evening says that the *Franklin* was nearing Saipan and most likely was already within sight of it. It is much easier to decipher those unwritten messages now than it was then, and the folks at home surely understood little of it. Elden seems to know that Bugeye is in the Solomon Islands, where the fighting has been over for a while, but he may not know that Bugs has boarded a warship that is by no means going to stay away from the combat zone.

He surely wanted to tell us that at 0500 that morning the *Franklin* had launched several planes to search for a missing land-based bomber, that they had found it three hours later, and that the men aboard it had been rescued.[10] He would have preferred to tell about the nonstop excitement of the past month, and he might even have told us that the weather was starting to turn bad, but he writes what he is allowed to write—that he has had boils lanced. His statement that he has come to not mind sea duty so much tells far more than the words themselves mean. Combat, once a fearsome future prospect, is now something he has done and something he knows he can do again. He knows also that Gerald has expressed what would become a lifelong interest in aviation, and the older and wiser Elden tells him in no uncertain terms not to join the Navy Air Corps.

August 1, 1944

Dear Mom, Dad, & Bros,

Well, mail will probably go off any time so I'll try writeing a few lines to let you know everything is O.K. out here and hope it is the same at home. I have got one letter since the 27th of June It was from Virginia. I'll probably get some tonight. I hope so anyhow. Virginia gave me the good word about Tom Steward being in the states again I sure was glad to hear it. Mary [Tom's and Bugeye's mother] won't have to worry about him anymore. She needent worry about "Bug Eye" as he is in one of the safest places in the Pacific. There wont ever be any more action there.

Well there is not much to write about out here. I have had two Boils in less than a month. I had one on my right elbow and one on my right knee. They sure were sore for a while but the Doctor fixed them up in a hurry.

Well I guess Geralds school will be starting pretty soon after this letter gets there. He will be a sophmore this year won't he? How old is he now 16 aint he.

Well does Gerald still think he wants to be a pilot? If so don't let him get in the Navy air corps, as its not a joke to land on a carrier. It has strickter qualifications in the navy air corps. He could make the grade easier in the army.

If he don't want to fly get in the navy as it is good duty. This tip is in case he ever has to go.

I guess Six is gone to the service by now hasn't he? He is probably about through boots by now. I haven't heard from him since the middle of June.

How did the harvest turn out? Good, I hope.

Well I lost my fountain pen over the side so I'll have to buy a new one pay day. I don't like to write with a pensil. They are still just paying $10 a month I should have quite a batch of money when we hit the states.

I am getting to where I don't mind sea duty so bad. I like the Idea of saveing money out here if I was in the states I would be broke continually. They are letting the boys draw $50 in checks to send home now. I think I'll draw one and send home for the watch. Say I was thinking the other day and I think I owe Taylors two or three dollars at the café. How about paying them for me. I sure hate it that I forgot it. If you'll pay them I'll make it right with you. How about Sending me 2 Levis 32x34. I like them better than the navy's and they are permitted.

If you will do all this I'll draw my money and send home.

Well, not much news now so I better close. We have to put our name at the bottom now.

With Love
Elden

We know of one personal experience Elden had when he drew the money he mentions here and on other paydays every two weeks—he had to sign a receipt for the money and leave the inked print of his right index finger.[11]

Mail did come that evening. A destroyer brought it to the *Franklin* just a mile off Saipan's west coast, and after so long a time it was a great boost to morale. The anticipated resupply did not happen, however. Choppy seas were making that operation difficult, and it appeared that the bad weather was going to continue. When Davison learned that a Japanese convoy including a light carrier had been located up near the "Jimas," he took his task group and went after them. In rough seas it was easier to fight than to resupply, and an opportunity of this sort could not be missed.[12]

The captain shared news with the men on the morning of August 2 that the downed bomber that *Franklin* planes had helped to locate had been more than just a bomber. It had been carrying Admiral Charles P. Cecil, and he and the others on board were all well. The bad weather was getting worse, though, and scuttlebutt had it that they were on the outer edge of a typhoon and might soon be in its midst.[13] Typhoons were dangerous to smaller ships up to and including destroyers, but they were unpleasant even to men aboard great ones like the *Franklin* and could return bouts of seasickness to men who thought they had outgrown it.

Two days later, on August 4, the typhoon and the war were both present in full force. A few minutes after the men arrived at battle stations at 0451, the captain warned the crew to expect an attack, and in the midst of the storm the *Franklin* launched planes to strike the threatening enemy.[14] Although waves occasionally broke over the flight deck, seventy feet above the waterline, west of Chichi Jima the *Franklin*'s planes sank a Japanese cargo ship and the destroyer *Matsu*. In contrast to the American admiral they had helped to save, Japanese rear admiral Takahashi Ichimatsu went down with the *Matsu*.[15] One pilot did not return.

While the storm still raged, *Franklin*'s planes hit fuel supplies, ammunition dumps, a radio station, an airfield, a seaplane base, and ships at Chichi Jima. This kept the crew at battle stations Sunday, August 5, for more than sixteen hours. Adrenaline surged in midafternoon when a bogie, slang for an unidentified aircraft, was spotted five miles dead ahead. At combat airspeed five miles means on top of you, and both the *Franklin* and the *Wasp* opened up on it with their 40 mm quads. Luck prevailed, however, as the bogie turned out to be an American fighter trying to get home to the *Lexington*. The plane was not hit, but we can be sure its pilot had some choice words once he got down.[16] We can also be sure that Elden participated in conversations about the event.

The irony of being downed by friendly fire was just one of the many risks pilots had to accept. A warship, especially a carrier, was vastly more important than a plane, and it was unacceptable to allow any unidentified plane to approach within striking distance. As though to drive home the point, not long afterward ships in the outer "screen" of the task group shot down six more planes, and these were Japanese bombers coming after the fleet.[17]

The *Franklin* lost four planes and six men in this stormy action, but destroyed several enemy planes and hangars and sank or damaged twenty-two enemy vessels of various sizes. The weather was still very bad and supplies were even lower as the task group again sought resupply, this time not at Saipan but all the way back at Eniwetok.[18] On the front line not long ago, Eniwetok was now far behind the westward-moving combat zone, and it was a great relief to be going there.

12   A Welcome Break

THE *Franklin*'s Plan of the Day for August 7, 1944, read: "We will hold a general field day throughout the ship during the balance of our trip to Eniwetok. This means that all hands will turn to—morning and afternoon—in order that our ship may be highly presentable on arrival."[1] This tells us that Elden spent some of his time spiffing up the ship, a duty that often focused on painting, on the day he wrote his next letter. His statement that there had been no mail for thirty-nine days and then all at once eight letters from home and six from others was the nearest he could come to saying he had been in a lot of action. His comment that he is getting to like this kind of life probably reflects having come through a great deal of danger without being hurt—a situation that can produce feelings of exuberance and bravado—and he probably felt both as he sat at some open-air spot in the waning light of evening. In the category of "It's a small world" stories, he has discovered among the *Franklin*'s crew a boy from Amarillo against whom he played basketball in school.

August 7, 1944

Dearest Mom, Dad & Bros,
Well I received 8 leters from you the fifth they were the first since the 27th of June.

I sure was glad to hear from you. You ask how often we get mail. We don't get any till we hit port. Sometimes we get it off another ship tho. The same way with this letter It won't leave the ship till we hit port or trade with another ship out here. I got three letters from Virginia, one from Rowena, one from Frances & one from Six.

I got the pictures you sent. I sure was glad to get them. That one sure was good of you and Pauline [Blasingame]. I have them taped up on the inside of my locker door.

Well I guess R.C. and a bunch of them are gone by now. It will nearly kill them in boot camp. I thought they would kill me when I was there. I don't see what those slackers are afraid of. I am getting to where I really like this kind of a life. I am saveing more money than I ever did in my life. You can get along O.K. in the navy if you take orders right. I haven't got a black mark on my record and I don't intend to ever have any.

Well I haven't saw any of those guys from Vega yet. I may run on to them sometime tho. I don't ever come into port where I think Krahn is.

I got the prayer card you sent it sure was pretty and had a nice verse. I sure would have liked to have been there to go down on some of Geralds Birthday cake. I had my last liberty on Gerald's birthday. I sure would have liked to have seen E.L. but I didn't have his address then. I cant think of anything else to write. I have told everything I know but where I am and what I'm doing. All I can say is I'm doing my part. Don't worry about me as I'm not in any danger. I'll be O.K. Say how about sending me the Amarillo Sunday paper once in a while. I never thought of it until I saw some other guys getting them from home. Just Roll it up and mail it

Well It was getting pretty dark outside so I had to come in to finish this up.

I met up with a guy the other day from Amarillo. I ask him where I had saw him before. I asked him where he lived and he said Amarillo. I found out I had played basket ball against him at a tournament at Price Memorial in 1939 or 1940. I sure was glad to get acquainted with him. He lives on east tenth street. Well I'll close for now and write to Virginia. So long for now.

Lots of Love,

Your son,

Elden

Although Elden felt relief at getting out of the Marianas action, this did not mean he was safe. On Tuesday, August 8, at 1440, as they passed by the Philippine island of Leyte, and as Elden very likely had Bish McKendree in mind, three Japanese planes strafed the *Franklin* and killed several men.[2] Real relaxation finally became possible when they slipped into Eniwetok's lagoon on August 9, joining a large array of American ships including at least five other fleet carriers and five light carriers as well as battleships, cruisers, destroyers, and support vessels.[3]

Best of all, Elden could put his feet on solid ground.[4] Accustomed by now to the wide-spaced swaying walk sailors unconsciously adopt to cope with the moving platforms beneath them, they might have looked and felt strange except for the fact that everyone walked the same way. Liberty was not very exciting where no one lived except other military personnel, but it was good to be taken to the atoll's main island of Runit, to receive their allotted three cans of beer each, even though it was 3.2 percent alcohol rather than full strength, and to swim and relax on the beach.[5] A guy could sell his beers for up to ten times their value back in the States, but Elden is more likely to have bought rather than sold. Fistfights are almost universal by-products of the combination of beer and young men in large numbers, and we must hope that Elden avoided these. The open air and the cool water must have felt good on the heat rash that had been endured by virtually every man of every rank. Looking around the island, Bob St. Peters took note of a graveyard with rock slab tombs above the ground level, and took time to wonder about the people who had lived there before war swept over them.[6]

Elden very likely took advantage of permission to sunbathe on the flight deck when off duty but not on liberty—enlisted men aft and officers forward. Movies on the hangar deck were much more frequently available than normal, and one that was presented during this interlude was *Hitler's Madman,* starring Alan Curtis, Patricia Morison, Ralph Morgan, and John Carradine.[7]

Other leisure time was filled with boxing and wrestling matches; games and even tournaments of baseball, softball, basketball, volleyball, and horseshoes; and concerts by Saxie Dowell's twelve-piece orchestra. Dowell played the popular big band style of music that characterized the 1940s, centered around his saxophone. Elden enjoyed it but preferred the very different genre of country music. It may have been during this period that Elden evoked laughter by shouting from the audience during such a concert, "Play something by Ernest Tubb."[8]

And there was news—good news. On August 10 they heard that the 54,000 Americans on Guam had prevailed against the 19,000 fiercely fighting Japanese defenders. The celebrating sailors would not have heard that several thousand of the defenders had faded into the jungle rather than surrender. A full year later a Japanese lieutenant colonel and more than a hundred subordinates would still be at large there.[9]

The *Franklin* was at Eniwetok for some badly needed maintenance and repair. It may seem strange that a new ship that had been afloat less than ten months, in combat barely five weeks, and never hit by anything larger than machine gun bullets would need repair, but three factors explain it. First, think of the ship as a machine that had been running constantly for ten months with its switch almost never in the "off" position. Most of that time she had actually been in motion, going from somewhere to somewhere else, sometimes at high speed. Thousands of times she had lifted, launched, recovered, lowered, refueled, and re-armed aircraft, and the planes themselves had flown hours upon hours at high speed and under high stress, not to mention hostile attack. She had fired her guns countless times in training and in deadly earnest, each time with metal abrading metal. Second, she had done these things as a steel vessel in salt water, a combination guaranteed to produce deterioration of ferrous metal. Third—and key to the American victory—she needed an occasional time out to catch up on technological innovation. As soon as a radar or a catapult or an elevator lift or an aircraft engine could be put into action, someone somewhere was developing an improved version of it. From the low point of December 1941 to the total victory of August 1945, the U.S. Navy became better and better, faster and faster, and occasional time away from the combat zone was required just to keep up. So for nineteen days between August 9 and August 28, 1944, the *Franklin's* own crew, crews from specialized repair ships, and crews from the Eniwetok facility brought the great carrier up to standard, topped off her tanks, and packed her storerooms and magazines to the brim.[10]

In the book and movie *The Caine Mutiny,* missing strawberries caused a warped captain to punish a crew, and the punishment motivated men to risk life and honor in an act of mutiny. Nothing like that happened on the *Franklin,* and yet a real-life incident aboard the *Franklin* shows the plausibility of the fictional story.

Young men relieved of stress and on light duty were sure to engage in pranks and worse. On one occasion Seaman First Class Pierce Brown told a buddy how good he felt after getting a dose of cold medicine (no doubt containing alcohol or codeine) in sick bay, and the next morning the buddy beat Brown to sick bay, pretended to be Brown, and enjoyed the high that Brown had anticipated.[11] Joseph Springer quotes Jim Metcalf saying, "Food was always a big deal aboard ship. One time (during this stop at Eniwetok) I watched this guy pick up a whole crate of fruit, throw it up on his shoulder, and he took off walking right down the hanger deck. Nobody questioned him. Not a word."[12] This was not Elden, in light of his determination never to get a black mark on his record, but it was probably someone in one of the V divisions. It might have been someone he knew, and he might even have gotten a taste of the purloined fruit. In any case, he certainly heard of it because there was more to the story.

In another of Springer's interviews, Joe Anderlik tells of what might have been the same incident: a shipwide search for a case of melons missing from the admirals' pantry.

They looked all over the ship but couldn't find the melons. The next day we were flying submarine patrol. Of course the island was full of brass watching the launch. The fighters took off first. Then a TBM torpedo bomber taxied out in front of us. He got into takeoff position, revved up his engine, and opened the flaps, and—boom—out rolled the melons from where one of the plane mechanics had hidden them. They hit the deck and the prop wash blew them into our propellers and everywhere else. They didn't do any damage, but they sure were messy.[13]

The *Franklin,* fortunately, did not yet have a captain who might make too much of such misbehavior.

August 11, 1944

Dear Mom, Dad & Bros,

Well Here I am behind a stack of fifteen or twenty letters wondering who to write first. The best news is that I am only one mile from Bob W[censored—surely Walcott]. I have been trying to get over to see him but can't I may get a chance in a day or two. He is probably trying too come over too. I have a feeling we will see each other in a few days I hope so. I got a letter from Krahn he said that Him, Carlton Buck and Speck [Leon Price from Vega] went on liberty together the 21st of July. I sure wish I could have been with them. I haven't saw anyone from Vega since Krahn left Boot Camp. I got Red Deweeses and Forrest Brents addresses I have nearly everyones address I'll surely run into some of them out here.

Say What is Geralds Red Heads name? It couldn't possibly be Billie Dove could it? She is about the only Red Head I know out there.

Well don't worry about me getting homesick as I know It wont do any good & besides I don't have time for that.

So R.C. is Going with the million Dollar Baby now. He thinks a lot of her I think. He will Probably marry her and Get that Seventy Five Thousand old Chafe left.

No I don't get Seasick any more Ki [probably Kenneth Robinson, of Vega] wouldn't if he was on a ship of this size. He is on a small ship which rides pretty Rough.

Yes the Bonds are to be sent home You should get the first $25 bond before long.

No Those Guys weren't the one I had the Picture with at the owl Bar. He is going into training for V-12 he will be an officer some of these days.(a 90 day Wonder) The Guys with me are Bob Bamberg & Roy Tredaway. Bob Wrote to Rowena and got an answer Roy wrote Francis but hasn't answered him she Told me she was going to tho.

I guess Gerald went to the 4-H camp didn't he. I know he did have a lot of fun if he got to go.

I got a letter from aunt Eva she said that Dale and his wife is there. How is Dale? He is Probably in Limited service aint he?

I got three Letters From Virginia and one from Howard Blasingame was sure glad to hear from them. Well I had better close for now. Don't worry about me. I'ts not as bad over here as you Probably Think.

I'll try Writeing again Tomorrow.

With Love

Your Son

Elden

Elden has made wistful references to several Vega people, in the service and at home. The meeting of Krahn, Buck, and Price almost certainly happened in Honolulu as Price's submarine chaser passed through on the way to duty farther west. Bob Walcott by now is serving aboard the destroyer tender USS *Piedmont*, which Elden knows is at Eniwetok and only one short mile away. Unlike the *Franklin*'s crew, however, the men of the *Piedmont* have little time for liberty, for they are kept very busy performing maintenance and repairs on various destroyers similar to what the *Franklin* is undergoing. Gerald has written as has Grace, and one of them mentioned Gerald and a redhead; Elden guesses it might be Billie Dove Cribbs, but Gerald in 2004 believed it had been Wyneth Wetsel. "R.C." would have been R.C. Valentine Jr., and the "Million Dollar Baby" would have been Jacque Glasscock, daughter of local rancher Chafin Glasscock. She did indeed marry Valentine, but soon divorced and after the war married Jack Dewees, the "Red" who is occasionally referred to in these letters. Howard Blasingame is Howard Jr., who will be eighteen years old and subject to the draft in five months, and who is normally known to adults as Junior Blasingame and to his friends as Snails. Elden's tone now is lighthearted, and he knows he is better off than many others.

Better off, for example, than Bish McKendree; and even Bish was doing better than usual because on August 15 another letter had reached him from the folks at home.[14] As he held in his hands the thin sheets that had come all the way from Texas and read the words of the family he had left three long years before, one of the poems he had been collecting and saving probably reflected his thoughts.

I Wonder

I sometimes wonder if my dreams
Of home will all come true,
And if the nightmare of these days
Will vanish in the blue.
I wonder when the Yanks will come,
And when the Japs will run.

I wonder if the folks at home are having any fun.
I wonder just how long we'll wait.
We won't be here forever.
Perhaps quite soon our luck will change,
And we'll be free—I wonder.[15]

Elsewhere, Bugeye Steward began duty on July 2 aboard DD-533, the destroyer USS *Hoel*, which was then at Purvis Bay in the Solomon Islands with a task force that was preparing to support the invasion of Palau. He will be spared that experience, however. Back on February 4, when Bugeye had already become unhappy with the navy, Virginia had guessed he might get out, saying, "He's pretty lucky that way." She was right, for on the day Elden next writes Steward is transferred off the *Hoel* for discharge because he had been significantly underage when he enlisted. How very lucky Steward had been we will see from the *Hoel's* experience ten weeks later.[16]

On the evening of August 15, Saxie Dowell's orchestra played at a "smoker" held on the hangar deck to announce the opportunity for crewmen to participate in organized boxing matches.[17] Elden attended and on the next day wrote about it.

August 16, 1944

Dear Mom, Dad & Bros,
Well I'll try to write a few lines before supper. I received two letters from you since I have wrote one of them was Gerald's I sure was glad to hear from all of you.

I hope everything is O.K. at home the same as it is here. I have been Painting for the last two days so my clothes are nearly solid white.

I was glad to get Bug Eyes address Yes marys guess was right he is on a destroyer. D.D. stands for destroyer. The number 533 is the number of the ship. If I ever see the Ship he is on I'll try to get to see him.

I am still trying to get to see bob but haven't got to yet. He may can come to see me I sure do hope so. I would give nearly anything to get to see him.

I went on a recreation party a few days ago. I really got filled up on Coconuts. I had a lot of fun. Tell Jerry the monkeys didn't throw any at me Tho. <u>Ha</u>

Did You tell mamie [Mamie Price of Vega] about E.L. and Speck running together and going on liberty. I might get to see Speck out this way before long. I imagine he will come my way.

We had Boxing and wrestling on the ship last nite. There are some Pretty good fighters on here.

We really have a good Band & orchestra here they play every nite. I really enjoy it. We are going to have a show tonight I forgot the name of It.

We have quite a lot of fun out here. It is not as bad as everyone thinks. They are all afraid of being drafted.

Well I would like to be home but as long as this war is on there isn't any use for a civilian at my age. It can't last too much longer. We will whip them in another year it's a cinch then I'll be ready for that $500 mustering out pay.

I guess Six has gone to the navy or something by now. I sure hope he got the navy as he will never be sorry of it if he did.

I heard N.S. Bought a 38 Cheverolet he must be saveing his money.

Say How about getting Don Milburns address from Roarks for me. I might happen to run on to his ship sometime and not know it. I must close for now.

Love to all,

Elden

Elden was not alone in his uncertain relationship with a girl—many men in many ways were coping with their own versions of another guy's "car, money, and plenty of gas." Everything back at home was changing, so much that it was hard to count on anyone or anything. Not enough men were available to do all of the jobs that had always been considered men's jobs; women were doing those jobs and doing them as well as any man had done. In contrast to the Great Depression, the economy was beginning to boom. It was not particularly pleasing to hear that men not in the service were making money, acquiring land, and doing the things many sailors would have liked to be doing. While most wives and girlfriends waited loyally for their servicemen to return, more of them than expected succumbed to loneliness and opportunity, sometimes abandoning faraway lovers for others who were near, available, and newly prosperous. Everyone shipboard knew someone who had received a "Dear John" letter, and the *Franklin Forum*'s articles reporting the changes back home caused many of its readers to feel they were missing out. Elden's preoccupation with "slackers" probably not only reflects his personal perspective and his relationship with Virginia, but also tells us what he was hearing from others in daily conversations.[18]

As evidenced in the letters from Eniwetok, mail seldom caught up with a ship when it was in the middle of a serious mission that involved combat and rapid movement. Elden's mention on September 27 of Virginia's August 17 letter suggests that it has taken five weeks to reach him.

This is the second letter in which Virginia has used the term "sister" to describe her aunt.

August 17, 1944

My darling Tex,

I received a letter from you today and was sure glad to hear from you again. I really should write more often but I was getting ready to come down here to Kansas. I've been here about two weeks now. I'm visiting my sister & her two kids, they live out on a farm and have 11 cows to milk every morning & night. I finally got a little stream of milk out of one old cow but I just about squeezed her tit off. I'll learn how before I go back to Las Animas. When you come back you'll have a professional farmer girl on your hands. I haven't went with a boy for about a month now. I sure wish this war was over so you could come home.

Tex, do you really love me or are you just kidding. So many boys feed you along & then drop you and play you for a sucker and that really hurts. I've learned from experience. I think I've loved you ever since I first met you over in the park that day Maureen and I were dropping those letters to get your attention.

I have a room of my own down here and its up-stairs, it sure is spooky. I'm writing by a coal-oil lamp. Its sort of lonesome when I sit here and think of you and the good times we had together. There wasn't very many but they were swell while they lasted. I must be getting sleepy. I can't even write decent.

Say, sweetheart, are you going to marry me when you come home. You never have said anything about it for a long time. I don't drink or smoke even if they beg me to. I'm keeping myself decent & clean for you, honey, so please don't make me break my good word by saying you don't love me any more. I guess you can't make yourself love some one. It just happens that way I guess.

Well, darling, I'm pretty sleepy but remember me in your dreams and don't forget I love you with all my heart.

Goodnite Darling,

Virginia

P.S. Write soon, I know you have a lot of work to do but write when you can.

On the day Elden next wrote, Vice Admiral William E. Halsey Jr., who disliked the nickname "Bull," became commander of the Central Pacific

Forces, replacing Vice Admiral Spruance. The Fifth Fleet was redesignated the Third Fleet, Task Force 58 was renumbered Task Force 38, and the *Franklin* was now flagship for Task Group 38.4.[19] MacArthur was about to return to the Philippines, and Halsey's forces were going to be there.

⚓

Home for Christmas, Elden hopes! Christmas is four months away. Is the final line in this letter merely the serviceman's universal wish, so often expressed as to be a cliché, or does it represent something more? Elden and every other sailor at Eniwetok knew the fleet was getting itself into shape for a big push. Two weeks of R & R had been good for the men and good for their morale. Conversation on the *Franklin* and on the beach with sailors from other ships is likely to have been optimistic. Elden is probably expressing a scuttlebutt consensus that all would be over for Japan as soon as the Philippines were retaken.

It was common for navy men on shore duty to wish they were in the fight at sea and men on ships and in the fight to wish they were safely ashore. E. L. Krahn, whose office duty at Pearl Harbor Elden envies, is trying to get assigned to Leon Price's vessel, the Patrol Boat USS *PC-1260*. Price has been in the navy for almost two years at this point, and the *PC-1260* has been patrolling areas from South Carolina to the Caribbean and the Gulf of Mexico, but Elden is right in his guess that now she is bound for the western Pacific. Aboard her, Price crossed the international date line on August 22. The transfer attempt was a long shot for Krahn, however, as these little craft carried crews of only fifty-nine men, and he did not succeed. Although called submarine chasers, their top speed was only two-thirds that of the giant *Franklin*. They carried only one three-inch gun plus three antiaircraft guns, and served primarily as reconnaissance vessels—during the entire war only one of them actually sank a submarine.

August 26, 1944 [mistakenly dated August 28]

Dear Mom Dad & Bros,

Well I can think of nothing better way to pass away the morning than writing to you.

I haven't had much to do lately it sure is nice for a change.

I guess Gerald's school will soon start. I know he is just dieing for it to start. <u>Ha</u>

I haven't heard from Bug-Eye in a long time. Does Mary ever hear from him? Where is Tom at now? Stationed in the States I imagine.

I guess Gerald made enough money to keep Goofey Goff [B. M. Goff, an old-time tent show clown and movie theater operator] in business all winter. <u>Ha</u>

I got a letter from Krahn he was trying to get transferred to the same ship Speck Price is on but he isn't having much luck I don't think. I guess he is getting tired of just sitting around and doing nothing. Krahns are trying to be big Buisness men I guess moving to Amarillo.

What is Sweed [Swanson, from Vega] going to do in Hereford? Has he got a station down there or something?

I was really surprised this morning I went down to breakfast and they had Ham & Eggs for the first time since I've been on this Ship. They have pretty good chow sometimes. I haven't saw Bob yet. Well I better close for this time. Don't be worrying about me as I'll be O.K. and still hopeing to be home for Christmas.

Your Loveing Son,

Elden

"Dinner" in Elden's next letter, as in our family back at home, meant the midday meal, so before dinner and just after church means he was writing at about noon. The "Sprouce" mentioned in the letter was Jim Sprouse, who by this time ran the Conoco gasoline station on Route 66 on the southeast corner of the intersection with present Highway 385.

Jim's son Harlow Sprouse later explained that "Little Cook" refers to the Cook family member who ran the Mobil station on the west side of the same intersection. Both establishments were popular loafing venues for teenaged boys, who Elden surmised would now be in school instead of buying cokes and candy bars there. Elden gives a positive one-sentence review of the movie *Iceland*, a 1942 romantic comedy starring Sonja Henie and John Payne, and featuring Sammy Kaye and his orchestra.

Repairs on the *Franklin* have been finished, the island liberties are over, and she has been on test runs in the final stages of preparation to head into action, first at Palau and then the Philippines—more action than anyone then imagined.[20]

August 27, 1944

Dear Mom, Dad & Bros,

I just got back from church and will try writing a few lines Before Dinner.

I wrote to you yesterday but put the wrong date on it. I put the 28th on it and wrote it the 26th its hard to keep up with the date out here.

I just finished writeing to Virginia I haven't got any mail for about a week now. I should get some in a day or two tho.

I guess Six is in boot camp by now. They will nearly Kill him carrying that 90 pound pack & Rifle

I went to the show last night it really was good. "Iceland" was the name of it Gerald may have saw it.

They have been having Basket ball tournaments the last few days my Division is playing this afternoon. I guess I'll play.

I ran out of paper and had to borry this sheet.

Did you ever get to take Sixe's Picture? He promised me a picture of him in those new boots. But he never did send it.

I heard from Grandma about two weeks ago and answered it. Everything is Fine her way.

Has Dad ever got the car overhauled I know it sure does need it by now. You could get another motor or fix the one I had.

Who is working for Jim Sprouce since Six left, anyone?

I Guess little Cook & Sprouce's business has folded up since school has started or I guess It has started by now. I better Close & go to dinner. So long for now. Write soon.

Your loveing Son,
Elden

1. Oldham County Courthouse. Courtesy Panhandle-Plains Historical Museum. 1857-34x_001.

2. Gasoline station, Vega, Texas, ca. 1927. Courtesy Panhandle-Plains Historical Museum. 1982-1-76-2_001.

3. Elden D. Rogers, December 29, 1944. Courtesy Gray's Studio, 004.

4. Elden D. Rogers in cowboy attire, December 1944. Rogers family photo.

5. Ancell, Elden, Grace, Jerry, and Gerald Rogers, December 1944. Rogers family photo.

6. Army recruit Bishop McKendree, March 1941. Courtesy of the family of B. D. McKendree.

7. USS *Franklin* (CV-13), showing Captain Shoemaker's lucky number, February 1944. Naval History and Heritage Command, 80-G-224596.

8. Bunks, USS *Hornet* (CV-12), identical to USS *Franklin*. Courtesy Nancy Burgas.

9. Prop trails on an F6F Hellcat aboard USS *Yorktown*, identical to USS *Franklin*. Naval History and Heritage Command, 80-G-204747-A.

10. SB2C Helldiver takes wave-off, USS *Franklin*, 1945. Naval History and Heritage Command, 80-G-397939 A.

11. Commemorative Air Force SB2C Helldiver in USS *Franklin* pattern. Courtesy Elvin D. Rogers.

12. USS *Franklin* operating near the Marianas, August 1, 1944. Naval History and Heritage Command, 80-G-367-248.

13. Belly tank detached on landing spreads fire on USS *Franklin* flight deck, 1945. Naval History and Heritage Command, 80-G-423418.

14. USS *Franklin* after kamikaze hit, October 30, 1944; USS *Belleau Wood* in distance. Naval History and Heritage Command, 80-G-326798.

15. Elden's duty station, Hangar Deck Control, showing windowed compartment at upper right. USS *Yorktown*, identical to USS *Franklin*. Courtesy Gerald Rogers.

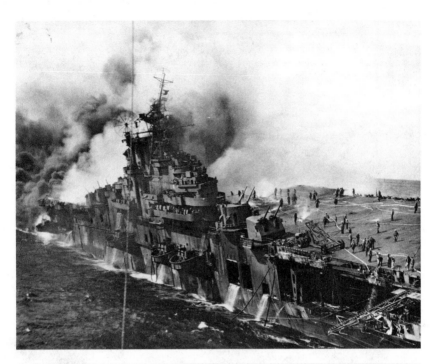

16. USS *Franklin* from USS *Santa Fe*, March 19, 1945. Naval History and Heritage Command, 80-G-273882.

17. Sad words: "Return To Sender." Courtesy Nancy Burgas.

18. Ancell, Grace, and Elden Rogers grave marker, Vega, Texas. Courtesy Nancy Burgas.

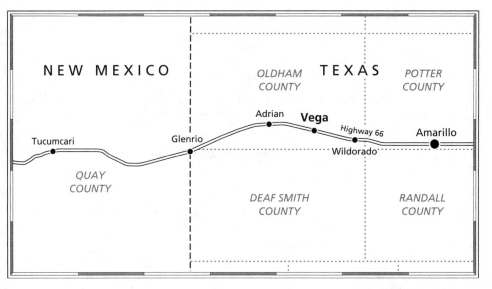

Map 1. Vega, Texas, on U.S. Highway 66. Map by John Gilkes. Copyright © 2017 University of Oklahoma Press.

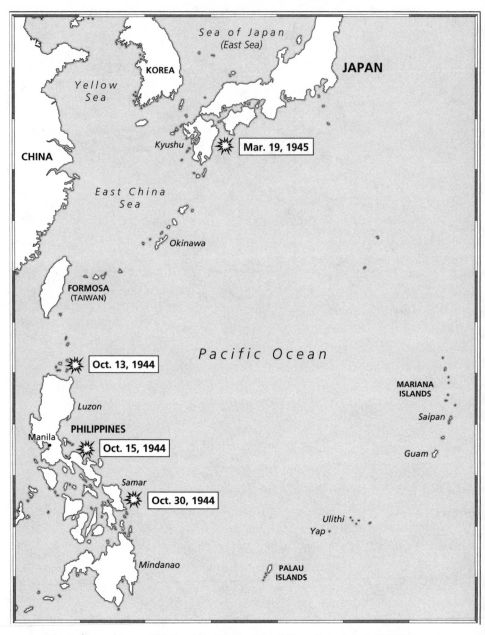

Map 2. Enemy hits on USS *Franklin*. Map by John Gilkes. Copyright © 2017 University of Oklahoma Press.

13 Palau

This Time for Real

The *Franklin* left Eniwetok on August 28, with the *Essex*-class carrier *Enterprise* and the light carrier *San Jacinto* in her task group, and sailed through very heavy seas directly back to the Bonins and Marianas area they had left three weeks before. The ship was carrying Australian correspondent for the *London Daily Express* Wilfred Burchett, who a year later will become the first newsman from the Allied countries to denounce the use of atomic bombs.[1] The ninety-one strikes the task force flew against Iwo Jima and nearby islands on September 1 and 2 were in part intended to keep Japanese strategists from deducing that the real target was Palau.[2] On one such strike, four Avengers flew off the *San Jacinto* on September 2 to bomb a radio station on Chichi Jima. One, hit by antiaircraft fire, managed to reach open waters before the crew bailed out. That evening Elden and the *Franklin* crew would have heard that two crewmen died and that the pilot was rescued by the submarine USS *Finback,* but he would have had no reason to take note of the pilot's name, George Bush, who would live to become the forty-first president of the United States and father of the forty-third president.[3]

September 4, 1944

Dearest Mom, Dad & Bros,
Will try writeing a few lines tonight in answer to the three letters I got from you a few days ago. I sure was glad to hear from you. I also got

one from Myrn [Ancell's sister Myrna Rogers Moore] and one from Six. I haven't got Sixes marine address. We took on more mail a few minutes ago so I should get more letters. Well School started today. I hope Gerald stays in there and pitches so he can make an Officer when he goes into the service.

I never got to see Bob Walcott. I sure did hate it. I doubt if he will still be around when I get back.

I have a hunch I'll see Krahn in six or Eight weeks I don't know its just a guess. I sure do hope so.

Six said that Slim Mitchell got married I don't guess he will ever have to go to the service now.

Myrn said that Dale took an overseas exam and didn't pass it. I never figured he would after he had the operation.

Beryl told her that the weither was pretty bad there at times I don't know how it got through the censor. We can't tell about the weither or anything.

Well I had better close for tonight. Don't be worrying about me as I am O.K. The Japs don't have a thing I am afraid of. Write soon.

Your Loveing Son,
Elden

Elden's hunch that he might see Krahn in six or eight weeks is a coded message that he thinks the *Franklin* might be going to Pearl Harbor. Like the earlier "home for Christmas" guess, it tells us what he was hearing from buddies in daily conversation, but we are left to wonder if the guess had any basis in reality or was only wishful thinking. Ironically, the guess turned out to pretty good, as the *Franklin* docked at Pearl Harbor ten weeks later, though for reasons he could not have anticipated—and he would not get to see Krahn.

Elden's mystification over how his cousin Beryl Moore's letter about weather got through the censors may reflect a difference between the army and the navy. Fast-moving ships and even fleets had the advantage of being able to lose themselves in the vastness of the Pacific, and information about weather might provide a clue as to their general whereabouts. Beryl was in the army in Europe, and in general both sides knew pretty well where the far less mobile division-sized outfits were located. Consequently, navy censors were probably much more restrictive than army censors, and general comments about weather may not have been of concern to the army. In any case, the point emphasizes once again why Elden's letters are so uninformative.

After a few short, sharp attacks on the Bonins, the task force stopped for a day at Saipan and then swung away southwestward toward the Palauan Islands.[4] Dark smudges on Elden's next letter are probably his first, though unintentional, communication about his new job in the ship's incinerator, about which he will write later. The Mr. Vincent he mentions is maternal grandfather to the Walcott boys.

September 8, 1944

Dear Mom, Dad & Bros,

I'll try to answer your last two letters. I sure was glad to get them.

Did mister Vincent ever get any better? I sure do hope so.

I see I am messing up this paper a little Its only Sweat & dirt I haven't taken a shower yet tonight. You have to excuse that.

I guess Gerald is in full swing now at school by now.

How are the pigs? Do you still have all nine of them? You hadn't told me Joye & Ralph had moved but I got a letter from her the same day I got yours. She said that Delton wanted to Go back with Gerald. Did he get to?

I guess Six is rubbing his sore feet tonight. <u>Ha</u> I thought navy boot camp was rough but its nothing to the side of the marines. I'tll probably kill him. The marines give three months of boot. Did you ever get his picture before he left? I sure do hope so & hope he had on the new boots.

If you haven't already got the Levis Just let them go as they are more trouble than they are worth.

Well today was payday I went down and drew my Five. I'll try drawing about Seventy next time. I figure I owe you that much if not more.

I was Glad to hear McKendrees Heard from Bishop. I really feel Sorry for Him I know he went through misery in the hands of the Japs. So long For Tonight.

With Love,
Elden

Clearly Grace had written Elden with the joyous news that the McKendree family had heard from Bish. It was only a card, one of five he was permitted to send during the four years of his imprisonment. It was minimally communicative, carefully designed to prevent transmission of any useful information, with no writing space but only a few multiple choice statements the prisoner had been permitted to underline. To his family and their supporting network in the community, however, it carried a world of news that he had not yet starved, died of disease, or been shot or bayoneted. Today the cards are in the Barker History Center Archives at the University of Texas at Austin.[5]

Elden, the *Franklin,* and the task group, seldom in any one place for long, were steaming southwestward toward Yap, at the western tip of the Caroline Islands group. They probably passed not far from the great atoll of Ulithi, with a lagoon large enough to allow construction of yet another major shipyard and supply base like the one the United States had just built at Eniwetok, but this one was on the enemy's doorstep.[6] They did not know that this atoll, well worth being fought for, was being vacated by Japan and could be had for the taking.

Passing Yap not quite so quickly, they slowed enough on September 6 for the *Franklin* to launch 168 sorties. Seaman First Class Clayton Alvin Pike, from Elden's V-1 Division, was injured by a propeller, but he was lucky because the prop was coming to a stop and it left him with a contusion rather than without part of his body.[7] They hit Yap again the next day, and the raids easily destroyed the airfield. As had been the case at Truk, these attacks plus earlier high-altitude bombing by MacArthur's B-24s made Yap useless to Japan. Again, rather than waste strength invading it, the Americans left the garrison isolated there with nothing to do and no one to fight.[8]

Almost exactly thirty years later, on September 18, 1974, I saw Ulithi from the window of an Air Micronesia Boeing 727 and then landed at the same airfield on Yap that had been hit by planes from the *Franklin* and the other carriers. In berm-sheltered slots alongside the runway were the remains of the Japanese fighters that had been destroyed in those attacks, and I wondered at the time if this might have been the work of the *Franklin*. I thought then that it was remarkable that the wrecks were still there, in silent witness of the work of war. I hope they are there today.

Japanese air defenses were noticeably weak here as they had been back in the Bonins. Palau was about to be invaded in order to deny Japan an air base from which to resist MacArthur's big Philippines landing, and some admirals now wondered whether it was necessary. The question was academic, however, because things had been set in motion and would not be stopped. By September 9, the task group had left Yap behind and had moved southwestward to the Palauan Islands.[9]

September 10, 1944

Dearest Tex,

I guess I owe you a letter. You must not of gotten any from me since I came down here to Kansas because Mom has been forwarding your letters to me all along. I guess I'll be here for a long time because my sister has to have an operation and I have to stay here with her two kids. It sure is lonesome here. I've been here for a month and haven't even seen a boy that looked like any thing. I'll sure be glad when you get to come home.

I fell down the stairs today and skinned my back all up. I landed down at the bottom of the stairs in a heap & knocked the door open and every one laughed till they cried, it wasn't very funny for me tho.

Tex, I wish I was home & you got a furlough. We would really have fun wouldn't we.

I can't think of much to write about since you don't know any body here. I can really milk now. I would make a good farmers wife I bet.

Well, I'm pretty sleepy so will quit for now and try to dream about you.

Goodnite Darling,

Love,

Virginia

On that morning of September 10, the *Franklin* sent her first fighter sweep over Peleliu to prepare the way for the ground troops who would land five days later. Early the next morning radio brought word that one of the *Franklin*'s bombers had been hit and had a wing on fire. The pilot ordered his gunner to bail out and was preparing to do so himself when the flames died out and he decided instead to save his plane. With neither flaps nor wheel locks working properly, at 0830 the plane hit the flight deck and skidded to a stop on its belly. The first order of business then was to get the pilot out quickly and safely, and then the plane was swarmed by a salvage crew that rapidly removed usable parts before the wreck was pushed overboard by men in Elden's division. The gunner was rescued and returned to the ship a few days later.[10]

There was now a new task to be done in the area covered by the V divisions, and a task that Elden might have witnessed. It was the mixing and loading of the new firebomb called napalm, dangerous in its handling and terrible in its effect. Every man on board would have heard and spoken of it, especially those who worked on or near the flight deck. Made substantially of gasoline, the stuff was mixed in a tank that had normally been used for washing engine parts and then was poured into the oblong containers that normally served as detachable auxiliary fuel tanks for fighters. The mixing was done in the open air of the port catapult sponson (a small protrusion from the deck that extended over the water), with nearby hangar deck curtains closed. If anything went wrong, the volatile gel could be dropped from there into the sea; and if there were a fire, it would be in the least dangerous location. The improvised bombs were not actually attached to the planes until just before launching, and only then were they actually armed with ignition fuses. This stuff was "handled with kid gloves."[11]

Over a seven-day period of ceaseless action, the *Franklin*'s planes flew 750 sorties and dropped half a million pounds of explosives, including the napalm. Some planes actually returned carrying mud splatters that had been blown into the air by their own guns and rockets—undoubtedly a subject of conversation among Elden and his buddies in the V divisions. For American troops on the ground, it would be a bloody slog. For Elden and the shipboard crew, it was an endless cycle of arm, fuel, launch, and recover; arm, fuel, launch, and recover. The frenetic work was interrupted from time to time by minor accidents like when two planes crashed into the barrier with only minor damage ten minutes apart on the morning of September 12. And then there were the major accidents like the one that followed a fighter's tailhook missing the cable at 2104 that evening. That plane smashed into four other planes, destroying all five. This stopped operations for more than two hours, as Elden's division cleaned up the mess and jettisoned the wreckage. Just before noon the next day yet another plane crashed into the barrier, although this time with only limited damage.[12]

Even with all the care devoted to handling napalm, there were bound to be accidents, and the first one happened on September 14. Fortunately for everyone except Seaman J. Z. Kaczetow, it was the kind of accident that can happen when dealing with any large, heavy item. While loading the tanks, the poor lad had two fingertips crushed.[13]

On September 15 a plane botched a landing attempt and went into the water.[14]

Elden's "job," as he will describe it on September 21, was in the ship's incinerator, which was located on the hangar deck next to the uptakes, to take the smoke away, and adjacent to the 40 mm antiaircraft guns of Quad Mount 13.[15] Presumably, Elden had a battle station at some place that is unknown to us, but in any case it was his V1 division that launched and recovered planes, operated the cables, dodged the crash landings, moved planes around, and pushed wrecks overboard. Buddies in the not very different V-5 Division loaded the napalm and suffered the crushed fingers. Elden would have known about, witnessed, and perhaps participated in deck action of this sort, and the intensity of the activity explains why he wrote no letters between September 8 and September 18.

I visited Palau September 20 through 23, 1974, to help the local government develop its counterpart to a state historic preservation program in coordination with the National Register of Historic Places. Our airliner landed at the old Japanese airstrip on Babeldaob, from which we crossed a causeway to the Continental Hotel on the island of Koror. Although local people were trying hard to reclaim their nearly extinct aboriginal culture, a close look into the green and tangled jungle revealed that most of the visible historic things were from World War II. It was not uncommon to walk through the forest and find the remains of a tank, a destroyed bunker, or a twisted gun.

The Palauan Islands are formed of uplifted limestone soft enough to be eroded by the surf, creating on many of them a slight overhang of solid land eight to twenty feet above the water level and giving each individual island the appearance of a white-stemmed and green capped mushroom. Few more beautiful places or more exotic landforms exist in the world. To get from a boat onto land in such places, a person must climb a ladder of several feet. There are only a very few beaches with small deposits of sand, and not many places where landing craft could deliver men for an assault. I rode a boat into a large natural cavern, perhaps one hundred feet deep and equally wide, hollowed into the side of an island at water's edge so that seawater filled the bottom of the cavern several feet deep. The Japanese had used it as a seaplane hangar, and fuel drums stood on a dry ledge around the inside edge of the cavern. Not far away, through clear water I could see a seaplane about twenty feet down, where it had been sunk by carrier planes.

We sped one day on a small boat called a Boston whaler all the way to Peleliu, which itself was an overgrown tangle of green. Later I described the visit to two of my colleagues, state historic preservation officers William Pinney of Vermont and Charles Lee of South Carolina. Both said that the last time they had seen Peleliu, as marines at the end of the battle, the island had not a tree standing. All of the vegetation had been chopped down by gunfire as a lawn mower chops grass, after almost 13,000 Japanese had fought to the death. Only 301 defenders survived.[16]

Probably before Elden put pen to paper on September 18, the destroyer *Patterson* came alongside the *Franklin* at 0830 to return two rescued pilots and to deliver mail.[17]

Dear Mom, Dad & Bros,

I received your letter last night dated aug 7th. I sure was glad to hear from you.

I was sorry to hear that Six was Put in the marines. But it is not so bad. He will get three months of boot camp then he may get five or six months duty in the states after that. He may get a break and be a seagoing marine. We have marines on this ship they don't have much to do. It's a cinch he will get more duty in the states than I did.

I guess Gerald had a big time at Buffalo lake. He is probably telling some big Fish stories by now isn't he? <u>Ha</u>

Say does Irene Have gill now or has Nick got him? Did you see him? I bet he sure is a fat kid by now.

You said Lucille [La Munyon] & kids come over where do they live. Tucumcari? Oran [La Munyon] is in the army isn't he?

I still haven't got to see Bob I am about to give up. I really would like to see him.

Has Odell come home yet? Personally I don't think they need to look for him until he finishes his V-12 school. I know a guy who went up for that and they told him he couldn't get a leave until after his school was over.

I am figuring on drawing fifty or Sixty dollars and sending home before long I'll send it all home.

Could you get the Levis I ask about? I like them better than what the navy has and everyone else has them.

Well I better close for now.

With Love Always,

Elden

14 Metamorphosis

Magazines and fuel tanks that had been filled to the brim three weeks before were empty now, and Task Group 38.4—carriers *Franklin*, *Enterprise*, *San Jacinto*, and *Belleau Wood*; cruisers *Biloxi* and *New Orleans*; twelve destroyers; and other supporting ships—pulled away southward to the Admiralty Islands for another big resupply. This took them across the equator in the early afternoon of September 20, triggering an initiation "ceremony" so ancient its roots are lost in opaque antiquity. With danger far away and tension again relieved, all hell broke loose on the *Franklin*.[1]

In the rank-conscious navy the equatorial crossing initiation is an anomaly, for at that moment only two categories matter: people who have never before crossed the equator are "polliwogs," and those who have done so are "shellbacks." Polliwogs of high rank as well as low are initiated by shellbacks of high rank and low—especially low. By general acclamation one shellback was designated King Neptune, and thus assumed "command" of the spontaneous chaos that followed. Polliwogs were pursued, caught, held down, rendered baldheaded, smeared with grease, and dragged before the diaper-clad "Royal Baby," who minutes before had been just a fat shellback, and required to kiss his navel. Resistance by a polliwog, even an officer polliwog, invited greater abuse and even beating. George Sippel was part of a group of seamen whose heads were shaved, and who were then hung upside down while their scalps were dipped into a bowl of mercurochrome to eyebrow level, dying their scalps bright red. "There ya go," their tormentors declared, "now you are all cardinals."[2] It was all done in fun, but a risky kind of fun, and the captain had fire hoses turned on one group that got too far out of hand.[3] It is interesting that the deck logs mention the hour of the equatorial crossing but make no mention of the unofficial activities that followed.

Elden endured all of this, but we do not know what he thought of it. Cautious of writing anything that might reveal location, he does not mention the equatorial crossing in correspondence until more than a month afterward and then only cursorily.

Now a shellback with a card in his wallet to prove it, Elden arrived in the Admiralty Islands, at Seeadler Harbor on Manus on September 21.[4] The base at Manus was enormous and routinely held one hundred ships or more. Now the whole task group, plus others, were there, and Bob Walcott's *Piedmont* was there to repair damaged destroyers. The beach at Manus offered few attractions; it had high breakers, a dangerous undertow, and too much coral for comfortable barefoot walking, but it was land and that was attraction enough.[5] Liberty was brief, however, only five hours, but this time the beer was not limited.[6] Exchanging stories with men from other ships was always interesting, and the prospect of meeting friends from home was exciting. Elden was not lucky enough to connect with any Vega boys there, but Bob was. Walking along the beach, Bob ran smack into his brother Charles.[7]

As before at Eniwetok, the rest, relaxation, and resupply were only fringe benefits of what was really going on. The task force was joining up with almost all other movable elements of American power on that side of the world for operations that would eclipse anything done in the Pacific before. The focal point would be the Philippines, and all that Elden had experienced since joining the *Franklin*'s crew had been small by comparison to what was coming.

There, in the targeted islands on the day Elden arrived at Manus, Bish McKendree heard a flying boat hurry to get off the water of Manila Bay and then pass at low altitude over his camp. The unusual sound shook him from the boredom of prison routine and drew him outside in time to hear the contrasting sound of machine guns and to see the seaplane catch fire and fall. A high-pitched whine grew higher; then American planes burst through the clouds in formation and dived in to bomb and strafe everything Japanese—ships, aircraft, facilities, and men. He counted fifty-six attackers and felt an elated retribution as Japanese planes exploded on the same runways where American planes had been sucker-punched so long ago. The few that managed to get airborne were quickly slammed back down. It was beautiful, he thought, beautiful— a rare and bright moment in a long and dismal imprisonment.[8]

War was a combination of boredom and fear, elation and sorrow. At the same time it brought renewed hope to Bish, on faraway Manus Elden heard the sad news about Vincent Walcott. He had time on his hands, and he used some of it to write two letters to the folks at home.

September 21, 1944

Dear Mom, Dad & Bros,

Well I received three letters a few days ago They were Dated aug. 27, aug. 30, & Sept 3. So I have been getting them pretty regular.

I sure was glad to get the pictures. Can you get films often? Tell me what your camera takes & I'll try to get some if I get in port. Service men can get all they want.

How is Joice Roark [a polio victim] getting along? I hope it don't get spread around Vega.

Has Six ever went to boot camp yet? I heard they wasn't taking them in the marines anymore he may get the navy yet. I haven't wrote him in a long time. I sure hate it. I didn't know what to do. I figured He'd be gone before the letter got there.

I guess I was pretty close to Dub Mc [McKendree] quite a while & didn't know it.

I never got to see Bob. He wrote a few days ago & said that he had tried to get over to my ship but didn't have any luck. He told me about Tub being missing in action & mr. Vincent being in the Hospital.

Did Everett's ever go for his physical? I sure do hope so.

I have a new job for Three months. I work in the Incenerator (Trash Burner.) I sure do get dirty but I like the job. I'll be on it for 3 months. I work from 12 at nite to Six in the morning. I get to sleep all day if I want. I sure do enjoy the short hours.

Don't hope on me being home for Christmas too strong. I may & I may not. I nearly know I'll see you before my Birthday.

Don't worry about me I'm O.K. & will be.

Your Son,
Elden

September 21, 1944

Dear Mom, Dad & Bros,

I wrote you a letter a few minutes ago but didn't have room for the paper. So I'll write a little more with it [apparently he sent a copy of the *Franklin Forum*].

I wish Bug Eye hadn't got transferred. I might have got to see him. I am pretty close to where he was I think. of Corce we don't know where he was before he got on the ship.

Page 7 & 8 of the paper was restricted So I had to tear it out.

Well I better close and write to Virginia & Bob then go to bed.

Don't worry about me the only difference in This and the states I aint running around so much. Ha.

Your Son,
Elden

And then the next day he produced a long letter full of light-hearted chitchat about Vega people and reports on several of his other correspondents. Gerald has traveled by train that summer from Amarillo, Texas, to Alva, Oklahoma, to visit cousins, especially double cousin Rowena Coin, and has returned long before.

September 22, 1944

Dear Mom, Dad, & Bros,

I'll write a few lines in answer to the three letters I got from you Today. They were wrote the 5th, 9th, & 12th of Sept. They are getting here pretty quick now. I sure feel a lot different wrighting with a pen. I findally found the guy that Borrowed it.

I sure was glad to hear that those Dodgers Passed their Phisical. I hope they put them in the marines.

I didn't figure the Spinhirne boy would pass he always looked to me like he had T.B.

I sure was glad to hear that Tom Steward got his discharge. He deserves it. He Probably saw more action in one day than I'll ever see.

I sent you a "Franklin Forum" (The Ships paper) It was too heavy to send air mail so I sent it Free. You'll probably get this before you get it.

The Ship has a Boxing Team and they are going to Box against another Ship. I don't know whether to try or not. I'd probably get my ears nocked down.

I got a letter from Bob & he said that he had heard Bill had lost so much weight that I wouldn't know him if I saw him.

Who worked for Frank Foster this summer, anyone? He didn't like it cause I joined the navy. He said to wait for the draft. If I had I would be a "Bell Hop" (marine) just like Six.

Say why don't Gerald get a job for Foster for the weekends? He might get in good with that good looking girl. Ruby I think is the one he thinks is good looking isn't it. <u>Ha</u>

I heard from Six yesterday I haven't wrote to him for a long Time. I figured he would be gone. I better write to him tonight. I guess his mother will foreward it if he leaves before it gets there.

Metamorphosis   197

I also got a letter from Rowena she said Carl [her father] came home. Just walked in. They didn't expect him. I guess Gerald was home before he came & didn't get to see him. Did he?

Well news is scarce around here So I better close pretty soon. Is major Jones Still after Mrs. Murphy? I bet Charlie Hammer beats his Time now that he has a car. <u>Ha</u> So long for now.

Lots of Love,

Elden

We have already noted how rivalry among branches of the armed forces led Elden to call marines bellhops. The marine contingent aboard the *Franklin* at this time numbered seventy-two enlisted men and three officers.[9]

Among the long string of bloody battles to conquer strategically important specks of land in the Pacific, there was one happy exception. At Ulithi, on September 23, Americans waded ashore unopposed and began to build an advance fleet base like the ones at Eniwetok and Manus.[10]

15 "Thirty Days Leave Coming in on the Port Side"

History holds many examples of lucky, sudden, and decisive turns in the momentum of conflict. Japan was rapidly and steadily losing the war, but the militarists who had shaped and been shaped by a tradition of fighting to the death deliberately blinded themselves to reality. Hope for a miracle was congealing into a form of faith, and faith—as it is prone to do—was overcoming reason. Plunging deeper and deeper into their bloody cultural mythology, the leaders of Japan focused on hope that bold, unexpected, and daring steps might create luck and bring a sudden and decisive turn.

Most of the best Japanese pilots were dead, and surviving ones were being killed faster than new ones could be trained, so their average skill was declining as the average skill of American pilots increased. American submarines were so thoroughly interrupting Japan's petroleum imports that scarce aviation fuel had to be reserved for combat and could not be used for training new pilots.[1] Japanese planes improved moderately as American aircraft improved vastly. Japan's navy was almost gone, and with her flyers losing six of every seven encounters, her once formidable carrier-based airpower had become insignificant.

American admirals would not expect the Japanese to give up carrier power entirely and to move all planes to islands within flight range of one another. A chain of interconnected island air bases would be vulnerable, in that loss of a single key island could break the connection, but such an approach would allow their few remaining carriers to be used for entirely different purposes. The step was bold, daring, and unexpected, and so they took it.[2]

What naval power Japan had left consisted of big ships that carried big guns: battleships and cruisers of the type that had been dominant in World War I but were now secondary to airpower. Bringing those men-of-war to bear in an effective way against the more modern power of the American navy required bold, daring, and unexpected plans, and so they began to make them.

Other ideas, equally bold and desperate and more deeply rooted in mythology than these, were simmering and would soon boil to the surface.

⚓

For Elden the brief time at Manus had been nice, but aircraft not flying and fast carriers not sailing are unimportant, and the *Franklin* got moving on September 24.[3] At "bloody Peleliu" Japanese defenders were still sacrificing themselves and making the Americans pay a heavy price, but it was clear that those defenders would soon use themselves up. Without reengaging in that lingering combat, in the Caroline Islands Admiral Halsey regathered Task Force 38 as the largest fleet in history, carrying more than 1,100 aircraft.[4] MacArthur's Philippine landing was set for Leyte Gulf on October 20, and to minimize Japanese ability to resist, Halsey sent those planes against all enemy airpower within plausible reach. Davison took his task group first toward Okinawa, a Japanese island only 350 miles south of the country's main islands.[5]

September 26, 1944

Dear Mom, Dad & Bros,
Well I received one of your letters a few days ago. Sure was glad to hear from you. I got it four days after you wrote it. Sure surprised me.
That's the quickest I've got one since I've been out here.

Life has been pretty easy for two or three weeks I haven't done much but Eat & sleep. Sure seems good for a change.

I would have wrote sooner but I let a guy use my pen and I never saw him again for a week. I think I'll quit loaning things.

I haven't got to see bob Walcott Yet I guess I might as well give it up.

I heard from Grandma about a week ago. Everything was O.K. up her way.

I imagine Six had left by now. I cinda feel sorry for him as marine boot camp is really rough. But he can take it.

Tell Jerry I hope that his tooth turned into a dime. <u>Ha.</u>[6]

Has Odell Ever got to come home yet. I hope he did as I know how it is not to get one.

I guess I'll have to go to the show tonight. We have some Pretty good ones sometimes but I have saw a lot of them before they get to us.

I sure will be glad to get back to the states. I don't know when that will be. I should get a pretty good leave. They are supposed to allow you 2½ days for every month your out I think. I will probably come home on a plane if I ever get leave.

The news looks pretty good I sure will be glad when the war is over. I don't think it will last over six or eight more months

Well I must close and go to eat Chow (supper). So Long.

Your Loveing Son,

Elden

The news was indeed good. In the "other war" Brussels had been liberated and the Belgian government in exile returned to its home soil. A large force of paratroopers had landed behind German lines in the Netherlands, and in France Allied forces from north and south had linked up. There was a lot of talk about the war in Europe being over by Christmas, just three months away. When that job was finished, forces could be concentrated in the Pacific where, Elden knew, big things were already afoot.

Headed toward the next of those big things, Task Force 38 moved as usual in three task groups, one of which was commanded from the *Franklin*. In the center of each task group was the airpower, in the form of two big carriers like the *Franklin* plus two smaller light carriers. Arrayed around them, and substantially for their protection, were two or three battleships, each carrying big guns and the names of states; six or seven cruisers, named for cities and also sporting big artillery plus antiaircraft guns; and thirty or more nimble and fast destroyers, named for naval heroes and ready to use torpedoes and depth charges. There were other small ships of various types. The ocean surface was flat like a prairie, and a task group may be visualized in Texas plains terms as measuring a little less than four miles on a side. When topside on a big ship in the center, Elden could easily see every ship in the task group. A sailor on a smaller vessel on the outer edge of the task group could usually but not always see smaller ships on the far side. A combat air patrol circled constantly overhead, ready to hit any enemy plane before it could reach the vital carriers. Two other task groups, similarly composed, sailed maybe a dozen miles away, usually within sight of one another.[7]

Probably reflecting the earlier observation that Japanese airpower was diminishing, and taking some cover from a typhoon, the task force fearlessly put itself within striking distance of Japanese fighters and bombers on Okinawa, Formosa (now known as Taiwan), and Luzon all at the same time.[8]

With the *Franklin* not yet in action, Elden's work appears to be fairly undemanding. On this particular night, if not on others, he is able to write a letter while on the job. From information in his earlier letter of September 21, we can deduce that he is writing at about 0400, or four o'clock in the morning.

September 27, 1944

Dear Mom, Dad, & Bros,

I received your letter a couple of days ago so I'll try answering it tonight. I am on the job now only have about two more hours then I can hit the sack. I'm about ready as I am pretty sleepy. I sat up and read a book till midnite so I never got any sleep before time to go to work.

This finds everything O.K. out here & I hope it is the same at home.

I heard from Virginia and she is in Kansas visiting Her Uncle & aunt. Her Mothers Brother. His name is Rogers Too.

I heard from Six & answered it I sure do hope he Gets it before he is Called I would have written sooner but I figured he would already Be gone before now.

I heard from Krahn. He was Telling me about going on Liberty With all of those Guys. I wish Bob & I could have been there. Choctaw [Bob Walcott] could have called a Pow-Wow and almost every Vega Sailor in the Pacific would have been there.

I was glad to hear that Gerald would have a hundred dollars when School Started. He should get him one of those Sport Coats like I had last winter. You know that tan one. When I get out of here That & a pair of boots will be the first thing I'll buy. I sure don't like to wear Shoes all the time.

I got the picture of "Ode" & Wife [Odell and Verda Mae Mathes Price] I thought it was pretty good.

Don't be worrying Too much about me. I know you can't help but Worry some but don't worry much as I am O.K. & will be. Thanks to the Navy I doubt if I could truthfully say that if I was in the army or marines.

With Love,
Elden

Prison camps on Luzon throbbed with anticipation of freedom after the carrier plane raids Bish McKendree had witnessed on September 21 and 22. The Japanese, however, not ready either to give up their prisoners or to allow them to be a distraction in a combat zone, set about moving them to more secure locations. Unable to provide humane care and morally indisposed to do so, Japan took the survivors of Bataan from a bad situation to one much worse and then to one unspeakably horrible. On October 1 Bish and other Cabanatuan prisoners were loaded onto trucks and driven to a dock in Manila. As they were herded onto a small freighter named *Haro Maru*, they got a glimpse of the bay and saw that it was full of sunken ships.[9]

Crammed into a cargo hold below deck, the prisoners soon gave the ship a more apt name, *Benjo Maru*. *Maru* in Japanese is a suffix traditionally attached to ship names, and *benjo* refers to a latrine or the excrement deposited therein. Told they were taking a seven-day voyage to Japan, the men instead endured twelve days at sea with barely enough room to sit down and with only one brief time on deck. Twice each day they were fed one mess kit pan of rice, level full, and once a day they were allotted a single quart canteen of water. Recognizing that this would not sustain life, McKendree wisely drank the water he used to wash his mess kit after each meal. Others, weaker or less resourceful, began to go insane by the fourth day and soon after began to die. It became a morning routine for the living to fix a rope to the newly dead and to hand them up to be thrown into the ocean.[10]

⚓

Back on the *Franklin,* Elden's cushy night job has come to an end long before the three months he had anticipated. Perhaps he still has incinerator duty, but the day shift is busier.

October 6, 1944

Dear Mom, Dad & Bros,

I got a letter & the paper a few days ago So I'll try writeing Tonight.

I also got a letter from Virginia. She is visiting her aunt & uncle in Mapleton Kansas.

No I haven't Sent any money yet as I have been pretty buisy and haven't had much time. But I'll take time some Day soon.

The took me off the job at night I sure did hate it. I am working days again. Those Same old long hours.

How is Gerald likeing School by now. Did R.C. & the Millon Dollar baby ever get married, I doubt it? I don't see how he's staying out of the army so long.

Has Six left yet? Tell him to be sure & write as soon as he got his new address.

Tom Steward is living in Vega now aint he? Does mary ever Here From bug-Eye? I haven't heard for two months.

I better close for now as I don't know anything to write but I'm O.K. & Don't Worry. I'll be seeing you for Xmas (I hope)

With Love,

Elden

Elden sometimes mentioned being close to Bish McKendree as a way of hinting his own location. He does not say so now, because he does not know that he may have been closer to Bish at this time than at any other. If the convoy of hell ships out of Manila really was headed toward Japan, they may have been sailing almost into the path of Task Force 38. Wherever the convoy was, American submarines found them on October 7 and again two days later. The subs, naturally, attacked, unable to know that these supply ships carried human—and American—cargo. The *Benjo Maru*, smaller than other nearby ships, was not targeted, but a tanker and other ships carrying prisoners went down. One American near Bish, pressing his ear against the hull, claimed to be able to tell from the sounds that a U.S. sub had been sunk by depth charges.[11]

Monday morning October 9, the *Franklin* and the other carriers launched Hellcat fighters against Okinawa. Japanese searches for the source of the attacks were fruitless, and for the time being the *Franklin* remained safely concealed by the vastness of the Pacific.[12]

Getting far more serious the next day, the Americans flew almost 1,300 sorties of fighters, bombers, and torpedo planes against Okinawa and Nansei Shoto. This kept Elden and his shipmates busy all day in the now familiar bustle of launching, recovering, rearming, refueling, and relaunching. The work was worth it, however, as task force planes destroyed a hundred enemy counterparts, sank nineteen vessels, and virtually destroyed the port of Naha. Success always came at a price, and one plane from the *Franklin* was among the twenty American aircraft lost.[13]

Near the end of the second day of attacks, Japanese planes finally located the American fleet. Having already suffered so much damage, they chose to make a rare and spectacular night attack by the light of flares that floated slowly downward under small parachutes.[14] It must have given sailors like Elden an eerie feeling to see their ships exposed in the strange brilliance of burning phosphorus, and to know that enemy fighters, bombers, and torpedo planes hidden in the darkness beyond could see them. The most thoughtful among these sailors, however, may have recognized that the situation illustrated the tremendous technical advantage the United States had developed since 1941. Fighting visually by flarelight was primitive compared to radar-guided American night fighters seeking out and destroying Japanese ships and planes under blackout conditions and then finding their way back to home carriers. As it turned out, this was mostly a light show. Although Elden and other sailors ran to battle stations several times during that night, no Japanese plane managed to hit an American ship.[15]

Japanese warplanes, scattered among islands and diminishing in number, needed to be concentrated in order to deal with anything as large as Task Force 38. Denying the enemy a chance even to guess where to concentrate, Halsey used the speed of his fast carriers to hit them in places far apart but only hours apart. Immediately after the night fight near Okinawa, the *Franklin* led Task Group 38.4 far enough southward to strike an airfield and a seaplane base almost eight hundred miles away on Luzon.[16] Not a single Japanese plane even got into the air as the *Franklin*'s planes destroyed ten to fifteen of them on the ground and strafed a merchant ship and a destroyer. Torpedo planes then came after the fleet but hit nothing. Even so, Tokyo Rose claimed yet again that the USS *Franklin* had been among many American carriers that had been sunk.[17] Sailors listened to her, and Elden would either have heard his ship mentioned or likely would have cracked a joke as he heard the story hilariously repeated by fellow crewmembers.

There were no radios to relieve the misery on the *Benjo Maru* as she entered Hong Kong Harbor on October 11. Bish's worry was somewhat relieved by the assumption that land presaged the end of the ordeal, but it was not to be so. The prisoners were not disembarked, and the ship simply sat there with nothing happening other than the occasional splash of a deceased prisoner being dumped overboard. One of these most likely was thirty-seven-year-old Alvin W. Sharp, from Clovis, New Mexico, a place much like and not far from Vega, Texas. Excitement returned for a while on October 14 when American planes bombed shore facilities and other ships in the harbor, but for ten long days more the prisoners remained confined aboard the motionless *Benjo Maru*.[18]

As Bish arrived at Hong Kong, the *Franklin* and other carriers unleashed enormous power upon Formosa, where he did not yet know he was headed. Further strikes on October 12 and 13 damaged installations, destroyed five hundred planes, and sank forty ships.[19] Japanese forces responded more effectively this time, getting at least 650 planes airborne, and the battle went on into the night.[20] Even though American pilots were now dropping most of these planes into the water with almost recreational ease and before they could inflict harm, a few of the enemy managed to have effect. The cruiser *Canberra* and the light cruiser *Houston* took torpedoes, but both were towed to the new forward base at Ulithi for repair.

October 13 became important for two reasons other than this fight, one involving hundreds of ships and the other a single plane. First, a different American fleet of enormous size, largely comprising troopships and supply vessels departed Manus on a seven-day voyage to the landing beaches on Leyte in the Philippines.[21] Second, a new and desperately different mode of warfare began when a Japanese pilot deliberately flew his plane into the *Franklin.*[22]

Quiet consideration had been given for some time within the Japanese admiralty to an ultimate weapon. It had become futile to send outclassed planes and pilots against American counterparts, but there was a way to give their remaining planes and pilots a measure of success. Even rickety planes could be loaded with explosives, and even raw pilots could guide them through the defenses directly into the very centers of American power—into the carriers. They would not engage in combat with American planes, but would bore unwaveringly toward their targets and toward their deaths. Most would be shot down, but if only one got through it could accomplish far more than the diminishing impact of recent conventional combat.

Rear Admiral Masafumi Arima had been raised in England, educated in its public schools, and trained in the Royal Navy,[23] but he was thoroughly samurai. Certain that Japan had no choice other than to use this extreme tactic, he was one of those talking it up, and he knew he had to set the example. Other studies more detailed than this reconstruction of one sailor's experiences dispute the proposition that Arima was at the controls of the first plane that seemed deliberately to hit an American ship, but the *Franklin*'s crew believed it was none other.[24] They took unsurprised delight that the best effort of an admiral proved clumsy.

The attack came as daylight waned in the early evening of Friday the thirteenth of October, 1944.[25] The *Franklin*'s attacks upon Formosa were over for the day. Bogies had been spotted during the day, and scrambling fighters had found and destroyed them. At 1727 Captain Shoemaker had allowed the men to leave their battle stations, but because the *Franklin* was not far from the island and a mere 450 miles due north of Manila, he had followed his standard protocol of leaving the 40 mm antiaircraft quads manned during daylight hours when within range of attack from enemy airfields.[26] Fighter planes coming home were hitting the flight deck one at a time at the precise spot where they must hit it, being jerked to a stop, then hustled by men in Elden's division to an elevator and lowered to the hangar deck for refueling, rearming, and if necessary, repairing.[27]

To the north a few miles a wall of falling rain hung from a cloud. Through this barrier at 1826 burst four twin-engine Mitsubishi bombers of the type Americans called "Betty." They were flying barely above water, beneath the searching beams of radar, and far below the watching combat air patrol. With targets aplenty, they ignored the older *Enterprise,* rejected mere light carriers *Belleau Wood* and *San Jacinto,* and went after the new one with the admiral's flag.[28] Antiaircraft guns on the *Franklin* and every other nearby ship opened fire and quickly knocked the first plane down. The other three, carefully spaced and in staggered formation to maximize the chances that one might get through, came into the fire with their own guns blazing.[29] Hit repeatedly and burning but still flying, the second one dropped a torpedo. Al Cole, in the engine room near Roy Treadaway and below the waterline where torpedoes would hit, heard over the intercom: "Thirty days leave coming in on the port side."[30] All who heard this knew it meant they were about to be hit.

William Brunner, in a chow line that as usual stretched up onto the hangar deck, saw "bullets hit the steel hangar deck and ricochet all over," and men in line "picked off like crows on a fence." He could see the torpedo coming and felt almost paralyzed as his mind gave him conflicting instructions: "move . . . run . . . stay."[31]

The common metaphor "like turning a great ship," meaning a change that happens very slowly, was not applicable that day to the well-commanded *Franklin.* Treating his one-sixth-mile-long giant as though it were a speedboat, Captain Shoemaker wrenched the wheel ninety degrees just as the second plane dropped its torpedo and continued on a course toward the *Franklin* at the flight deck and hangar deck level. "Everybody ducked and said their prayers."[32] Tilting in response to the captain's maneuver, the port side dropped just enough to put the flight deck beneath the would-be first kamikaze's trajectory. Instead of entering the open curtain wall and crashing inside the vulnerable hangar deck the plane ricocheted upward off the flight deck and exploded a hundred feet beyond.[33] The ship was unhurt, but there was still the torpedo. Luckily, it had entered the water at a steep angle that made it go deep, pass under the *Franklin,* and then bubble away on the opposite side.[34]

With two Bettys down and two still coming, the defense was only half done. Probably because of Shoemaker's sharp maneuvering, a second torpedo missed the ship's rear so narrowly that it passed under the overhanging fantail. The third Betty was taken down near the *Belleau Wood* by gunners from that ship and from the *Enterprise.*[35]

Still in the air and a minute behind, the fourth Betty's pilot carefully led the moving *Franklin* in his sights as a hunter leads a flying duck, and sent his torpedo where the *Franklin* would soon be. Shoemaker ordered another sharp turn and "back full" on the starboard engine; Roy Treadaway's buddies down in the "black gang" put the order into action. Great power, suddenly reversed, slowed the ship as the turn swung it away from the path of the torpedo, which passed just in front of the bow. Hopping over the *Franklin*, the Betty got between her and the *Enterprise.* Guns from the two carriers chewed it to pieces and gnawed at one another in the process.[36]

It takes but one torpedo to sink a ship, and one of the four found its mark. The crew heard a resonating "bong" as it struck the *Franklin*'s hull, but they did not hear an explosion. A dud! They were saved by the torpedo's own internal flaw.[37]

We cannot know where Elden was during this action, but we can guess that he heard the ominous "thirty days leave. . . ." We can be certain that the guns told him the ship was under attack. He felt the ship suddenly tilt, and he heard or maybe even saw the Betty carom across the flight deck. He may have been thrown off balance when the ship suddenly slowed and swung back, and he may have heard the changing pitch of the engine's whine. He may have been on the flight deck to dodge both hostile and friendly fire, he may have been in the chow line with Brunner, and he may have seen others hit. He may have heard the dud torpedo strike the hull. Wherever he was, he knew this was extraordinary action, and he knew more or less why it was happening. Afterward he knew, as every man knew, this had been an extraordinary experience. He surely believed his life had been saved by the captain, and in light of the dud torpedo he probably mused about "lucky 13."

The suicide plane—if indeed it was a *suicide* plane—had done no damage to the *Franklin* beyond scars in the flight deck planks, but it had killed Harold Stancil, a member of Elden's V-1 Division. Friendly fire from other ships had wounded several people, and the attackers' guns had hit others. One man was dead and eleven were wounded, all very possibly friends of Elden's, and one shipboard aircraft had been destroyed.[38]

"Everyone's favorite story," wrote Steve Jackson, was "that of Lieutenant Winters," who had hit the deck to avoid being struck by the "Betty" Arima was flying. As it bounced off the flight deck and over Winters before crashing into the water, the plane came just close enough for a piece of it to tear the seat out of Winters's pants. Standing and with his rear end showing, the lieutenant yelled, "'Scratch another Betty,' as though he or his derriere had been responsible for the kill." Like good stories everywhere, this one grew better and better over the next several hours. Someone started a collection to tattoo a Japanese flag on the lieutenant's butt, representing the enemy plane it had brought down.[39]

On the adrenaline high that follows a narrow escape, Elden probably said his part in the hubbub that night about the flyer who seemed to have tried to kill himself in order to kill them. They told one another where they had been when it happened and what they had seen, heard, and thought; and they wondered what had been wrong with that fool pilot. But the one man lost from a crew of 3,000 had been a workmate, a messmate, a bunkmate, a pal; and the V divisions' loss was heartfelt and personal. "Why him," people wonder at times like this, "and not me?"

16   Three Strikes and Out

Giddiness was suspended for a while the next day when the men stood for a solemn service and then watched a weighted sailcloth bundle slide from beneath a flag down a slanted board and drop seventy feet into the sea. One year to the day after the *Franklin*'s launching, she buried the first crewman who had been killed by enemy action. She also steamed toward Luzon, attacked Aparri airfield there, and had one plane crash-land on the flight deck with only slight damage.[1]

According to a printed program Elden sent home three weeks later, the crew observed the anniversary with a celebratory ceremony and an outstanding meal. There was cream of tomato soup, Virginia baked ham with pineapple sauce, cream whipped potatoes, buttered asparagus, creamed corn, cabbage and apple salad with mayonnaise dressing, ripe olives, hot graham rolls, mince pie, ice cream, bread, butter, lemonade, and cigarettes.

The war, of course, went on, and pilots who struck Luzon that day returned with word that they had been very successful and had seen the damage from their strikes of three days before.[2] In Elden's short life this day of mixed emotion was probably unlike any other, combining celebration and sorrow, laughter and solemnity, and a heightened awareness of being alive based on recognition that it might have been him under that flag rather than poor Stancil.

Since the days when the crews of sailing ships used artillery to disable enemy vessels and then boarded them to fight with pistol and cutlass, naval warfare has steadily grown less personal and more institutional. In 1944 men were still fighting men but did so ship to ship, plane to plane, and even fleet to fleet. Unless you were a marine on the land, it was seldom man to man. Sailors on smaller ships like destroyers sometimes saw individual enemies whose ships had been sunk floating in the water, but even then it was rare enough to be an occasion of special note. Sailors on big ships like fleet carriers almost never saw their enemy, so we can be sure that Elden took note when three captured Japanese were brought to the flagship for interrogation. One of the three, the pilot of a Betty that had been shot down, had lived in Ohio until just before the war began, and spoke English. Jack Lawton remembered that he asked to sit in the cockpit of the plane that had shot him down and was allowed to do so.[3]

The prisoners went first to sickbay for physical examinations and were found to have jock itch, like nearly every other fighting man in the tropics on both sides. Although gentler treatments were available for the skin fungus, the medics had them apply salicylic acid, which stung mightily when applied to tender parts. Onlookers laughed as the prisoners yelped and hopped.[4] More indicative of what was important to sailors, Robert Ladewig recalled that marine guards always took the prisoners to the head of the chow line as sailors waiting their turn hooted and jeered.[5] Generally humane handling, aside from the acid treatment, included fresh-air breaks on the flight deck, which probably inspired some grousing or at least joking among Elden and his buddies. Eventually the interrogation was over and the three were transferred to a destroyer that would take them to a prison facility. The first one to go over, the pilot, saved his honor and wasted his life by jumping into the sea halfway across. He was not rescued, but the other two thereafter were handcuffed to the line and successfully transferred.[6] Elden, with duty topside, almost certainly witnessed some of these things personally, and scuttlebutt being what it is, he heard about the rest.

On October 15, *Franklin*'s planes flew 150 miles westward to hit Nichols Field at Manila.[7] This time the enemy quickly located and went after the source of the attackers. Bogies first showed up on the *Franklin*'s radar at 0720, and the fight was on. The combat air patrol did its job well as the morning went on, splashing Japanese planes as soon as they were spotted, and men on the *Franklin* knew that things were working the way they were supposed to.[8]

Then suddenly they were not. At 1046 three bombers were detected in the least desirable way—visually—and in the worst possible position— overhead. Looking up, one of Elden's division comrades "saw a picture book look of an engine and two wings," one of two enemy planes that were diving straight at the *Franklin*.[9] Again the captain took evasive action, wheeling his giant out of the path of carefully aimed bombs. Guns on the *Franklin* and other ships apparently hit the lead plane, which continued its dive straight into the water at a point where, without the captain's action, the *Franklin* would have been. The bomb of the second plane was almost dodged, but it barely hit the outside edge of the deck elevator and exploded.[10]

Elden needed no explanation as he adjusted his own equilibrium to the evasive maneuver. He heard the guns and felt the ship vibrate to their rhythm, and he heard and felt two bomb concussions.[11] He might have been one of those who saw strange little puffs of flame on walls where minute bomb fragments struck with speed and heat enough to ignite the paint.[12] He might have seen gasoline begin to pour out of shrapnel-pierced airplane tanks and soon afterward catch fire. He might have seen water fall in curtains as automatic firefighting systems kicked in, and he might have been among those who grabbed hoses and sprayed the flames. As a member of V-1, he might very well have helped to push three damaged aircraft overboard, and he might have seen, known, or directly aided the two men who were killed or some of the thirty who were wounded. He surely was pleased to learn that little damage had been done to his ship, and he surely again thought that this captain knew what he was doing.[13]

At 1253 a damaged plane found its way back to the *Franklin* and landed without flaps or wheels—a crash landing worthy of the name that required V-1 Division sailors to push the wreckage overboard. Then five minutes later another returning plane made a water landing off the starboard quarter.[14]

Three hours later, relieved that the fires had been extinguished, Elden heard the captain announce that two very large enemy squadrons were approaching. Only minutes away—seventy miles—fifty planes were coming from the northwest and thirty from the southwest, as the *Franklin* sent additional planes to intercept them.[15] On the speaker system he heard the ominous countdown of their approach: "now at twenty miles and closing . . . now at ten miles and closing." He heard report after report of American planes shooting some of the enemies down, and he heard and participated in cheers each time. Then he heard the order to take cover, and depending on where he was, he took it. The running narrative of the intercom "frightened the hell out of you," Glenn Davis and Steve Nowak said, and "wore your nerves down more and more."[16]

The defenses worked just barely well enough that day. The *Franklin*'s pilots took down twenty-nine planes and her gunners bagged one. Pilots from other carriers shot down fifty-five more. All in all, the Americans had been very successful, but things had been close. In the evening the men heard Tokyo Rose again say the *Franklin* had been sunk, and this time it was not funny.[17] Everyone had seen that the *Franklin*'s elaborate defenses could be penetrated. Some had seen the dead and wounded, and some of those had been friends. Many had seen firsthand that the hangar deck's concentration of planes, fuel, and munitions made the ship a floating bomb waiting to be ignited. As a mythical Murphy had written into a mythical law, "What can go wrong will go wrong."

October 17, 1944

Dearest Tex,

How are you darling? I'm home again. I got here yesterday noon. I stayed down there about three months and wish I had stayed all the rest of the year. I sure like farm life. Some day I think I'll live on a farm, after I get married.

Do you know Wilma H? Shes married now & so is Clara W. and a whole mess of kids have gotten married while I was gone. I heard Chuck Steward was discharged & was here in Las Animas for a while but he must have went back to Texas for I haven't seen him. Maureen & Wanda and Bernice all went to Texas with him I guess. I guess you know Earl is married & Kial & Virginia are. Nearly every one is.

I sure hope you get a furlough before very much longer. You should, you've been in long enough. Make them give you a real long one when they do for making you wait so long for it.

I'm going to get my picture taken & send you one as soon as I get to La Junta again.

I hope you can read this. The table shakes every time I start writing.

I'm going to send you a Christmas package. What do you need? A shaving kit or a box of candy & cookies or cigarettes or what. I read in the paper that all the boys needed sun glasses & soap worse. You tell me so I'll send the right things.

Well, darling, take care of yourself for me and don't fall in love with those girls out there, remember theres one back here waiting for her sailor boy to come home. It seems like you've been gone for years.

With all my Love,
Virginia

The only girls "out there" were the pin-up images taped inside locker doors plus fantasies of individual sailors, though those girls were many and all of them beautiful. Elden has already learned from Carlton Six that Bugeye Steward has gotten out of the navy and is back at home where real girls were abundant, and this news must have inspired its own wistful and envious fantasy. Work, however, drove such thoughts away as on October 17, planes from both major commands, Nimitz's and MacArthur's, began three days of preinvasion attacks.[18]

If eighty planes at a time coming at the *Franklin* seemed like overwhelming force, every Japanese defender in the Philippines faced that many times over. Amazingly, their families back at home believed the opposite, as the same claptrap with which Tokyo Rose taunted American servicemen was used to prop up domestic morale. Who would not believe that in the action near Formosa eleven American carriers, two battleships, three cruisers, and a destroyer had been sunk when they had heard it on the radio from the divine emperor himself? It was lies—all lies. While facts pointed toward defeat, the streets of Japan's cities were filled with people gullibly dancing toward doom.[19]

Nimitz and his men at sea heard of this nonsense, and on October 19 Elden surely heard the admiral's ironic response read aloud to the *Franklin* crew: "Admiral Nimitz has received from Admiral Halsey the comforting assurance that he is now retiring toward the enemy following the salvage of all the Third Fleet ships recently reported sunk by Radio Tokyo."[20]

As MacArthur's men hit the beach on October 20, the *Franklin* sent fighters and bombers to hit the islands of Cebu and Negros.[21] The next day she and her task group moved away eastward to refuel as, over on the west side of Leyte, American ships continued to pour ashore 133,000 men and 200,000 tons of supplies.[22]

With his own death, Admiral Arima had made his point. For Japan, conventional air defense had become futile. Now, at Mabalacat airfield north of Manila Bay, Vice Admiral Takejiro Onishi reconciled his own mind to the fact, and on the day Elden next wrote, the use of suicide missions became official Japanese policy.[23] To rationalize the tactic, leaders would call upon a centuries-old myth of a wind by which divine providence protected Japan even when in battle all had been lost. The divine wind, called *kamikaze,* would enable a warring nation to hang on for nine and a half more months until fact piled upon fact, defeat piled upon defeat, and needless death piled upon needless death, bringing the deception to its inevitable end.

October 22, 1944

Dear Mom, Dad, & Bros,

I will Write a few lines tonight in answer to your Two letters & the Paper. I sure was glad to hear from you. I got a letter from Six he was telling me about Bug-Eye being in Vega with Berneice and two other girls from Las Animas. You may not have heard about it as he didn't want it known. How did he get out do you know?

I guess you bought Cal & Ivas house as one of your letters said that. You were thinking about getting it & the other said you would have moved it if it Hadn't Rained. What did it cost you for the Lot & all? At least It will be a place where bose or no one else can be telling you what to do.

How is the oil well comeing I guess they are still drilling aren't they?

I went to the show last nite. "Barnacle Bill the Sailor" It sure was good.

Well Jerry is a pretty good artist at least I could tell what it was.

Yes you may as well send the Levis as they will shrink some.

Has E. L. Krahn on a sub now or do you know?

I wish Bish was still where he was as I would like to see him.

I have thought Several times that I had it bad here but I think of him and Jim & it just makes me that much madder at the Japs. They are Going to start Hollering some of these days and I hope we don't have any mercy on them.

I get the "Franklin Forum" every two or three months I'll send all them.

It looks like Odell will be on a carrier some of these days to. As that is a naval air station there in Calif.

Must Close

Lots of Love

Elden

"I wish Bish was still where he was as I would like to see him," Elden writes to tell us he is near the Philippines. Everyone in Vega knew that Corregidor was where Bish and Jim had been, but neither Elden nor anyone at home knew that Bish on that day was departing Hong Kong in the fetid hold of a shitpot ship, bound for Formosa.[24]

Virginia, with no understanding of how Elden's mail reached her and no way even to imagine what he was experiencing, was pouting over something she has heard indirectly from Steward. As misinformation and infrequent mail plant doubt in her mind about Elden's devotion, her expressions of love grow stronger.

October 23, 1944

Hello Darling,

Its been so long since I've heard from you. I hope you haven't forgotten me. Chuck told Maureen he seen you in Hiawii or some place with two girls. If you don't love me Tex, just tell me so, because I would feel a lot better knowing the truth, altho it would ruin me to think you didn't love me.

Tex, I would do anything to make you respect & love me. What have I done that has made you change your mind? Maybe I'm just not the type of girl you want, only I've been keeping myself for you. No smoking, drinking, or anything. Please write & tell me Chuck was lying when he told Maureen all about how you felt about me now. Whatever you do tell me just how you feel & I will just have to take it I guess.

Every single girl in town is married now, except me.

I heard Chuck & Janet were going to get married. Shes really crazy about him.

Write & remember I'll always love you in the same old way.

Lovingly yours,

Virginia

P.S.

I'll send you some pictures next time I write. Send me some more of you. I'm so proud of my sailor boy. I like to show your pictures to people & say "Hes my guy, isn't he handsome."

Bursting with the urge to express what he has experienced, Elden quickly writes again. He can tell only a little—that he has been south of the equator and he is still near the Philippines, and the frustration he feels from the restraint is almost palpable. It comes out in open and perhaps envious resentment of others his age who are not doing what he has been doing, and perhaps even in his rare mention of going to church. His comments about destroyer duty reflect what he had seen firsthand— that carriers were the enemy's primary targets and destroyers certainly were not. The destroyers he most frequently saw were the ones following in the *Franklin*'s wake to rescue air crews after a plane had been ditched or a landing or takeoff botched.[25] These destroyers got to shoot at enemy planes, but the planes were not coming for them. From his spot in the bull's-eye, that looked like good duty.

There was much about destroyer duty that Elden was not taking into account. To the enemy, carriers were indeed the primary target, and therefore to the United States they were the primary focus of defense. So powerful was this focus that the captain of a destroyer would be duty bound to sacrifice his own ship and crew if doing so might save a carrier. Destroyers less visible to Elden formed the outer ring of a carrier's "screen" and were sometimes hit as alternate targets by attackers whose attempts to reach a carrier had been frustrated. They were tossed about in bad weather and sometimes even capsized by typhoon waves. The United States lost scores of destroyers in the Pacific War and no *Essex*-class carriers at all, though the carriers sometimes suffered enormous casualties while remaining afloat. In fact, only two days after Elden wrote this letter, the destroyer USS *Hoel*, from which lucky Bugs had just been transferred, boldly attacked enemy ships of vastly greater size and power and sank after taking as many as forty hits from Japanese guns as large as sixteen inches in diameter. It was one of the most heroic acts of any ship in the war, and it was a conscious act of sacrifice to save several light carriers.[26]

October 23, 1944, fell on a Monday, so the church reference suggests that this letter and the previous one may be erroneously dated.

October 23, 1944

Dear Mom, Dad & Bros,

I hope to have time to write a few letters this A.M. I will write yours first in case I don't get them all wrote.

I got a letter from Six he dated it Sept. 28th. He talked like he had got his notice. He said he was leaveing in a few days but didn't say when.

He told me about bug-Eye Getting Discharged. He didn't say how or why he was out. He also told about him and herman Ward & those Girls being in Vega. Tell bugs to write me if he hasn't already ran off somewhere before now.

Did Edd Murphy ever get his yellow band fixed? I hope he never does. I guess Bugs is pretty thick with Him ain't he? Six Said Murph wanted me to write to him. I never did & don't think I will. If I do I will really read him off. (Get him Told in other words.) He sure is yellow or he wouldn't be sitting at home. I would like for him to get a taste of this out here. Bugs had Destroyer Duty. The best duty in The navy if he can't take that he can't take anything. I would jump at the Chance to get duty on a destroyer.

This Duty I have is hard work but is just as Safe as anything in the navy. I kinda like it. I'll stick it out. I won't do like Bugs & Edd if it kills me. I can remember Bugs Talking when He got in about his being a hero or Something. Then he turned out to be just like Murphy. Or I guess he did as I don't think He was wounded or any thing like that.

Well I have $179 on the books but can't draw it now. I would like to send some of it now but I can't do it now. I will when I can Tho.

Say How about sending Odell Prices address if you can get it.

I was South of the Equator once So my hair is only ½ inch long again.

When you go across the First Time You are initiated. You are a Polly wogg as they call you then you become a Shellback.

The navy Seems to be agreeing with me. I'm not getting much heavyier but my mussles are a lot harder than when I left the States.

I have got two of the Amarillo Papers So far. They just haven't caught up with me yet.

I wonder where Bishop Mc is now. I sure would like to See him if he is still where he was. I might get to see him sometime.

Well I must close as it [is] time for church. Don't worry about me as I am O.K. & I will be. Those Japs don't worry me in the least. Was sure Glad to hear of the Philipine Invasion.

With Love,
Elden

As Japan shifted her planes from carriers to land bases and changed the missions of many new pilots from combatant to suicide bomber, she made a third major shift in order to use what was left of her navy. One scholar called the change a reversion, of necessity, to pre–World War II ideas,[27] and indeed it was. With their carriers now unimportant but a number of battleships and heavy cruisers still afloat, the admirals would try to engage American ships in old-fashioned artillery duels. This was not the way World War II had been fought in the Pacific, but it was the way navies had fought for the two centuries before 1941. It was the only way Japan could still fight on water.

Reckoning that Halsey would focus on the carriers, Japanese planners devised a daring and comprehensive strategy to get the only kind of naval battle Japan could still fight. They would dangle their carriers in front of Halsey like a fly on a line in hope of drawing his airpower away. Then they would send their remaining surface ship power to trap MacArthur's fleet and catch his landing force from behind.

The decoy force approached the Philippines from the north. Six carriers looked formidable, but they hauled only 116 planes, all topside so they could be seen. Three light cruisers and eight destroyers tried hard to look like a "screen" for the carriers. In fact, they all expected to be sunk. Their leader, Vice Admiral Jisaburo Ozawa, expected to go down with them.[28]

The real power lay in two groups of big ships carrying big guns. A Southern Force and a Central Force would slip into the Philippine archipelago from the west. If the plan worked, few American warplanes would be in the area, and MacArthur's seven-hundred-ship invasion fleet might be caught at its most vulnerable stage, hit simultaneously from north and south, and destroyed the old-fashioned way.[29]

It was a cold-blooded strategy carefully calculated to produce the needed sudden, lucky, and decisive turn in momentum, and it almost worked. It brought on what was initially called the Second Battle of the Philippine Sea and is now remembered as the Battle of Leyte Gulf.

Radio was a wonderful tool in World War II, enabling instant and direct communication over great distances, but radio signals could be used by the enemy to locate and destroy the broadcaster. To confer using a primitive but safer method—megaphones—two American submarines surfaced side by side toward the western edge of the Philippines just after midnight on October 23. Radar could be detected too, but a few minutes on the surface was a valuable opportunity, so while the skippers of the USS *Darter* and the USS *Dace* shouted to one another, their radar operators sent signals into the darkness and read the returning echoes.

One of them recognized something in motion. It was a fleet, and a big one—the "Center Force" under Admiral Takeo Kurita—moving into the Philippines from the west and hungering for MacArthur. The *Darter* alerted Halsey's Third Fleet on the opposite side of the archipelago about 260 miles northeast of Samar Island, and both subs went after the enemy. By dawn they were within visual sight and torpedo range, and they sank two heavy cruisers and damaged another in the strait known as the Palawn Passage.[30]

It is likely that the *Franklin*'s crew heard the reason why search planes were being launched, and it must have been a long and suspenseful day as they waited to learn what enemy was out there. About twenty-four hours later it finally paid off when they found not just Kurita's fleet on the west but another to the south as well.

Planes could only stay in the air as long as their fuel lasted, and a shorter distance to the targets meant less time reaching the enemy and more time attacking him. With crews at battle stations, the carriers moved westward in the early hours of October 24 to maximize the time their planes could spend in attack mode. Long before daylight the first planes were launched from only twenty-five miles east of Samar. They circled as one by one their number grew and their formation filled out, then they went after the enemy.[31]

They found Admiral Shoji Nishimura's Southern Force between the islands of Negros and Mindanao and promptly inflicted significant damage upon a battleship and a cruiser. Then they hit the Central Force, which was now in the Subuyan Sea, and did serious damage to the superbattleship *Musashi*.[32] The new Japanese air strategy emphasized offense against U.S. carriers. Planes and poorly trained pilots would no longer be wasted in futile defensive air cover, and the strategy left these fleets wide open to attack. Except for the flak of antiaircraft guns, the American pilots found their targets easy to hit.

Determined offense—to the point of suicide—meant going where the American ships were, and they were to the east. Most of the hard-charging Japanese attackers were successfully countered, but one managed to put a bomb through the flight deck of the light carrier *Princeton*. As the *Princeton* burned, the cruiser *Birmingham* and the destroyer *Irwin* (DD-794) came alongside to rescue her crew. Then the self-destructive potential of a carrier took effect as one of the *Princeton*'s magazines exploded, causing extensive casualties on all three ships.[33] After it became clear that the *Princeton* could not be saved, she was abandoned and then torpedoed to eliminate any possibility that the enemy might learn anything from her hulk.

Even after the American air strikes on the Southern Force, Japanese strategists got the old-fashioned surface ship battle they had sought, but it did them no good. In the Surigao Strait, Japanese and American battleships and other heavy vessels pummeled one another the way ships-of-the-line had done for centuries.[34] This last battle of its type in history, based on a bold Japanese gambit, nonetheless ended in a U.S. victory. Two Japanese battleships went down, one of them taking Admiral Nishimura with it. The remnants of the Southern Force moved away from the action.[35]

Halsey's pilots were returning to their carriers east of the Philippines with good news on the afternoon of October 24. Whatever the Japanese had been up to with those strange fleets over to the west, they appeared to have been stymied. The Central Force had stopped its forward motion, causing it to seem perhaps to be a feint. Meanwhile, other pilots discovered the approaching Northern Force of enemy carriers. As Japanese strategists had anticipated, Halsey assumed that the carriers constituted the main attack, that he needed to hit them before they could hit him, and that this was his chance to finish off the last of Japanese airpower at sea. At 1600 he took the Third Fleet, including the *Franklin*, speedily northward to meet Ozawa. The next day, October 25, American carrier planes easily eliminated the sham air defense sent up by the decoy force, although it cost the *Franklin* three planes lost and others damaged.[36]

The Center Force, though damaged and disrupted, had not been stymied and certainly was not a feint. Pulling itself back into order, the flotilla resumed its course and on October 25 entered the San Bernardino Strait. To the great good luck of the United States, Kurita did not know that Halsey had gone too far away to do him harm. He also did not know that between him and his objective was a force much weaker than his own.

What admirals don't know can hurt them. The six American light carriers, three destroyers, and four destroyer escorts in Kurita's path, like small dogs raising their hackles to appear more formidable, puffed themselves up and fought with such frenetic energy that Kurita seems to have believed he was fighting Halsey's big carriers. With grim selfless courage, Bugeye Steward's recent ship, the USS *Hoel*; another destroyer, the USS *Johnston* (DD-557); and the even smaller destroyer escort *Samuel B. Roberts* (DE-412), with guns blazing, went straight into Kurita's battleships and cruisers. The light carriers had to be saved, and these three little giants sacrificed themselves to save them.

They were not the only heroes. When planes from the light carriers had dropped their bombs or torpedoes, and after they had used up all of their machine gun ammunition, the heat of battle gave them no chance to land and rearm. In one of the great bluffs of military history, they kept big enemy ships on the defensive by diving toward them as though to attack. One ultimately brazen pilot opened his canopy, drew his .38 revolver, and banged away at the Japanese dreadnaughts as he flew past.[37] The bluff worked. Kurita, just as he was about to overwhelm this thin defense but having lost two heavy cruisers, turned around and withdrew to the west.

The Battle of Leyte Gulf was over. The United States had lost the light carrier *Gambier Bay*,[38] and the *Roberts*, the *Johnston,* and the *Hoel* had gone down—in history as well as in fact. MacArthur was safe. Halsey was chagrined.[39] Of Bugeye's recent shipmates, those few who still lived floated on or clung to life rafts.

On the next morning of October 26, Halsey sent a few more air strikes against the decoy force. A torpedo threat was perceived, and the *Franklin*'s screening destroyers *Gridley* and *Maury* dropped depth charges, then the *Franklin* was refueled at sea.[40] Word went around the fleet, through the *Franklin* crew, and to Elden Rogers that other Japanese planes had clearly tried to crash into American ships.[41] One had hit the escort carrier *St. Lo,* and she had sunk very quickly.[42] Elden and his buddies on the *Franklin* thought back to what had happened to them just thirteen days before, when everyone had said the plane that had ripped Lieutenant Winters's pants seemed to be trying to crash into them. It wasn't funny anymore, and it wasn't a relief. It was frightening, disgusting, and a little nauseating.

It helped to hear on October 27 that the *Franklin*'s planes found and sank two destroyers.[43]

Ground forces on Leyte by now had captured some airfields, but heavy rains had made the unpaved runways useless. This required carrier planes to continue a little longer than planned providing air cover for ground forces, and in doing so the *Franklin*'s planes shot down eight fighters over Luzon on October 28. Then the weather became so bad that even the navy planes stopped flying for part of the day. By October 29, when the *Franklin* maneuvered to avoid another submarine that was being fended away by the *Gridley,* fatigue was becoming a problem throughout the fleet, and like everyone else, Elden experienced it.[44]

At sunrise on October 30 the island of Samar was visible fifty-seven miles to the west. The *Franklin*'s crew began with the usual dawn call to general quarters and then afterward remained on alert. Some of her planes were flying defense for other parts of the fleet. As noon approached, two low-flying Bettys were spotted, sending everyone running back to battle stations, but after a time things were clear enough that the readiness condition was relaxed so the men could eat, visit the head, or take care of other needs. In the meantime, the *Franklin* had moved slowly westward cutting the distance to land in half.[45]

Because we do not know where Elden was, except that he was in the division that handled planes on and near the flight deck, the recollections of others are particularly useful. The orchestra was aft on the hangar deck rehearsing, and the notes of Tchaikovsky's 1812 Overture carried far and wide.[46] Stanley Graham was on the starboard side helping to bring fuel from another ship onto the *Franklin*. In the relative calm a perceptive officer near Graham pointed to the no-longer-rotating radar antenna and said, "We are under attack."[47] Then came the shattering signal for general quarters at 1419. Bogies were thirty-seven miles out, and Hellcat fighters were being launched as rapidly as possible to join the combat air patrol in going after them.[48] Such experiences were no longer new, but neither were they calmly accepted. Thirty-seven miles was close, and Elden and many others probably made the mental calculation that things could really get popping by the time they reached their battle stations.[49]

The captain certainly made that calculation. Radar told him there were six attackers, which could be seen to be Judys and Zeros. A plane diving almost straight down at extremely high speed would lose some of its maneuverability, and when he guessed that they were about thirty seconds away and committed to a trajectory, he took action to dodge them. Men on the *Franklin* heard the ship's guns and those of every nearby ship open fire; they felt the vibration; and they shifted body weight to keep balance during the now familiar twists, turns, speedups, and slowdowns. The first attacker, ripped apart by antiaircraft fire, came toward the *Franklin* in pieces and created a great splash barely twenty feet away. A voice on the ship's speaker system screamed, "Hit the deck!"[50] Louis Bonitatibus, like Elden a V-1 sailor, recalled, "I saw the kamikaze coming down, so I ran across the flight deck to the port side of the ship and jumped into the catwalk."[51]

From directly behind this hail of debris a second plane found its mark, slamming through the flight deck near Elden's buddy Nelson Myers and exploding on the gallery deck. Myers was slightly wounded.

A third attacker aimed a bomb at the *Franklin* and pulled out of his dive. Top brass on the bridge watched it sail past them and explode when it hit the water to starboard. The plane then wobbled a couple of miles through hot fire from several ships and crashed into the light carrier *Belleau Wood*. Shells other ships had aimed at the attacker hit the *Franklin,* and shells the *Franklin* had aimed at it hit other ships, but the *Franklin*'s shipboard gunners took credit for downing two planes.[52]

The gallery deck, where the kamikaze had exploded in a ball of fire, shares open space with the hangar deck where the fires quickly produced scenes of rapid action and stark horror. Automatic water curtains deployed on the hangar deck, and men grabbed water hoses. A man completely covered in flames begged Stan Butryn to shoot him, then ran over the open side into the air, into the sea, and we can only hope out of his pain. In places, some of the fires actually penetrated two decks below the hangar deck. One group of men trapped by flames escaped by climbing knotted ropes up the outside to the flight deck.[53] When the fires were out after two and a half hours, thirty-three planes were tallied as destroyed, the Japanese plane dangled with other wreckage in the gallery deck with its dead pilot still seated in the cockpit, and fifty-six charred bodies of his victims lay about, all amid a smell of burned flesh, fuel, paint, and metal.[54] In one final burst of excitement, men returned to battle stations after bogies appeared on radar. When they came close they were fired upon, but happily were recognized as friendly before harm had been done.[55]

Almost in shock, as the *Franklin* listed to starboard, the crew began the work of recovery, collecting the dead, pushing ruined planes and equipment overboard, getting rid of water, and cleaning off the soot. Every man knew that he and his ship had narrowly escaped death and destruction. Elden and the others who worked on the hangar deck and above, especially his wounded buddy Myers, knew it best of all. On October 31, with all hands on deck, the *Franklin* lowered her flag to half mast, held a solemn ceremony led by the Catholic and Protestant chaplains, and dropped the dead six at a time into the sea. Then a seven-man honor guard of marines fired three volleys, and the bugler played taps. It is virtually certain that Elden stood in rank for this ceremony, filled with emotion like everyone else. But in war it is always back to business; the *Franklin* rejoined the tanker fleet, completed the interrupted refueling, and with damaged little sister *Belleau Wood* headed for Ulithi to be further evaluated.[56] Billy Gwin probably spoke for Elden and many others when he remarked to his buddy Robert Tice, "Bobby, I sure wish I was back home with my mama."[57]

The galley had been destroyed, and no cooking could be done. Munching sandwiches of spam, bologna, or maybe canned Vienna sausages, trying to absorb what he had seen and comparing notes with buddies, Elden probably cursed when he heard that the captain who had saved the ship repeatedly was to be replaced.[58] The men may have been grateful to Shoemaker, but the admirals saw it differently. Three times in seventeen days Japanese planes had found their way past radar and through the combat air patrol. Admiral McCain, in reviewing the action report for October 15, had reprimanded Captain Shoemaker for not stating whether the bogies had been spotted on radar.[59]

Virginia wrote of Halloween, and how well she was behaving.

October 31, 1944

My Dear Tex,
This is Halloween night. They had a big party for the little kids up town. I went up for a while and came home right quick because it was so cold. I bought some new records too. I have 101 now, I counted them this evening. I sure wish you could be here to listen to them with me.

I haven't heard from you for so long it seems like you've been gone for ages.

Where are you now or can you tell me. When do you get a furlough or do you know. I wish you would get one real soon now.

Tex, I love you so much and I only hope you really love me too. Someday when we meet again we will know for sure I guess. I've been home about 3 weeks now and I've been staying home every night except when I go to the show with mom. There just isn't any boys here anymore. Maureen wrote and told me when I was in Kansas there was a lot of new boys but I haven't seen any of them & besides I'm waiting for you Tex, darling. I don't want anyone but you.

I hope you don't think I'm silly writing like this but I mean it all. Someday I'll prove it to you.

Write when you find time. Be good.

With Love,

Virginia

At some point, Elden, like many other men, took a small souvenir fragment from the suicide plane. Martin Kassover saw English letters on his piece and deduced that it must have been an old American plane salvaged from three years before. Being a kamikaze required a lot of the pilot, but it did not take much of a plane, and any old craft that could carry explosives into the air would do.[60]

17 Three Cheers—and the End of Cheer

ELDEN was most likely topside, standing in rank order with the *Franklin*'s crew, as she pulled into Ulithi lagoon on November 2 to the sound of three cheers from the crew of the *Wasp*.[1] Bish McKendree would have given a lot to be topside anywhere, even on the *Benjo Maru,* as it arrived at Formosa on the same day, but there was no such luck. The prisoners stayed in their cramped holds for another week.[2]

November 2, 1944

Hello Tex, Darling,

I finally got me some air mail stationery. They hardly ever have any in this town. I got a letter from you today that was mailed Oct. 20 & here it is Nov. 2, it sure takes a long time for letters to get from you to me, maybe this air-mail will go faster, I hope so.

Yes, Tex, I can come to Vega when you get your leave. I'll be glad to. I know you want to be with your mother & father while you're home and I just have to be with you so we'll all try to be together, just let me know when to come. I hope its real soon, it would be nice if you could be home for Christmas but I don't suppose you'll be that lucky.

I'll be waiting for you even if they don't let you come home for 10 years, because I love you so much.

I guess I have told you Maureen was in Vega and saw Carl Six. She said that was the smallest town she ever saw. She said Carl was working at a gas station there.

My brothers will be home from school in a minute & want some dinner, so I had better finish this up. Everything is about the same here, just as dead as ever. Write and be good.

Lots of Love,

Virginia

P.S.

When you write to your mother tell her "hello" for me. I might write to her if I ever find time.

Bish McKendree later guessed that his ship had probably docked at the Formosan port of Takao. Even then the hell continued for another six long days before the prisoners were let out. When they finally debarked after thirty-nine days, even the strongest were weak and many literally crawled ashore. All were loaded onto trains that they rode through the night of November 9. With death imminent for some and approaching in the distance for nearly everyone, they at last got a small break. Guards at this new camp were more humane, and the work was less onerous. Those lucky enough to be alive had a chance to begin to recover strength.[3]

At Ulithi the *Franklin*'s crew took turns by watch group visiting Duffy's Tavern during liberty on Mog Mog island.[4] It was just the usual hot dog or hamburger, two cans of warm weak beer, surf, and land beneath their feet, but the navy called it liberty.[5] The interaction of men from various ships surely would have produced a higher than normal level of storytelling. No one yet fully understood what had just happened, but there were plenty of opinions. The "escape" of the Japanese carriers and whether Halsey had erred either in going after them or in letting them go would have been a primary topic—especially in contrast to the unparalleled heroism of the small ships that had fought off battleships and cruisers. It is virtually impossible that Elden did not hear and join in talk of this matter, perhaps criticizing Halsey or perhaps defending him. Lou Casserino, however, provides one interesting insight into the conversations: "When you went ashore . . . you never talked about your ship—with anyone. It was a superstition," he said. "You talk about your ship when you're *on* your ship."[6] In any case the interlude provided a rare chance to write letters, and also revived hope of running into Vega boys from other ships there. A shuttle boat was available to take men from one ship to another, and Elden had high hopes of seeing hometown friend Red Dewees. Elden's reference to being close to where Bugeye had been may have been a veiled reference to the now-martyred USS *Hoel*. One wonders whether the little cold Elden mentions was actually the effect of smoke inhalation during the fires five days before.

November 4, 1944

Dear Mom, Dad, & Bros, & Grandma,

Today is an unusial day as they have blew mail call Six times and will probably blow two more. I really have been getting mail the last two days.

I have Six of your letters I haven't answered. There wasn't any writeing paper on the ship for quite awhile so I didn't write many letters only borrowed a little once or twice. That's why I didn't for so long. But now I set in a stock before the Hoardeers got it. Ha!

I bought a Sheaffer's lifetime Pen from a buddy so I am having a hard time getting used to it. So you will have to excuse this letter.

No, I don't get a bond a month I get one every three months. You should get another by the first of January or maybe a little later.

I guess you have got moved by now, haven't you? How about a garden will you have one next spring? I hope so as it sure helps.

Well, I just had a big surprise. I found out Red Dewees is here & I rate liberty tomorrow so I will get to see him if he isn't gone on liberty or Something. So wish me luck.

I got three letters from you and one from Virginia today so this was a pretty good day all the way through.

I think I was close to where Bug-Eye was twice. I would have liked to have saw him.

He went to Las Animas & told Virginia He saw me in Honalulu with two girls she wrote me and ask about it. She didn't like it much. I don't know why he would tell a thing like that. I haven't saw him since he was on his boot leave.

I am O.K. Except I have a little cold. I am about to get rid of it tho.

I sure was sorry to hear about Tubby Walcott. It sure is bad but no one will ever say he didn't do his part.

I got the Halloween Card. Thanks a lot Jerry, It sure was cute.

Tell Bug-Eye He don't know what He's talking about when he said there wasn't any trash burner on a ship. There is on here. A ship like he is on don't have enough trash to amount to much. It is a rule on the ship to not throw anything over the side that floats. The enimy might see it and they could tell where you were going.

Well Everything is O.K. & I have to sign off so So Long For This Time.

Lots of Love

Elden

As Elden wrote, battle damage was being assessed to determine how best to get the *Franklin* back into action. The question was whether she could be repaired at Ulithi or whether the work would have to be done back at Pearl Harbor or even on the U.S. mainland. The fire on the *Franklin* had been the most serious that any U.S. naval vessel had survived up to that date, and Halsey himself came aboard to check things out.[7]

This was not a simple job. Facilities in the Pacific were fully occupied with other work, and it was decided to do the job at Bremerton, Washington. Over the speaker system Elden and the crew heard in the great admiral's own voice: "Well, boys, you can go home for Christmas." He warned them not to tell anyone, not even the folks at home, how badly the ship had been damaged or what had caused it.[8] The *Franklin* was filled with happy, cheering young men.

Halsey, always aggressive, dealt with the kamikaze phenomenon by becoming even more so. Combat air patrols could be improved, better fighter planes could be deployed, and the screen of ships that protected carriers could be tightened up or increased, but it was clear that if enemy pilots sent against carriers in large numbers were willing to die doing so, some of them could sometimes get through. Hitting enemy aircraft while they were on the ground therefore became not only a matter of pride but the only completely reliable way to deal with the problem. The first kamikazes had taken off from Luzon, and the day after Halsey inspected the *Franklin* at Ulithi (the day Elden said he would have liberty on Mog Mog) he had Task Force 38 go after whatever planes could be found on Luzon. On November 5 and 6 they destroyed an amazing 439 Japanese airplanes and sank a number of ships.[9] Naval task groups would then go in closer and hit harder. This tactic would prove important to the *Franklin*—and to Elden—after the ship returned to the fight.

Having missed his post-training leave, Elden would have been very happy that he was not one of approximately one hundred unlucky crewmen who were needed aboard other ships and who were transferred rather than allowed to head home. Also, he, like most others, would have felt combined regret and curiosity as Captain James Shoemaker relinquished command. The "old man" whose lucky number had been thirteen had taken the *Franklin* into dangerous places, attacked with success, dodged bombs and torpedoes, kept the men informed, instilled a sense of pride, and had earned their loyalty and admiration.[10] Who could know what would come now?

Elden almost certainly attended a November 8 ceremony on the hangar deck where a very different man took command, a man who wanted everyone to see the difference.[11] Some of the difference could literally be seen, as the new skipper was six feet four inches at a time when six feet was considered tall. Only three others (one of them Roy Treadaway) among the 3,000 men aboard were as big. Captain Leslie Gehres had started his career thirty years earlier as an enlisted man and worked his way up—but if a seaman second class like Elden hoped that having "one of them" in charge might mean increased understanding, he soon learned better.

The first negative sign was a résumé posted here and there detailing everything Gehres had done in his career. Men reading the posting took it as braggadocio, and noted that Shoemaker had never shown such airs. These seasoned veterans had earned by now the right to be cynical about higher-ups, and the posting invoked ridicule when officers were not around.

Gehres's story was actually quite impressive. He had seventeen years' experience as a flyer and had been so good at it that he had been a member of an early version of the navy's exhibition flying team—predecessors of today's Blue Angels. He had held high rank and important commands, but this was his first ship captaincy. The trouble was that the captaincy impressed no one else quite so much as Gehres himself. Like so many others new to an elevated and exclusive brotherhood, he was self-important, and the swagger showed.[12]

Arrogantly careless, or perhaps craftily intentional, he declared in the presence of enlisted men that lax discipline had been a factor in the October 30 hit, and that he would soon fix that problem. Elden and every other crew member heard this within hours as Gehres surely knew they would. It was a damned-fool way to begin, insulting not only a respected predecessor but also a crew that had engaged in four major actions in four months, destroyed three hundred enemy aircraft and seventy-five enemy ships, with the ship's own guns shot down three planes, endured the worst fire survived by any American ship to date, and lost many buddies who were close in the way only combat buddies can be.[13]

Gehres's intention, no doubt, was to lay down a marker, to make November 8, 1944, a day everyone above him and below him would remember. The *Franklin* had already done some great things, but she was almost certain to have the opportunity to do great things in the future, and those accomplishments would be his. Battered and burned when he took over, the ship would soon be renewed and, he thought, strengthened. This was not the sort of captain anyone could imagine sharing his own sense of relief with the crew after a near miss, or jokingly promising better chow after a day's work well done. He wanted a clear and crisp new beginning.

What Gehres accomplished instead was the sorry beginning of a tragic end. The wrenching change from a leader who lifted men up to one who weighed men down created a vicious circle in which negative fed negative, sapping the crew with energy-draining attitudes. For five months the *Franklin* had come unscathed through scrape after scrape, and then suddenly had been hit repeatedly with extreme damage. Men had seen with their own eyes how explosive a carrier could be, and how vulnerable they were aboard it. Superstitions spread by sailors who talked too much held that a ship hit once would be hit again. The enemy had begun to use what was by American standards an appalling tactic, and in the first few days that tactic had succeeded twice against the *Franklin*. People began to rethink the "Lucky 13" legend that a more upbeat captain had cultivated, and soon they were finding negative significance in the string of thirteens attached to the ship. She was CV-13, had the number painted large on her flight deck, carried Air Group 13, had been hit the first time on Friday the thirteenth, and so on.[14] The bully Gehres bullied on, unaware of or unconcerned about the dead weight he had dropped on his crew.

But for now the thought of home offset those things, as on the afternoon of November 11 the *Franklin* left Ulithi for Pearl Harbor.[15] The next day each man filled out a questionnaire about his travel wishes in order that advance arrangements could be made. Elden had said before that he would fly home to save leave time, but the men learned now that air travel was overbooked to the point of unavailability, and that even seats on trains were hard to get.[16] Tantalizingly, the Plan of the Day for November 13 reminded him that the correct uniform, blues and watch caps or flat hats, was mandatory when on leave or liberty.[17] The long-delayed dream began to seem real.[18]

November 19, 1944

My darling Tex,

This is Sunday night and I'm here all alone. My father went to the show and I seen it once in Kansas so I have to stay home. I'd go again but it wasn't very good.

I guess I've told you I got on at the air Base and am going to training school. Its kinda hard to learn every thing they try to teach us but I guess I'll get by O.K. We took our Physical examinations yesterday & took a blood test and got vaccinated for small pox.

I saw Chuck the other day. He said he was going to write & tell you he took me out and got me drunk, don't believe it. You know how much he lies. I think he was lieng about you and those Haiwiian girls too.

I sure hope you get to come home before the first of the year. Honey, I miss you so much and wish I had one of those big kisses you give.

Write, darling, and I'll be looking for you around Christmas. Remember that I love you with all my heart & write real soon.

Loads of Love & Kisses,

Virginia

At 0930 on the day Elden wrote his next letter, he most likely attended a nondenominational memorial service for all lost ship's crew and air crew, conducted by both chaplains on the hangar deck with 1,000 to

1,500 men present.[19] The dentist with whom he has an appointment might have been Dr. H. R. Magnuson, Dr. R. E. Wales, or Dr. H. W. Richardson, who were the ship's dentists in March 1945.[20] The bracelet he mentions, now in my possession and engraved "E. D. Rogers, U.S. Navy, 357-53-50, 1944," tells generations to come that Elden's wrists were small, consistent with his slender, though not slight, build. The reference to "this port," where Krahn was located, tells discerning readers at home that he is approaching Pearl Harbor. Together with the urgent query about the address of Odell Price, known to be stationed in San Francisco, and the wistful question about the length of Gerald's Christmas vacation, Elden did his best to say he was on the way home.

November 19, 1944

Dear Mom, Dad, Bros & Grandma,

I don't have anything to Do so I can't think of a better way of Spending the afternoon than writeing letters.

I am getting an appointment with the Dentist to have another Tooth filled. It don't hurt me yet but I'll get it fixed before it does. They won't do anything to the one with the corner broke off.

I haven't had much to Do So I have been making me a bracelet out of Stainless Steel. I sure am going to Like it when I finish it. Sure takes a long time tho.

Say How about Getting Odells address for me and Send it in Your next letter. Don't forget. I sure do want it. I might get to See him Sometime.

How long is Gerald getting off for Christmas? I sure would like to be there but all I can do is hope.

I wrote to Virginia a few minutes ago, to you, Myrn & Rowena & I will be caught up for awhile.

I haven't Got Sixes address yet. We will get mail in a day or two so I may get it then.

I sure hope I get to See Krahn. He was at this Port The Last time I was here But I didn't have his address Then.

How is Gerald & Gooffy by now? I guess Gerald is Still keeping him up. Ha Or has Goff come back yet?

Well I Better Close & Take a Shower, Eat Supper & Go to The movies. So long for today.

With Love,

Elden

In wartime no waters anywhere were safe, but farther each day from the combat zone work became less serious, and some days were even fun. On November 20 officers presented a play called "Franklin Frolics" with Dowell orchestra music on the hangar deck at 0900; one improvised song, probably enjoyed by Elden because it was in the country music mode, was raunchy enough to provoke Chaplain Harkin to anger.[21] Afterward there was a volleyball tournament. Elden and the others heard it announced that a crewman had been found with seventy-five pairs of loaded dice. The point was to avoid shooting dice, as presumably the sailor had been selling them and if so no crap game anywhere on board could be safe. A day later the prescribed uniform was dungarees as the *Franklin* put in at Pearl Harbor for a quick inspection to assess repair needs.

Although Elden would have enjoyed seeing Krahn, he was by no means disappointed when they cast off the very next day heading eastward. It was Thanksgiving Day that November 23, and nothing lay east of Hawaii but the mainland United States. Ironically, as the battered warship took its fuzzy-cheeked crew away from the life-threatening dangers they had learned to consider routine, each morning's Plan of the Day began to emphasize dangers that were altogether different. Young men taken from home in boyhood and jerked by sudden experience into a maturity unlike any other, at a stage in life when most strongly attracted to the opposite sex, but who had not so much as seen a girl for almost half a year, might be particularly vulnerable while on leave. Venereal disease, the plans warned, could be anywhere—emphasizing *anywhere*—even with one's sweetheart back home as well as with the working girls in ports. Preventative condoms could be purchased on board.[22]

The back of the envelope enclosing Virginia's next letter, along the line of the seal, bears the letters "W.W.A.P.S.W.A.K.I.L.T.S.T.O.T." Letters five through eight may be interpreted as "sealed with a kiss," but the others remain encoded. Elden, we presume, might have understood the message.

November 24, 1944

Tex darling,

How are you honey? Are you still on "big ben"? Do you still love me like you used to? Have you heard from Chuck? He said he was going to write to you.

Mary & I finally got on at the Air Base. I bought a bond today. I'll buy all the bonds if it will get you home sooner. I've been working about two weeks now and I've stayed home every night. I haven't even went to a show. I'm always so tired I just come home & eat supper & go to bed. I've found out I can't run around and work too. Did you have a nice Thanksgiving dinner? I had to work so it didn't seem like Thanksgiving day to me.

I'm hoping and praying that you get to come home before the first. I can hardly wait to see you in your uniform. I'll bet you are the handsomest man on the ship.

Is Carl Six still here in the states? I sure feel sorry for him if he hates the army or what ever he's in. I know nobody likes to be in the service but I think he would take it harder than most other fellows. Earl was home from Boot camp for a little while. His wife is sure cute.

Chuck & Kial & Herman are still here. Herman goes steady with Wanda. She hasn't got her divorce yet tho. Andy & Barbara got a divorce & Pat & Florence have this divorce now & Pat is getting married again.

Bernice bought her a car and wrecked it the night she bought it. She works at the air base too. She is about to get married to Freddie P. Do you know him?

Everyone around here is either getting married or divorced.

That's all the news there is I guess. I heard Chuck Steward was going to start working at the air base. He lies so much you can't tell whether he's lieing or not.

Write when you have time and I hope you get a furlough pretty soon. I'll be waiting for you, my darling. I love you with all my heart & hope you can come home soon to your waiting sweetheart.

All my Love & Kisses,

Virginia

It is hard enough to keep a secret at any time but especially hard when the secret consists of wonderful news. On November 25 Elden redoubled his signals, in ways that would not violate censorship rules, that he is headed toward home. Even the mention of listening to the radio broadcast of a football game that morning was one such signal, for had he still been in the western Pacific the football game would have been played in the middle of the night, and the broadcast would not have reached that far anyway. "I have given up hope on seeing Bish now" is a signal that he is no longer near the Philippines. "I might see Odell" tells us he may be near San Francisco. That he has opened his Christmas presents a month prematurely is not a confession of misbehavior but rather a statement that he may be at home by the magic day. Our parents were a bit puzzled by some of these repeated hints, but they knew he was trying to tell them something and they began to nurture hope that they might see him before long.[23]

November 25, 1944

Dear Mom, Dad, & Bros,

as I have five letters from you that I haven't answered I'll try to do so now. Everything is ok out here. Hope it's the same at home.

I sure hated to hear of Jackie Worsham Getting hurt. Has he got any Better or have you heard?

What kind of work is Bug-Eye doing in Tucum do you know?[24]

I listened to a football game on the Radio This morning Ohio State V.S. Michigan. Was pretty good.

Well Thanksgiving is over. I would have liked to have been home. I had a good Dinner. We had Turkey, Dressing, Cranberrys, Pie, Ice Cream, Lemonade & I can't Think what Else.

I have given up hope on seeing Bish now. I might See Odell sometime tho.

I never got to see Red.

I never knew Six was in Arkansas. His letter hasn't got here yet. I haven't heard from him since he went into the Service.

I was Glad to get the picture of Rowena & Margie. All The Guys in my Div. wanted Their addresses I told them I didn't know Their address. If I hadn't told them That They would be Getting letters from every Guy in the Div.

Yes I have The watch You sent[25] & The Other Package. I was going to wait till Christmas to Open them but the Temptation was to Great. I really am proud of it. Thanks a million for Everything. But I really Didn't expect to much. I got a package from Myrn Too.

Sure did Hate to Hear about Bill & Loretas Baby. They sure have a lot of bad luck.[26]

Yes, we are going to get Certificates like Dub got. I saw one This morning They sure are Pretty. I'll Send mine Home when I get it.

Well I Kinda Doubt if I get a leave for Christmas But I may Get one before Too Long Tho. Wish me luck.

Well Must Close for Now and Write Virginia & Myrn. Aunt Myrn said Bill Roberts was in The Navy at Great lakes Ill. He won't never be sorry he Got in The Navy. So Long For now.

With Love,

Elden

From Virginia came a Christmas card, with the printed words "Christmas Greetings to One in the Navy. Ahoy there Mr. Navy Man! May Christmas bring good cheer, And good luck. Keep the watch for you, All through a grand New Year." Handwritten "Forever yours, Virginia" Inside a fold of the card is the following note.

November 26, 1944

Dearest Tex,

Boy, this is really a dreary old day. It snowed yesterday and is about all melted now. Some kids are coming down this afternoon and we are all going Pheasant hunting. I wish you were here to go with us.

I haven't heard from you for a long time. How often do you get the mail, every time you come in to San Francisco? Maybe you haven't been getting my letters.

This is kinda early to send a Christmas card but it might take till Christmas for it to get there.

Write, darling and send me another picture of you when you get them taken.

With all my Love,

Virginia

News that Halsey had awarded the *Franklin*'s crew a unit commendation for their October 30 response would have offset somewhat the new captain's insinuations about the crew's culpability, but for now that dominating personality daily grew less important. Every young heart thrilled when land became visible, and a comforting feeling grew as the *Franklin* sailed into Puget Sound and was embraced not just by land, but by homeland. A different emotion was present at Orchard Point on November 27, as Air Group 13 left for other duties, never to rejoin the *Franklin*. Then, at 1700 on November 28 the wounded warship settled into her own hospital bed for the next several weeks, dry dock number 5 at Puget Sound Naval Yard, Bremerton, Washington.[27]

Everyone could not just head for home at the same time, but half the crew left immediately for twenty days' leave. Elden was among those who had to contain his eagerness and stay for the second round, but in compensation that meant he could be at home on Christmas Day. Although he must have been filled with yearning to hit the road, after where he had been and what he had seen, he also must have felt a sense of ease just being inside the United States. With his ship the subject of repair rather than a home to its crew, he slept in barracks for the first time in six months, finding strange the immobility of the floor beneath his feet and equally strange the eerie quiet that replaced the constant metabolic roar of a ship under way. For once, he and his buddies had plenty of leave. On some days he could see Mount Rainier in the distance, and every day beautiful Seattle rose up sharp little hills from a charming waterfront. The young women there were amazing things just to look at—works of art—and they also knew that these men had earned friendly attention. Elden had remarked about it being easy to save money while at sea, but it cannot have been so easy in this favorite port of most sailors.

18   "Anybody Home?"

Hello!!!

Bremerton, Washington
December 3, 1944

Surprised?

I'll bet you are.

I am at Bremerton, Washington now. Will be here quite ahwile.

I am comeing Home. I may not make it by Christmas but if I Don't I'll be there Shortly after. I'm O.K. I never Received a scratch all time I was gone. I will get 20 Days Leave. I will make it Home This Time I Think. I have signed the papers & have the money in my Pocket for my Ticket. So Don't wory about me any more. I know you Couldn't help it. But as Murph Says You can rest assured I'll Be O.K. Now.

I went to Seattle last nite I sure did feel funny with women around I just couldn't get used to it.

I guess Murph is still in jail aint he? I sure Wish He could have saw what I have. He would Think his Duty in Idaho was a Pleasure.

So Long For Now.

See You Soon

With Love,

Elden

Grace had not yet received this wonderful news when she wrote a long "line or two" on the back of a salvaged *Longhorn News* in order to share tidbits about Elden's friends who were still in Vega High School. Elden's only surviving grandparent, Julia Tegarden, was in Vega, and suffering from a cold. Dr. O. H. Lloyd had prescribed something for her sore throat, most likely a diluted opiate that made his patients feel good no matter what ailed them. Doc Lloyd and his wife, Lulu Mills Lloyd, had arrived in Vega in 1908, six years after its founding, and he had been the attending physician at my birth thirty years later. Among the many services he provided was tooth extraction, and it was said that he kept every tooth acquired in this manner in a quart jar on a windowsill of the office in his home.

December 6, 1944

Dear Son,

Ill write a line or two on this School paper & send it on. Gerald said he didn't happen to get one last week So he got this one out of the Waste Paper basket at the post Office—hope this finds you fine & dandy. We are all O.K. only Mama she has a sore throat. I went & seen Loyd & he gave me some Medicine for her. She sure feels tough. She wanted to go home this week but don't look like she will for a few days.

Well this is Thursday Dec 7. I never got this finished last night So will see if I can tonight. Mama is some better. But Not too good yet. She will go home soon as she is able. I may go with her if she don't want to go alone.

I washed & Churned today & about a Jilllion other things.

Billy Valentine was hurt very badly the other day. She had gotten off a bus & a Car struck her some how. It broke both legs & she has a skull fracture. It happened Sunday & she is still unconscious. They don't think she can possibly live.

Well Gerald never came home from school this evening So guess he went with the bunch to Canyon to play basketball. He didn't know if he was going to get to go or not.

We had a letter from Cloe [Cloria Roberts] yesterday. She said Billy [Cloe's son Billy Roberts] was at the Great Lakes—she said he sure was glad to get the Navy. She said he tried it once & Couldn't make it. She said La Veta [Cloe's daughter La Veta Roberts] Carried your picture in her Billfold & shows it to every one & tells them that's her good looking Sailor Cousin.

Well I don't know much to write. We had an awful Snow Storm Monday & the highway guys Just got all the snow off the roads today. Sure was bad in places.

I'm going to send this Common Mail as this paper is so heavy. You'll probably get it as soon any how.

Bye. Mom & all[1]

Young Billy Valentine died two days later.[2]

Elden informed his parents by letter that he was back in the States, but he had sent Virginia a telegram, which should have made her feel special. Her December 11 letter to him is folded inside a Christmas card printed: "Christmas Greetings to my Sweetheart in the Service. To tell the joy, I wish for you, No card could have the space, But Merry Christmas, Sweetheart Dear, There's no one takes your place." And handwritten: "Loads of Love, Virginia."

December 12, 1944

Dearest Tex,

I have to go to work in about an hour. I work nights now & don't even get to go to a show. When you get your leave I'll quit my job & go to Vega with you, my darling. I sure hope you get it real soon. Write & tell me a few days ahead of time so I can kinda get things ready.

A lady just came in to see Mom & I can't write very well with them setting here gossiping so you'll know whats the matter if you can't read this.

I saw Chuck up at the Main Café yesterday afternoon. He sure likes himself. He stood there & looked at his-self in the mirror & tried his hat on different ways. Maybe he was drunk or something.

I haven't seen Kial or Charlie for about two weeks now. They haven't gone to the army yet. Where is Carl Six now? In the same place? Tell your mom hello for me when you write to her. I sure like her even if I have never met her. The letter she wrote me was so sweet & friendly. I would sure like to meet her.

My dad went to Kansas last week on the bus. My grand mother fell & broke her hip. I wish you were here & we could use the car while hes gone. Mom said we could. She really likes you. She knows you are a nice boy. She doesn't like Chuck very well I don't think. He lies so much.

Tex, darling, I love you so terribly much & miss you more than any thing in the whole world. I hope you get to come home in a few weeks.

Good bye my darling & write.

Love & kisses,

Virginia

On December 19, 1944, the *Franklin*'s executive officer, Commander Joe Taylor, distributed two memoranda to that part of the crew that was about to go on leave, one providing transportation plans and one warning the men to resist the urge to tell family and friends of the many things they had experienced. In the first memo Taylor says that it appears that the *Franklin* crew would be allowed a special train from Seattle to Chicago and back. It reminds us today of how young these people were when he relates that railroads are reluctant to provide special trains for groups like the crew of a specific ship because buddies tend to be rowdier and more destructive of property than servicemen traveling individually. He counsels the men to behave well. The train was to leave Seattle and proceed eastward through Cheyenne, Wyoming, and then to Milwaukee and beyond, and would return via the same route.[3] We are no longer certain just how Elden got to Vega, but we recall that he hitchhiked at least part of the way. It seems likely that he rode this special train to Cheyenne, which must have been a heady experience, and then took other trains to Denver and thence to Amarillo, probably hitchhiking from Amarillo to Vega.

A match flared in the dark, "Anybody home?" asked a baritone voice. "My son!" Grace exclaimed as we all jumped up and surrounded Elden. We had been asleep in the small lean-to on the north side of our little board-and-batten house on Sixth Street at its corner with East Main. A cloth curtain made of old sheets divided the space into two bedrooms. Mom and Dad slept in a bed on the east side of the curtain, and Gerald and I in a bed on the west side. Elden had entered the house silently, dropped his duffel bag, and stepped into the room before waking us. It was the happiest moment of this story.

Although Elden had already written that he had been at Bremerton, Washington, Taylor's memorandum said he was not to be specific about the location of his ship beyond that it was "in a west coast port for overhaul and alteration." Concerning his experiences, he could only say that his ship had been part of the fast carrier fleet operating in the western Pacific, including the campaigns in the Marianas, Palau, Formosa, the Philippines, and the big battles in the Philippine Sea. He could say the *Franklin* had been under enemy attack, but could not mention either damage or casualties. He could not mention the names of other ships associated with the *Franklin*. He could not mention Air Group 13, engage in guesswork about where they might go in the future, or mention by name the islands of Eniwetok, Manus, or Ulithi.[4] A slogan of the era, "Loose Lips Sink Ships," was fully in play. Elden complied with the order and did not mention these things, but he did draw ink lines on a map of the Pacific showing where he had been.[5]

Elden surely must have felt the sense of unreality reported by others during this brief period at "home." What was home, anyway? We lived in a different house than the one he had left to join the navy, and he had lived away for the best part of a year before that. He could not release emotional burdens, whether of pride or fear or loneliness or grief, by telling what he had seen, and if he had doubts about his Colorado sweetheart he kept them to himself. He knew that even if he had been free to talk, the communication would have been frustrating because much of what he might have described could only be comprehended by others who had experienced something like it. *Franklin* pilot Willard Gove told Steven Jackson that friends and family back at home had little concept of what had been happening in the Pacific, and the things they could talk with him about such as coping with rationing and shortages, eating margarine rather than butter, and collecting scrap metal seemed to him trivial.[6] It could not have been different for Elden; he could be grateful for statements that people at home were supporting their men in uniform, but behind his polite smile and respectful response there must have been an unspoken "If you only knew." The more sensitive among the hometown people must have recognized the communication gap, aware, although only faintly so, of how little they could understand. The fools who did not, and there were some, must have been insufferable.

But it was home, after all. This was his place and these were his people. More importantly, it was not the combat zone. The talk would have included sympathetic mention of Bish McKendree, whose new, more humane captors at about this time allowed a group of British prisoners to put on a variety show including costumes, skits, songs, dancing, and jokes.[7]

Elden's heavy woolen blue uniform was right for that Christmas season, and he wore it as directed. He also wore it for the pleasure of his mother, who thought he looked especially handsome in it. She saw to it that he went to nearby Amarillo and sat for a studio portrait, and she paid extra to have it hand-tinted (as was common in the days before color photography).

Elden also got into civilian clothes when he could, no doubt enjoying the comfort of cowboy boots and Levis and the feel of a white Stetson hat borrowed from his dad. Even then, though, his sailor's stance and walk were noticeable. He and Junior Blasingame posed for Kodak pictures while brandishing a big pistol in Wild West settings at the Rock Island Railroad's livestock shipping pens (see fig. 4). There is a photo of Grace, Ancell, Elden, Gerald, and myself on the front porch of the house (see fig. 5). These photographs convey the appearance of sunny and relatively warm weather for December.

December 30, 1944

Dearest Tex,

I hope you had a merry Christmas & will have a happy New Year. I'll bet you will really throw a big one New years eve won't you? I don't blame you tho. I guess I would too if I was in the Navy & knew I probably wouldn't be home again for a long time.

I thought you had forgotten all about me after you went home. I didn't get your letter until today.

Don't worry about the ring you are going to get me because I still feel the same toward you even if I don't have a ring.

I guess I'll see you about the 6th won't I? I have a roll of films that I want to use up on us when you get here so come down in the afternoon & we will be hoping the sun shines nice & bright. I bet your folks were glad to see you & they will hate to see you leave again so soon.

Well, bye now & I'll be looking forward to next Saturday.

Loads of Love,
Virginia[8]

Virginia was right: we had been glad to see Elden, proud for other people to see him looking so good in his uniform, and we were very sad to have him leave again after so short a time. None of us could know that on January 3, 1945, Admiral Raymond Spruance had completed his plan for the capture of Okinawa or that this plan would take Elden from us forever.[9] Nor could we know that on that same day Bish McKendree took heart from seeing American warplanes over Formosa for the first time.

With the substantial risk of error in the memory of a freshly minted six-year-old, now dimmed and altered by the passage of seven additional decades, I recall taking Elden to the train station in Amarillo in the very early morning darkness of January 5, 1945. Our family car was a 1930 Ford Town Car, a big sedan as Model A's went. Electrical wiring was not in those days what it is today; insulated by rubber wrapped in fabric, it had a tendency to short out various circuits, resulting in a sudden temporary electrical failure. If the wiring in the ignition switch, for example, shorted out, the engine would die as we were going down the road. Ancell's remedy was to grab a pair of pliers kept always on the floorboard by the driver's seat and rap on the dashboard with them. This would somehow restore the circuit, the engine would catch up, and we would continue chuckalucking along with the sound unique to the Model A engine. Lights were subject to similar quirks, and as we followed Route 66 home from Amarillo in pitch dark, and at a point just west of today's junction with Loop 335, the headlights blinked out. As Ancell jiggled the light switch, trying to fix the problem without stopping, the car drifted off the right shoulder of the pavement and struck a mailbox in front of a farm house. The lights came back on, and a chagrined Ancell continued down the road, turning the nearest he ever came to an accident in a lifetime of driving into a hit-and-run of sorts.

Elden took the Fort Worth & Denver Railroad northwestward from Amarillo through Dalhart, Texline, and Clayton to Pueblo, Colorado, and then caught a bus eastward to Las Animas to see Virginia. Telephone service beyond almost any immediate locality in those days was expensive and sometimes difficult. Elden tried without success to call ahead, but once again he arrived in Las Animas without Virginia know-ing he was there, losing part of the precious and dwindling time for the two to be together.

January 5, 1945

Hello,

I got here at 5:30 This afternoon. I tried to call Virginia 3 times today But couldn't make connections. I will see her when she gets home. Will write more at Puebalo.

Love,

Elden[10]

P.S. I Phoned to Puebalo just now and don't have to leave till 9:40 in the morning.

The ever-patient Elden appears to have decided to enjoy the little time he could have with Virginia rather than to fret about why she did not join him until 1:30 A.M. Six weeks later, in a letter to Grace, Virginia will imply that she had been at work. In any case, they spent the next five and a half hours together, presumably in her living room. Then he made his way back to Pueblo, probably by bus unless he hitchhiked or some-one in Virginia's family drove him, to resume his railroad journey to Denver. From there he mailed this postcard, then perhaps continued to Cheyenne to reconnect with the *Franklin*'s special train on January 7 in order to reach Seattle on January 8.

January 6, 1945

Dear Folks,

Well the train was to leave Puebalo at 9:40 but it left at 11:30. Sure Glad it was late or I wouldn't have made it. I have about 2½ hours layover here. I leave here at 5:10. I was with Virginia from 1:30 till 7:00 This morning. I sure am sleepy.

Love,
Elden

Elden, like servicemen everywhere, needed to feel the love and commitment of a girl "back home." These young men and women, at the hormonal peak of mutual attraction and wrenched by the magnification that war could produce—by the terrible recognition that any moment together might be their last—took chances they might never have taken in settled times. Many liaisons led to unintended pregnancies, and many more to ill-founded marriages. A boy and girl meeting at a USO dance shortly before the boy was to ship out might marry at once on impulse. It was virtually a patriotic duty for girls at home to correspond with lonely sailors and soldiers, as Elden's cousins Rowena Coin and Frances Rogers corresponded with his buddies Bob Bamburg and Roy Treadaway. The acuteness of danger, loneliness, and sense of obligation could produce very poignant letters, and these could produce feelings of love and commitment entirely out of proportion to a couple's actual compatibility.[11] Elden and Virginia were no different, and something about that night made things different than they had been before.

January 12, 1945

Dear Mom, Dad, & Bros,
Well I'll try to write a few lines tonight before I go To bed.

I made it back O.K. The Train was two hours late or I wouldn't have caught it in Puebalo.

Virginia & I had quite a bit of fun even if we didn't have much time.

I think I'll get married the next time I come home. I haven't decided yet whether to Wait Till The Duration or not.

Well I hope to Stay here ahwile. We are supposed to get The job Completed the 29th. I hope we don't tho.

I haven't Got to see Bryan Yet. I Guess I will Go see him monday.

I really was tired when back. I got back at 4 P.M The 8th.

Well I better close & Sleep a while as it is 10:30

Lots of Love,

Elden

Bryan was probably Bryan Williams from Vega, who was actually a distant cousin, though so removed that the families hardly regarded one another as kin. Duty in Bremerton was good, as duty for enlisted men went, living in barracks with lots of elbow room rather than in the cramped spaces aboard a ship, enjoying fresh fruits, vegetables, milk, and eggs rather than the shipboard canned, condensed, or powdered versions.[12] Seattle had the reputation of being the best liberty port during the war. Girls there were glad to meet sailors, and grateful civilians would often pick up bar or meal tabs.[13] With little work to do, frequent liberty in Seattle caused Elden to hope the ship's repair might not be completed on time.

Meanwhile, on the day Elden next wrote, Bish McKendree, wearing a newly issued woolen British army overcoat and new shoes, boarded a less hellish ship called the *Melbourne Maru* bound for Japan. He arrived there two weeks later and was taken by train through Tokyo with window blinds drawn to prevent the prisoners seeing the bomb damage. As the month ended he reached Odati, a mining camp on the far northern part of the island of Honshu where snow was three feet deep.[14]

January 13, 1945

Dear Mom, Dad & Bros,

I guess I'll try writeing a few lines tonight & put it in with these things.

I am O.K. & doing fine. Ted Hickman made a $5.00 bet on quitting cigarettes. I haven't smoked a one since the 9th & have only smoked my pipe four or five Times. I guess I'll stay quit for good.

I am going over to see dale Pingel in a day or two. Tommorrow maybe.

Well I worked all day & I am Pretty Tired so I'll Sign off for Tonight. So Long For now.

With Love,

Elden

Dale Pingel's family farmed southwest of Vega, and Ted Hickman was a crewmate from southeast Texas whom Elden had known since boot camp. Quitting smoking is a hard thing to do, requiring some short-term suffering in return for long-term better health. It would be particularly hard amidst the stress of tense and dangerous situations, and one would think it was a sign of Elden's optimism about having a longer and better life after the war was over. There was plenty to be optimistic about: the Japanese navy was virtually gone, and the American navy was growing at an amazing speed.[15]

19   I Don't Think I'll Make It

As the *Franklin*'s crew reassembled and the relief of leave dropped away, a somber mood reconstituted itself and began to spread; a mood shaped less by war than by the authority figure from whom leave had been a respite. Captain Gehres, tall, broad, arrogant, pompous, openly contemptuous toward those he should have been energizing, cast upon his crew a pall as large as his outsized shadow. Trailing anxiety among officers and enlisted men everywhere he went, he was sought out only when necessary and avoided whenever possible.[1] Under this cloud the scuttlebutt of superstitious sailors picked up where it had left off. When repairs at Bremerton were nearly done, a substantial number of men "went over the hill," risking dishonor and imprisonment in the hope of getting away from Gehres, his ship, and its destiny.[2]

Technically better than ever, with a new and improved catapult, the *Franklin* was back in the water by January 28, 1945. For three days she conducted tests up and down Puget Sound, past the lush islands and inlets, with Seattle draped downward from hilltops to water, and, if the weather was clear, with Mount Rainier looming in the southeast.[3] Then on February 2 she left Port Townsend and in early afternoon exited the sound southbound through cold weather and rough seas along the Washington, Oregon, and Northern California coastline. There was one more stop to make stateside, and on February 4 they sailed under one of the world's most unmistakable landmarks, the red-orange and graceful Golden Gate Bridge, into San Francisco Bay. Passing the prison island of

Alcatraz on port side and the city starboard, with all hands who were free to do so surely taking in these great sights, just before noon the *Franklin* docked at the carrier pier of Alameda Naval Air Station.[4]

It seems likely that Elden felt a derisive contempt, this sailor who was determined never to get a black mark on his record, as he saw or heard about deserters being marched aboard under guard. These were the clever fellows who had gone AWOL at Bremerton. As soon as the *Franklin* was out of sight, they had turned themselves in, believing they would spend a few days in the brig and then be reassigned to another ship. They had reckoned without railroads, however, or the possibility of another mainland stop, and were astonished to be hustled aboard a train bound for San Francisco. Returned to their tormentor, they were deposited in Leslie Gehres's brig in the bowels of his ship.[5]

The *Franklin* was at Alameda to take on her new fliers and their planes: Air Group 5, which numbered 110 planes, 20 more than the ship had carried before.[6] Piloted by marines and crewed by marine gunners, none of whom would be called bellhops, Air Group 5 brought the standard Curtiss SB2C Helldiver bombers and Grumman TBM-3 torpedo planes, but it also brought the magnificent Chance-Vaught F4U Corsair fighters. These navy-blue powerhouses could exceed 400 miles per hour in level flight, and seriously outclassed the Japanese Zeros. As part of an anti-kamikaze strategy, a higher percentage of a carrier's planes now consisted of fighters for the defense of the ship. This air group included the Black Sheep Squadron, later made famous by a television series, but its commander, "Pappy" Boyington, was now in a Japanese prison camp after having been shot down and replaced by Stan Bailey.[7]

Elden looked for but failed to find Shorty Green from Vega, but with effort he located the duty station of Odell Price and quietly walked up and tapped him on the shoulder as he pecked at a typewriter. Price was so delighted that he (somehow) took the rest of the day off and took Elden home to see his wife, Verda Mae, daughter of Grace Rogers's neighbor Iva Mathes.

That evening of February 6, 1945, mellowed by alcohol and a home-cooked meal with people who were from home but who were in the navy, Elden could at last let his guard down. He knew too many things to keep them all in. He knew he had come close to death during the October hits. Fleet carriers were the enemy's primary targets. No amount of surrounding defense could shield them completely from fliers who were willing to die reaching them. Even the fearless Halsey kept his flag aboard a battleship rather than a carrier.[8] That the *Franklin* had been hit by a dud torpedo meant it could be hit by functional ones. A carrier was its own form of floating bomb that only required ignition from an accident or an outside source, and his new duty station in Hangar Deck Control was squarely in the volatile core. Enemy bombs had exploded only feet from the *Franklin,* one had barely struck it, and others might be better aimed. The captain was a jerk, and soldiers' tales said thirteen was no longer lucky and a ship that had been hit once would be hit again. It is commonly said that men in combat are keenly aware of death all around them but that they always think it will happen to the other guy. Maybe Elden had felt that way when he and Hickman quit smoking, but not on this night. Weeping, probably from pent-up emotions he had been unable to release either with shipmates or people back at home, he told Odell and Verda Mae that if he sailed on that ship, he did not think he would see home again.

Odell had a colleague who wanted sea duty, and here was a friend from home who wanted shore duty. In a flurry of activity during Elden's brief time at Alameda, they tried every way they could think of to arrange for Elden and Odell's colleague to exchange duty posts. They almost had it done, but in the end Elden's division officer refused to concur. Weeks later, Ancell would observe that the request was denied because Texans like Elden know how to do things. Decades later, we attribute the denial to a combination of two factors: that the division officer had a high opinion of Elden as a dependable person in a significant job, and that the *Franklin* already had too many new crewmen who still needed to be trained in their jobs.[9]

Elden was by no means alone in his premonition. About the many partings taking place as he said goodbye to Odell and Verda Mae, the *Franklin*'s first postwar history says, "There was something fateful about that last evening; many who lost friends or loved ones on Big Ben have spoken of an overpowering feeling that these goodbyes were final."[10]

As the Golden Gate Bridge fell out of sight behind them on the next afternoon, Elden wrote a long letter filled with references to relatives and to people from Vega. Probably to remind readers always to look for hidden messages, he almost emphatically fell back into the old coded language to say he is en route from San Francisco to Hawaii. His mention of Verda Mae's mother getting a telephone reveals something of the state of "progress" at home. He tells of a new job, which he does not say is in a small compartment hanging on the port side wall of the hangar deck, with three large windows looking out on an enormous mostly open space 654 feet long by 70 feet wide.[11] He guesses that the new post is a relatively safe place in battle, as indeed it was safe from many of the dangers he had seen before. The bullets of strafing enemy planes were unlikely to reach this duty station, nor were the "friendly" shells that other American ships might fire at such planes. But he knew well what a hangar deck can become, and he was not going to tell his parents the truth about his intuitions.[12]

February 7, 1945

Dear Mom, Dad & Bros,
Well I guess you thought I had forgotten You I haven't written in so long. I haven't I've just been buisy.

Well Luck was for me for a change. I got to see Odell last nite. He was supposed to work but he got off & we went and saw Verda Mae. Little Shorty green was gone so I never got to see him. I ate supper with them I really enjoyed a home cooked meal for a change.

Odell really has a good job. He don't do anything but peck a typewriter.

He says he thinks he will get to stay two years. And I guess he will unless he fouls up his record.

I walked in the office and he never saw me until I walked up beside him and started to tap him on the sholder.

He really was surprised and tickled to Death. He reached over for his Hat & Told the officer in charge That he was leaving. He does just about what he pleases. The lucky Devil.

I lost my address book and never got to see Bryan or Dale. I sure did Hate it. I just remembered enough of "odes" to find Him. It took three hours to find him then.

How about sending me a small address book I really do need one & cant buy them on the ship.

Have McKendrees Heard from Bishop any more? You can never Tell He may have been one of the prisoners who was rescued on Luzon.[13] I sure do Hope so.

I got a letter from you and you said Iva was putting in a telephone & Iva wrote Verda and said you helped her paint.

You have wrote me about three letters since I have ans them.

I work in a small office on the hangar deck now. I like it a lot better. All I have to do is answer the telephone and a few things like that. I'ts a pretty safe place to be in battle I guess.

I should have more time to write letters now. I will be able to write oftener than the last time out.

Say Gerald that place sold out of knives I tried three different times to get one for You. I'm sorry.

I have saw "Ode" so I hope to be lucky enough to find Krahn some of these days.

I sure was glad to hear that Vega won the Basketball Tournament. I haven't had time to write lately so I owe almost everyone a letter Myrn, Frances, Virginia, Rowena, Grandma, Six, & Snails have all wrote letters I should answer pretty soon. Well maybe I will have time tonight I'll Try.

I guess I had better sign off for This afternoon.

So Long for Now.

Lots of Love,

Your Son,

Elden

Oahu was sighted at 0459, just short of an hour into the second watch on February 13, and at five minutes past noon the *Franklin* tied up at Ford Island's pier F-13, on the opposite side of the island from the present USS *Arizona* Memorial. There was time for liberty, but not much. Wig Price, Odell's cousin, spotted the *Franklin* moored not far from his own ship and tried unsuccessfully to get aboard. He reached Elden by telephone, and as they talked Elden said: "Things were so bad in our last tour out there that I don't think I will make it this time." Although Elden would see at least two other Vega friends while in Hawaii, he and Wig would not succeed in getting together before the USS *Copahee* took Wig to sea on February 22.[14]

In addition to ten more planes, the *Franklin* now carried four hundred more men than before. A greater number than that were new, the old hands had grown rusty, and the air group was new to the ship. Training was necessarily a much higher priority than liberty, and for three weeks they got plenty of it. In waters off Hawaii gun crews used up huge amounts of live ammunition to make the practice as realistic as possible. As just one example of the need for practice, the power of the new Corsairs took some getting used to.[15] A landing pilot whose approach was slightly wrong might be waved off at the last instant by the landing signals officer. In lesser planes a pilot might instantly apply full throttle to pull the plane back to flying speed, but the resistance of a thirteen-foot propeller against a 2,000-horsepower engine could roll these planes over and send one crashing onto the deck or upside down into the water. Statistics tell the story—in sixteen days with no enemy involved there were three fatalities, one midair collision, and twelve planes lost.[16] Crewmen like Elden would have remarked on the irony of dying in practice when there were battles to be fought.

Vernon Gayle Bowen from Post, Texas, who later lived in Canyon, Texas, was one of the "green" crew members who had come aboard at Bremerton. He was quartered on the fourth deck, but his battle duty was as a loader on a gun mount. "I had to go from the 4th deck up ladders to the hangar deck, and then on up to the gun mount when we would go to battle stations." He and Elden were not far apart, and might even have met during Bowen's brief service aboard the *Franklin*.[17]

Elden had high hopes of getting to visit Vega friends E. L. Krahn and Carlton Buck, but the zealous censor who used a razor blade on the next letter seemingly believed that telling their names might somehow help the enemy.

February 15, 1945

Dear Mom, Dad & Bros,

I have four un-answered letters from you I think. I had better Get Buisy and try writeing for a change.

I got the Valentines also. Thanks a million. I was rather surprised to hear from Jerry. I was really Glad to hear from you Jerry. I hope you are over your cold & can go out and have a big time by now.

I Get [censored] tomorrow or the next day I am going to Try to find [censored]. Of course you don't know where either of [censored] are. I'm Sorry but I cant tell you. It helps win the war so I don't mind not being able to say anything much.

I am still Hopeing for an Early Victory and it looks like we will get one if Those Russians keep going.

I broke the stem out of my watch a few days ago. I will have to wrap it up and have it censored and send home. I would like to have fixed. I sure am lost without it.

I found out about the allotment I cant take one out for Dependency. I am going to take out more bonds & a self savings allotment in a few days. That is when they just take so much out of your pay and send it home. Maybe I can Get you Payed up that way. I sure was glad to hear that Six Got to come home wish he could got longer & Got it sooner. Say about Christmas. That would have been a good Deal. Sounds kinda bad Reporting back to Baltimore.

I think that is a good Idea about getting another big Picture made & Sending Virginia one of them. I will want one of them sometime so I'll Get Half interest in one that way. Ha

I really do think Gerald should go to work for Georgie That way he could work up an all summer job & I imagine he might get Dad to milk The Cows for Him. Ha.

What is the dope on Bugs & Snails are They Going To the merchant marines or not?

Snails should grab that if He has the chance. I sure would if I had the chance.

I really must close for now & write Virginia. I wrote everyone in Okla. Last week or whenever I wrote You last. So long for now.

P.S. I got a letter from Rowena with two pictures. One of Gerald & Her and one by herself. There really good.

Lots of Love,
Your Son,
Elden

Given that we know the ship was at Pearl Harbor or in Hawaiian waters from February 13 to March 3, and given what was not cut out of another letter six days later, we can easily infer that the words perceived somehow too dangerous to be shared were "liberty," "Krahn," "Buck," and "them."

"Those Russians" that Elden mentioned were indeed going. The big news two days before was that they had captured Budapest and in doing so had killed 49,000 enemy troops and captured 110,000 more. The far eastern German city of Dresden, heretofore beyond the reach of Allied bombers, where the Wehrmacht had concealed war production in the smug belief that the city could be passed off as a "neutral" center of international architectural heritage, had just been firebombed into rubble by British and American planes. The enemy powers that had generated this war were collapsing even faster in eastern Europe than in the western Pacific.[18]

On February 16, as the *Franklin* prepared to reenter the fray, the other fast carriers of Task Force 58 daringly approached a point only sixty miles off the Japanese main island of Honshu. They destroyed 190 planes on the ground and shot down 341 with a loss of 88 American planes.[19] This both reduced Japan's ability to defend Iwo Jima and tested the counter-kamikaze strategy, which included significantly tightening the defensive screens that surrounded the carriers. Another part of the strategy seems to have been to increase the aggressiveness that Halsey had been showing. By taking the carriers close in to a mere ten minutes flying time from land, Americans could reach farther inland and destroy more airplanes on the ground before they posed any danger to anyone.

Something transformative had happened in those five and a half hours Virginia and Elden spent alone in her parents' living room before dawn on January 6. In sharp contrast to her treatment of Elden when they were last together almost a year earlier, Virginia is now so worried about her relationship with Elden that the teen confesses her fears to the woman she had been too shy to meet not long before. The worry seems misplaced, as Elden had just written his parents not of whether he would marry Virginia, but when. In all likelihood, her letters had been chasing him since the *Franklin* got under way on February 2.[20]

Cultures require certain rituals of the people who are part of them. Italians tend to avoid important subjects until a social relationship has been established. Mexicans solicitously inquire after the health of relatives and friends before coming to the point of a meeting. On the Great

Plains the weather determines the difference between prosperity and poverty, even life and death, and the farm- and ranch-oriented Anglos who dwell there are required to comment on and ask about it. Virginia meets her cultural obligation between paragraphs devoted to more emotional subjects.

February 17, 1945

Dear Mrs. Rogers,

I'm awfully worried about Elden. (I call him Tex) He hasn't written for a long time, he wrote once right after he left & I've been writeing to him but he doesn't answer. Have you heard from him? I thought maybe he got shipped out or some thing & was unable to write or maybe I don't have his right address. He didn't put a return address on that last letter he wrote. I would sure like to hear from him. Maybe he's mad at me about some thing & I would like to get things straightened out. I think a lot of Tex. He is one of the nicest boys I have ever met & I would hate to lose his friendship without knowing what happened.

How is your weather down there? It has sure been nice here until last night. It snowed a little but is all melted now & its sort of cloudy out. I'll sure be glad when summer comes. I don't like cold weather at all.

Tex said he had some big pictures taken when he was home. I don't have very many good pictures of him & if you have an extra one would you send it to me? I would sure appreciate it.

I didn't get to see him very much when he was home but I realize that he would rather spend his furlough at home. I know I would & besides I was working on the night shift & I wouldn't have gotten to be with him very much even if he had of stayed in Las Animas longer.

I guess I'll quit. Write to me. I enjoy your letters very much & when you write to Tex ask him to please write & tell me what is the matter.

A true Friend,
Virginia

The U.S. landing on Iwo Jima had begun on February 19, the day before Elden's next letter, and we can be sure that he knew. By saying he had not given up on seeing Krahn, he says in effect that he is still at Hawaii. Much more directly important to this sailor's story, however, is his explanation of his new job. Together with his February 7 letter, this clearly describes Hangar Deck Control. His buddies teased him about being a racketeer because the job did not involve getting dirty, doing physical labor, or dodging the crashing airplanes as flight deck sailors had to do on average about every three days.

February 20, 1945

Dear Mom, Dad & Bros,

I will Try to write a letter this morning since I don't have much to do. We get paid This afternoon so all in all this is a good day. I get 25$ I was last paid the fifth. So that isn't So bad for fifteen days I don't think. I don't think I need any money for quite a while so I will get an allotment & more war bonds taken out in a few days. The first time I'm not buisy & when I've caught up on my letter writeing.

I wrote & said I was going to send my watch home, well don't expect it Yet as I think they can fix it at the Instrement Shop. I've Got to find out about it as soon as I Get time.

I haven't run on to Krahn yet but I haven't Gave up hopes Yet. I sure would like to see him.

I wrote to Virginia Yesterday & also Rowena. I have been taking it easy lately I have a different job now I sit here and watch airplanes & write down on a piece of Paper if they are in flying condition or not. If not I send someone to fix it. I really do like the Job. I am what all the fellows call a "Racketeer" or I have a racket.

How did you like it hearing about carriers bombing Tokio? That really sounded good to me. I wasn't lucky enough to be there tho.

Have you heard any more about Snails & bug-Eye going to the merchant marines? I doubt if They go until they Get Drafted. They really should Go ahead now. They would get a better deal if they did.

I had better write Snails while I have time.

I really should write To Odell. I will write him if find time Today.

I must Sign Off for Now. So Long.

With Love

Your Son

Elden

P.S. Send me Six's new address if You can get it.

This easy new job is actually a link in a somewhat longer chain than Elden has explained. Airplanes often returned from their sorties in need of attention because of damage, wear, or accident. They might have holes from bullets or flak, or they might have burned spots. They might have oily streaks from leaking hydraulic fluid or engine oil. They might have blown tires or broken glass. Or they might sustain dents, breaks, or worse in one of the frequent on-deck "crash landings" or collisions with barriers. Any time planes were being recovered, a V officer was on the flight deck to watch for such damage, and to initiate action for repair. That officer's telephone was connected to one of the four phones in Hangar Deck Control, and his instructions were taken by Elden or one of his three companions, noted on a piece of paper, and then precisely relayed to others who would quickly get the plane lowered to the hangar deck and moved to the proper area for repair. The same information would then be relayed to a master Flight Deck Control office high up in the island structure that kept track of the location and status of each individual plane. The duty seems much more like the normal work of the V-3 Division than of the V-1, but apparently the officers did not allow such technicalities to prevent their assigning men wherever they chose.[21]

February 20, 1945

Dear Mrs. Rogers,

I received that picture of Tex & its really swell. I sure do appreciate it. You certainly have a handsome boy. I'm really proud of him. I wrote to you the day before I got the picture & didn't put your right address on it so you probably won't get it for awhile. I finally heard from Tex. He has been out to sea I guess & couldn't mail any letters, anyway hes O.K. & that's all that really matters. I was awfully worried when I didn't hear from him for so long. Yes, he sure looked swell in his uniform. My mother sure likes him. She said he was such a nice boy & handsome & clean looking. It would take a whole box of stationery to tell you how much I think of him so won't tell you. Ha

It rained all night & is still misting today, & it looks dark & cold outside & its only about 3:00 o'clock & we have to have the lights on to see. I don't like days like that very good.

I thought Chuck Steward was going to join the Merchant Marines. Hes pretty changeable I guess. He was in the Navy for a while wasn't he? I never got to see him in his uniform tho.

I'm going to send Elden a birthday present pkg I don't know what it will be yet. Its hard to know what to send I think.

When Tex came home he sent me a telegram from Washington so I knew he was coming & I could hardly wait. I guess he wanted to surprise you.

I guess I will sign off now. I was sure glad to get the picture & your letter too.

Love,
Virginia

This is the last we have of Virginia's letters. Does this merely demonstrate the difficulty of mail catching up with ships on the move in the war zone? Elden will soon be receiving letters from home that had been mailed four months earlier, and at about the same time receiving one letter a short twelve days after it had been mailed. Perhaps all of the letters Virginia wrote after this were returned undelivered, as Grace's were. Perhaps not.

Still exercising his penchant for surprise visits, Elden has at last gotten together with Vega friends E. L. Krahn and Carlton Buck. This letter and another one three days later tell of the meeting, which clearly happened somewhere within the Pearl Harbor Naval Base and during duty hours for Krahn. They took the opportunity to exchange news about two other boys from home. Russell Adcock is either duty stationed in Hawaii or on a ship Elden knows to be there at the time, and Red Newman, sadly, is missing in action.

Ancell hardly ever went to movies. Doing so required a trip to Amarillo and an expenditure of time, money, and gasoline coupons that could be used for more practical purposes, but he has heard of a movie that might show him some of what Elden was experiencing. Grace has mentioned it to Elden in a letter; Elden has seen the movie and he recommends it. *The Fighting Lady* was a navy documentary narrated by Robert Taylor and released on December 31, 1944. It showed live action by the USS *Yorktown* (CV-10), and it won the Academy Award for the best documentary that year.

February 21, 1945[22]

Dear Mom, Dad & Bros,
I received your letter a few days ago So I'll try to answer it. Luck was with me yesterday I got to see krahn yesterday. Him & Carlton Buck are on an Island over here of corse I can't tell you which one.

He had to work so I just stayed there and talked to them. I was within three feet of him when he saw me. He sure was Surprized. He had saw Wig the day before But he left so I never got to see him.

I found out where Russel Adcock is. I think I may get to see him before long.

I am thinking strongly on trying to get in the Submarine Forces. I found out all about it & I know it's the best deal.

I haven't had a chance to find out about getting my watch fixed yet. I sure hope I can have it fixed on the ship.

Krahn Sure does look good. Its sure agreeing with him as he has gained twenty pounds since he has been over here. But I guess I would too If I didn't have anything to do but eat. That is about all he does. He works in a fruit & Vegetable Ice box.

Have McKendrees heard any more from Bishop. The Japs turned some more of them loose a few days ago. I have sure been Hopeing He would be one of them.

I don't guess Newmans have heard any more from Red have They? Or have you heard? I sure did hate to hear about him being missing in action. But I don't guess all can come through it ok.

Well I Guess I better close for now. Wish me luck on getting to see Russell. So Long for Now.

Lots of Love,

Elden

P.S. I think that's a good idea of Dad's Seeing "The Fighting Lady" I sure liked it. The only bad part is it is too Real. Its about a ship like mine.

As these visits were happening and these letters were being written, a battle was raging for the small and strategically located volcanic island of Iwo Jima. Long-range bombers flying from Tinian had been striking the Japanese mainland, but troops on Iwo Jima were observing them and giving advance alert to defending fighters. Furthermore, many of the bombers being damaged by defenders could be saved if only Iwo Jima could be made an emergency landing spot. We at home would have heard on our radios that American troops had gone ashore on February 19 after a terrific bombardment but that the resistance was powerful, terrain was difficult, and American casualties were high. Elden may have known, as we may not have known, that on February 21 kamikazes flying among Japanese fighters and bombers sank one American ship and damaged others. We may all have known that on February 23 the summit of Mount Suribachi had been captured and the American flag had been planted there. We did not know that Herman Sifford, who would live to become my father-in-law, was among the thousands of U.S. fighters whose spirits were lifted by the sight. And no one then knew that a photograph of the flag being raised would win a Pulitzer Prize, become the stuff of legend, and come to be represented in bronze as the United States Marine Corps Memorial in Arlington, Virginia.[23]

The first payoff from this terrible fight, the emergency landing on Iwo Jima of a crippled American B-29, would come only eight days later on March 4. This battle was still far from over, but the lesson from it, being repeated in each battle for an island, was that Japanese defenders would fight long after their cause had become hopeless and would have to be burned out with flamethrowers from each individual defensive position.[24]

February 24, 1945

Dear Mom, Dad, & Bros,

I cant think of a better way than writing to you to use this spare time this afternoon. I think I told you I got to see Krahn & Carlton Buck Didn't I? Krahn saw wig Price The day before I saw him. I never got to see wig. Sure wish I could have saw him. I think I'll go look up Russel Adcock some of these days. Krahn said Wig Talked like he'd get to see Charlie Robinson.

I got a letter from Grand-ma a few days ago. I better try to answer it today. Everything was O.K. with them.

You was talking about the Show "Since You Went Away." I saw it last week on the Ship. It sure was good I thought.

Have you got Six new address yet? be sure to send it when you get it.

Also send Joye & Ralph's address. I have more time now so can write on the job & can wright oftener.

How is mrs. Landrum? Getting Better I hope. Krahn Said that Red Dewees Had been in fourteen major Battles. I wouldn't tell mrs Dewees tho if I were you as it would just worry Her. I sure would like To See Him Get a leave.

I heard They Released 2146 more Prisoners on the Philipines today so McKendrees surley will hear from Bish some of these days.

My Ship is in That show that dad wanted to see when it came to Amarillo. It show it once ancored with a bunch more ships.

I sure hated To Hear from about Red Newman being missing in action. Krahn Hadn't heard it when I told him. Krahn was tickled to Death to get the longhorn News. They haven't put out the Franklin Forum in a long Time I'll send them when I get one.

Love,
Elden

Neither Elden nor anyone at home knew that Bish McKendree had left his tropical hell for an opposite kind of misery and was working in an open pit mine in northern Japan amid bitter cold. Neither Elden nor any enlisted men knew that "Big Ben" was about to leave "Somewhere in the Pacific," code for Hawaii, but he is looking forward to another visit with Krahn on March 2 and hoping they can both have the day off.

What Elden cannot write, as he scribbles of buddies, Virginia, springtime, and a broken watch, is that twenty-four hours earlier a plane had crashed on the flight deck. The impact had dislodged and ruptured an auxiliary gasoline tank and flames had engulfed the plane. The extraordinary firefighting capability of this ship had the flames out in only thirteen minutes, but during that interval V-1 Division sailors on the flight deck had seen the pilot roasted in his cockpit. This time, however, Elden would have been in his new "safer" job in Hangar Deck Control, a few feet beneath the action rather than in the middle of it. He would have heard this crash, the fire alarm, and the commotion, but he probably remained at his post and did not see it.[25] Afterward he heard others say how it had felt to be able to see the pilot but unable to save him. In the rough and clumsy business of war, even on a training exercise in American waters, no one was ever really safe.

February 28, 1945

Dear mom, Dad & Bros,

Well I haven't written for several days so I'll try to do so this morning. I think I told you I got to see a couple of my Buddies didn't I? I didn't Get to go anywhere with Them as They couldn't get off. I get off day after tomorrow so think I'll phone Krahn (one of my Buddies) & see if He can get off then I sure hope so.

We just Got the news that they were still bombing Tokio area.

I still haven't been lucky enough to get in on it yet.

I haven't got any mail for about a week but I imagine we will get some tonight tho.

I haven't had too much to do lately it sure does seem nice.

I heard from Virginia about a week ago she isn't working anywhere now. They laid off a bunch on the air Base job & she was one of them.

I wrote to snails quite a while ago but haven't got an answer yet. Is he & Bug-Eye still at Vega?

Well here it is The last day of feb. Spiring will soon come for you & you will have some warm weather for a while.

I haven't found out about getting the watch fixed yet. I'll do that today if I don't forget it.

I can't think of much more so I'll close for now as I cant think of anything else to say & I must try to write Virginia today. Well So long for now.

Love,

Elden

20 "Would You Like to Have a Transfer?"

"TELL it to the chaplain," a sailor is apt to hear when complaining of personal problems. On March 2, as Elden again visited Krahn, Captain Gehres transferred Chaplains Harkin and Chamberlin off the ship and replaced them with Catholic Joseph T. O'Callahan and Protestant Grimes Weldon Gatlin.[1] These new pastors probably found much of their time occupied with crewmen unburdening themselves of the sin of hatred, for the captain's behavior had made the feeling widespread.[2] Going so far as to scream at officers in the presence of their enlisted subordinates, the captain accomplished the nearly impossible task of making enlisted men actually feel sorry for officers.[3]

March 3, 1945, brought to a close the interlude of daily voyages out to sea for takeoffs, landings, and live-ammunition training followed by evening telephone conversations and occasional actual meetings with buddies from home. The *Franklin* was ready to return to combat, or had better be, because Task Force 58 was reassembling at Ulithi and she was needed there. As the big ship was nudged away from Ford Island's mooring quays F-2 and F-3, at 0640 that morning the cheering crews and deep-throated whistles of other ships bid her good luck. A choir of fifty WAVES singing their farewell added emotion to the moment. The feeling was heightened for Elden by the sight of his buddy Seaman Second Class Nelson Allison Myers from Colorado City, Texas, standing near them.[4]

Elden and Myers, two among a small number of Texans in a 3,400-man crew of mostly northeasterners, had commiserated about their desire for other duty. Probably Elden longed for an office job back in the States, such as Odell Price and Pumper Boydstun had (while Odell and Pumper longed for sea duty), or even one in Norman, Oklahoma, such as he had heard of long ago and from where he could visit home on a thirty-six-hour pass. They knew they were daydreaming, and they underestimated the dangers of many other duty stations, but they wanted off a carrier. Myers had been wounded slightly in the October kamikaze hit, and both were acutely aware that they lived in a bull's-eye. On February 28 Elden's division officer, probably Red Morgan, had walked up to where he and Myers were working and said, "Say, Myers, would you like to have a transfer?" Myers had leaped at the chance and had been assigned to the USS *Houston,* which was not yet fully repaired from the torpedo hit back on October 12 near Formosa and was now bound for the mainland.[5]

As the space widened between the *Franklin* and her mooring, Elden spotted Myers in the crowd, waving and fighting back tears. Neither Myers, who was glad to have his transfer but felt the tug of friendship and loyalty, nor Elden, who was happy for Myers but would gladly have traded places with him, could realize the full poignancy of the moment.

March 3, 1945

Dear Mom, Dad & Bros,

I'm not Very buisy this morning so I'll write a few letters. I got to see one of my buddies Yesterday. (a Guy by The name of Krahn.)

I sure was Glad to see him. I hope to see him again sometime he sure is a swell guy.

That Guy on the ship said he would fix my watch if he had the right size stem. He thinks he has it. He is checking up on it today. I went down to take out an allotment this morning & the fellow said to come back at 1:00 so I'll Get that Squared away. It's a self savings allotment so they will take out $22 a month and send it to You. I should have you payed up in Six or seven months then you can Deposit it in the Bank for me.

Well the fellow just phoned me up about the watch & he has the stem for it. He will have it fixed in about three days. They say he does good work. He was a watch maker for five years before he came in the navy. It will cost me about five dollars.

I'm sure Glad I have Charlie Robinsons address as I may run on to him over here & maybe so wig Price Too. I sure would like to see Them. I never Got to see Russell Adcock I sure hated that.

Virginia Wrote & said she had heard from You & also Received The Picture.

I received a letter & Picture from Francess

I better close for now as I don't know anything to Say. So long For now.

Love,
Elden

Hangar Deck Control would not have been a very busy place as the *Franklin* slipped out of Pearl Harbor and took a westward heading. Things may have been relaxed enough for Elden to stay topside and watch high and beautiful Oahu gradually slip below the horizon, perhaps with regret at leaving American soil one more time and perhaps with a longing to return there as soon as possible.

Safely away from gossips and spies who were always ready to wheedle information from a talkative sailor, the crew was allowed to know that they were about to go after the enemy in his lair—in Japan itself. They were headed first for Ulithi, where the *Franklin* and the heavy cruiser *Guam* sailing with her were to become part of the most powerful naval force in history.[6] Task Force 58, under Admiral Mitscher and part of the Fifth Fleet, would get its general direction from Admiral Spruance, who had taken Halsey's place. Following the precedent of the recent bombings of Tokyo from a mere sixty miles offshore, they would hit Japan hard again and again with the intention of destroying kamikazes on the ground and crippling the nation's ability to manufacture aircraft. They may not yet have been told, but most men probably guessed, that Okinawa was next to be invaded and that the task force intended to eliminate Japan's ability to defend the island from its mainland air bases.

There was work to do that evening, however, as at 1826 a plane crashed into the barrier and was damaged slightly.[7] A V-1 officer on the flight deck would have noted the damage and telephoned Hangar Deck Control with instructions for dealing with the plane. Elden or another person in that little office with the big windows would have taken the call, noted the instructions, and relayed them to the appropriate parties.

March 4, 1945

Dear Mom, Dad & Bros,

I wrote you a letter yesterday but I got one from you today so I'll answer it. I just got back from Church and don't have anything to do but stand by (Be here in other words) Yes I really do like my new job. It isn't a dirty job & isn't long hours so that is right down my alley. I guess I will have this job from now on. I hope so. I have been pleasing everyone as far as I can tell. There hasn't been any complaints. I just have to take orders then Relay Them on to someone else, like some officer tells me a certain plane needs to be worked on Then I tell someone what it needs & send them to fix it.

Tell dad That he can keep the knife. Ted had two and he let me have one. I would sent it To Gerald but it is sold at a reduced Price & is supposed to be for our own use.

I'll tell you what I like about this job is That I can write two or Three letters a day. I've wrote at least two every day since I've been here.

Yes I got to see [censored]. I sure was glad to see him. He is looking Good. He has gained 25 or 30 pounds since he has been There.

The guy told me to come back the other day & he would fix me up on the allotment. He said He was too buisy Getting Ready for Pay Day. Said to wait until after Pay Day. Pay Day is tomorrow so I'll Go down Day after tomorrow.

The other fellow said my watch would be fixed about The Seventh. I'll sure be glad when I get it back. I'm lost without it.

Take out what I owe you from the allotment. Also Take out for the Pictures.

Say if you see any dark blue or black canvas Baseball Caps How about sending me a size 7 or 7 1/8, They Issued us one & I lost mine & can't Get another.

Another thing. Send me Joye's address I have time to write to her now.

I knew mrs Six would worry about Carlton You can't blame her. But its not as bad as its made out to be over there or it isn't in the Pacific at least. They will have their Part done over there before we do I think.

I was Glad to hear that Virginia Had wrote to you. But sorry to hear that She hadn't Got a letter from me. I just was working so hard there for a while that when I had a minute off I didn't feel like doing anything but resting. But Both of you will hear more now. They may be all in a bunch Tho. I wrote to krahn this morning & sent him The clippings about Bill Newman & Pat Livesay. How is Pat Have You heard anymore

Pete Livesay is on the same Island as Russell Adcock & Krahn is on another one near by.

Yes I know Virginia worrys a lot about me. I know she thinks a lot of me too. I could Tell that when I first walked in on her in Las Animas when I came home on leave. I'll bring Her down with me on my next leave which I hope won't be too long.

Well So Long For now.

Lots of Love,
Elden

P.S. Don't worry about me as it won't be any worse this time Than last time out. If not it won't scare me any. I may Get a little nervous at Times but That won't hurt me. I'll be O.K.

Elden has just given us perhaps his most informative letter of all, both directly and indirectly. In a direct way he tells far more about his new job than his letter of February 20, explaining what he had meant when he said that he watched airplanes. We now know exactly what he did and how his work fit into the total job being done by the 3,400 men now aboard the *Franklin*. In particular, we can see that this would have been considered a plum job compared to others in his division. The flight deck officers from whom Elden took messages might have been Lt. Fred Harris, Lt. D. M. Winters, Lt. (JG) G. L. Hassig, or Ens. F. M. Hall, and perhaps plane captain Irv Dahlen, with whom I corresponded years later, might have been among the individuals to whom he relayed orders about planes that needed attention.[8] Pieced together with a drawing provided later by Odell Price and with information from the surviving ships most likely to have been identical to the *Franklin*, USS *Yorktown* (CV-10) and USS *Hornet* (CV-12), we know precisely where his duty station was located. From the description, from other references, and from a letter from Roy Treadaway's mother, we can be confident that the duty station was called Hangar Deck Control. Much later, this information will come to be of almost stunning importance.[9]

We venture here farther than before into the risky territory of indirect communication—what we *believe* Elden wanted to say but could not, and for which evidence is limited. This letter, written on Sunday, contains one of the rare references to church. He has been to services, which we have guessed before that he did not routinely attend. Perhaps he was checking out the new Protestant chaplain, but very likely he was seeking to assuage the foreboding we know he felt. Things had been very bad last time out; Elden had used those words to tell others that he thought he might not return. By his comment that "it won't be any worse this time" was he was saying he expected the worst? In admitting to a little nervousness and in saying it would not scare him any, was he attempting to reassure himself as well as those who would read the words?

⚓

How drastically different Vega, Texas, in 1945 was from rural America today is evidenced by events described in fifteen letters written by Grace between March 7 and April 12, 1945. It seems a safe assumption that her many other letters that do not survive were similarly full of the petty happenings deemed worthy of remark in a town whose city limit sign announced a population of 515, in which Route 66 was the only paved street, and where few people had telephones, no one had television, and farm homes only a little way out of town had no electricity.

One thing was astonishingly similar between then and now, however; teenagers were uncontrollable and their parents worried about them. The Brents family were close friends and former neighbors whose house was diagonally across the original Route 66 from my birthplace. As if the two sons they had in the war were not enough to worry about, one of the two other sons at home was acting up. Fifteen-year-old Odell Brents, dubbed "Eggs" by friends in childhood, had sneaked away in the night with Bugeye Steward. Oldham County Sheriff John Haliburton, who held the office for thirty of the thirty-six years between 1916 and 1952 and whose approach to law enforcement was rooted in a still earlier era, did not take the matter very seriously and counseled Eggs's mother to wait for her son to realize his error and to return home on his own. Grace has given Eggs's mother a few hints at detective work that later will bear fruit, and in one sentence she reveals that Bugs seems to be a considerable problem for his own parents.

My Dear Son,

Well I think I should take time out right Now & write you a few lines. We received 3 letters from you yesterday. Sure was glad & surprised to get so many at once.

Sure glad you got to see E.L. Mrs Robinson told me the other day that Russell was on a ship now. Did you know that? She said he wasn't satisfied till they put him on a ship. Some people don't know when they are well off do they?

Well about you getting into the submarine Corps. Of course you know more about that than we do. I don't think I would want to be on one. Is E.L. still in the Sub Corps? A job like his wouldn't be so bad. Be sure & find out for sure if it what you want before you Change. Im sure I don't know what to tell you.

Well Brents are having a little trouble with Eggs. He ran off with Bug eye last Friday night to Colo Some place. Paul Author saw them in Raton. Bugs told Mary he was going to Denver But he told her he had a Job helping drive an Oil truck up there. It was just a lie. Eggs slipped his clothes out while there wasn't any one at home & told his folks Friday night that [censored] was having a party that night & wanted to go—and he never Came back. Mrs. Brents was up here yesterday evening & told Me about it she sure was broken up over it. She was wanting Haliburton to wire up there & have him picked up but John just stalled them off & said he would be back in a few days. Well Bugs will have him drinking & every thing else. They are a pretty good pair but I don't blame Mrs. Brents for wanting him brought back as he isn't yet 16 yrs old. Mary told me Sunday that Bugs shipped his trunk. So I told Mrs. Brents she might find out where the trunk was sent to from [Rock Island Railroad depot agent] Shelton as he sent it from there & that way she might find out where he is & Could wire up there herself & have him picked up. I also told her Bugs went by the name of Chuck in Las Animas so I think they can find him if they try. Mary said Bud was trying to locate Janet. She had been to Calif, but wasn't back to Las Animas but had left Calif. But you Cant tell a thing about what he says. Well guess that's all I know about that.

Mrs. Brents said Pete went back to Ponca city day before yesterday & hes joining the Navy right away. He don't like Ponca City & said his Mother didn't either. I was afraid they wouldn't. Junior took his physical & passed. He told Gerald he didn't know when he would have to go. He is trying to get in the Navy (or army) he told Gerald.

We are having some windy & kinda foggy weather this Morning & sure is Cold. I sure am glad I washed yesterday.

Helen Stewards folks & a Brother & 2 sisters Came down & stayed a Couple of days. The sister stayed a week or More. Letha & I went up to see her & Helen Monday evening—They were over to Marys So we went on over there a while. She was planning on Going back to Las Animas yesterday. If she did Expect Stewards would find out by her if Bugs was up there. They probly wont try tho as I think they are always glad when he is gone.

Well I don't have time to write Much. But as you wanted Carltons address Ill go over & get it & get this mailed. Valda said Yesterday morning down town that Carlton was Gone they guessed as they had his A.P.O address.

Will sign off for now. Love.

Mom & all

While the *Franklin* churns steadily westward, her turbines rumbling day and night, Elden writes, as Grace has written on the same day, of land-based sailors who want sea duty while sailors at sea long for onshore assignments. The reference to Howard Blasingame trying to keep Snails (Howard Jr.) out of the service until after the early July wheat harvest reinforces the importance of food production jobs in the fates of individual young men. The senior Blasingame owned no farm land but did own a truck and perhaps a combine that were vital to the harvest, and even this connection gave hope that Snails's induction might be postponed.

March 7, 1945

Dear mom, Dad & Bros,

I wrote you about three days ago I think so I'll write again to let you know I'm O.K. & Doing fine.

I wrote to Virginia Yesterday (Monday 5th) & wrote to Francess the same day I think. That's about all I do anymore is write letters. I've decided That is as good of a passtime as any.

Today was Pay Day I drew $25 & had Ten left from last Pay day So I'm doing pretty Good I think. I have eight dollars loaned out. I'll collect it Today Too. My watch will be fixed Tommorrow That will cost me five Dollars. Then I guess I'll buy up enough clothes to last me for this Trip then I won't have any clothing to worry about.

I guess you know I have almost a year in The navy. Starting next Pay Day I'll Get $12 every four months for clothing allowance. That is an extra $36 per year on my pay check It will help.

I think I'll make S 1/c before long Then that will be twelve bucks more a month.

I am going down tomorrow or the next day & take out that allotment.

Say Have you got Six'es address Yet? I sure hope he hasn't Gone overseas yet. That overseas duty is Plenty rugged for the army.

Say if you see any maps of The Pacific for sale I would like for you to send me one. I was figuring on getting one when I had the chance but I forgot it. Mabye I'll get everything I need sometime then I can quit bothering you for something in every letter.

I don't Guess Snails has left yet has he? I expect Howard will try to keep him out till after Harvest but I doubt if He can that long. Bug-Eye will be 18 the 13th of July so I bet he will have to go the fourteenth.

I don't Guess John L. Has left yet has he? Everyone who writes me says they think he will have to go yet. I sure Hope so. He is no better than the rest of us.

I would like to see Pumper Boydston if he is Craveing Sea Duty I would trade with him any time I had the chance.

I think I told you I tried to trade duty with a guy didn't I? Well They wouldn't let me. This is The first ship I ever Heard of that won't let you swap. I sure wish it would have went through. I would been with a buddy. They call him "Ode." He is a swell Guy I wish you could meet him. Hope This finds everything O.K. With You. So Long For now.

Love Always,
Elden

In his book *Lucky Lady*, Steve Jackson graphically describes what Elden is likely to have experienced during this peaceful outbound voyage: "But for the knowledge that they drew nearer to the war with each swell that passed beneath the hull, the voyage would have been pleasant. The seas were calm, the sunrises and sunsets painted in spectacular arrays of colors . . . As the nights grew warmer, men congregated on the flight deck to enjoy the breeze, a smoke, conversation, and the stars above the ocean."[10]

Feathers were ruffled at home, however, where Grace has heard, and does not at all approve, that Elden and his first cousin Geneva Roberts may have exchanged flirtatious letters. Directing unduly harsh language toward the niece as a way of scolding the son, she admonishes Elden not to be inviting gossip. In other feather-related news, the brooder that kept Ed Murphy's baby chickens warm has overheated, burned the chicken house, and threatened to explode the thirty-gallon butane bottle that provided his cooking fuel. Grace predictably assumes that Ed was drunk. And Hot Dog McKendree is to have his appendix removed.

The most beautiful thing in Vega in those days might have been the fire truck. Of 1920s vintage, it had been purchased before the Depression took all the money away, and seeing it was worth a visit to the Volunteer Fire Department where it was on display. Open, without a cab or doors, its black leather seats perfectly matched the black rubber tires. Most of it was a deep and shiny red, except for the radiator shell, lights, bumpers, racks, and rails, which were nickel-plated and even shinier. It always looked good, and because it was hardly ever used the battery was often dead. There were not many fires, and when a siren on the water tower summoned volunteers to their duty, they sometimes had to push the truck into the street, hook it up to a chain, and tow it to start the engine. Most likely this full routine was followed, and then the truck raced with bell clanging and siren wailing the full five hundred feet to Murph's house in time to hold him back from following his chicks into eternity.

March 8, 1945

My Dear Son

Well seems as tho Im in the letter writing business today. This is My fourth. I got another letter from you today Dated Feb 28. sure was glad to hear as we always are.

I hurried so with my letter yesterday I don't think I half way wrote it so I thought Id start in on this one this evening. I even forgot to send Joyes address. Here it is. Mrs. Ralph Winters. Medicine Lodge, Kans. Route 2. I know she will be glad to hear as she hardly ever sees any of the rest that does hear.

Mrs. Six said she had been sending Carltons letters to his old address as the Card never said he was leaving the states. But I know they intend to have it sent to the New address or they wouldn't have sent the Card out. She said maybe I better send you the old address too. But if I was you Id use the new one. Ill bet he is gone or soon going—she sure is having a fit about him going over seas. I told her I knew how she felt. But she said Yes but you have others to occupy your Mind some. But I don't think that makes any difference. Ill bet she writes & gripes to him about every thing & makes him feel Blue. Well I don't see any use griping about things we can't help. Just hope and pray for it to Come to an end soon.

I hope you Can get your Watch fixed there as it probly would'nt take near so long.

Well Im glad you was'nt lucky enough to be in on Bombing Tokyo & I don't think Im wishing you any bad luck either.

Gerald said he heard that Bugs & Eggs was in Denver. Dad said Jeff never said any thing about it yesterday. I talked to Snails yesterday Morning. He said he had heard from you and Answered it. He said he guessed he would have 21 days.

Wish you could have seen Wig. Had I told you he was going to be Daddy.

Grace & Floyd Bixler stayed all night at Ivas Night before last. They were on their way to San Diego. All 3 of their boys are there. One of them has had Jungle fever & is getting a discharge. They don't think he will ever be well.

Mrs Dunning & Don Came with them & will be here a while.

No I don't think McKendrees has heard any thing from Bish. Hots was to be operated on for appendicitis a day or so ago. But I haven't heard how he is doing O.K. I suppose.

I don't know if Newmans has heard any more from Red or Not.

Mrs Landrum is slowly improving but has to stay in bed part of the time.

Boy Red Deweese sure has been in the Battles has'nt he. No I wont tell his Mother. But I sure hope he gets to come home & he can tell her. I think he should deserve a leave.

Well we sure have had a beautiful day. Just like spring But I Can take a lot of them. We have been having so much Changeable Weather.

Gerald got the Cellar dug down about 2 feet & Now he always manages to find something else to do. We want to get the water line dug—soon.

Dad says we will try to have a garden. I bought a little push garden plow last week.

Whats all this I hear about you being so sweet on Geneva. Frances told me you had written her & said Geneva took you too serious. Well I would'nt be feeding that water Brain Much dope as she will be telling the whole town. & I know you Couldn't possible mean it.

Don't think I ever told you about Ed Murphys fire last Saturday Night. He had his brooder house right close to his Mansion & some how the brooder house got on fire & burned up 75 Chickens that would weigh a lb each. It burned a feed stack & his house got so hot the paint raised up in blisteres & the Window Cracked & that was what woke him up. It was about 2 oclock in the morning. His Butane Bottle was right Close too & it's a wonder it hadn't blowed up & the whole thing would have went. Ill bet it griped him to loose all of those chickens. I imagine he was half drunk is the reason he never woke up sooner.

Well this is Friday Morning and I don't know Much More to say. Iva Came over & said Verda Mae & Odell had an apartment in Alameda Now & he comes home nights. Goes to work at 7 AM & gets off at 5 PM (I think she said).

Well I will sign off & go Mail this.

Love & all good wishes from home.

Mom & all

On March 8, Elden and everyone else not essential to keeping the ship moving slept late. As Elden writes on March 9, the *Franklin* is passing thirty-nine miles north of Eniwetok, this time not stopping because she is already fully supplied and urgently needed farther west.[11]

As usual, however, Elden writes of hope to see guys from Vega, this time Red Dewees and Charlie Robinson, whose ships he anticipates will be in the big fleet assembling at Ulithi. Usually positive about navy chow, Elden expresses dismay about having to eat fish on this Friday, but then after interrupting his letter for the meal reports that the salmon has not been bad at all. He has bought a case of pineapple juice, presumably back in Hawaii, for seven and a half cents per can and has finished drinking the last of it, and he shares the story of his buddy Myers. It is a brief interlude of luxury and laziness, and it will not last.

March 9, 1945

Dear mom, Dad & Bros,

I haven't wrote for several days so I'll do so now. I am waiting for the other guy to get back so I can go to chow. We have to relieve each other for Chow. Today is Friday so I guess we will have fish. I hate to see Friday come anymore as I don't like fish.

I wrote to Virginia Yesterday so I won't have to write her until tomorrow. I have Written you and her about ten letters each since There has been any mail left the ship. So I guess you will get them all in a bunch. Im still hopeing to See Red Dewees or Charlie Robinson. Don't know if I will or not. Of course you don't know where they are. I am hopeing Reds ship is in where I saw it last. I doubt it tho. I don't know who I'll run onto First Red or Charlie. I'm just Guessing.

I'm hopeing I don't get back before December as that would be nineteen months & I would have a pretty good chance of getting some State Side Duty. I sure could stand some of that.

I don't know tho I guess it is just luck. I think you heard me talking about my Buddie From Dallas (Myers). Well My Division Officer walked up and Said: "Say Myers Would You like to have a Transfer" and Myers said Yes. So he is on the way Back to the west coast I guess. I guess some guys are just luckyier than others. Oh. Well, I'll Get a break someday I guess. Myers wanted to Go but Yet he almost Cried. He was on the Dock Waveing at us when we Pulled out. You could tell he couldn't hardly take it. I sure was Glad to see him Get to go even if I couldn't go with Him.

Did I tell you I bought a case of Pineapple Juice? I finished it up last nite. It sure was good & Plenty Cheap. I paid $1.80 for a case of number two cans. Twenty Four Cans. I thought that was Plenty Cheap.

I don't know how to guess as to when I will be home. I'm just hopeing to make it by Christmas & I'll be satisfied. I haven't missed a Christmas with you yet & I'm hopeing I don't this one.

I have almost a year in the navy now & almost nineteen years old. It doesn't seem like I've been in near that long. Time sure passes faster than I figured it would.

Well Yesterday was one of Those days all sailors look foreward to. All Hands may sleep in all afternoon. I really Did Catch up on my sleep.

I have wrote to everyone since I've heard from anyone. We haven't brought any mail on the ship in about ten Days. We will get some in three or four more days Tho I think. I should hit the jackpot when we do.

I saw some films for your kodac in my last Port but I can't bring films or send them off any naval ship or Station. I could have got five Rolls. I sure wish I could have sent you some.

Well This is after dinner The Guy Got back so I went to Chow. We had Salmon, Tomatoes, Spuds, Soup, Rasin Pie & Iced Tea. So It wasn't as bad as I thought it would be. I guess I'll Go down & see if my Watch is fixed This afternoon. I sure do hope so.

Have you heard any more about where Six is Yet. I hope he is still in Maryland. I better sign off for now. I'll write again Tommorrow or the next day.

So long for This Time.

With Love Always,

Elden

P.S. I ask for a baseball cap in one letter well skip it if you haven't already Got it. I found mine. I had sent it to the laundry & forgot about it.

On this same March 9, American B-29s were headed toward Tokyo with terribly destructive intent. German Luftwaffe planners had invented a method for setting large sections of a city on fire in a manner that would create a firestorm—a fire so powerful that it could not be suppressed or even minimized. They had used it against Warsaw on September 13, 1939, and then against Coventry and other cities in England.[12] Royal Air Force generals figured out what had been done at Coventry and thereafter applied the technique against many German cities. With Japan resorting to such desperate tactics as banzai attacks and suicide missions, the United States applied ever more destructive offensive approaches to force them to acknowledge the fact that they had lost the war. Japanese cities were even more vulnerable to fire than European cities, and the firestorm on the night of March 9, 1945, destroyed a quarter of a million homes made of easily combustible material and killed 84,000 people, mostly civilians.[13] The destructiveness of this raid was virtually equal to the atomic bombings that would come five months later, but the utter newness of split atoms quickly pushed this early form of mass destruction from public memory.

The *Franklin* now passed through an area that had once been dangerous—within flying distance of Truk. Once the Japanese counterpart to Pearl Harbor, it had been so devastated by carrier planes' attacks in February 1944 that it was no longer of concern to the Allies, but that did not keep scuttlebutt from spreading worry among the crew.[14] By the time I landed there on September 13, 1974, the sunken warships in the clear blue waters had become an international destination for recreational divers.

It is likely that by the time Grace wrote on March 11, we at home and Elden at sea knew of the firebombing raid, and it is likely that we were pleased about it. War had come to be recognized as *total* war, and its harshness had suppressed feelings of sympathy for fellow humans who were perhaps necessarily demonized as enemies. If their nation was willing to attack other nations, kill civilians, starve and abuse prisoners, kill your boys, and threaten you, you felt justified in viewing them as unworthy of pity and undeserving of life. As one would expect, the concern in Grace's mention of Tokyo's bombing is for her boy and not for the burned civilians of every age and sex.

There is a great deal of chatty little news, however, of other boys home on leave, of the Williams family filling two entire pews at church that morning, of Hot Dog's appendix, of the scarcity of nylon hose, of me and my girlfriend Jane Russ. The detective advice Grace gave Mrs. Brents a few weeks back has helped her locate her wayward juvenile son, who is still under the sway of Bugs. After getting no help at all from the Old-ham County sheriff, Mrs. Brents has taken her complaint to the police in Amarillo, who seem to have responded more satisfactorily than had our own old-time lawman.

But the tragedy of war is present at home as well. The letter conveys the loss of boys from the Newman family, south of Vega; and the Mil-hoan family, east of Wildorado; and of Pauline Blasingame's fear that her boy might be pulled into the maelstrom.

March 11, 1945

My Dear Sailor Boy,

I will write you a line or two this P.M. How does this find you? Fine I hope. Guess we are all O.K. but Dad. He has a Cold & has been working so hard he sure feels tough. He has been working over by Pan Handle. Goes to work at 7.30 am. & don't get off till 7 P.M. So that's nearly a day.

Well we had 2 sailors and a Soldier at Church. Charles Junior McNabb & Junior & Bryan Williams. Bryan got to Come back to see Junior as he had'nt seen him in over 3 years. Im surprised he got to Come as he was here, you know, since you was & stayed till Feb 14. But Im glad he got to Come. Junior flew from New York home. There was 2 seats filled at church with the Williams & their kin folks. Some how or other I admired the Sailors more than the soldiers. (I wonder why) & just wished Mine Could be right along with us.

We had a hundred in Sunday School & there was 25 or 26 in our Class. Sure was Nice.

I am sending you a clipping from the Hereford Brand about the Newman boy. This is all we have heard so far. The piece right below it. We don't know him but thought it was interesting any how. Here is also a Clipping about a surprise on Nina. From the Alva paper.

There has been a Milhoan boy killed in Europe. I don't know his name. But it was a Cousin to that Milhoan girl that stayed at Frankies & I may hear more who it is later.

Jerry & I went to Amarillo yesterday With Iva & Edward. Helen went too. Gerald stayed here & worked on the cellar some. I had to go to get me some hose Mine was shot & there is'nt a pair in Vega. I got 2 new pairs so I guess I can go to Church a while.

Guess Hots hasn't been operated on yet. Will be Next Wednesday some one said. Linda Come to take Care of the Kids while Marie stays over to Amarillo with him a few days. Linda has been to Colo springs & to See Earl. So Earl & Annabelle brought her back down here.

About Bugs & Eggs—They found out they shipped their suit cases to La Mar but they thought they were in Denver. Mrs Brents went to Amarillo the other day & turned it over to the Police over there & had them to pick them up. But I haven't heard any More. So don't know if they have them yet or Not.

Jerry has gone over to see Jane. She must have been at home as he has'nt Come back. Gerald went down town a while.

I talked to Snails the other day. He said he had heard from you.

Pauline said it sure was hard to see Junior go for his physical. She said she Just wanted to come over here & Cry. I asked then why didn't she & She said "Well you went through it alone & I Just as well." I felt sorry for her. But I Cant think Junior will see too much of it & hope he don't. I hope its too near over for him to see much. Well how glad I am that you are not (Lucky) would you say lucky enough to be bombing Tokyo—Id Just as soon you would stay where you are.

Hope you an E.L. got off together. I know you really enjoyed it if you did.

Hope you did get your watch fixed. It would be much quicker than sending it home.

Well here it is Monday Morning & a pretty one at that. Im nearly ready to wash. Will go after the towels then I will be.

Well it was in the Yesterdays paper about the Milhoan boy. It was Chester Milhoan the son of Miles Milhoan of Wildorado. You will see it when you get the paper. But this will get there first.

Well I must Quit for Now.

Love as ever.

Mom & all

Julia Ann Evans Peeler Coin Tegarden is Grace's mother, Elden's grandmother, and the only grandparent still living after 1930. She had a long and hard life, and was much loved and deeply respected by Grace. Born in Decatur County, Indiana, two and a half years after the Civil War ended, Julia attended such rural one-room schools as were available— ones clearly not strong in language or spelling ("ought to have" comes out as "otto of"). In her teen years her family moved to Kaufman County, Texas, where she married Jesse Samson Andrew Jackson Peeler and bore him a son named Burt. Peeler was abusive, however, and she divorced him and with her parents moved to Kansas, where she married widower John Coin. Coin brought four teenaged children into the marriage, and they had five more together, the last of whom was Grace. She took care of her children and her husband as Huntington's disease gradually reduced him to helplessness and then death. Then she married John Augustus Tegarden and outlived him as well. Now she lived with her increasingly disabled son Charlie Coin, who was eroding away with the same disease that had taken his father, and with daughter-in-law Junnia in the little story-and-a-half frame house that had been built about 1910 by Burt (Peeler) Coin, the same house in which Elden and Gerald had been born. In 1945 the house drew its drinking water from a cistern that caught rainwater shed by the roof, and it was lighted by kerosene lamps, connected to the outside world via a party line by a big wooden telephone on the wall, provided with news by a radio that was sparingly used because battery powered, and heated for comfort and for cooking by wood fires in iron stoves. She writes of farm things— butchering needs to happen during cold weather, and she wonders if it is growing too late in the year—and of the ubiquitous concern about the war.

March 12, 1945

Dear grandson I will now try to scrible you a few lines as I am tired of working out in the yard and to answer your letters was truly glad to get this leaves us all as well as common I have been well all winter but to day seems like Spring we haven't got our butchern done yet was going to day but got arond to late and put it of until tomoro Jim & Tom McConkey was going to butcher for Chas as he cant do that eny more. It is hard for him to do eny thing eny more

I got a letter from your Mother last Saturday they were well and we got your pictures they were just fine and when I look at it looks like you are smiling at me and every body say it is sure fine.

One of Junnia nephews were here last night it was Leo Butler he has three brothers in that war they are all over sea but him in May one has been over Seas 3 years & [one] 2 years and the other 1 year and their father is not expected to live long. You Said that you thought you would get Married when you get your next leave you are pretty yong but if you do I hope you get a good woman.

Well I hope you get to See Some more of the Vega boys and I hope & pray that this old war will soon be over and you soon get to come home to stay.

Rowena boy got a GI haircut the other day and you otto of seen her She sure did get mad I was down there 2 weeks but I am at home now you write when you can and I will try to answer but I will try to get some better paper if you will excuse this from Grandma with lots of love

As Elden writes, also on March 12, he knew the *Franklin* would arrive at Ulithi the next day to join a great assemblage of ships. He might have a chance to see Bob Walcott, Jack Dewees, and Wig Price. The destroyer tender *Piedmont* would be working at Ulithi, and he anticipated that the cruiser *Pensacola* and the light carrier *Copahee* would be part of the task force the *Franklin* was joining. He was right about the three ships, but there would be no time for socializing.

March 12, 1945

Dear Mom, Dad & Bros,

I Guess I better write you this morning to let you know that I'm O.K. & doing Fine. I hope you are The same.

I haven't been doing much lately just the same old thing day after day. That is why it Gets so monotonous at Sea. There very seldom have anything unusual happen. We have a movie every nite but I decided I had a lot rather sleep than to Go to Them.

I am hopeing to See a buddie of mine tomorrow a Guy They Call "Red Dewees." That is if he's at the same Place as last time. Of course I cant tell You where That was. I guess we will Get mail tomorrow. I sure Hope so. The ten or twelve letters I've wrote to you will Go off also. You will Get Them all in a bunch I guess. I think you will be more satisfied with my writeing This Time out. I have been writeing at least every two days at least. I'm Glad I have time to write more. Last cruze I didn't have any Time Hardly at all To write.

Oh. Yes! I took out The allotment day before yesterday. I will Send twenty-Five Dollars a month home. It starts comeing out next month so I don't know when you will Get the Check. It leaves me Thirty-Seven Dollars a month. I am recommended for the S 1/c exam the Twentyeth of next month. If I make it I am Going To take out more war bonds. I wont need any money out here. You should be Getting another bond before long Hadn't you.

That money should pay you up in five or six months. Then You can put it in the bank for me.

I think I told you that I got the watch back. I feel like a diffrent guy now with it. I felt like I was lost when it was broke.

I wrote to Bob Walcott & Wig Price Yesterday and told Them to keep a lookout for me as we might Get Together Sometime.

I Guess I had better close for now as I can't think of anything else to write. So long For now. Don't worry about me. I'll be O.K.

Love,
Elden

21   "So Long for Now"

THE monotonous time at sea ended when the *Franklin* steamed into Ulithi lagoon on the morning of March 13. The men knew that liberty could sometimes be had at Mog Mog, one island of the low circular atoll, and crews of ships that had been there for a few days had probably enjoyed that privilege. The *Franklin* was a latecomer, however, and her crew had no time for liberty or visiting friends on other ships or pleasures of any kind. She took her place at berth 21 in a line with a full dozen fleet carriers. The line was called Murderer's Row, and every ship there was engaged in the deadly serious business of getting stocked and loaded for what was to come.[1]

Big things were afoot—unbelievably big things. That much could be seen by every sailor in the enormous array of naval power assembled in the lagoon, but on the thirteenth Elden and the *Franklin*'s crew learned the full amazing story. Okinawa, the doorstep to the home islands of Japan, was going to be invaded on April 1 in an enormous move called Operation Gunto.[2] To keep Japan-based kamikazes from countering the invasion, Admiral Mitscher would lead Task Force 58 the next morning on an aggressive mission called "Lucky Day."[3] They would sail northward for four days, get in close with overwhelming force to the Japanese home islands of Kyushu and Honshu, and destroy every airplane and airplane-related thing that could be found. The *Franklin*'s code name during the operation would be *Dixie*.

Walcott, Price, Dewees, Robinson, and other Vega boys Elden knew were nearby must have been much on his mind. Some of them were probably nearer one another than they would have been if all were back in their homes on the other side of the planet, but there would be not even a minute to see them or to talk by phone. The whole outfit would sail at 0730 the next morning. The few hours before then were used for reviewing what to do in emergencies and how to handle casualties—and to take on and send out precious mail.[4]

"In close" meant in danger, but it must have been thrilling and somewhat reassuring to hear that sixteen carriers of various sizes were involved, wielding power that truly was overwhelming to a deteriorating Japan. Great care was to be taken for defense, especially of the carriers. For example, the task force would move in four task groups, each with four carriers in its center, and each with a larger and more powerful screen than ever before. The carriers also hauled more planes than ever before, and a higher percentage of them were fighters devoted to knocking down attackers.[5] The pilots, already by far the personnel in greatest danger, would bear extra risk for the good of the carriers because their planes would have to be positively identified before they could approach. Even if wounded or damaged, any unidentified plane would be presumed an enemy and shot down. Shipboard sailors like Elden understood what this meant and respected the fliers for their courage.[6]

Elden's shipmate Bob Blanchard felt very secure amidst such power.[7] Elden had seen enough to know better, but despite his earlier statements of concern, he is not morose or entirely pessimistic, as evidenced by the fact that on the first day out he went to the commissary and bought enough new uniforms for the next six months. Both new chaplains held services every day; at this point there was still not much work to fill the time, and Elden may have attended.

March 14, 1945

Dear mom, Dad & Bros,
I just got back from Chow so I'll write a few lines. I'm never buisy anymore. I just have to sit here and answer the telephone is about all.

I haven't had a letter in about twelve days. Oh yes! I'll take that back as I had a letter from you, One from Gerald & One from Joye. I got them day before yesterday. They were mailed in November. They must of followed me all over The Pacific. Geralds letter had Two pictures in it. They were his School pictures. One in his football Suit & one plain. I already Had two of them he Gave me. So I'll send them back so he can send them to someone else who don't Have any. I was Glad to Get them even if they were out of date. I Got Joy's address that way. I had been wanting it so I could write her.

I think I told you I Got the allotment taken out for Twenty Five Dollars.

I'm hopeing to Get somewhere where we can bring mail on the ship. We sent it off Yesterday so you Probably Got a dozen letters in one bunch. Unless Six has had some Good luck he has probably had to Go across by now. I feel sorry for him as the army is plenty rugged duty overseas.

I went down yesterday and bought all the Clothes and things I'll need for the next six or eight months so I won't be bothered with them for some Time now.

We have to Go down and get Inoculations or booster shots today. Whatever you want to call them. I have to take two each Year I think it is. I am kinda Dreading it. I don't like them.

The Pacific War seems to have Changed a lot. It don't seem like it is as bad out here as it used to be.

Gerald said in The november letter he would like to Get to play enough to Get a basketball jacket. Did He? I hope so.

I Guess I better close for now as I don't know what to write. So long For now. Don't worry about me I'll be O.K. & a lot safer than I was The other time out here. Besides the war will be over sooner if I'm out here. Then I can come back to stay.

Love,

Elden

P.S. Luck was with me They sounded mail call a few minutes & I Got a letter from You mailed march 3. It got here in a hurry. I better close. Mabye we will Get more mail Tonight I hope So.

It was a mark of pride to crewmen like Elden that Admiral Ralph Davison commanded Task Group 58.2 from his post aboard the *Franklin*, though he occasionally moved to other carriers. His command included another carrier, the *Hancock*, of equal size to the *Franklin*; light carriers *Bataan* and *San Jacinto* (with George H. W. Bush no longer aboard); battleships *Washington* and *North Carolina*; cruisers *Baltimore*, *Pittsburgh*, and *Santa Fe*; and well over twenty destroyers and destroyer escorts. The amount of protection was extreme, but so was the danger as they approached the homeland of pilots willing to ride their flying bombs directly into great ships. Elden's mood may have swung from hour to hour between confidence and concern, or it may have been a mixture of both at all times.[8] As before, Tokyo Rose was on the air telling the sailors in an almost personal way that their approach was known, and that they had no chance of surviving the coming encounter. Mike Sansone said the men noticed that her reports corresponded so well with information in the ship's daily bulletin that it was almost as though she were watching.[9]

On the afternoon of March 15, Elden surely would have heard a crash above as a plane wrecked on the flight deck, damaging itself so badly that his buddies in V-1 had to push it overboard.[10]

Back in view of Ed Murphy's place, Grace opines that the visible construction activity is to produce a new house for baby chicks. She has not "heard anyone say" what it is, but her syntax indicates that normally she would have expected to hear. Such was the subject matter of conversation in that small place and different time.

March 16, 1945

Dear Son,

I will try my luck writing a few lines this morning before the kids gets up. I am going to let them get their nap out. But Gerald will make up for lost time when he does get up. Im going to get him at the cellar digging. There is no school today as they are having teachers meeting.

It 8:30 A.M. & I feel as tho I had done a half days work. Have the Chores done & hung out a line full of Clothes. I washed the Barber towels last night after supper.

I will send the Longhorn News. There isn't much in it but will give you something to read. I don't know much to write but to let you know every one is O.K. at home and hope you are too.

We got our share of Vitamin K yesterday.[11] The wind & dust blew Nearly all day So I have a lot of house cleaning this morning.

You'll have to excuse this letter. This pen don't want to write & there seems to be a grease spot on the paper it wont write on. Maybe you can make it out.

I have been in the soap making buisiness this week. I made up 11 cans of lye for myself and 14 cans for Mrs. Brents on the shares. So guess I'll have enough soap to do a while. They hadn't yet heard anything from Eggs and Bugs Tuesday evening when I was over there. She sure has been worried about him. But I believe Mary worries more when Bugs is home than she does away. I am glad I don't have a boy I would rather be away than at home.

I had a card from Mama the other day. Thanking me for your picture. They thought they were really good.

Well, today is Iva's birthday. Guess Ill have to go over there & see if I can whip her & yours will soon be too, Wish you were here. I know I could bend you. ha. Hope you have got your birthday box.

One year ago this morning my Boy left to join the Navy. and what a long year it has been. expect it has been for you too. But I know it has been well spent serving your country & mine & I'm always proud of you but surely hope and pray that victory is not far off.

Charles McNabb, Charles Wiseman & Toots Everts has been home, Dad said they were to leave last night on the train for the West Coast so guess they are coming your way. I talked to Charles Mc but never seen the other two. he sure didn't like Army life but said there was nothing you could do about it But to make yourself satisfied. He said he wouldn't be long going over seas Now. Didn't seem to mind too much.

Well there is a new building going up over to Ed Murphy's place. so I reckon its another brooder house. I haven't heard any one say. I don't know when Snails is having to leave. Im going over to Paulines soon as I can.

I don't know whats keeping Gene Murphy around. Ill bet he don't never go.

Bose Came over the other night and fixed Dads income tax out. Dad has some Coming back that has ben held out. About $8 I think. I went down & paid the Back Taxes on this place & this years too. It was only $7.60 in all Well I Cant think of any more to Write So will bring this scribbling to a Close.

Oh yes I do too. Nick Thomas Came thru Vega the other day on his way back to Calif—He is in the Navy and has been 2 years. Has been in the South West Pacific. He went to see Iva, Mary, Mrs. Dunning & Don here. Dad saw him down at Jims. He seems to think he might get out. Said he had Arthritis. Dad said he never said much about where he had been only Pearl Harbor he had been home on a 3 day leave & had to see Bill & Irene. He don't like the Navy.

Well I will quit this time. Write when you can.

Love as ever. Mom.

March 16 began auspiciously, as the USS *Owen* came alongside with mail. The screen protecting the *Franklin* had grown to include sixteen destroyers, and the *Owen* was one of them.[12]

Elden heard over the ship's speaker system on March 16 that they were passing to the west of Iwo Jima and that U.S. forces were prevailing in the battle that was raging there. He probably heard that a terrible price in American lives was being paid to secure the island, but that bombers and their crews were already being saved as a result. He may have reflected that his present mission was intended to reduce the price that American troops would pay when they landed at Okinawa sixteen days later. By this stage in the war he would not be surprised to hear that defenders on Iwo Jima were fighting to the death, long after all hope of victory was gone. The American attitude had become "If death is what they want, we will oblige them." Had he lived, he might not have been surprised to learn that the last Japanese soldier on Iwo Jima did not surrender until 1951.

Elden wrote a long letter in lazy, chatty language that conveys the inaction that prevails when a ship, already fully prepared for action, is approaching combat. The remarks about the ships of Wig Price and Russell Adcock having been near though he had been unable to see them help us understand the frequent hope and frustration concerning seeing friends from home. The Don Buchanan Elden mentions is another Vega boy who a few years later will be the representative of the *Amarillo Times* who recruits me as the paper's delivery boy for Vega. A bit of the nickname factor comes through in the mention of "Herks." This was Herman Brents, called "Hercules" because of his muscular physique, who had joined another branch of the service because he was pathologically afraid of water. We are not sure today who "N.S." was, but Gerald believed the initials represented a nickname "Never Sweat" for a lad who at some point had been accused of avoiding hard work.

"Things are peaceful out here," Elden writes, apparently in late morning, but he surely knows that will last for only a few more hours. He is acutely aware that they are sailing into more than ordinary danger, and most likely into extreme combat. The length of the letter, longer than most, may suggest a worry-driven longing for connection with family, or it may simply reflect time on his hands. Perhaps we should take the reassurances as meaning the opposite of what they say, but the leisurely and peaceful nature of the letter seems genuine. In any case, this will be the last such peace in Elden's short life, and his last letter home.

Dear Mom, Dad & Bros,

I don't think I've written for several days so I'll do so now. I Got a letter from you a few days ago. Also Got some that were mailed last November.

I haven't heard from Virginia in quite a while. We may get some before long. I think we will trade with another ship in a day or two. I hope so.

I have been reading the paper all morning. They sure haven't been Telling whats Going on in Germany for The last week or ten days. I've been wondering about it.

I had to Go down & take two shots yesterday my arm is sure sore. They put them in my left arm or I probably wouldn't be writing this letter. Oh Well I won't have to worry about any more of them for another year. Tommorrow at ten minutes after five I will Have a Year in the navy. It don't seem like any Time at all.

I sure hope I make S 1/c then I can take out more bonds. I guess They will have a forth of July bond drive this year. If they do I'm Going to put all that I have on the books in on it. They are going to let us draw all our money if we want it but I Guess I'll just draw five of mine a month.

I'll bet bug-Eye won't Get out of the army or navy this time if He is Drafted. I sure hope he don't.

I'm libable to write him a letter and ask him whats the matter is he yellow. He sure makes me mad at Times.

Your last letter was dated March 2 & I got it day before Yesterday. It sure did come in a hurry. Yes I got to See Krahn & Buck. We had a lot of fun even if we didn't Get liberty together. Wig left the day before I got liberty. Wig Told Krahn he thought I was there but they couldn't find my ship. They must not have looked Very Hard as I was only about a quarter of a mile from Wig all The Time & was about two hundred yards from Russel Adcock at one time & didn't Get to see Him. I didn't Go by to see Charley Robbinson either. I sure would liked to have saw him.

I Guess luck can't be with me always. Did you ever hear any more about N.S. Going to The navy? I Guess he will be Getting into something before long as he was eighteen Yesterday I hope he gets the navy if He has to go. He shouldn't have to go as his mother needs him at Home.

I Guess That's right about herks being afraid of the water. He has said that ever since I've known him.

I Guess Gerald has the cellar dug by now. Just Stay right in there. That's the way I Got my Start. (Just look where I am now) Ha! What are you Going To do? You never did say wheither You were Going to Re-build the House or Just move it. Did You ever Get to buy the Chicken House from Chas Hammer? I hope You did. You needed one, didn't you? How big of a Cellar are You digging?

I don't like the sound of Don Buchanan's ship. That is a Personal Attack it is Called. They haul troops across and up to some beach & send off landing craft. Of course buck don't leave the Ship. So it isn't too bad. He is a gunner.

Say Jerry That was a Good picture of the Garden Plow You drew. Thanks a lot.

I Guess Gerald is going To hate for school to turn Out & Jerry will Get to Go next year. I'll bet You'll be Glad won't you Jerry?

Francess Said in Her last letter This was her last Year of School & she sure is Glad. She said her & Bill was Going to get married. She said she hadn't asked her folks but she Talked like it wouldn't make much diffrence what They Said. Now Don't You write & tell Eva about it. Francess don't want them to know I don't think. So long For now. Don't be Worrying about me. Things are Peaceful out here now. To the side of what it was the last time I was out here.

Love,
Elden

Despite the claims of Tokyo Rose, the task force was not yet aware of any enemy contact, but the crews had been warned to anticipate being discovered by an enemy submarine. They would know they had been spotted when the first torpedo exploded against the side of a ship, probably in the night. An enemy sub commander might have to settle for one of the destroyer escorts or destroyers that surrounded the cruisers that surrounded the battleships that surrounded the carriers in an almost solid wall, but he would want the carrier if he could get it. Everyone knew this, and it caused lookouts to see things that were not there and to call the crew needlessly to battle stations. Extreme caution seemed better than its opposite, and sailors were used to losing sleep. It was not a big deal at first, but it would become a bigger deal as real reasons appeared for not sleeping. Also lost that night was any remaining sense that things were peaceful.[13]

Going to battle stations at dawn was routine, but doing so closer each dawn to Japan was not, and adrenaline was high as March 17 began. Moving day and night without pause, they were twenty degrees of latitude farther north than at Ulithi, and the weather was cold, cloudy, and windy. Elden's buddy from the Louisiana Cajun country between Shreveport and Natchitoches, Fireman First Class Robert Leon Bamburg, who had been corresponding with Rowena Coin, had early chow. His normal duty was in engineering (E Division), but this day he was to relieve watch in Gunnery Department, Division 6, Section I, under Section Leader Louis Casserino.[14] Elden's best buddy, Roy Treadaway, worked in the engine room far down below the waterline. Roy's job (which if done at all today would be done by a sensor and monitored remotely) helps us understand why such a huge crew was needed to run this ship. He monitored the heat of bearings on the shafts that turned the screws—not with instruments but by touch. If he felt a bearing getting hot, he would have another sailor grease it.[15]

Generally sailors on a giant ship became buddies with others they saw every day at work. Treadaway and Bamburg worked in the same division, but Elden was in a different division seven decks above. They were friends for deeper reasons than mere daily association, and they had been close since boot camp.

Japan had planted minefields to turn aside such flotillas as this, and danger became more palpable as the task force sailed into one. Now the smaller ships, destroyers and destroyer escorts, really began to earn their keep, getting out ahead of the other ships, finding the mines and exploding them with gunfire. The sounds of this action were audible to men on the *Franklin*. At 0600 Elden heard the 20 mm machine guns open up on one mine only five hundred feet away that the smaller ships had missed, and he felt the great ship shiver as the mine's concussion vibrated through it. This was one more reminder that even a large and diligent screen could not find and fend off every threat.[16]

On this fourth day of the voyage, Catholic sailors by the hundreds sought a moment of confession with Father O'Callahan. It was not a good time to be carrying burdens one might be asked to explain on Judgment Day. From his duty station perch Elden surely saw this line stretching halfway down the hangar deck, and he must have shared some of the thoughts of those men.[17]

A Japanese plane found the task force that day. It must have been shot at and pursued, but you cannot get them all and this one got away.[18] Soon others were back to reconnoiter, and the enemy knew everything they needed to know.[19] At 2154 a bogie twenty-five miles out caused the *Franklin* to go into torpedo defense, waking everyone.[20]

As we try to comprehend Elden's experiences during the waning hours of his life, it seems strange that one of the things we know best is what he was eating. The *Franklin,* aware that its presence was known and that it was within easy range of land-based planes, went on Red Alert. Among other things, Red Alert meant that there was no time for normal chow. Looking slightly incongruous wearing helmets with their white mess uniforms, men on galley duty brought sandwiches and coffee when they could to men at battle stations. The choice among types of sandwiches was not great, mostly flavorless spiced ham (Spam) or the more flavorful bologna, called "horse cock" by sailors because of the size and shape of the unsliced sausages.[21]

We know that he was sleepy. Jittery lookouts had interrupted sleep several times the night of March 16 with false alarms. There was less sleep for better reasons the night of March 17, and on the eighteenth the men were at battle stations three times between midnight and 0730.[22]

We also know what sorts of things he saw. Because Elden's normal job was a fundamental part of the air operation, we can be confident that it was also his battle station. Every time the alarm sounded he jumped from his bunk on the third deck, got into his shoes, and ran up two ladders (staircases) to the hangar deck, then up one more level to a little steel box hanging on the wall. Through glass windows in the box Elden could see planes being repaired, fueled, and armed by crews of men who were specifically assigned to care for individual planes. He could have seen the plane captains who headed each crew, our informant Irv Dahlen among them, giving their planes a quick final check, and then he could see the planes being pushed to the elevators for lifting to the flight deck.[23]

His flotilla having been discovered and thoroughly reconnoitered, Mitscher's option was to strike or to be struck, and he naturally went for offense. He gave his orders to his task group admirals, Davison relayed them to his four carrier captains, and with an hour of darkness remaining in the early morning of March 18, Gehres swung the *Franklin* into the wind and began to launch fighters and bombers. Once airborne and in formation, the planes raced landward at high speed and low altitude to evade Japan's primitive radar. They hoped to hit planes at the Kagoshima and Izumi airfields on Kyushu before the inexperienced but dangerous pilots in those places could get off the ground.[24]

It was never only a matter of offense or defense, however, but always both. There was little realistic hope of catching all of an alerted enemy's planes on the ground, and at the moment American planes were getting off the flight decks, some enemy planes were getting off the runways. The beefed-up American fighter defenses got busy dealing with the twenty-five bombers and twenty-seven kamikazes that came after the fleet. These were handled with general success, but the *Enterprise, Yorktown,* and *Intrepid* were all hit, albeit without sustaining significant damage.[25]

Those carriers, all counterparts to the *Franklin,* were in other task groups.[26] The *Franklin* seems not to have come under direct threat during the day, but her fliers knocked down eighteen of the attackers. Her offensive squadrons also had success in their attacks on the mainland, destroying many potential kamikaze planes on the ground. With planes being launched, recovered, launched, and recovered all day long, Elden and his three companions in Hangar Deck Control were at the ready to receive orders and to relay them. One of them took a call at midday with word that a returning plane had crashed on the flight deck and with directions for dealing with the slight damage it had sustained. Other than that one, it appears that few if any planes returned to the *Franklin* that day in need of special attention. Elden heard the day's events broadcast over the ship's speakers by Father O'Callahan like a play-by-play description of a baseball game, and he must have been pleased.[27] One did not have to be an officer to know that the Japanese defense had been anemic, which must have boosted his confidence. Only two American planes had been lost, and their crews had been rescued by submarines.[28]

That evening the men heard Tokyo Rose announce that the task force had been successfully attacked, and they heard once again that the *Franklin* had been sunk.[29] They also heard a report about the war in Europe, most likely that Cologne, Germany, was now in Allied hands and that the railroad bridge at Remagen had been captured and crossed, putting the battlefront east of the Rhine River. Hearing this, young Nick Turcic was moved by thoughts of ground combat to comment about how much better off sailors were with steady meals and clean bunks. Embarrassed by the almost palpable glare directed at him by an older and more experienced sailor, Turcic clammed up, realizing that the other man knew things that he did not yet know. He was about to learn.[30]

At midnight, as March 19 began on the far side of the international date line (it was midday March 18 back in the United States), the task force reversed a temporary diversionary course it had followed for the past few hours and resumed a course directly toward Japan.[31] In the forty-first minute of the new day the torpedo defense alarm routed Elden from his bunk in response to an enemy plane. At some point, as he gathered his wits, he became one of a statistically predictable nine men among the 3,400 on board to realize that it was his birthday.[32] Sleep, not birthdays, mattered now, but he got little, for the alarm repeated at 0135 and again two hours later. Perhaps there was a moment for rest after that, but a brief one if so because the fighters of the combat air patrol, the overhead screen, were launched between 0535 and 0555.[33]

Sometimes a fellow really needs a drink. Liquor was not to be had by enlisted men, but everyone knew that the forward motion of torpedoes was fueled by alcohol. It was methanol, which could cause neural blindness or worse, but scuttlebutt had it that straining it through bread would make it as safe as bourbon. At some point during this hectic night, tension got the best of a sailor named N. J. Bennet and he knocked back a slug of this torpedo juice. Bennet died from the drink, and at 0650 the attention of Commander Joe Taylor, Chaplain Gatlin, and some others was diverted to conducting a burial ceremony for him on the fantail. In all likelihood, Elden and the three others in Hangar Deck Control heard of this, or read it in the Plan of the Day, and shook their heads at the seaman's foolishness. Life was too precious to waste, and too easy to lose in more purposeful ways.[34]

Sleepy people do not think well and by now everyone, including the captain, was sleep-deprived. They were also hungry and sick of sandwiches. The prior day's action had been reassuring, and it led Gehres, the iron-pants martinet who had blamed the previous captain and the Franklin's crew for having been hit back in October, to make his own fatal error. He told the galley to cook a hot breakfast, and relaxed the ship to Condition 3, which meant attack was believed to be unlikely. Able to decide for themselves how to use their time, many men took to bunks on the third deck or lower. Others went to the head to relieve bladders or to perform the morning biological function. A great many ran to be first in line for the hot food in the galley two decks below the hangar. The galley quickly filled and a line stretched outside into a passageway, up two sets of steps, and across the hangar deck. Some men, guessing that the break would be short, napped where they were.

Access to a telephone was one of the things that made Elden's job enviable, and he used it to invite Roy Treadaway to come up for a while.[35] Not relishing several decks' worth of steps, Roy declined and sat down with his partially read novel, *Kings Row*. One of the four guys in Hangar Deck Control—we do not know who—went somewhere—we do not know where. Three stayed in their little office, and Elden's call to Roy suggests he may have intended to stay there. Perhaps they were leaning forward to sleep with their arms and heads on the desk in front of them. Or perhaps they were awake and on duty, because the *Franklin* had just recovered one combat air patrol, launched another, and was set to launch its first strike at 0700 just as Bennet's funeral ended.

The action was topside, and the V-1 Division was doing its usual efficient work, having launched seven planes in the six minutes following 0700. Thirty-one planes were on the flight deck with engines warming up for takeoff. Twelve of them were Corsair fighters, each with a "Tiny Tim" rocket ready to fire, powerful enough to destroy an enemy ship. The others were Helldivers and Avengers, carrying 500-pound bombs. Below, on the hangar deck, twenty-two more planes were armed and being fueled, ready for their turn to go topside and take off. Fueling during launching would have been visible through the windows of Elden's office. He might have known it was contrary to safety regulations, but everyone knew the captain liked to set records for speedy launches, and such matters were not for a seaman second class to second guess.[36]

More important this time was what was not happening topside. Although the *Franklin* was sixty-five miles from Japan, within quick and easy reach of land-based planes, only two of its guns were manned. Two officers on the hangar deck watched a kamikaze being shot down and almost hitting the *Yorktown*. Why, they wondered, was the *Franklin* not at general quarters with such things happening only four miles away.[37] Seaman Second Class Ray Bailey saw the mountains of Kyushu, and recalling that sunrise was a common time for attack had the same question in mind.[38] The battleship *North Carolina*, a thousand yards directly behind, warned the *Franklin* that her radar showed bogies approaching.[39] *Franklin*'s companion carrier *Hancock* gave a similar warning, and repeated it saying that one unidentified plane was just over twenty miles away. Official records do not fully support Captain Gehres's later claim that he had no reason to believe bogies were nearby, but apparently *Franklin*'s own radars showed none.[40] He merely told the two gun crews to keep their eyes on a cloud bank and to fire at any unidentified plane.[41]

The twin-engine Yokosuka D4Y3 Suisei (Comet), called Judy by Americans and faster than any American dive-bomber, was twelve miles away and hidden in clouds by the time *Franklin*'s radars found it.[42] Everett Beaver left his radar on the *North Carolina* and stepped out on the signal bridge to see for himself; on the bow in front of him Bob Palomaris ran to his deck machine gun; photographer's mate first class Al Bullock and marine corporal Andy Anderson looked up from their battle stations on the *Santa Fe*—all saw the Judy, canopy open, perform a snap roll to the left and approach the *Franklin* from dead ahead in a high-speed dive.[43] The *Hancock* radioed a last-second warning: "*Dixie, Dixie*, there's one coming in on you!"[44] Frank Albro, checking wing locks on planes about to take off from the *Franklin*, glanced upward. "I saw the bombs fall," he later recalled.[45]

Halfway around the world, it was still Sunday evening, March 18. Supper over, dishes washed, dried, and put away, Grace Rogers sat down at her oilcloth-covered kitchen table to begin a birthday letter to her son. In this pretelevision era the high school senior class play and the sophomore class play were big events (there was no junior class until 1946), and, in this time so different from ours in other ways, Gerald would play a part in which his face was blackened with burnt cork. Bugs and Eggs had been located, and young Eggs is about to be brought home by the law. One of Elden's friends has made a drunken spectacle of himself. One of our first cousins, Dale Moore, may have been about to ship out, and another, Jack Farley, a tank driver in Europe, had been wounded twice and might get the oak leaf cluster. Ancell and Grace had heard about the bombing of Japan, and they correctly guessed that Elden was part of it. Lovingly, poignantly, they wondered how he was spending his birthday, and they hoped he had received the box of sugar cookies Grace had sent.

March 18, 1945

Dear Son.

I want to write a few lines tonight & will finish up in the Morning. I feel like I just have to get a letter off in the morning & say Happy Birthday to the Best Sailor boy in Uncle Sams Navy. That May be saying a lot but you really Mean Just that to us. Surely hope by Another Birthday rolls around that all will be peaceful & Calm & I Can bake you a big birthday Cake. I really think it will be over long before then. The sooner the better. I hope you got your birthday box by now.

I went down & got Mrs Landrums Clothes while ago & I told her I was going to write you that tomorrow was your birthday & she said Give him our love. She is feeling better & is able to be up quite a bit now.

We went to the Senior play Friday Night it sure was good. Mumbo Jumbo was the name of the play.

The sophomores are going to give theirs Friday April 13 how do you suppose they will make out. Ha. The name of it is Nuts & Bolts. Gerald is a Negro boy.

Well Mrs Brents said yesterday that she had found out that Odell [Eggs] was in Las Animas. So she Called the Police up there & was having them to pick him up the sheriff was to call back as soon as he got him. Helens Sister wrote to Helen & said Bud & his buddy was staying at a Hotel. So I don't think they will have any trouble finding him. Mrs. Brents said she probly would go up there after him.

Mrs Brents told me that Junior Blassingame was going to have to leave April 2nd. I am having some more of those Kodac pictures finished for him. Junior turned the pickup over here a while back & was down town drunk & Howard Sr. told Junior to go home with him & he told his Dad he wouldn't do it so the old Man Slapped his Jaws for him & he went home with him. That's what we heard.

I wrote Cloe a letter today & fixed up a picture to send them.

We had a letter from Myrn this Morning she sure thought the picture was good Dales wife & baby was there. They hadn't heard that Dale had shipped out yet. She had a letter from Jack & he was going to get the Oak leaf Cluster for being wounded in action twice.

Myrn thought that Carroll Might be deferred but they did'nt know yet. She said she wouldn't be surprised at anything.

Sonny Morris is home Now. I talked to him in the Barber shop. He said he sure was glad to get back. He has to report to Fort Ord Calif the same place Son Wiseman & Charles McNabb went to.

Mildred Wells said this morning that Major was in Georgia. She said he had been taking schooling & still has to take his basic training.

Well Ill quit for tonight & see you in the morning.

Well here it is Monday Morning and your birthday. Wish You was here. We would take you out & roll you in the Snow. It sure is snowing and acts like it might keep up all day.

We sure are having changeable weather Thurs & Friday we had strong Winds & dust blowing. Saturday was a fair day Yesterday was too hot to be comfortable outdoors & today its snowing. But it isn't so very cold.

We are wondering how you are celebrating your birthday. The radio tells us about so many Carrier planes bombing Japan today & the last few days. Dad said if his guess is right he expects you are in on it. Wonder if his guess is right.

Well I have written all I know for Now So will Close with a birthday Wish that you are O.K. and Always will be.

All our Love. Mom & all

In Wakefield, Massachusetts, the grandmother of one *Franklin* sailor so powerfully sensed danger to her grandson that she made note of the day and time so she could ask later what he had been doing at that moment.[46] In Chicago the mother of seaman second class James L. Pipolo awoke in tears and described a nightmare. She had seen her son. "I saw no legs . . . a lot of smoke, he was reaching out for me. He tried to touch me."[47]

If Elden were awake, at his duty station, and looking through his office window into the hangar deck, he saw the plane captains and crews of twenty-two planes hustling to get them ready to go topside. Directly in front of him he saw men in a chow line that came up the ladder from decks below and strung out onto the hangar deck. Beside him were two other men, Utahan Carl Edward Coleman and Alabamian Paul Joseph Marino. He heard a few shots from the two 40 mm antiaircraft guns that were manned. And he might have seen the first of two bombs crash through the flight deck at an angle, ricochet off the hangar deck to a point just above the end of the gallery deck a few feet almost in front of him, and there explode. In all likelihood he was dead before his brain registered what his eyes had seen.[48]

If Elden had decided to go for chow, as large numbers of others did in a great rush, he was too late to make it to the chow hall two levels below the hangar deck. Most of the men who made it to the hall, or even to that deck level, survived. If the momentary delay to call a friend caused him to be at the back of the line that strung out onto the hangar deck, the explosion happened above him and slightly to the left, with the same instant result.

22   Fire and Water

MEN throughout the ship were knocked off their feet by the concussions. Seven decks down and twenty feet below waterline, Roy
Treadaway had fallen asleep reading. Even down there he was bounced
into the air. He knew the explosions had been above, most likely on the
hangar deck. A few seconds later, oxygen-bearing air rushed back into
the giant hollow of the hangar deck, mixed with the fumes of gasoline
from ruptured aircraft tanks, and made the ship a gigantic bomb; an
even greater explosion rocked the ship. It left behind a massive fire,
which then began over a period of hours to detonate fuel tanks and
bombs, and to ignite rockets that sped around and exploded here and
there. Treadaway felt a terrific vacuum and heard a whistling sound as
air was sucked out of the lower decks. He inferred that it was caused by
a huge fire far above, and he thought of his buddy Elden, who was most
likely in that fire. His thoughts were right, for only two men among the
hundreds who had been on the hangar deck were alive at the end of
that day.[1]

Many men were blown overboard by the concussive force of the
bombs, others by the vapor explosions, and yet others by subsequent
explosions of fuel and munitions. The North Carolina had to make a
sharp turn to avoid running over men in the water, as her crewmen began throwing them anything that would float.[2] All over the vast carrier
in darkened and sometimes hot and smoky compartments, pockets of
trapped men lived out individual dramas mixing stark fear and quiet

heroism, thinking things like "I wonder how the people back home are going to talk about me when they find out I've been killed"[3]; and "Oh God, I hope my mom don't hear about this . . . not knowing what happened to me, or . . . just how I died."[4] Men reassured themselves and one another: "Just hold tight; just hold on and we're going to make it out of here."[5] In one example that would become well publicized, Lt. (JG) Donald Gary found a long and convoluted way to take a few men at a time from the mess hall to fresh air near the bow on the hangar deck, and he returned over and over until he had guided everyone out.

It was not that way on the bridge, where a rattled captain temporarily lost command of himself, let alone of the ship. Executive Officer Joe Taylor maintained his wits, and in a calm demeanor made suggestions to the captain, who agreed and ordered that they be done.[6] Even Admiral Mitscher helped fill the vacuum by advising the captain to reduce speed and turn the *Franklin* in a direction that would cause the wind to take some of the smoke away from crewmen who were trying to fight the fires. This new direction was landward, however, and this would gradually bring the burning ship within fifty miles of the mainland.[7]

It is not possible to exaggerate the scenes of horror. As Aviation Machinist's Mate Third Class Glenn Davis watched a river of fire—burning gasoline—pour off the hangar deck into the water, a man running to escape a cloud of choking and blinding smoke ran directly into a spinning propeller and was obliterated.[8] Through a telescope from the USS *Hunt*, Seaman First Class Ralph Packard saw men on fire running. He also saw a crowd of men run forward to escape the explosions and then be shoved overboard by others behind them.[9] Here and there men trapped by fire faced the choice of death or the sea. Some who had helmets on remembered to unfasten the chin straps before jumping because if one entered the water feet first, a secured helmet would catch enough water to snap the neck of its wearer just like a hangman's noose. Others did not remember. Aviation Machinist's Mate Third Class Nick Mady climbed from a trapped spot down a knotted rope to the water, but still believed he would die, thinking, "I never got the chance to get married and have a family."[10] A famous photograph caught the Catholic chaplain, O'Callahan, administering last rites to Bob Blanchard on the burning flight deck, though happily Blanchard survived. Another boy, dying, asked Chaplain Gatlin to read aloud the twenty-third Psalm from his pocket Bible, and then asked Gatlin to send the Bible to his mother: "Tell her I read it."[11]

Seaman Second Class William Smith awoke from a long period of deep unconsciousness with a tag pinned to his uniform. As he and his best buddy, Glenn Hashberger, similarly tagged, made their way toward the flight deck, an officer asked where they were going. "To help with the fire hoses," they answered. "You can't do that," said the officer, pointing to the tags. "You're dead."[12]

Here and there firefighting groups got themselves organized, led by officers like Elden's division commander, Red Morgan; Joe Taylor; and even Father O'Callahan. Men took brief turns at the nozzle ends of the hoses until they could stand the heat no longer, and then rotated to the back and the next man moved to the front. Automatic firefighting systems sprayed water everywhere. The engines shut down and the ship slowed to a stop. Some of the water from the flight deck and the hangar deck went over the side, but much of it found its way into internal compartments, more on the starboard side than the port, and the ship began to tilt.[13]

Captain Harold Fitz, in a heroic maneuver, swung his USS *Santa Fe* (CL-60) alongside the *Franklin* and began simultaneously to fight the fires and take men off the burning carrier. Everyone aboard the cruiser, including Don Rickey, who would live to become a National Park Service historian and my friend and colleague twenty-three years later, knew what had happened to the USS *Birmingham* five months earlier when she had tried a similar thing alongside the burning light carrier USS *Princeton*. That carrier's magazine had exploded and had almost destroyed the *Birmingham*. There were more men on the flight deck of the

Franklin than there were fire hoses, and many who could see no useful thing to do began to transfer to the *Santa Fe*. Others, seeing them go, thought the order to abandon ship must have been given, and joined them. Admiral Davison, before moving from the *Franklin* to the *Hancock* in order to continue his direction of the task group, had recommended abandonment, but Captain Gehres had recovered enough composure to decline the advice.

Water Tender Third Class Saul Gill, in the number 1 fire room, watched the huge boilers move from the growing pressure of pent-up steam, and thought they would soon explode.[14] Not far away, at the number 4 fuel transfer and booster pump, Roy Treadaway was more worried about the increasing list. When it reached seventeen degrees, he called Executive Officer Taylor and told him that he could transfer 29,000 gallons of fuel from a full tank on the starboard side to an empty one on the port side to counterweight the list. Taylor told him to do it, he did, and the list began to correct itself. Gehres remembered having the idea presented to him and saying, "Do it, for God's sake." The captain never learned that Elden's best buddy, a tall strapping lad from the Edwards Plateau of West Texas, was the one who saved the ship from further consequences of the captain's incaution.[15]

With engines dead, there was no electricity. Inner compartments went dark, and the internal combustion engine that powered an alternate generator automatically cranked itself up to provide emergency light and power. Unfortunately for Treadaway and his companions, that engine was located in their area, and its ruptured exhaust line began to fill their compartment with deadly carbon monoxide. As Treadaway contacted his superior to get permission to leave the space, a companion named Ralph William Reuter put on a rescue breathing apparatus (gas mask) and went looking for a way out to air. He soon returned to say that he had succeeded, and at about 0930 the two of them made their way up to the engine overhaul shop on the hangar deck. They saw only one living person, a sailor so painfully injured that he would not allow them to touch him. They slipped on the oily and tilted surface and slid down to a spot on the rail that afforded a bit of shelter from the explosions that were still happening. Thinking they might have to jump, but uncertain what to do, they removed shirts and shoes just before the Group Five ammunition magazine made the decision for them.[16]

The explosion sent them flying over the rail, far enough to clear a floating fire of gasoline atop the water. Treadaway pulled the pin to inflate his life jacket, but instead of feeling its sudden embrace, he heard its gas hiss away through shrapnel holes. He and Reuter began to swim, two among hundreds struggling to save their own lives or the lives of others. Some men shared life jackets; some gave their life jackets to others who appeared weaker; and some, like Yeoman Second Class John Franklin Brown who had done the latter, drowned as a result.[17] Others clung to the sides of the few lifeboats present, with the weakened and wounded inside, and some clung to anything that floated by. Ships picked up men when they could, and after Treadaway had kept himself afloat for about three hours, the *Santa Fe* came by and threw him some lines. He missed them, so the cruiser began to back up for him, but her screws created an undertow that started to pull him down. When he swam away to avoid being drowned, the *Santa Fe* gave up, cut loose a cargo net containing life jackets, and went on to rescue others who could be reached without threat. He and Reuter shared one life jacket for a time, and eventually found a sailor who gave them one of the two he had. Their body heat ebbed away for four more hours until finally the USS *Miller* (DD-535), having just delivered Admiral Davison from the *Franklin* to the *Hancock*, stopped for them. Roy let go of his life jacket and began to climb up the cargo net just as a Japanese bomber, one of many attracted by the column of smoke above the *Franklin*, dropped a bomb. The *Miller*, putting first things first, began firing at the plane and immediately went to flank speed, and the net jerked out of Roy's grasp. He swam again, without flotation, for another half hour before the *Miller* was able to return and at last drag him on board at about 1600.

Tired when the day had begun, and having spent seven hours in the life-draining cold of the water, Roy was hardly aware when they cut his remaining clothing off, injected him with a sedative, and treated the burns and shrapnel wounds he had not even begun to feel.[18]

Eventually the fires were out, and the cruiser *Pittsburgh* took the wallowing *Franklin* under tow and began to move her slowly away from Japan. Later she was able to fire up one turbine and to move slowly under her own power toward Ulithi, accompanied by other ships carrying rescued crewmen. Barely one-fifth of her original complement was still on board to operate the ship, with another fifth wounded, two-fifths missing, and another fifth dead. At one point during the worst of the fires Captain Gehres had signaled Admiral Mitscher, "If you will save us from the Japs, we will save this ship," and the message became the first block in the building of a legend. The captain's composure had returned, and unfortunately it returned with a vengeance.[19]

23 "There's Dead People in There!"

Saving the *Franklin* from the Japanese still took some doing. The enemy sent forty-five planes out on March 20 to finish her off and to hit other ships, and forty-one of these were shot down by angry defenders swarming from sister carriers. While that statistic reveals the near-total dominance of America's expert pilots at this stage of the war, it also reveals the effectiveness of untrained but determined kamikaze pilots, for two got through and struck the carriers *Essex* and *Wasp*. These giants fell in with the sad procession back toward Ulithi; the destroyers *Hunt*, *Tingey*, *Hickox*, *Marshall*, and *Miller* (on which Roy Treadaway slept unaware) wound up the rescue effort.[1] More than 1,700 men had been rescued, almost half of them from the water.[2] New and different forms of hell awaited almost all of them.

For those still on board the *Franklin*, this might have been the right time for a tough and unfeeling captain, because the reality that had to be faced required everyone to be that way. The top two decks were a hellish shambles of twisted steel, wrecked airplanes, and dead friends everywhere in every imaginable—actually unimaginable—condition. Some compartments below the hangar deck were filled with water, and some with bodies of men who died of smoke inhalation. This was a time to confront a tangible reality that was enough to destroy the sanity of any man who allowed himself to think or to feel. The captain put the men to work and drove them hard. A moment of rest might permit a moment of thought, and a moment of thought might pull the most rational mind over the brink. There was water to be pumped, wreckage to be pushed overboard, and bodies and remnants of bodies to be gotten off the ship.[3]

The two chaplains valiantly performed solemn funeral services and traditional burials at sea, but they were soon overwhelmed by the magnitude of the task. The ship reentered a tropical climate, and warmth and moisture turned human remains from objects of respect into hazards to the living. Garbage cans became mortuary vessels; scoops, brooms, and mops became instruments of removal. Over the next five days, four hundred bodies went over the side in ways no one could call burial.[4]

Grace, unaware and thankfully never to learn of the situation just described, sent an Easter card. The letter enclosed with it reveals how worry would build up at home when letters did not arrive regularly and also refers to our family's practice of milking several cows, separating the cream, and hauling that cream in specially designed ten-gallon cans to a creamery in Amarillo. There, the cream, and perhaps a few dozen eggs, would be sold for enough money to enable Grace to buy a few personal items for herself or her kids. She worries a bit about Bish McKendree, gossips about two local women being pregnant, begins to accept Virginia as a possible member of the family, and then gives the latest news about Bugs and Eggs.

> *Easter Greetings*
> *Every Easter bud and blossom*
> *At this season will convey*
> *The message of true happiness*
> *That's sent to you today.*
>   Mom Dad. Gerald & Jerry (look inside)

March 22, 1945

Dearest Sonny—

I think Id better make an extra effort to write a few lines this morning. We got 3 letters from you yesterday. Sure was glad to hear & that you was O.K. We hadn't heard for 2 weeks. So it pepped us up Considerably. Hope you have heard from us & sure hope you got your birthday box. Did you get the address book.

I got your letters yesterday morning as I was starting to Amarillo with Marie, Linda & Mrs McKendree. So I read them on the way. I got a Map & hope it is like you want. Will try to get an envelope of some kind to send it in. if I Cant Ill wrap it up. Now don't worry about asking for things as those little things we Can do for you is Certainly a pleasure. Only wish we Could do More.

Well our storm only lasted a day & we are having beautiful weather again. Sure hope it stays this way. I took my cream to town. Got some materiel for me an Easter dress & the kids some clothes.

I went by Jack & Lauras [Krahn] place yesterday. She waved at me. I went in a minute. They have a right cute place. She ask about you. I think she already knew you had seen E.L. She said she never seen you while you were home.

Hots was operated on last Friday. He is doing fine will get to Come home Monday. If hes still doing O.K. McKendrees are sure Blue about Bish. But are still hoping he is O.K. They said Dub wrote that he was due a 30 day leave this summer Sure hope he gets to Come as it would help his folks as well as him.

Melba Joe (Hobbs) Williams is working in the Red & White Store Now. Ruth W. had to quit. They are telling she is pregnant. Also Old Lady N.[5] Ha. Can you beat that. I know this is all interesting to you but thought Ill tell you. Ha.

I haven't heard any more from Virginia. Did I ever tell you that Grays had your photo in their Window. That made me rather proud.

Now we don't intend for you to pay for those pictures. That was My Idea & I done the giving to Who I wanted too—so you are not paying for them. Its Nice of you to send the allotment home, and you can be sure we wont take any More than we have Coming—how much do you say it is? I don't know for sure. Its Nice you are getting the extra for Clothes. It will help out & I hope you get the 1st Class rate too. That will mean quite a bit. You know if you are going to be Married When you Come back You will be Needing all these extra pennies—as who knows you may be saving up Coupons before too long.[6] Ha. Ha. Well I don't know Virginia only thru her letters but I think she sure is nice & I think Ill be proud of her as a Daughter in law. I sure hope you do Make it home by Next Christmas & hope its for good.

I haven't saw Sixes lately but the last I heard they had'nt heard from Carlton. Well I guess you Got My letter with his address in it & Joyes too. Ive sent them both.

I sure am glad you are getting the watch fixed there. Its so much quicker than you Could send it home.

Say how about the smoking habit? Did you quit or go back?

I hated to hear you & your buddy was Separated but it will be O.K. when he gets acquainted again. Is Ted Hickman still with you?

Guess Junior Blassingame will leave April 2 & for the infantry Ill bet.

Well as to Bugs & eggs—Brents got a telegram from the Las Animas Sherriff that he was holding Eggs in Jail & Mr. Brents has gone now after him—he probly wont feel so smart now or Bugs either. Probly Bugs will come tagging back as he has to have a buddy or he wont go.

Well I am out of time & space so will go Mail this & Write another right away.

Love,
Mom & all

The following day, Chaplain Joseph O'Callahan wrote on behalf of the captain to the next of kin of all who were killed or missing in action. I am not sure whether this letter ever reached our family, or any others. Knowing what we know now, we see the duty of a minister to comfort the afflicted taking precedence over the Ninth Commandment's admonition to tell the truth. Portions of its eight paragraphs follow.

> Your loved one did not suffer. The attack was so sudden and the resulting explosions so rapid and intense that there was time only for a short prayer and then death came.
>
> There is a further source of consolation—the reverence which enshrouds a military burial at sea, however abbreviated the ceremony might be. In times of great catastophy, the human soul penetrates directly to the important spiritual essence of things; in times of great catastrophy, reverence does not need the normal ornaments of ceremony. Had you been here you would have been indelibly impressed with the reverence of those who committed the body of your loved one to the depths of the sea. At the conclusion of the burials, and when the ship was beyond the combat area, there were held Catholic, Protestant, and Jewish Memorial Services with full military honors.[7]

True, most deaths had come quickly, but the stuff about the short prayer was wishful thinking and the good father knew full well that the description of the respectful burials was simply not true.[8] Decades later, Chaplain Grimes Weldon Gatlin, trying to record history rather than to comfort next of kin, came closer to the truth: "When we found a body it went over the side and this went on for five days until we reached Ulithi. All hands turned out for a memorial service for the dead."[9]

Over the years our family developed a generalized notion of a solemn and respectful ceremony and burial at sea, and Elden may have had that. Unquestionably he was honored in the one ceremony for all. On the other hand, he may have been among those for whom there was no time for formality. As we shall see, there are yet other possibilities.

Sad songs are a form of emotional insurance. Cultures accustomed to hardship use them as a means of preparation for future loss. Singing a sad song or hearing it sung is a sort of premium paid, a small increment of grief experienced in advance to make genuine tragedy more bearable. Drawing upon a tradition running back through hardscrabble Appalachia to Ireland and Scotland, country music in wartime America had produced such a song, called "The Soldier's Last Letter." About a mother, and too realistic in its time, it could wring tears from all but the hardest-hearted, and in a small way it could toughen in advance hearts that were more vulnerable.

The *Franklin* is approaching Ulithi at the center of a sorrowful convoy as Grace on March 25 finds time to write two letters. The first one, to go through regular mail for three cents postage, is only an enclosure with the high school newspaper that Elden had seemed to enjoy receiving. Acknowledging Elden's devotion to country-and-western singer Ernest Tubb, she lists the songs in an Ernest Tubb songbook recently purchased. Ironically she comments that Gerald knows one song—"The Soldier's Last Letter"—unaware of its poignant appropriateness.

March 25, 1945

Dear Son.

I will write a line & put in this letter with the Longhorn News & some Clippings (Jokes from the Furrow) & Ill send them 3 cents mail. Will Write a letter this evening to go off Air Mail in the Morning. This may get there as quick as the Air Mail letter. We got 3 letters from you Wednesday & Thursday & the one we Got thurs was wrote first. So We Cant tell how they will go.

We ordered a New Song book of Ernest Tubb Songs. Its Book no. 3. Will send it to you if you want it. It only has one song that Gerald knows & that's the Soldiers last letter. Ill send the names of the songs & you'll know if you Want me to sent it to you.

They are.

Soldiers last letter	Theres Nothin on My Mind
Tomorrow Never Comes	Just Rollin on
Ive lived a lie	My Mother is lonely
Mean Mama blues	Im Missing you
Careless Darlin	Ill Never loose you—Though youre gone
Sun down & Sorrow	That's all she wrote
Left all Alone	Married Man Blues
Im Waiting for you	Keep My Memory in your heart
Why do I Cry over you?	Just Crying to Myself
That's Why Im Crying over You	Swell San Angelo
	You wont ever forget Me

Now that's the names of the songs & there are Some pictures of Ernest Tubb his wife & 2 Children & others. So you tell me if you want it sent.

Well I see Bats Denny is back again. But I haven't heard how Come him to be back.

The kids & I went to Church this Morning. It sure was pretty this Morning but is a little Clowdy this afternoon. Don't know what it will do next. The wind blew 90 to nothing yesterday & day before. I will be glad when March is over & Maybe the wind will be too.

Today is Carls Birthday. He is 42.

Next Sunday will be Easter Sunday & also April fool. Will be 16 years since you told Charley Apricot. Ha. Ill bet he will think of it.

Well I will sign this off & Mail it.

Love from Home.

Mom & All

The *Furrow* was a farm magazine distributed by the John Deere farm implement company free of charge to customers and potential customers as a form of advertisement. Grace has clipped a page of jokes—corny and behind the times even for then—and enclosed it with her note above and the school paper. The "apricot" incident alluded to was covered back in chapter 2. "Bats" is Harold Denny; the origin of his nickname is now lost.

Some of the *Furrow*'s jokes:

Obvious. A reporter was interviewing a 100 year old man. As usual, the questions as to whether the old man had smoked, chewed, used liquor, were asked.

"I sure did," the centenarian bragged, "Been smoking and chewin and drinkin since I was 16."

"That's strange," said the reporter, "I had an uncle who was a tough old rascal and proud of it. But why do you suppose he died at 80? He always used tobacco and drank like a fish."

"Trouble was," retorted the 100 year old, "he didn't keep it up long enough."

Thought They Wouldn't Mix. Pat and Mike ran a coal yard. Pat was converted during a revival meeting. Although Mike was not a particularly "bad" man, he showed no interest in Pat's exhortations to attend revival sessions. When Pat became insistent, pressing Mike for a decision, Mike finally stated his position. "It's not that I'm agin religion, Pat," he explained. "It's just that I'm worried about the business."

"Faith, and whut harm would a little religion be in our business?" said Pat.

"Well, if we both go and get religion, who's goin't weigh the coal?"

Next, Grace turns to the information and, of course, the gossip that merit the higher postage of air mail. As always this includes information about who is in the war, who is not, and who is about to go. The patriotic fervor that had men lining up to volunteer three years earlier is now little in evidence. Most of the people mentioned are no more eager to volunteer than Elden had been, but the mother who has a kid in the service in 1945 sees things through a different lens than had the mother who had not wanted her kid to go in 1944. In southeastern Colorado kids far too young are still getting married, and Eggs has been saved from his wayward path by his dad having him clapped in the Las Animas jail and then fetching him home. Bugeye is told by the law there to keep a job or keep out of town. Castle is Charlie Castle, owner of a local feed store, who lives directly across Sixth Street from our house. Grace has gone to pick up barber Wallace Moore's towels in order to wash them for a small fee. Finding the barbershop closed, the teetotaling laundress guesses that he might be drunk—maybe an unfair judgment, but maybe not. Vega was a dry town in a dry county. Drinkers there had to be opportunistic, and this meant that a "special occasion" worthy of special celebration could be defined as any occasion when one had something to drink.

March 25, 1945

Dear Son,

Now Ill try Writing the Air Mail letter. Just in case you get this first Ive sent a 3 cent letter. With the Longhorn News, Some Jokes & a few lines in it. We are all O.K, at present & hope this finds you the same.

Well it wont be long now for Snails & Gene Murphy. They leave for induction the 2nd of April & Marvin Slutz & Dock Ivy goes for their physical the 2nd. Bellow was to go or he had his physical with Snails. But I don't know if he got deferred or Not. I have'nt heard anything about John L. But I doubt if he goes. I figured Gene M. would squirm out of it some way but I guess he is'nt.

I went to Amarillo Wednesday & saw Rankin. She said T.C. was on Guam. Guess you have his address. You might get to see him.

I sure was glad you got to see Krahn. Hope you got off on liberty together.

I guess you got your watch fixed by now. I sure was glad you Could have it fixed there as it was much quicker than you Could send it home.

Mrs Robinson told me that Russell was on a ship, or did I tell you?

Well I went down & Mailed the letter & I saw Winnie & talked to her a few minutes. She said Mr. Robinson had been pretty sick but was better. Mr. & Mrs. Robinson are going to Kansas in a few days to visit his Mother.

She also said Charley Robinson has a very Serious heart ailment. His wife told her. But Robinsons dont know it.

Well I sure am glad you like your new Job & I hope you get first Class soon.

I have been thinking Maybe I would hear from Virginia again but I haven't. Guess she don't have any thing to write.

Well Mr. Brents went to Las Animas & brought his little son back. He told Daddy that Eggs was plenty glad to see him. They put him in jail until Jeff got there after him. Jeff said he Couldn't tell the sheriff any thing about Bugs. Said they already had his Number. They had told Bugs this time he was up there that he would have to get a job & get to work & stay at it or to go back to Texas one. That they was'nt going to have any loafers around in these kind of times.

Bugs was working some where out in the country & Jeff never even seen him. Eggs has started back to school & he told Gerald that he was'nt going to run around with that Guy any More. So maybe he has learned a lesson. The law gave Eggs a good talking to when they locked him up & then another one when they turned him over to his dad. Eggs told Gerald he was going to get married if his dad had'nt come after him. Ha ha Said his girls name was Ruth H. Do you know her. He is'nt yet 16.

I hope you got My letter with Sixes address in it. I should have kept a Copy & sent it more than once but I went by there & Just Copied it in your letter so I don't have it here. But Ill get it again if you don't have my letter. I know he has gone overseas. They had'nt heard from him 2 weeks ago but I imagine they have by now. Ill go over in a day or two & get the dope on it & I can write it in my Next letter. I feel sorry for Mrs. Six. But I think she should realize she is'nt the only Mother who has a boy in the Service. But I feel more sorry for Carlton As his did'nt get his Choice about what he wanted in.

Well Al Campsey Anna & La Rue Came by a while ago. They were hunting Castle to get some Chicken feed. They are on a farm Now about 15 miles South west of here (McForesters Place). Doc & Lois is on one of their places too. Don't see why Al went on a farm. He is too old for the draft. Ha. He probly thought he Could Make More. It Costs so much to live in Amarillo—rent to pay & every thing.

Boy I guess the Pineapple Juice was Cheap. Wish I Could get some at that price. That was 7 ½ cents a Can. Its good for you too.

Yes Ill be satisfied if you can Make it back by Christmas. But hope its over sooner than that. But Ill be looking forward to when You'll Come in and wake us up again. & also planning on seeing Virginia too then.

Well Your Friday dinner sounded good to us. We don't get Salmon Much & I sure like it. We got some Black Pepper a day or So ago. That's another hard to get Item. I also got some oil Cloth. But Im Not Complaining about What I cant get. & Im Not a hoarder and I think we get along O.K.

Iva & Cal butchered a Calf & they gave us a Nice roast for todays dinner. It sure was good. Dad said to tell you that Texans was the ones they knew Could do things was probly the reason You Could'nt trade & get shore duty. But maybe you Can when you have been out this time & Come back.

From what the News tells us it looks like the war will be over in Europe in 2 or 3 more weeks.

Well here I am at the Post Office Monday Morning. I have my washing machine going & Came after Wallaces towels. He isn't there so of Course I wonder if hes drunk.

I got a Birth Announcement from Emma Turpin Brookshire. She has a baby boy born Mar 9 Named Tommy Ray. So I guess Ill have to send him something.

We are all O.K. this A.M. & able to work if we should want to as it Certainly is a lovely day.

Well I must sign off for this time hope you are O.K.

Love as ever—

Mom & all

⚓

Anger is a ready substitute for feelings of guilt, and all of the worst characteristics of a guilty authoritarian were now magnified in the seething anger of Leslie Gehres. The *Franklin* limped from Ulithi toward Hawaii, operated by a mere 704 men. These were the men who had not left the ship—for any reason, voluntarily or otherwise—on March 19. Surviving the fires, explosions, threatened capsizing, and the horrific aftermath had welded them into a unique solidarity. The captain named them the 704 Club, and would soon make the club a seedbed for discord.

During this voyage, any human remains found here or there within the wreckage were buried at sea with less urgency and with time for normal ceremonies.

⚓

Grace's letter is brimming with clues to the "different world" of 1945. In Ancell's job he was one of a small crew who kept about sixty miles of U.S. Highway 66, from east of Bushland, Texas, to the New Mexico state line, in good repair and free of snow, weeds, and trash. While at work, these men found a vast variety of items that had been lost or abandoned by the vast variety of people who traveled what was then one of the world's primary roads. Among the strangest of Ancell's finds was a lidded five-gallon bucket of hog fat. Grace, calling upon a skill that had been universal among pioneer women but was rare by 1945, promptly "rendered" grease by boiling the fat and then combined the grease with lye and hot water to make laundry soap.

She also canned beef for Mrs. Brents, perhaps for pay and perhaps "on the shares" in which she would keep a share of the canned beef. Homes did not yet have freezers. Many people still raised and butchered their own beef and pork, and what was not eaten within a few days had to be preserved by older methods.

Grace had made herself a new Easter dress and hopes to make a second one this day. She was an excellent seamstress, and on her foot-powered Singer sewing machine she made most of her own dresses and virtually all of the shirts worn by Ancell and the boys. The flour she used in baking bread twice each week and the feed for the chickens she fed twice a day came in bags made of good-quality print-patterned fabric that she collected until she had enough to make garments.

Evon is a daughter in the often-mentioned Brents family. The spelling is a phonetic rendering that in many places might have been spelled Yvonne, but the only person in Vega actually named Yvonne, a little girl who lived with Pop and Coogie Landrum, was called "Wye-vone."

The ever-present matter of rationing is mentioned. Audie Morgan, who was Ancell's boss on the highway crew, coworker Burt Ballard, and the Rogers family had applied for ration coupons that would allow them to purchase tires for their automobiles. Getting tires had been a serious problem throughout the war, and Grace's apparent optimism may reflect a diminished scarcity of rationed materials, or perhaps the Rogers family has earned a higher chance of approval by just waiting its turn.

March 29, 1945

My Dear Son.

Ill write a few lines this Morning. I don't think I know Much to write but feel like I should write you twice a week at least whether I know any thing to write or Not.

We are all O.K. at home and that's worth a lot I think. I hope you are O.K. too.

I went over to Mrs. Sixes yesterday evening to see if she had heard from Carlton but she was'nt at home. So I will go by there this Morning as I go to Mail this. Then I Can write a few More lines—

Well I thought I was through Making soap. But of all things to find on the highway Dad came home with some soap grease. Ha. It was Clean hog fat that had never been rendered out. It is strong but Not spoiled so I am going to Make it up today. It will Make up 6 Cans of lye. So if I keep on I will have enough soap to Wash Clothes for My Grand kids. Ha. It May last that long. But it will keep & I sure do use lots of Soap.

Well I have a Job for Friday or Saturday Canning beef for Brents. I don't care much about the Job but she is working so guess Ill take pity on them. She is Working at the Conoco Café. Since Evon went to Clarence.

I made Me a New dress yesterday. Guess its My Easter dress & have another one I want to Make today. If I get around to it.

Well I went to the Ration office Tuesday & put in for 2 New tires. But haven't got the returns Yet. We should get some if Ballard & Morgan does. I think they put in too.

Mrs. Dunning & Don has been down here Visiting the past Month and are going home Friday.

Dad Morris is in bad shape in the hospital. They have to set up with him every Night. I doubt if he Comes out of it.

Charles McNabb tried to Call Bose & Vada last Sunday Morning while they were at Church. & of Course Pop Landrum Never went after them. Then after Noon Vada tried to Call him & they told her he Couldn't Come to the telephone then Unless it was a sick or death Message. So they figured he was shipping out. I don't think it would have hurt Pop to go or send after them. But that shows what kind of an American he is. I would do that for Any body.

We sure had a pretty day Yesterday but it acts like the Wind Could blow today if it half tried. Well March is Nearly gone so Maybe the Wind is too.

I have been trying talk Dad into laying off Saturday & getting the Water put in here. But don't know if I Can or Not. It sure would Make the home work lots easier for Me & it has to be done some time any how.

Well I will quit for Now & will write More at the Post Office.

Well I am at the P.O. I went over to Mrs Sixes & she wasnt home again So I stopped at Mrs. Corseys (She lives where Valta did) & she said Mrs Six was gone to Okla & had been for 2 weeks but they hadn't heard from Six any More when she left so Ill have to see her when she gets back.

I Must Close—
Love. Mom & all

Pop and Coogie Landrum, down at the telephone exchange, were close friends of the Rogers family although Pop sometimes annoyed Grace by his curmudgeonly nature and by his irreverent references to Holy Scripture. "Like it says in the Bible," he might prevaricate with a hidden grin, "a fool and his money soon part." The telephone exchange was located in the middle of the first block of West Main Street, in the spot now occupied by the back end of the bank building. The front room of the building contained a hand-operated switchboard shaped like an upright piano and containing perhaps 100 connections, a telephone booth, some heavy mission-style furniture upholstered with itchy black horsehair, and almost always a cloud of smoke from Pop's cigar. Behind the business room was a succession of rooms serving as living quarters for the Landrums, who could be roused from sleep at any hour of the night if a call had to be made. The exchange finally became obsolete in the mid-1950s, and the building was later moved to Iron Well Camp on the Bridwell Ranch.

The First Baptist Church, of which Vada McNabb was a "pillar" and Bose a deacon, was located about three hundred feet north of the telephone office. Grace is much put out with Pop because when Charles McNabb called his parents just before shipping out, Pop refused to leave the switchboard, walk over to the church, interrupt services, and bring Charles's parents to the office telephone booth for a farewell conversation with their son. In the continuing theme of "a different world," it seems amazing today that anyone would even have thought such a degree of personal service possible, let alone be annoyed that it was not performed. The difference is also evident in the indication that people generally did not expect to make telephone calls during the night. But such was small-town 1945, and that past is a foreign country.

The "Queen" Grace mentions on April 1 is a milch cow. The Jersey cow with a new calf was unimaginatively named Jersey and gave somewhat small quantities of milk exceptionally high in cream content. A third cow, a Guernsey named Sally, had a mean streak and was prone to kick or butt. Blackie, the fourth and by far the best cow, was a Jersey-Holstein cross who provided enormous quantities of extremely rich milk.

April 1, 1945

My Dear Son.

Well I am Not going to April fool you by writing a letter as I know you will be looking for one. We are all O.K. this fine Easter Sunday and sure hope you are too. I wish you Could have been along this morning at Church. We surely had a nice Easter Sermon. And some how it Made me more Thankful than ever for our Savior that died on the Cross that we Might have life More abundantly. And I Never forget to Thank him for a Son like you. An All American Sailor. So Brave & True Blue. I always ask him to Watch over you & keep you from harm & expect you to do the same.

Well Junior Blassingame & Gene Murphy leave tomarrow for induction (in the walking Army I expect) & Dock Ivy & Marvin Slutz goes for their physical. Gerald said he hoped his Class gave Marv a party if he passes & has to go. It don't seem possible that he is old enough.

Well Jerry has had quite a bit of fun with Easter eggs. He has hid them several times. Gerald will hide or hunt them for him But he comes in the house if a car comes by. Gerald has gone down town he has been going up by Joe Russells Most every Sunday & plays Ball a while. The Whole Neighbor hood plays—even the girls including Ruby & Frances Foster. Ha. Think that's what Makes it interesting for Gerald.

I seen Loreta Ferguson down to the Post Office & she ask me if I had heard What you Wrote Junior & she said You wrote him that you were going to get Married When you Come back again. So I reckon it will be all over town if she knows it. Well Maybe you don't Care. But I kinda hated it for her to know it.

This sure is one Beautiful day. Hope its this pretty tomarrow & Ill wash.

I really have been busy this past week. I washed 3 times. Ironed. Made 2 dresses & a batch of Soap. Kept Lethas baby while she went to Amarillo & helped Mrs Brents Can beef a half a day.

Well our Jersey Cow had a bull Calf last night. It's a Red Bull. Sure is pretty. We are going to go out to Prices after while & Bring Queen in here. We will have 4 Cows and 2 Calves here then. Sure is lots of bother without the water in here. Dad did'nt lay off yesterday & Pipe the water in here like I wanted him to. Im going to have a fit if they don't get it in pretty soon.

Well Gerald is getting along Slow but Sure with the Cellar. I guess he got it deep enough yesterday. It isn't so very big-about 7 by 8 unless they make it bigger but it will hold all my Canned stuff Meat lard Soap & all that Junk.

Well I doubt if we get to do any thing about the house this summer & we wont move it either unless we Could make a Concrete Basement. When we get the Cellar done & I can move my Junk out of the Bed room. Im going to paper & paint it & build in a Closet.

We got a letter from you Yesterday & talk about speedy Service. You wrote it Mar 16. It was post marked the 24th & got it yesterday. Just a week later. Sure was glad to hear from You. It probly was peaceful & Calm When you wrote that letter but we think it probly Was'nt so peaceful a few days later & since then. I am wondering if you got your Birthday Box. I got some more pictures finished of those you & Snails took & gave them to Dollie to give him Yesterday evening.

You never did say if you got the kodac pictures I sent You or not and the address book.

Hope you got the Map & was like you Wanted. Guess the old November letters didn't seem much the News. Wonder where they had been all this time. I think I told you that Emma Turpin Brookshire has a baby boy. Named Tommy Ray. I sent it a gift box powder Soap & Oil.

Well I wish you Could have seen Wig & Russell & Charley or in fact any one from home.

No we never bought the Chicken house from Charley. Dad rigged up another we Can get by With. He will have to fix a place for little Chicks one of these days but we don't get them till May 1st.

Mrs Buchanan told me one day that Don had Written her that he had one star on his pin. So she said that meant one Battle.

Well I think Eva is expecting Frances to get married. She told me before Xmas that Frances said she Might get Married but she wasn'nt wanting her too for a while.

Well here it is Monday Morning and the Weather is some what different from yesterday. The wind is in the North and 49 Degrees. It's a little mist in the Air. Im going to wash whether I dry them or not.

Edward M was playing ball yesterday & sprained his Ankle. So he is laid up in bed this morning Cant walk on it. So wont get to go to school & there is a Base ball game this P.M with Adrian. Gerald said he bet it griped Mathes because he would'nt get to go. I think he would rather play ball than to eat. Gerald took him over a bunch of funny books to read.

Well I Will Close for this time & go mail this & get Mrs Landrums Clothes & Wallaces towels.

Bye Bye, Mom

Roy Treadaway had remained aboard the USS *Miller* until the convoy reached Ulithi. There he was then placed on the Coast Guard recovery ship *General Hugh L. Scott* (AP-136) and after a few days moved again to a liberty ship. The USS *Cushman K. Davis* delivered him to Pearl Harbor, where he was admitted to the Red Hill Hospital just up the mountainside from the base.[10]

After the *Franklin* had undergone a minimal cleaning up at Ulithi and set out for Pearl Harbor, word of her tragedy spread within the navy. High-ranking officers assembled at Ford Island to see for themselves what was not yet publicly known. At the harbor's entrance on April 3, a pilot boarded to steer the ship through the channel to berth F-12, but the captain scorned the service. Other ships saluted with their whistles, and the choir of WAVES who had sung the crew away exactly one month before was ready to welcome them back. There are good reasons why pilots routinely steer ships inside crowded and complex harbors. Gehres passed too close for comfort to other vessels, and then approached the mooring at too great a speed. As the WAVES began to sing, the captain suddenly yelled, "Back full," and "Right full rudder," then the women and admirals alike scampered to safety before the crippled giant crashed where they had been standing. Gehres, true to form, later attempted to blame the mooring detail for the consequences of his arrogant ineptitude.[11]

Grace writes on April 5, 1945, passing along gossip that her circle of friends found scandalous, and sharing a snippet of Ancell's understated sense of humor (Gerald has done such a good job digging that Ancell bought him a new spade). Junior Blasingame, now two months past eighteen, has at last gone away to war. Grace allowed Junior's mother a little private time that morning and then went to her home to offer support. Mrs. Brents, who had three sons in the service, also soon arrived.

In perhaps the most touching passage of the whole body of correspondence, the three mothers sat together and wept.

April 5, 1945

Dear Son.

I will try writing a few lines this morning. We got a letter from you Yesterday. Dated Mar 12. It was older than the one we got last Saturday the one we got Sat was dated Mar. 16. We sure was glad to get them. I haven't as yet got over 3 letters at one time. I have been getting some Nearly every week. I don't imagine You have been Getting Many from the way you Write. But hope they will soon Come in. I am still wondering if you got the birthday box. Also the kodac pictures. Address book & Map.

Winona Blassingame & Betty Milhoan Came over here Yesterday & got the Negatives of those pictures you & Junior taken. They wanted to have some more Made. I had one each Made for Junior. They also borrowed my kodac as they had some films & wanted to take them up. I sure hope they take Care of it. I still have 1 roll of films you got. I will take some some these days But I don't know what to take them of.

Brents folks are looking for Forest to Come home one these days. Louies training is almost Complete now. So they are thinking he'll be Going over seas before long.

I saw Valta down to the store the other day & she said they had a letter from Carlton last Saturday. He was still at Sea & Could'nt tell where he was.

I went over to see Pauline Monday after noon after Junior left. She sure was broken up. She said she thought she knew what it was to give up a boy by the Neighbor boys going But she Never had any Idea until she gave up her own. I sure felt sorry for her. Mrs Brents Came in too while I was there & we all Cried together. I know Pauline will feel better after she has time to hear from him. Pauline said Junior wanted her to write to you as he had'nt heard in quite a while and she had written to you. So it would be Nice if you Would write her a letter & give her a few words of incouragement.

Well Easter Sunday was sure beautiful but we have paid up for it since. We have had Mist & Ice freezing & snow to Cover the Ground twice & is still Chilly but the sun shone Yesterday & is today.

Gerald got the Cellar deep enough but they haven't dug the stair way or put a roof on it yet. So he is digging ditches Now for the Water line. Dad said he had done so well he went & bought him a new spade. Ha. Gerald didn't seem to appreciate it Much. See there will be post holes to dig too if we get it fenced and we want too. There sure is lots to be done.

We went out to Mack Prices Sunday & brought Queen to town So we have 4 Cows & 2 Calves here now. Queen will be fresh soon too.

Dad Morris is home from the hospital but he is'nt doing any good. He is in bed all the time. I doubt if he gets up.

I haven't heard any more from Virginia so I expect she is hearing from you too. I guess Bugs is still in Colo & working as they told him he would have to work or get out. The law said No loafers in war time.

Old Robert H got drunk the other day & was on Thelma Ruths porch Just Cussing a blue streak & Thelma Called John Haliburton to Come & lock him up & he did & while he was in Jail his wife loaded 7 kids in the Car & left for her folks. They let him out the Next Morning. I don't know what they will do. But they say he gets mean when he drinks any more & has whipped his wife & threatens his kids.

Well I guess Id better sign off for this time & get this Mailed.

Hope you are O.K. every thing is at home.

Love & all good Wishes from home. Sure glad you got your watch. Did you see Red Dewees.

Mom & all.

On this meaningful day Grace receives Elden's letter of March 14 and is motivated to write him a second time. Dr. Oscar H. Lloyd and his wife, Lulu Mills Lloyd, pioneers of the still young Vega, are about to celebrate their golden wedding anniversary, and young Gerald, who in a few years will be a nationally recognized college basketball star, has not been allowed to play enough in the past season to win a Vega High School letter jacket.

April 5, 1945

Dearest Son

I mailed you a letter this morning & then got one from you. So I think you diserve another letter. Yours of today was dated Mar 14—We was glad to get it.

We are all O.K. and hope you are too. Gerald has gone to the school house to play practice. They are supposed to give it Friday the 13th. They sure will have to work at it if they expect to have it ready.

Marvin Slutz got back from his physical but he didn't pass.

I talked to Ruth Murphy this morning down town. She had'nt heard from Gene Yet. She said she was going to start working at the Drug Store tomarrow. She said it was too lonesome up there by herself. Their little girl is in school this year.

We went to the school house for a play 2 weeks ago. The Eastern Star lodge had it put on. The players were from Amarillo. I am putting in a paper about it & who helped about putting it on. I sure hope you Make s 1/c & I expect you Will.

I am glad you get so Much good out of your Watch that you are lost without it. I expect it is quite a bit of Company to you.

I am so sleepy I Cant see to write so Ill have to finish in the morning. Well here it is Friday Morning April 6. Ill try to finish this up.

Dr & Mrs Loyd are Celebrating their golden Wedding Anniversary Next Tuesday April 10. They are holding open house to all their friends from 3 till 7 P.M. We got an invitation it said No gifts. Mrs Landrum Said he would'nt let them have it if they were to bring gifts as he did'nt think it was right when there was a war on. The ladies who are sponcering it is Mrs. Williams, Wiseman, Ivy, Landrum, Wimberly, Thompson, & Godwin. I think it will be nice.

It seems a little Windy here this Morning, But I will wash Wallaces towels if he isn't out.

I heard that Gene & Mrs Murphy had a big fuss Just before he left & he Cussed her to every thing he Could think of & even told her he would'nt Write to her—that if he wanted to tell her any thing he would write Ruth & She Could tell her. Guess that's some more of Harrys blood in him. Ha. I don't think I could be proud of a son that would talk that Way to me When he was leaving for war. Ed got drunk too along about the same time & John Haliburton locked him in his house over night.

How often do the bonds Come. We have had the Dec one for a long time. & I expect there soon will be another. They will be a Nice little Nest egg for you When the war is over.

I hope you have gotten some Mail before Now. Besides old ones. Im going to get Sixes address again & send it Just in Case you Never Got that letter.

The savings allotment will soon Count up—but hope the war ends soon. I Cant think it will last too long.

No Gerald Never got a Basket Ball Jacket as he was on the B string & None of them got any. No Matter how Much they played. He will be on the A string Next Year. You see he will be a Junior. School sure flys by. He said it sure seemed short this year. School will be out June 1, he said.

Have you heard from Virginia lately?

Well Ill quit and go by Mrs Sixes & get Carltons address & put it in & go Mail this. Love and Prayers from Those who Care.

Mom Dad & all.

A double shock awaited Roy Treadaway when he was released from Red Hill Hospital and reported for duty to the *Franklin*. Wondering why his locker was empty, he learned that the *Franklin* had reported him "missing in action." The destroyer *Miller* had saved him but had failed to tell anyone. The *Franklin* had sent his sea bag to "graves registration," which meant he was presumed dead. Suddenly alarmed that his poor parents, who had already lost one son in the war and had another wounded, might suffer the devastation of a telegram from the navy, he contacted a hometown girl who worked in the army censor's office in Honolulu and asked her to warn his parents that he was well. She did so immediately and just barely in time.

His second shock was to learn that a huge percentage of the *Franklin*'s crew was no longer welcome aboard. The captain honored his 704 Club but treated all able-bodied men who had not stayed with the ship as deserters. Hundreds who reported for duty were lined up and told that they would be court-martialed and that they had twenty minutes to retrieve gear and "get your butts off my ship." Men who had been blown overboard by explosions, men who had gone over to the *Santa Fe*, men who had jumped to escape fiery entrapments, men who had given their life jackets to weaker comrades, men who had kept their wits when the captain had not kept his, even the men Ralph Packard had watched being shoved overboard by panicked crowds behind them were scum in the scum-encrusted mind of Captain Gehres. Roy was spared this indignity only because he had been presumed dead.[12]

Checking quickly on Elden and Bob Bamburg, Roy heard that Bamburg had been killed. The death toll on the hangar deck was so nearly universal that it was hard to get information about the V divisions, as there was hardly anyone left to ask. He knew that Elden's duty station had been Hangar Deck Control, he knew that four men normally worked there, and he heard that three unidentifiable bodies, with dog tags melted, had been found there.[13]

Mercifully, Grace does not know as she writes that she is answering her sailor's last letter.

April 8, 1945

Dear Sonny boy.

I will try writing a few lines tonight. We are O.K. and hope this finds you the same.

Mrs Six and Valta Came over yesterday afternoon They had 2 letters from Carlton yesterday. He is Some Where in France. She said his address was a little different from the one I sent you. So Ill send it too. She said she expected Next time she heard it will be different again as She thinks he will go to Germany. I expect he will see a plenty. Only hope he Comes back O.K. It will be quite a glad Meeting When you two gets together again, wont it?

Well the news sounds good to us in both directions So hope it wont be too far off till its over.

Pauline Came over Yesterday afternoon a while. She had had a letter & a Card from Junior. He was in Arkansas, Camp Chaffee but would'nt be there long enough to get a letter. But would write again soon as he got to where he would be. He said he sure was mad as he qualified for the Navy but they Came along & Changed it. So he is in the Army Now. Pauline felt better I think after she heard from him. I sure feel sorry for her in her Condition. Think her baby is to be born in May.

We went up to Bose's Ranch this afternoon & brought down some old Iron & stuff. He sure is in big business. He has 3 hens setting in the basement. I think he takes Care of his hens about like he used to his horses. He said Charles Mc shipped out Friday April 6 and Charles Wiseman too. Charles Houseman would have went too but his wife was out there & was awful sick. So they gave him emergency furlough to bring her home. So Now he will be separated from them.

Thomas Brents is home Now on a Ten day furlough. They are looking for Forest home soon. He wrote that he would have his feet under his Mothers dinner table May 20th. They are afraid Now Thomas wont get to see him.

Dad isn't going to work for a Couple of days. He is getting a sick leave and is going to get that other tooth out & get his new ones Made. We probly wont know him. But Ill sure be glad for him to get them.

Dad Morris is still awful bad. He don't know any one. Most of the time.

They are taking up Clothing in Vega to send to War torn Countrys. I ram sacked every thing Yesterday and found a few things I could spare.

They taken up tin Cans a while back & are going to pick up Waste paper right away. Well its O.K. if it will end the war sooner.

I Cant think of any More to write tonight so will sign off & go to bed.

Mom.

Oh yes—When you get todays paper April 8 be sure & Notice some things we have drawed around in red. Its Some sports events the Vega boys won in track. And a poem by Mrs. O. H. Loyd.

Well its Monday A.M. Ill finish this & get it Mailed. Im, ready to wash & the wind acts like it will blow—so may not get to dry them.

Dad Just Came back from down town. But never got any Mail. Our latest letter from You was dated Mar 16—before your birthday.

Dad wants to go to Amarillo but Never Seen any one going—So far.

Well I will Close for this time & go Mail this—Love & Best Wishes from home—

Mom & all.

Dad said tell you he guessed you got in on bombing Okinawa. We are guessing.

Dad said 3 kids (strangers) run into Staggs Car as he was crossing the tracks Saturday evening. Tore the fenders off his Car & got away. He Never even got their license Number. So don't guess they can do any thing about it.

This letter opens yet another window into 1945. It tells first that Ancell's job involved a six-day workweek and that the "weekend" in which he could run errands, rest, or pipe water into the house was limited to Sunday. It tells that our little house had not even the rudiments of "indoor plumbing." The water faucet outside the back door was a major improvement over the barrel and trailer tank that had stood outside the McNabb place, but there was not so much as a kitchen sink inside. Water for drinking, cooking, and hand washing came indoors in a white-trimmed-with-red-granite enamel bucket that resided on a small wash-stand in the kitchen. Beside the bucket were a matching long-handled dipper and a small wash pan. Dishes were washed in a larger and deeper "dishpan," rinsed in an adjacent "rinse pan," hand dried, and put away in a breakfront cabinet. Bathing was done every Saturday night in a round galvanized washtub in the kitchen. Hot water for these activities plus laundry, including Wallace Moore's barber towels, came from a teakettle and a twelve-gallon copper "boiler" heated on the burners of a kitchen range fueled by kerosene, which we called by its nineteenth-century name "coal oil." Bodily functions associated today with plumbing were performed in a Works Projects Administration pit toilet about seventy-five feet from the house, and during cold nights in lidded chamber pots called "slop jars" that were hidden beneath each of the two beds. But times were getting better. Three bull calves meant that next winter there would be one to butcher and two to sell, and it meant there were at least three "wet" cows providing plenty of milk and thus butter and leftover cream to sell. With chickens for food and providing eggs for use and also to sell, pigs for pork and also to sell, and with Ancell's job now a "steady" one, the Rogers family was distinctly better off than it had been since the onset of the Great Depression.

April 12, 1945

Dear Sailor boy.

I will write a few lines & send the School paper. I thought I had sent it but ran across it yesterday in My letter box.

How does this find you? Fine we hope. We are all O.K. Dad went to Amarillo Monday & had his last upper tooth pulled so he is ready to have his plate made in 2 or 3 weeks. He layed off Tuesday too. Guess he will get paid for both days as they put it in the sick leave. When you have to go to a Dr.

He thinks he will take off Saturday & get the Water in they have the ditches dug but Will have to help Armitage (Robert Willis Armitage) tap it in. Ill sure be glad when we get it in. I sure am tired Carrying it.

Dads going to try again this evening to get his truck drivers license but he'll take off work long enough for that.

Old Queen has a Bull Calf. We have 3 Bull Calves Now. We are going to put 2 Calves on Queen & wont have to bother feeding them.

Archie Castleberry has been trying to sell Dad some insurance. He was supposed to Come down yesterday evening to see him again but he never Came. Dad may take out a thousand. I don't know yet.

Well Iva & I went over to Dr and Mrs Loyds Golden Wedding Anniversary I think they had around 80 Callers that afternoon & got some phone Calls & Telegrams. They sure seemed to appreciate it a lot. There was several out from Amarillo including Horace Griggs & his Wife.

Well Wallace Just came hollering for some towels to be washed & I had to stop & put on some Water. So Now I don't have Much time left to write.

We have had several dusty days expect you Could stand dust to what you are standing but I sure Get tired cleaning it out.

Well Ill sign off and go mail this & Write again soon.

Love. Mom & all.

⚓

The *Franklin* at this point has been headed for three days toward the Panama Canal and then New York. During her six days at Pearl Harbor, dockworkers had brought cutting torches on board to remove some of the most dangerous wreckage. Some of these workers went up to an office structure on the wall near the gallery deck, a place called Hangar Deck Control, and ran back out yelling, "We're not going up there! There's dead people in there!"[14]

This incident, discovered decades later during research for this book, would become extremely important, especially when coupled with knowledge that at 1330 on April 7, the body of Charles Edward Coleman was found, identified, and removed for burial ashore; and that at 1250 the next day the body of Paul Joseph Marino was identified and transferred to the Naval Hospital at Naval Base 10, Pearl Harbor. To our family it would become absolutely important that at 2010 on April 8, 1945, the remains of an unidentified person who had been killed in action March 19 were transferred to that same hospital.[15] *Franklin* survivor Sam Rhodes told historian Joe Springer that these bodies were buried in Hawaii, in the Punchbowl Cemetery.[16]

It gives one pause!

Elden's parents, while still living, incorporated into their own gravestone a white marble Veterans Administration marker saying that he had been buried at sea in the Pacific. During their waning years, they found comfort and a sense of union with him by visiting this marker on warm summer evenings. His brothers had kept to themselves the gnawing thought that "buried at sea" might have implied something different than what might really have happened. Now, at last, this remarkable information suggests that Elden might neither have been buried ceremonially in Asian waters nor callously scooped overboard. The chances approach 50 percent that he has lain all these years in American soil in a beautiful national cemetery under a bronze marker bearing the single word "Unknown."

24 Holding On to Hope

THE telegram came on Friday the thirteenth of April 1945. Here the flaws of human memory become more likely to intrude—particularly a likelihood that I may have conflated what happened around the time we received the "missing in action" telegram with things that happened later, after the October 13 telegram confirming Elden's death.

Beyond a sniffle at a funeral, I am not sure I had ever seen my mother cry, but my six-year-old mind registered her as weeping inconsolably on an old wicker-backed horsehair divan in our small living room. Although it cannot be correct, and Gerald Rogers assured me that it was not, it seemed to me three full days before she even arose. During those days I visited my playmate, Jane Russ, who lived three blocks away. Jane's mother, Letha Russ, and one or two other adults told me I was too young to understand. True, I did not understand quite what "missing following action" meant, but I knew what death meant and figured out for myself that it had almost certainly come to our family.

The grief spread quickly among the extended family. Grace's pioneer mother, Julia Tegarden, knew firsthand what hurt was, and how it felt. Rudimentarily educated, she used phonetic spellings that require extra attention to decipher, but as she tries to console her youngest child and only daughter, her heartbreak is clear.

Dear Grace Ancell & boys,

'tis with a heavy heart I try to answer your letter we received this morning found us as usual but cant have words to express my simithy but
let us all hope and pray to God for his return I said that I wished I was
down there & Charley and Junnia said for me to get on the train and
go I have not got eny letter since the 24 of Feb. O I cant hardly write.
I tuck his picture and folded it up I cant hardly stand it to look at it Chas
& Junnia have gone up to the other place to see after their cattle Charley
isent very well eny more his chest hurts him since he got hurt he has
been talking about going and having a exra taking I sure wish he would
I should of written sooner but waited four your letter I was sure glad that
you folks has so many friends down I wouldent hafto have eny one to
come with me down there our garden looks pretty good but we have had
so much hard rains it hurt some of it I will quit and let Junnia write some

    your loveing Mother

    good by

    PS I was sure glad that you and Gareld was to be baptized next
    Sunday I wish I could have been there go rite ahead & don't
    look back

An untimely death among the young is particularly difficult for parents to accept. In a wise and compassionate policy, *Franklin* crew members who had survived were encouraged to correspond with and when
possible to visit the parents of shipmates who had not. Such offerings of
sympathy did not always turn out well, as when Seaman First Class Gib
Martin reached out to the parents of a dead shipmate from his hometown in Illinois. This devastated mother, helplessly jealous that Martin
was alive when her son was not, could not look the sailor in the eye—
not during the visit and not for the rest of her life.[1] Grace Rogers, a new
member of the First Baptist Church of Vega and a practical person who

knew there were still children to be raised, work to be done, and the second half of her own life to be lived, was the opposite. When she arose from her grief, surely far sooner than her six-year-old would recall, she not only took care of her family but reached out to Elden's buddies and other young servicemen in mothering ways and sought to learn as much as she could.

In reaching out, she planted in her own heart a seed of hope that lived as long as she did. She was sad to learn that Bob Bamburg was dead. She inquired after the welfare of Ted Hickman, whose knife Elden had passed along to Ancell. One buddy, Ed Shroba from Cleveland, Ohio, wrote twice from the Hawaii hospital where he was being treated for what we now call posttraumatic stress disorder. Ed wrote kind things about Elden, with whom he had stood many watches and shared many laughs. He promised to visit our family in Vega, but was careful not to give false hope for Elden.[2] The Amarillo newspaper mentioned that a boy named Thomas Ellis from the Vega-sized town of Kress, Texas, had been on the *Franklin,* and she wrote to ask if he had known Elden. He had not, but he answered in a warm manner.[3] She found hope, however, in Roy Treadaway's remarkable experience, as recounted in several exchanges of correspondence with Roy and his mother, Elsie Treadaway, of Miles, Texas. That family had received an urgent letter warning them to expect a telegram such as we had received, but the letter said it was all a mistake and Roy was actually alive! The horrible but happily erroneous telegram came the very next day.[4]

Newspapers and radio often carried stories of "miraculous" reversals of tragedy. Four months earlier a New Orleans family's holiday joy was overwhelmed by fear and grief when a December 22 telegram brought word that their son, carrier pilot Tommy Lupo, was missing in action. When Tommy knocked on their door, alive and home for Christmas, it seemed more like the act of a merciful God than an error by the navy.[5] In Benton Harbor, Michigan, Agnes Smith learned that her son William's best buddy, Glenn Hashberger, had been listed as dead. She reasoned that William was almost certainly dead as well. Her grief was relieved when she received a Mother's Day card.[6] Such happenings were not common, but nationwide news coverage of such heartwarming stories made miracles seem plausible, and they had their effect on Grace.

Information from the Treadaway family, slightly garbled by the time it reached Grace, became very important. She heard that three unidentifiable bodies had been found in Elden's little Hangar Deck Control office—men who had not suffered because they were killed instantly by the concussion of the bombs. Four men were supposed to be there. Roy himself had been reported missing in action and had been presumed dead; his parents had even received the awful telegram, but he was not missing and was not dead. Something like what had happened to Roy, and to the others who were so often in the news, might have happened to Elden. He too might have been blown overboard! He might have swum to some nearby island and might be living there the way George Tweed had lived on Guam for three years before being rescued. With a life jacket, he might have drifted to Japan, or been picked up by a Japanese ship and delivered to a prison camp. Even Elsie Treadaway said so! Bish McKendree's family believed, or at least had reason to hope, that Bish might be alive somewhere. Why not Elden?[7]

Information about major damage to major warships was top secret, but the *Franklin*'s devastation had been seen by many witnesses at Hawaii, and then by a few at the Panama Canal. Soon she would be at New York City and visible to the world. Her captain had left her briefly vulnerable in the most precarious waters imaginable, costing at least 724 men their lives and many others their health, and costing the United States one of her most useful warships. He had spread bitterness over the tragedy by declaring a specific set of his surviving crew members to be heroes and whole categories of others cowards and deserters whom he intended to punish. Back on October 30 the *Franklin* had survived the worst fire any American warship had ever survived, and then on

March 19 she had broken her own tragic record by orders of magnitude. After an unbelievable ordeal she was still afloat.

The story was leaking out, and the navy needed to be in control of the story. Top brass knew it was the captain himself who should be court-martialed, and they quickly quashed his intention to punish others. But they also knew what kind of story the country needed to hear and they decided to go with the flow. The *Franklin* would become "The Ship That Wouldn't Die," and Gehres would become the fearless captain who dismissed his admiral's advice to abandon ship, with the words "If you will save us from the Japs, we will save this ship!" On May 17 with full navy approval, newspapers everywhere began to spread the word, and to show dramatic photographs. A long and solemn broadcast of the story by Gabriel Heatter, second only to Edward R. Murrow among wartime radio newsmen, was heard across the nation.[8]

⚓

Elden had died in an operation that was the advance stage of the invasion of Okinawa, launched on April 1 and followed by twenty days of fighting. Takeshi Maeda, who had been the navigator on a Japanese torpedo plane in the Pearl Harbor attack, was one of the lucky few still alive and flying in 1945. His seat behind the pilot faced backward, giving him a view of where he had just been. At Pearl Harbor, as he much later told National Park Service historian Art Gomez, his plane had dropped its perfectly aimed torpedo, and as it pulled up and away he saw the torpedo's wake, plus six others, headed toward the battleship *West Virginia*. He knew the American dreadnaught was doomed. Three and a quarter years later, his plane pulled upward and away from a similar run at Okinawa. There he saw from his rear-facing seat the same USS *West Virginia*—raised, repaired, and firing away—and realized, "That's when I knew we could not win."[9]

Most people knew it long before that. Seventeen days after Japan lost Okinawa, victory in Europe was final and official. Hitler was dead, the last casualty of his own murderous hand. The people of Japan were just beginning to figure out the extent of lies they had heard from the Japanese war machine. That war machine was perceived to be doubling down, becoming more fanatical than ever and preparing to sacrifice everything and everyone with only the hope of being saved by divine intervention. Even though victory was almost certain, many Americans believed their greatest costs still lay in the future, to be paid in blood in an invasion of the Japanese main islands.

In the predawn darkness of July 16, 1945, thirty miles southeast of San Antonio, New Mexico, the adobe village where Conrad Hilton had worked in his father's hotel, a light flashed hundreds of times brighter than the sun, a shock wave greater than any before created by humans roiled the desert, and a fireball rose to 40,000 feet. Newspapers reported that an ammunition dump had accidentally exploded. Twenty-one days later the world's second atomic bomb exploded over the Japanese city of Hiroshima, and after three more days a third one destroyed Nagasaki. Japan's emperor put an end to the madness. On August 14 Japan surrendered unconditionally. It was over.

Everyone in Vega knew that the war's end would be proclaimed by a long blast on the siren on the water tower, and thus both V-E (Victory in Europe) Day and V-J (Victory in Japan) Day were announced. Grace Rogers came to the front porch to listen to the sound as I ran, jumped, shouted, and turned somersaults in celebration. Good news, but it came as our family, embraced by our neighbors along with a few other families, feared the worst and gradually came to expect it.

The worst finally came on October 13, 1945. Another telegram told us that Elden had been confirmed dead, though we knew that the confirmation was not based on hard evidence but really meant only that the navy could come to no other conclusion. The brand-new weekly newspaper, *Vega Enterprise,* announced an October 28 memorial service for Elden in a two-inch-high headline, and the community filled the First Baptist Church and spilled out onto the sidewalk. The Reverend J. A. English read from this obituary.

Our Son Elden Duane Rogers enlisted in the Navy Mar 17-1944, received his Boot training in San Diego Cali, went aboard the great Air Craft Carrier Franklin & Sailed over seas. Saw his first action July 4th of the same year. Saw action at Eniwetok, Guam, Palau, Bonin Islands, Formosa, Leyte and the 2nd Sea and Air battle of the Philippines. Returned to the States early in December for ship repair and was Granted a 20 day leave & spent Christmas at home. Reported back for duty Jan 9-1945—Lost his life on his 19th birthday Mar 19-1945 At that time was on Duty in the Inland sea Just 38 miles off the Coast of Japan when the Carrier was hit by Japanese dive bomber at 7 A.M. less than 800 men were left from a Crew of 3,000 We received a message April 14 that he was missing in Action and Oct 13 we received the death message[10]—A Beautiful and empressive Memorial Service was planned & Given in his honor at the Vega Baptist Church Oct 28-1945. There is a Great Vacant place in our hearts & lives but our Sweet Memories of him and his Bravery Causes us to Carry on for the rest of our Family & Friends—

   Mrs. A. R. Rogers (Mother)

At Hardtner, Kansas, near the Oklahoma state line, Ancell's younger brother Deyoe Elvin Rogers was making a living shoeing horses. A few miles west, on the Farley Ranch, Elden's cousin Jack Farley was beginning a struggle with "shell shock," or PTSD, manifested in alcoholism that would sadden and shorten his life. Jack's brother, Howard, was breaking a team of mules to pull a hay wagon. At Vega, Ancell had paid $500 for a spiffy 1930 Model A Ford Sport Coupe with a rumble seat and with its spare tire located in a wheel well on the passenger side. Amazingly by today's standards, he paid approximately the same price that the fifteen-year-old car had cost when brand-new. The Model A's hardiness and good gas mileage had entirely offset depreciation during depression and war, but a year or two later, with gasoline rationing gone and American industry again producing new cars, the Ford would be worth just $35. Grace is still making soap, I am entering first grade, and Ancell for the first time in his life gets a *paid vacation*—twelve days! Everywhere the Rogers family went in Vega, people spoke to us in soft and respectful tones.

Boys who survived the war were coming home, and life in general was seeking to become whatever "normal" might be after all that had happened. The only certainty was that it would be a new normal, never again as it had been before. Like every other small town in America, Vega had had its own share of the uncertainties, immature loves, ill-founded marriages, early divorces, and disruptions like those Virginia had described in Las Animas. Too many of the boys who had gone away did not return. Of those who did, too many suffered quietly in ways that only those closest to them could see and only another veteran might understand. Those who did readjust and find a new normal did so quietly. Probably the tightest-lipped generation of veterans in history, they did not want to talk about the war or to think about it; they just wanted to live. The community held in its heart each veteran and his or her family, jointly grieving those who were lost, celebrating those who returned, and worrying about those whose fates remained unknown.

Not everything became clear on V-J Day. Some answers took time, especially for those who had been in prison camps where administration simply collapsed after the surrender. With each passing day after combat had ended, concern for those not yet accounted for grew into worry, and with each passing week worry grew into anxiety. As time dragged on, to the McKendree family no news did not seem to be good news.

Sometimes the strength of human exuberance can seem to go beyond our mortal bodies and find expression through inanimate objects— even the machines we use. So it was with the automobile that in late September 1945 fourteen-year-old Merle Denny, operating a tractor in a field, saw tearing northward from Vega along a dirt road that was normally traveled at a more careful speed. He recognized the car as belonging to Marian Montgomery, whose husband "Boots" ranched just north of the Denny place; and from its speed, from the dust plume it threw into the air, or from something less explicable, Merle knew something was out of the ordinary. He was right—the driver carried news wonderful beyond containment, so wonderful that it had to be shared— with everyone, with anyone. As the driver spotted a human on the tractor, she screeched to a stop, exited the car, crossed the barbed wire fence, and strode through the soft soil toward him. Merle throttled down his machine, dismounted, and ran to her. When they were a few feet apart, Mrs. Montgomery shouted: "They've found Bish McKendree! He's alive!"[11]

Epilogue

No longer with scoops and garbage cans, but with full and solemn ceremony, human remains were still being buried at sea after being discovered aboard the *Franklin* even as she drew near to New York.[1] As probably anticipated, the extensive repairs that would make the ship useful could not be completed before the rapidly approaching war's end. Having earned four battle stars (Marianas, July 3 to August 5, 1944; Western Caroline Islands, August 8 to September 24, 1944; Leyte, October 10 to 26, 1944; Okinawa, March 17 to 22, 1945), on June 15, 1946, she joined the "mothballed" fleet at the Bayonne Navy Yard in New Jersey. Margaret Mydosh, the late mother of my wife, Nancy Mydosh Burgas, worked in that navy yard during the 1950s. Margaret and Nancy too surely would have seen the *Franklin*, though without taking particular note of it among the gray mass of so many ships. In 1969 the *Franklin* was towed to Norfolk, Virginia, and dismantled, having been sold as scrap for the grand sum of $228,000. Ancell, Grace, Jerry, Peggy, Tiana, Houston, and Elvin Rogers visited the ship about halfway through the process. Legend has it that the demolition crew found the last human remains in an air duct.[2]

The Gehres venom ran its toxic course. Warships abandoned during combat were routinely torpedoed by American ships to ensure that their technology would not become available for study by the enemy. Predictably this practice generated legends among sailors to the effect that a few living Americans still on board had been killed by American torpedoes. Logically, such legends caused some *Franklin* crew members who had worked on lower decks to conclude that Captain Gehres's refusal to abandon ship had saved their lives. This, together with Gehres's division of the crew into heroes, traitors, and the dead, caused some members of the 704 Club to adhere loyally to the captain's honor. Decades later, at a reunion banquet of the USS *Franklin* Association, former plane captain Irv Dahlen remarked that the captain should have been court-martialed. His former shipmates asked him to leave the table. He did more than that—he left the association. He never attended another reunion, but he generously contributed information for this book.

Such loyalty did not endure within the majority of survivors, however, and no admirers of Captain Gehres were noticeable during the six such reunions Elvin and I have attended. Most of the veterans preferred to enjoy one another without thought of Gehres, but when they did mention him it was not in flattering terms. As years passed, and then decades, and then finally the war-bloodied twentieth century itself was behind them, these veterans never lost their appreciative reverence for the shipmates who had died in combat, but they did regain a sailor's ability to laugh about things. Ernest Scott, joking in 2005 about the period just after the bombing when the captain was frenzied, said that when he and his buddies in the number 2 engine room decided the engines were capable of being restarted, they telephoned the bridge. "Request permission to blow tubes," they said, meaning to blow air through the boiler tubes to clear obstructions before raising steam pressure. The captain allegedly turned to his bugler and ordered him to "Blow Tubes." Frank Turner said that as the very last pilot was about to fly off the burning flight deck, with the captain shouting, "This is my ship and I am going to save it!" the pilot catapulted into the air shouting, "This is my ass, and I am going to save it!"[3]

"I guess some guys are just luckyier than others," Elden had written on the tenth day before his last. The duty exchange he so badly wanted back at Alameda had almost but not quite been achieved, and then this different transfer opportunity had gone not to him but to the guy next to him. That guy, Nelson Allison Myers, in his sixty-five and a half bonus years of life after waving goodbye to Elden and the *Franklin* on March 3, 1945, never forgot how lucky he had been. The light cruiser USS *Houston,* only partially repaired after a torpedo hit back in October, was out of the war, bound for the States, and he was on her. Elden died on his nineteenth birthday in sight of Japan; Myers, who was five days younger, sailed on his nineteenth birthday under Liberty's lifted lamp into New York Harbor. In peacetime Myers returned to his West Texas home, married Verna Ruth Willborn, had two daughters and three sons, resumed the highway work he had learned before the war, and became a respected bridge construction superintendent. Ruth died in 2000, Nelson in September 2011, and both are buried at Colorado City, Texas. He knew what had happened to the *Franklin,* knew that he had escaped almost certain death, and he told others of his good fortune.[4]

Roy Treadaway, though he never returned to the *Franklin*, finished out the war and then completed a career in the navy that lasted into the Vietnam era. His service included time with the Seabees, and time as a navy recruiter in Texas. He married a girl from Slaton, Texas, had a daughter and a son, then settled near Lake Whitney at Laguna Park, Texas. On March 19, 1959, he published an extensive recollection of the *Franklin*'s bombing in the *Sweetwater Reporter.* Thirty years after that he contributed a similar piece to USS Franklin *(CV-13): The Ship That Wouldn't Die*, and he has generously provided additional information for this book. Roy's published recollections reveal the negative side to the sailor's advantage over infantrymen of having clean bunks and reliably good food. When a ship is hit, the people on it have few ways to look to their own safety. "There are," he wrote, "no foxholes on ships."[5]

Elden's sweetheart, Virginia, exits this narrative in an abrupt way that both is and is not a bit strange. It is not strange because we know mail delivery was so erratic that Elden received letters in March that had been mailed to him in November. From his letters we can tell that he was writing to her fairly often and seems to have written at least as late as March 10. His letters do not convey or imply that anything was out of the ordinary, and the last letter we have from her to Elden, back on December 30, fairly gushes with love. Letters that reached the *Franklin* after March 19 would have been returned to her undelivered, as several of Grace's letters were. Some items sent to Elden's family from his locker show water damage from the firefighting, and perhaps some letters were destroyed by fire or water. Of the letters that survived in the locker, Grace may have destroyed some in disapproval of their contents or she may have returned some to Virginia.

It is a bit strange, however, that on February 17, 1945, forty-two days after Virginia last saw Elden, she wrote to Grace, whom she had been too shy to visit not long before, in a familiar way that conveys a faintly muted panic because she had not heard from him. We do not know how and when Virginia learned that Elden was missing in action, but it is likely that word reached her very soon after we learned on April 13. It is very strange that on June 12, 1945, two months after that grievous news arrived, Virginia signed in unmistakable handwriting a return receipt for registered mail with the title "Mrs." and a different surname. We do not know who her husband was, when or under what circumstances she married him, or how long the marriage lasted. Apparently it did not last a very long time.

Virginia had hedged her bets that night back in March 1944 when she pulled a "cousin stunt" and kept her date with another man instead of going with Elden one last time before he went to war. Eventually she cashed in the hedge by marrying that other man. She bore a total of four children. Although her husband's many farms and money surely provided her a good living, it is less clear whether it was a good life. She eventually divorced that husband, and years later she married for a third time. When Gerald spoke with her by telephone on June 11, 1994, she was caring for her aged mother three blocks from the house where she and Elden had last parted an hour before dawn on January 6, 1945. She lived eighty-four years, and left behind the impression that she may never have completely escaped the central tragedy of this story. During the course of the telephone conversation, she said of Elden, "I think of him often."

Bugeye Steward, Virginia had written in February 1944, would probably get out of the navy because "Hes pretty lucky that way." She was right. He got off the USS *Hoel* just in time to avoid her sinking and the death of three-fourths of her crew. Some Steward family researchers believe he later joined the Marine Corps. All we know at present is that he had talked of joining the merchant marine and that he was working in Colorado as late as March 25, 1945. After the war he lived and worked in the Amarillo area and died there in the 1980s.

Bob Walcott's ship, the *Piedmont*, made it through the war and had the honor of entering Tokyo Bay soon after the capitulation. She got back to Alameda, California, in March 1946. As soon as he could, Bobby returned to New Mexico, settled in Albuquerque, built a career in the title insurance business, and became a respected citizen. In 1949 he married Ruth Pharris of Alamogordo and raised five children. Ruth died in 2006, but Bob lived to contribute to this story.

The Walcott boy who had left Vega as Tubbi probably remains somewhere on Saipan as Marine Private First Class Vincent H. Walcott—or he may rest in the National Memorial Cemetery of the Pacific in a grave marked "Unknown." He is memorialized on the cemetery's extensive marble tablets.

Between September 6 and September 29, 1974, I traveled for the National Park Service through the western Pacific, spending a few days each in Hawaii, Ponape, Guam, Yap, Palau, and Saipan; touching down on Johnston Island, Kwajalein, and Truk; and flying over Ulithi. I was keenly aware that Elden had sailed near most of these places, and I naturally wondered how many of the wrecked World War II aircraft, guns, and bunkers I saw had been attacked by planes from the *Franklin*. My usual habit of forming mental images of these places was sharpened by the likelihood that Elden might have seen them too.

Historic places will speak to those who listen. I stood in silence, on that trip, on a high point near the north end of Saipan. It was Suicide Cliff. In a view beautiful except for its history, I gazed across the flat where a fighter base had once been toward other cliffs with white surf at their feet and blue ocean beyond. The Japanese who had used the fighter base had warned local people that Americans were savages, and from those other cliffs, as American forces approached the island, many natives had thrown their children into that surf and then jumped after them. Somewhere not far away the banzai attack had ended 5,000 lives including Vincent Walcott's. Below and to my left was the cave where General Saito had committed ritual suicide. From the spot where I stood, the last few living and uncaptured Japanese soldiers had jumped, single file, to their deaths rather than acknowledge defeat. I was aware that this battle had been fought to secure the island of Tinian, and I was conscious of it a few miles over my left shoulder. Tinian was important because from it B-29 bombers could reach Japan, and from it the *Enola Gay* had reached Hiroshima with an atomic bomb. The morality of the decision to use that bomb remains debatable, but on that day Suicide Cliff clearly said to me: "Truman was right."[6]

We trace our family history back nineteen generations, and Elden's death was the unquestionably central event in one of them. Forty years afterward Grace would say that Ancell never managed to grieve out his pain, but had simply absorbed the blow. If he had been a happy man before, he would be less so until his death on one final unlucky thirteenth, in August 1985. Grace, until her death on November 28, 1993, consoled herself slightly by never quite letting go of a gradually dimming hope that Elden might someday show up at her kitchen door.

Gerald was convinced that his parents' acute disappointment at Elden's quitting high school, a mistake that because of his death could never be corrected, was the fundamental reason why he went to college, earning both bachelor's and master's degrees and having a career in education. If that is so, then that positive effect passed on to Elvin and me, as we both followed in Gerald's footsteps, as well as to children and grandchildren of all three. On the negative side, I believe one result of Elden's loss was childhood depression that persisted for many years and a romanticized notion of death as a key to love and respect. Elvin, the youngest of the family, born on Veterans Day in 1946, would come to recognize the effect on his life as well. I have often thought that if one wants to understand the impact of World War II, one might multiply by 70 million the awful effect of this one death on our family, then factor in how long the affected survivors would live and perhaps how they would unwittingly pass the effect along to their descendants.

Grace and Ancell joined their community in being happy for the McKendree family when Bish at last came home. After taking time to regain his bearings, Bish earned a degree from the University of Texas and had a successful career with Gulf Oil Company and the Texas Railroad Commission. Late in life he recounted his experiences as a prisoner of war, and under the title *Barbed Wire and Rice*, the Cornell University East Asia Program published the memoir along with the poems and songs he had risked his life to sequester.

Grace, who joined the Vega Baptist Church in the difficult year of 1945 and thereafter became an ever more devout believer in everything written in the Holy Bible, defined and generally disavowed superstition as unprovable beliefs not derived from scripture. She had to wonder, however, whether there might be something to the superstition that associated the number thirteen with bad luck. The *Franklin* had been CV-13, her first set of flyers had been Air Group 13, and she lost her first crew member to enemy action on Friday, October 13. The "missing following action" telegram had come on Friday the thirteenth, the telegram confirming Elden's death on October 13, and Ancell's death on August 13. She could not say what that meant, but it seemed just too much for there to be no meaning at all.

Peace among nations returned far sooner than it could return within hearts, but eventually it penetrated those inner spaces as well. Japan and its people, then called "Japs" and thoroughly demonized as a result of the excesses of her military and by the need to despise those whom one must kill, changed quickly during the postwar occupation. Seeming almost opposite of its earlier self, the nation became antimilitary, pacifistic, and pro-American. In our family, as in the United States at large, it took time and effort to turn off the anger and to replace it with the respect that is due to all humans of goodwill. Grace could never again eat rice or see a fish head without choking a bit in remembrance of what she had heard from Bish McKendree of prison camp diets, and without remembering Jimmy Bales.

Tough, gruff, and taciturn by day, Herman Sifford gradually recovered the ability to sleep through a night without screaming himself awake. Moving from place to place for several years, he eventually found his dream job as manager of the Bridwell Ranch west of Adrian, Texas. When in the 1970s he saw an Amarillo television station interview of a Japanese youth who wanted to be a cowboy, he immediately went and found the lad and brought him to the ranch. Kumazoe Kurata, who asked Americans to call him Larry, had only a tourist visa and was not legally permitted to work in the United States. That detail was ignored as for a few months he lived his dream, riding the range with a man who had been his own father's mortal enemy. Larry overstayed his visa and eventually was required to return home—the better, we hope, for the experience. Whatever good the relationship did for Herman went with him, unexpressed, to his grave, but something special was there—something most likely remembered from Saipan or Iwo Jima.

The Rogers family knew from information provided in 1945 by Roy Treadaway via his mother that three bodies had been found in Elden's duty station and that four men normally worked there. It was our understanding that all three were burned beyond recognition. We did not know until work on this book was half done that these bodies had been discovered while the *Franklin* was at Pearl Harbor on April 7 and 8, 1945, and that only one of the three was unidentified. We did not know that the three had been buried at Halawa Cemetery, just outside the navy base, and that Halawa Cemetery was later obliterated and its graves moved to the National Memorial Cemetery of the Pacific in the crater known as the Punchbowl overlooking downtown Honolulu. We did not know that two of the three were Radarman Third Class Carl Edward Coleman of Utah and Aviation Ordnanceman First Class Paul Joseph Marino of Alabama. We still do not know what became of the third one, which might have been identified and sent to relatives on the mainland, but more likely is buried in the Punchbowl.

Gerald, his wife Babs, and my wife, Nancy, and I have all seen Elden's name among the 18,094 American servicemen memorialized there as missing in action, lost, or buried at sea during World War II. The inscription reads: "IN THESE GARDENS ARE RECORDED THE NAMES OF AMERICANS WHO GAVE THEIR LIVES IN THE SERVICE OF THEIR COUNTRY AND WHOSE EARTHLY RESTING PLACE IS KNOWN ONLY TO GOD."

For six decades, including the times of our initial visits to that place, we had assumed that Elden's remains had been "buried at sea in the Pacific," as the white marble Veterans Administration memorial stone standing next to his parents' gravestone in the Vega Memorial Park Cemetery says. In fact, there is close to a 50 percent chance he is one of more than 2,000 unknown World War II dead who are interred in the Punchbowl. The task of tracing a specific one of them back to Halawa Cemetery and from there to the Naval Hospital at Naval Base 10 Pearl Harbor and then to the *Franklin* is daunting but perhaps not impossible.

Nor during those initial visits did we know of the complex molecule in every human cell called deoxyribonucleic acid, now well known and commonly called DNA. Should we succeed in identifying the grave of the third person whose remains were found in Hangar Deck Control, it might yet be possible to compare a close female relative's DNA with that of the grave's occupant. It might yet be possible to identify Elden's remains and thus to rebury them with his parents only a quarter mile from the home he left to join the navy.

Bish McKendree's tombstone, barely fifty feet away from that potential grave, reads:

> *Here he lies,*
> *Where he longed to be.*[7]

Enough, just enough, is known about what became of Elden to leave a sliver of hope that it could yet be so for him, validating his words in lieu of goodbye:

So Long for Now.

NOTES

Prologue

1. "Isoroku Yamamoto," q.v., *Encyclopedia of World Biography* (2004), Encyclopedia.com, http://www.encyclopedia.com/doc/1G2-3404706990.html.

2. Art Gomez, National Park Service historian, "Conversation with Takeshi Maeda, Oahu, Hawaii, December 5, 2006," e-mail to Jerry Rogers, February 5, 2013.

Chapter 2

1. Oldham County Historical Commission, *Oldham County: 1881–1981* (Lubbock, TX: Taylor, 1981; hereafter cited as OCHC); Elvin Rogers, with Gerald Rogers and Jerry Rogers, "A Session for Memories" (unpublished manuscript of memories from growing up in Vega, Texas, shared at Santa Fe, New Mexico, June 20–22, 2008).

2. Utley, *Lone Star Lawmen*, 122–23.

3. Rogers, Rogers, and Rogers, "Session for Memories," 66–68.

Chapter 3

1. Rogers, Rogers, and Rogers, "Session for Memories," 84.

2. OCHC, 125.

3. Rogers, Rogers, and Rogers, "Session for Memories," 27.

Chapter 4

1. OCHC, 285; McKendree, *Barbed Wire and Rice*, 151. McKendree's book provides a rare insight into the prisoner-of-war experience, the behavior of humans under extreme duress, and the story of Bishop McKendree and Jimmy Bales. Their timing in volunteering in order to avoid being drafted was good, as the *Oldham County News* reported on January 9, 1941, that Allen Stafford and Travis Fowler had been selected as the first two draftees from Oldham County. Copies of the

Oldham County News (hereafter cited as *OCN*) can be found at the Panhandle-Plains Historical Museum Research Center in Canyon, Texas.

2. McKendree, *Barbed Wire and Rice*, 155.

3. Manchester, *American Caesar*, 210–11.

4. The contempt implied in the sobriquet was genuinely felt but was by no means universal. MacArthur was greatly admired by members of all branches of the armed services and by the general public.

5. McKendree, *Barbed Wire and Rice*, 87.

6. Frank Hewlett, quoted in Stephen Bye, "Nobody Gives a Damn," U.S. Army Military History Institute, March 26, 2010, https://www.army.mil/article/36309 /nobody-gives-a-damn/ (accessed June 27, 2016). Hewlett was Manila bureau chief for United Press and the last American reporter to leave Corregidor before it fell.

7. McKendree, *Barbed Wire and Rice*, 166. American forces on Bataan had surrendered almost a month earlier on April 10.

8. Ibid., 167.

9. Ibid., 13–14.

10. *OCN* 35, no. 6, May 14, 1942.

11. McKendree, *Barbed Wire and Rice*, 169.

12. Ibid., 173; National Archives and Records Administration, World War II Prisoners of War, 1941–1946.

13. McKendree, *Barbed Wire and Rice*, 174.

14. Ibid.

15. Hoyt, *Nimitz and His Admirals*, 71–72.

16. Ibid., 72–73. The dividing line was adjusted to longitude 159° west to avoid splitting Guadalcanal.

17. Ibid., 76.

18. Ibid., 190.

19. Springer, *Inferno*, 18–19. Springer, Nilo and St. Peters, and Jackson have each collected and published oral interviews and written accounts from a wide range of veterans who served on the *Franklin* and the *Santa Fe*, and have done extensive research to place the statements into context. I have relied extensively and with gratitude on their work.

20. Springer, *Inferno*, 19; Nilo and St. Peters, *The Ship That Wouldn't Die*, 7.

Chapter 5

1. Bobby Walcott, in discussion with the author, July 15, 2005.

2. Ibid.

3. Ibid.

4. This communication was on a postcard, with a photo of the Royal Gorge Bridge on the back.

5. Hoyt, *Nimitz and His Admirals*, 299.

6. Grace's quilting frame is now in the possession of her granddaughter Tiana Lynne Conklin.

7. Grace did not know at the time that George Miller was a distant relative on her mother's side.

8. Hoyt, *Nimitz and His Admirals*, 316.

9. "That Ferguson kid" apparently refers to Morris Earl Ferguson.

10. Hoyt, *Nimitz and His Admirals*, 354.

11. Ibid., 346.

Chapter 6

1. "USS *Franklin*, May 31, 1944," 79, 83, Muster Rolls of U.S. Navy Ships, Stations, and Other Naval Activities, 01/01/1939–01/01/1949, RG 24, Records of the Bureau of Naval Personnel, 1798–2007, Series ARC ID: 594996; Series MLR No.: A1 135, National Archives and Records Administration (hereafter cited as NARA), http:search.ancestry.com/cqi-bin/sse.dll?h=276540&db=NavyMuster&indiv=try (accessed May 29, 2012). All muster rolls were accessed via Ancestry.com, an online research service providing access to images of original historical documents and to databases relevant to family history, available by subscription at www.ancestry.com.

2. OCHC, 337–38.

3. "USS *General John R. Brooke*, March 19, 1944," 44, Muster Rolls, NARA (accessed June 6, 2012); "USS *General John R. Brooke* (AP-132)," Wikipedia, http://en.wikipedia.org/w/index.php?title=USS_General_J._R._Brooke_(AP-132) (accessed June 6, 2012); Lt. A. R. Morrison, "Bombing Squad Thirteen, Complete Summary of Operations, July to October, 1944," in USS *Franklin* Museum Association, *USS* Franklin *(CV-13): Original Documents 1943–1946* (Paducah, KY: Turner, 1994; hereafter cited as FMA, *Original Documents*), 36.

4. Hoyt, *Nimitz and His Admirals*, 355.

5. McKendree, *Barbed Wire and Rice*, 175.

6. Walcott, July 2005.

7. "USS *Piedmont*, April 30, 1944," 32, Muster Rolls, NARA.

8. Walcott, July 2005; U.S. World War II Army Enlistment Records, 1938–1946, Ancestry.com, NARA.

9. Hornfischer, *Last Stand*, 67.

10. Friedman, *U.S. Aircraft Carriers*, 136.

11. Office of Naval History (ONH), "History of USS Franklin (CV-13)," in FMA, *Original Documents*, 80.

12. Rogers, Rogers, and Rogers, "Session for Memories," 9.

13. Roy G. Treadaway to author, December 5, 2005.

14. ONH, "History of USS Franklin (CV-13)," in FMA, *Original Documents*, 81; "Alfred F. Jmasch, Sr.," in Nilo and St. Peters, *The Ship That Wouldn't Die*, 91.

15. Deck Logs, USS *Franklin* (CV-13), May 24, 1944, RG 24, Records of the Bureau of Naval Personnel, January 31, 1944–September, 1944: ARC ID 594258, Box 3459, 118-A 1, National Archives at College Park, MD (hereafter cited as NACP); ONH, "History of USS Franklin (CV-13)," in FMA, *Original Documents*, 81; Springer, *Inferno*, 19, 65.

16. Hoyt, *Nimitz and His Admirals*, 372.

Chapter 7

1. These were not the only buddies from boot camp to be assigned to the *Franklin*; others included Robert Bamburg and Theodore Hickman.

2. In all references to shipboard times, we will use the four-numeral twenty-four-hour system used by the navy.

3. May 24, 1944, Deck Logs, NACP.

4. Elden is in error here; the actual length was 867 feet.

5. Friedman, *U.S. Aircraft Carriers*, 133–57.

6. Springer, *Inferno*, 19–20.

7. Friedman, *U.S. Aircraft Carriers*, 133–57; Hoyt, *Nimitz and His Admirals*, 288; Satterfield, *Saving Big Ben*, 60.

8. Friedman, *U.S. Aircraft Carriers*, 133–57; Jackson, *Lucky Lady*, 97.

9. The hangar deck was also called the main deck.

10. Friedman, *U.S. Aircraft Carriers*, 133–57; Jackson, *Lucky Lady*, 97–98.

11. Jackson, *Lucky Lady*, 98.

12. Fahey, *Pacific War Diary*, 357; Karig, Harris, and Manson, *Battle Report*, photos between 52 and 53. I have not documented problems with flour aboard the *Franklin* specifically, but have relied on Fahey, whose comments make it appear to be a generalized matter rather than specific to his own ship, the light cruiser USS *Montpelier*. However, Fahey also recorded having chow of poor quality and in inadequate amounts throughout the war. It appears that having good chow and plenty of it may have been a benefit of serving aboard *Essex*-class carriers, which were large enough to carry ample supplies and whose needs may have been given priority.

13. Friedman, *U.S. Aircraft Carriers*, 141; Jackson, *Lucky Lady*, 98. The range of a fast carrier's planes allowed them to strike targets at least 400 miles away and return to the ship; adding that distance onto both the beginning and the end of a 900-mile voyage created a potential for her to hit places 1,700 miles or more apart within twenty-four hours.

14. August 28, 1944, Deck Logs, NACP.

15. Nilo and St. Peters, *The Ship That Wouldn't Die*, 7.

16. Ed Shroba to Grace Rogers, July 25, 1945.

17. "Plan of the Day, August 9, 1945," in FMA, *Original Documents*, 137.

18. "Lou Casserino," in Springer, *Inferno*, 62.

19. Bowman and Warrick, *Big Ben the Flattop*, n.p.; Springer, *Inferno*, 27; "Nick Mady," in Springer, *Inferno*, 61.

20. Bowman and Warrick, *Big Ben the Flattop*, n.p.; Hornfischer, *Last Stand*, 90; Springer, *Inferno*, 27; Charles Varady, USS *Hornet* Museum, personal communication, May 21, 2015.

21. "Casserino," in Springer, *Inferno*, 62; September 22, 1944, Deck Logs, NACP.

22. "Steve Nowak," in Springer, *Inferno*, 219. "Poggy" meant a novice, or young boy, just out of boot camp. "Poggy bait" has connotations dating back to World War I of candy used to reward such novices for acquiescing in homosexual acts. Elden had written that ten cents would buy four candy bars, and that cigarettes were five cents a pack. His 1944 letter is better evidence of prices than Nowak's memory filtered through five decades.

23. Springer, *Inferno*, 28.

24. Friedman, *U.S. Aircraft Carriers*, 151. There were a total of forty-eight 40 mm guns.

25. Jackson, *Lucky Lady*, 128.

26. June 6, 1944, Deck Logs, NACP.

27. Jackson, *Lucky Lady*, 125.

28. June 6, 1944, Deck Logs, NACP. Alfred Jmasch, quoted in Nilo and St. Peters, *The Ship That Wouldn't Die*, 91, said that they tied up just aft of the *Arizona*, which would have been at mooring quay F-8, where the USS *Nevada* had been when the December 7, 1941, attack began. Carriers normally berthed on the opposite side of the island, and the deck logs seem a stronger source.

Chapter 8

1. *OCN* 33, no. 51, March 26, 1942.

2. Ibid., no. 43, January 22, 1942; and no. 49, March 12, 1942.

3. *OCN* 35, no. 7, May 21, 1942. "Maize" was locally pronounced "mays" and referred to grain sorghum rather than to yellow corn.

4. Rogers, Rogers, and Rogers, "Session for Memories," 35.

5. *OCN* 33, no. 46, February 12, 1942.

6. Ibid., no. 48, March 5, 1942.

7. Rogers, Rogers, and Rogers, "Session for Memories," 35–36.

8. *OCN* 33, no. 52, April 1, 1942; and 35, no. 17, July 23, 1942.

Chapter 9

1. June 16, 1944, Deck Logs, NACP; Hoyt, *Nimitz and His Admirals*, 383, 398, 399.
2. Hoyt, *Nimitz and His Admirals*, 392.
3. Springer, *Inferno*, 67; "Peter J. Brady Diary," in FMA, *Original Documents*, 226.
4. Jackson, *Lucky Lady*, 130.
5. June 22, 1944, Deck Logs, NACP.
6. "Byron Robinson," in Springer, *Inferno*, 90.
7. Jackson, *Lucky Lady*, 131.
8. June 30, 1944, *Deck Logs*, NACP.
9. William H. Russ, e-mail message to author, July 19, 2012.
10. Elden to family, September 18 and 22, 1944; Jackson, *Lucky Lady*, 203.
11. "Robert Ladewig," in Springer, *Inferno*, 88.
12. "Robinson," in Springer, *Inferno*, 89–90.
13. Satterfield, *Saving Big Ben*, 36.
14. Roy Treadaway to author, December 2, 2005. The gedunk stand was the canteen, same as the Poggy Bait station.
15. Paul Dalton and Ernest Scott, at USS *Franklin* Museum Association reunion in discussions with the author, Arlington, VA, October 13, 2005.
16. "Robert St. Peters," in Nilo and St. Peters, *The Ship That Wouldn't Die*, 133.
17. "Robert Shapiro," in ibid., 127; U.S. WWII Jewish Servicemen Cards, 1942–1947, Ancestry.com. Apparently yet other separate services were conducted for the 150 African American mess attendants who were on board.
18. "To the Crew of the USS Franklin," photocopy of memorandum attributed to Rear Admiral Ralph Davison, n.d., in Nilo and St. Peters, *The Ship That Wouldn't Die*, 33; Jackson, *Lucky Lady*, 328.
19. Springer, *Inferno*, 87; "Deane Kincaide," in Nilo and St. Peters, *The Ship That Wouldn't Die*, 96.
20. FMA, *Original Documents*, between 336 and 337; Dave Brown, USS *Hornet* Museum, e-mail to author, June 18, 2011.
21. Springer, *Inferno*, 67.
22. Karig, Harris, and Manson, *Battle Report*, 229.
23. July 1, 1944, Deck Logs, NACP; Olson, *Tales from a Tin Can*, 227.

Chapter 10

1. Springer, *Inferno*, 68; "Captain James M. Shoemaker," in Nilo and St. Peters, *The Ship That Wouldn't Die*, 128.
2. Springer, *Inferno*, 75.

3. "Brady Diary," in FMA, *Original Documents*, 226. Brady violated rules by keeping a diary during his service aboard the *Franklin*, from May 20 to August 8, 1944. It appears in *Original Documents* in facsimile from pages 225 to 236.

4. Jackson, *Lucky Lady*, 134; "N. Bently Folsom, Jr.," in Nilo and St. Peters, *The Ship That Wouldn't Die*, 72. Folsom provides a detailed account of what it was like to fly as a gunner in this first attack.

5. July 4, 1944, Deck Logs, NACP; *War Diary of the USS* Franklin *(CV-13)*, RG 38, Records of the Office of the Chief of Naval Operations Relating to Naval Activity during WWII, ARC ID 305242, Box 870, July 4, 1944, NACP; "William George Lloyd," in Nilo and St. Peters, *The Ship That Wouldn't Die*, 101; "St. Peters," in ibid., 133. Lloyd's and St. Peters's accounts differ on the death date of Mulligan. The barrier was a nylon net stretched across the flight deck to catch any landing plane that had not been stopped by the normal tailhook and cable apparatus.

6. Jackson, *Lucky Lady*, 132.

7. "Brady," in Nilo and St. Peters, *The Ship That Wouldn't Die*, 54; "Brady Diary," in FMA, *Original Documents*, 227.

8. Springer, *Inferno*, 78.

9. "Brady Diary," in FMA, *Original Documents*, 227–28.

10. Unidentified page about Vincent H. Walcott, Private First Class, Battery H, USMC, 3rd battalion, 2nd Division, provided by Bobby I. Walcott, July 2005; Karig, Harris, and Manson, *Battle Report*, 260–63.

11. McKendree, *Barbed Wire and Rice*, 60–61.

12. Jackson, *Lucky Lady*, 143.

13. July 9, 1944, Deck Logs, NACP.

14. Ibid., July 10, 1944; "Brady Diary," in FMA, *Original Documents*, 228–29.

15. "Brady Diary," in FMA, *Original Documents*, 229.

16. July 12, 1944, Deck Logs, NACP; "Brady Diary," in FMA, *Original Documents*, 229.

17. Americans heard that Japanese authorities had spread the story that as a prerequisite to joining the U.S. Marines, a man had to kill his own mother and father.

18. July 16, 1944, Deck Logs, NACP; "Brady," in Nilo and St. Peters, *The Ship That Wouldn't Die*, 54; Jackson, *Lucky Lady*, 145. Jackson says that more men from the *Franklin* were killed on the flight deck than in the air during July 1944.

19. "Brady Diary," in FMA, *Original Documents*, 230.

20. Springer, *Inferno*, 78; "The History of Bombing Squad 13," in FMA, *Original Documents*, 46.

21. "Casserino," in Springer, *Inferno*, 63.

22. Jackson, *Lucky Lady*, 146.

23. "Brady Diary," in Nilo and St. Peters, *The Ship That Wouldn't Die*, 231.

24. Ibid.; July 20, 1944, Deck Logs, NACP.

25. "Brady Diary," in Nilo and St. Peters, *The Ship That Wouldn't Die*, 231.

26. "Brady Diary," in FMA, *Original Documents*, 231.

27. Springer, *Inferno*, 79.

Chapter 11

1. Springer, *Inferno*, 79.

2. July 26, 1944, Deck Logs, NACP; "Brady Diary," in FMA, *Original Documents*, 233; "Brady," in Nilo and St. Peters, *The Ship That Wouldn't Die*, 54.

3. "Brady Diary," in FMA, *Original Documents*, 233.

4. Ibid. Brady misidentified the USS *Tingey* as the USS *Tingling*. July 28, 1944, Deck Logs, NACP.

5. July 31, 1944, Deck Logs, NACP.

6. Hoyt, *Nimitz and His Admirals*, 411.

7. Ibid., 413.

8. McKendree, *Barbed Wire and Rice*, 175.

9. August 1, 1944, Deck Logs, NACP.

10. Ibid.; "Brady Diary," in FMA, *Original Documents*, 234.

11. "Franklin Forum," September 6, 1944, in FMA, *Original Documents*, 196.

12. "Brady Diary," in FMA, *Original Documents*, 234; Jackson, *Lucky Lady*, 152; Springer, *Inferno*, 80.

13. "Brady Diary," in FMA, *Original Documents*, 235.

14. Ibid.

15. Jackson, *Lucky Lady*, 195; Springer, *Inferno*, 80.

16. "Brady Diary," in FMA, *Original Documents*, 235–36.

17. Ibid.

18. Springer, *Inferno*, 84.

Chapter 12

1. FMA, *Original Documents*, 101.

2. "Brady Diary," in ibid., 236.

3. August 9, 1944, *Deck Logs*, NACP.

4. "Walter A. Jordan, Jr.," in Nilo and St. Peters, *The Ship That Wouldn't Die*, 91.

5. Springer, *Inferno*, 85.

6. "St. Peters," in Nilo and St. Peters, *The Ship That Wouldn't Die*, 133.

7. Jackson, *Lucky Lady*, 173.

8. Roy G. Treadaway to author, December 17, 2004. Dowell's repertoire included "Shoot That Bogie Down," with fighting lyrics to the tune of the line "Lay That Pistol Down" in the song "Pistol Packin' Mama." FMA, *Original Documents*, 13.

9. Hoyt, *Nimitz and His Admirals*, 408.

10. Springer, *Inferno*, 85.

11. "Pierce J. Brown," in Nilo and St. Peters, *The Ship That Wouldn't Die*, 56.

12. Springer, *Inferno*, 86.

13. Ibid., 86–87.

14. McKendree, *Barbed Wire and Rice*, 175.

15. Ibid., 66.

16. "USS *Hoel*, July 9, 1944," 2, Muster Rolls, NARA; ibid., "August 16, 1944," 14.

17. "St. Peters," in Nilo and St. Peters, *The Ship That Wouldn't Die*, 133.

18. Jackson, *Lucky Lady*, 150.

19. "Cruising Disposition—Task Force 38," in FMA, *Original Documents*, 56; Springer, *Inferno*, 91. Bob Walcott's ship, the *Piedmont*, also sailed as part of Task Force 38, but was in a different task group, 38.1.

20. August 23 and 24, 1944, Deck Logs, NACP.

Chapter 13

1. August 28, 1944, Deck Logs, NACP.

2. Karig, Harris, and Manson, *Battle Report*, 298; Jackson, *Lucky Lady*, 174; Springer, *Inferno*, 91.

3. Springer, *Inferno*, 92.

4. September 3, 4, and 5, 1944, Deck Logs, NACP; Jackson, *Lucky Lady*, 174.

5. McKendree, *Barbed Wire and Rice*, 174–75.

6. Jackson, *Lucky Lady*, 174.

7. September 6, 1944, Deck Logs, NACP; December 31, 1944, Muster Rolls, NARA.

8. Action Reports, USS *Franklin* (CV-13), September 5–18, 1944, ARC ID 305242, MLR Number A1-353, Box 990, RG 38, Records Relating to Naval Activity during WWII, Action and Operational Reports, NACP; Springer, *Inferno*, 92.

9. September 9, 1944, Deck Logs, NACP; Hoyt, *Nimitz and His Admirals*, 418; Springer, *Inferno*, 95.

10. September 11, 1944, Deck Logs, NACP; September 18, 1944, Action Reports, NACP.

11. September 18, 1944, Action Reports, NACP.

12. September 12 and 13, 1944, Deck Logs, NACP; September 12, 1944, Action Reports, NACP; Hoyt, *Nimitz and His Admirals*, 418; Springer, *Inferno*, 95–98.

13. September 14, 1944, Deck Logs, NACP.

14. September 15, 1944, Deck Logs, NACP; September 15, 1944, Action Reports, NACP; Springer, *Inferno*, 95–98.

15. "Reon G. Hillegass, Jr.," in Nilo and St. Peters, *The Ship That Wouldn't Die*, 147; Brown to author, June 18, 2011.

16. Springer, *Inferno*, 98.

17. September 18, 1944, Deck Logs, NACP.

Chapter 14

1. September 20, 1944, Deck Logs, NACP; "Morrison," in FMA, *Original Documents*, 47; Jackson, *Lucky Lady*, 175; Springer, *Inferno*, 98.

2. "George Sippel," in Springer, *Inferno*, 100.

3. Springer, *Inferno*, 99–101.

4. September 21, 1944, Deck Logs, NACP; Jackson, *Lucky Lady*, 175.

5. Fahey, *Pacific War Diary*, 255.

6. Bowman and Warrick, *Big Ben the Flattop*, n.p.

7. Walcott, July 2005.

8. McKendree, *Barbed Wire and Rice*, 175–76; Karig, Harris, and Manson, *Battle Report*, 301–2.

9. "Nowak," in Springer, *Inferno*, 301.

10. Hoyt, *Nimitz and His Admirals*, 419.

Chapter 15

1. Karig, Harris, and Manson, *Battle Report*, 335.

2. Hoyt, *Nimitz and His Admirals*, 430.

3. September 24, 1944, Deck Logs, NACP.

4. Ibid., September 29, 1944.

5. Karig, Harris, and Manson, *Battle Report*, 323–24; Springer, *Inferno*, 109.

6. I had lost a baby tooth. Our family did not participate in the "tooth fairy" mythology, but rather embraced a sort of transubstantiation in which a tooth under a pillow literally became a nickel. Elden was plumping for an even better outcome.

7. Jackson, *Lucky Lady*, 176.

8. Ibid., 177.

9. McKendree, *Barbed Wire and Rice*, 176.

10. Ibid., 176–77.

11. Ibid., 178.

12. Karig, Harris, and Manson, *Battle Report*, 324; Jackson, *Lucky Lady*, 177.

13. October 10, 1944, Deck Logs, NACP; October 10, 1944, Action Reports, NACP; Springer, *Inferno*, 109.

14. "Jordan," in Nilo and St. Peters, *The Ship That Wouldn't Die*, 91; Karig, Harris, and Manson, *Battle Report*, 326.

15. Jackson, *Lucky Lady*, 178.

16. Ibid.; October 11, 1944, Deck Logs, NACP; October 11, 1944, Action Reports, NACP.

17. Jackson, *Lucky Lady*, 179; Springer, *Inferno*, 110.

18. McKendree, *Barbed Wire and Rice*, 179; World War II Prisoners of War, 1941–1946, NARA. The official record shows Sharp as born in 1917, enlisted at Santa Fe on March 18, 1941, held at Camp 504 in the Philippines, and died as prisoner of war. McKendree became acquainted with him in camp and seems a reliable source for his death occurring aboard the *Haro Maru* in Hong Kong Harbor in 1944.

19. October 12, 1944, Deck Logs, NACP; Hoyt, *Nimitz and His Admirals*, 430; Springer, *Inferno*, 110.

20. "Ronald Currie Noyes," in Nilo and St. Peters, *The Ship That Wouldn't Die*, 112.

21. Jackson, *Lucky Lady*, 179.

22. October 13, 1944, Deck Logs, NACP; Springer, *Inferno*, 323–24.

23. Jackson, *Lucky Lady*, 161.

24. Ibid., 188; Springer, *Inferno*, 323–24; Halsey and Bryan, *Admiral Halsey's Story*, 229; Karig, Harris, and Manson, *Battle Report*, 240. Halsey had witnessed a damaged Japanese plane try to crash into the USS *Enterprise* back in 1942, but that was a last effort by a doomed pilot rather than a premeditated suicidal sacrifice. Another plane had crashed into the USS *Indiana* on June 19, 1944, apparently intentionally.

25. October 13, 1944, Deck Logs, NACP.

26. Springer, *Inferno*, 110–11.

27. October 13, 1944, Deck Logs, NACP.

28. "Noyes," in Nilo and St. Peters, *The Ship That Wouldn't Die*, 112.

29. Preliminary Design Section, Bureau of Ships, Navy Department, "War Damage Report no. 56, U.S.S. *Franklin* (CV-13)," September 15, 1946, in FMA, *Original Documents*, 344; October 13, 1944, Deck Logs, NACP.

30. "Al Cole," in Springer, *Inferno*, 112.

31. "William Edward Brunner," in Nilo and St. Peters, *The Ship That Wouldn't Die*, 57.

32. "Robert Lee Tice," in ibid., 137.

33. "Noyes," in Nilo and St. Peters, *The Ship That Wouldn't Die*, 112.

34. October 13, 1944, Deck Logs, NACP.

35. "Noyes," in Nilo and St. Peters, *The Ship That Wouldn't Die*, 112; Springer, *Inferno*, 112–13.

36. "War Damage Report," in FMA, *Original Documents*, 344; "James M. Shoemaker," in Nilo and St. Peters, *The Ship That Wouldn't Die*, 129; Springer, *Inferno*, 114.

37. Jackson, *Lucky Lady*, 230.

38. October 13, 1944, Deck Logs, NACP; October 13, 1944, Action Reports, NACP; "Brief History: USS *Franklin* (CV-13)," in FMA, *Original Documents*, 76;

"War Damage Report," in FMA, *Original Documents*, 344; "Shoemaker," in Nilo and St. Peters, *The Ship That Wouldn't Die*, 129; Springer, *Inferno*, 114.

39. Jackson, *Lucky Lady*, 189–90.

Chapter 16

1. October 13, 1944, Deck Logs, NACP.
2. Springer, *Inferno*, 116.
3. "Jack Lawton," in ibid., 115.
4. "Robinson," in ibid.
5. "Ladewig," in ibid.
6. "Mady," in ibid.
7. October 15, 1944, Action Reports, NACP.
8. Jackson, *Lucky Lady*, 207.
9. "Mady," in Springer, *Inferno*, 117.
10. October 15, 1944, Deck Logs, NACP; October 15, 1944, Action Reports, NACP; "War Damage Report," in FMA, *Original Documents*, 344–45; Springer, *Inferno*, 116.
11. Jackson, *Lucky Lady*, 208.
12. "Robinson," in *Inferno*, 118.
13. October 15, 1944, Deck Logs, NACP; "War Damage Report," in FMA, *Original Documents*, 344–45. A third man later died of injuries from this bombing.
14. October 15, 1944, Deck Logs, NACP; October 15, 1944, Action Reports, NACP.
15. Jackson, *Lucky Lady*, 210.
16. Springer, *Inferno*, 119–20; October 15, 1944, *Deck Logs*, NACP.
17. Jackson, *Lucky Lady*, 217.
18. October 17, 1944, Deck Logs, NACP.
19. Karig, Harris, and Manson, *Battle Report*, 328–29; the authors opine that Japan may have been the victim of extremely faulty intelligence rather than propaganda alone.
20. Hoyt, *Nimitz and His Admirals*, 330.
21. October 20, 1944, Deck Logs, NACP.
22. Jackson, *Lucky Lady*, 221.
23. Ibid., 222–23.
24. McKendree, *Barbed Wire and Rice*, 182.
25. Olson, *Tales from a Tin Can*, 182, 192.
26. Hoyt, *Nimitz and His Admirals*, 442; Hornfischer, *Last Stand*. Hornfischer's whole book is about this heroic episode.
27. Hoyt, *Nimitz and His Admirals*, 432.
28. Karig, Harris, and Manson, *Battle Report*, 335; Hoyt, *Nimitz and His Admirals*, 433; Springer, *Inferno*, 129.

29. Hoyt, *Nimitz and His Admirals*, 431–34.

30. Springer, *Inferno*, 129.

31. October 24, 1944, Deck Logs, NACP.

32. Springer, *Inferno*, 137. The *Musashi* sank later on October 24 after many more hits. Her hulk has been identified at a depth of 1,000 meters and is being explored by officials of the National Museum of the Philippines.

33. Jackson, *Lucky Lady*, 227–28.

34. Hornfischer, *Last Stand*, 105.

35. Springer, *Inferno*, 139.

36. Ibid., 139, 143.

37. Hornfischer, *Last Stand*, 246.

38. Charles D. Walcott of Vega was a gunner in a plane flying off the *Gambier Bay*, but he was airborne when his ship was lost.

39. Springer, *Inferno*, 139–40. Admiral Halsey was chagrined because some of the Japanese carriers had been allowed to escape. No American yet knew the carrier force had been a decoy, or that Halsey's entire staff had fallen for the ruse.

40. October 26, 1944, Deck Logs, NACP.

41. Springer, *Inferno*, 144.

42. Hoyt, *Nimitz and His Admirals*, 445; Jackson, *Lucky Lady*, 252.

43. Springer, *Inferno*, 144.

44. October 29, 1944, Deck Logs, NACP; Springer, *Inferno*, 145.

45. October 30, 1944, Deck Logs, NACP; October 30, 1944, Action Reports, NACP.

46. "Kincaide," in Nilo and St. Peters, *The Ship That Wouldn't Die*, 96.

47. "Stanley S. Graham," in ibid., 84.

48. Springer, *Inferno*, 152.

49. October 30, 1944, Deck Logs, NACP; October 30, 1944, Action Reports, NACP.

50. October 30, 1944, Action Reports, NACP; "Donald Eugene Croft," in Nilo and St. Peters, *The Ship That Wouldn't Die*, 65.

51. "Louis Bonitatibus," in Nilo and St. Peters, *The Ship That Wouldn't Die*, 53.

52. October 30, 1944, Deck Logs, NACP; October 30, 1944, Action Reports, NACP; "War Damage Report," in FMA, *Original Documents*, 345; Jackson, *Lucky Lady*, 259–60.

53. Springer, *Inferno*, 155.

54. "War Damage Report," in FMA, *Original Documents*, 345; "Brief History," in FMA, *Original Documents*, 77; Jackson, *Lucky Lady*, 259–66.

55. October 30, 1944, Deck Logs, NACP; October 30, 1944, Action Reports, NACP; "Noyes," in Nilo and St. Peters, *The Ship That Wouldn't Die*, 112.

56. October 31, 1944, Deck Logs, NACP; October 31, 1944, Action Reports, NACP.

57. "Tice," in Nilo and St. Peters, *The Ship That Wouldn't Die*, 137.

58. "Plan of the Day, October 31, 1944," in FMA, *Original Documents*, 110; "Steve Jurika" and "Gerald J. Keegan," in Nilo and St. Peters, *The Ship That Wouldn't Die*, 94. The Vienna sausage reference comes from March 19 and 20, 1945, and is inferred as a possibility for 1944.

59. October 15, 1944, Action Reports, NACP.

60. "Martin Louis Kassover," in Nilo and St. Peters, *The Ship That Wouldn't Die*, 94.

Chapter 17

1. November 2, 1944, Deck Logs, NACP; "Alternate Plan of the Day, November 2, 1944," in FMA, *Original Documents*, 112; "Brief History," in FMA, *Original Documents*, 88; Springer, *Inferno*, 163.

2. McKendree, *Barbed Wire and Rice*, 179–82.

3. Ibid.

4. *Duffy's Tavern* was another popular weekly radio show of the era. "Casserino," in Springer, *Inferno*, 164.

5. Walcott, July 2005.

6. "Casserino," in Springer, *Inferno*, 64.

7. "War Damage Report," in FMA, *Original Documents*, 343.

8. "Kincaide," in Nilo and St. Peters, *The Ship That Wouldn't Die*, 96.

9. Hoyt, *Nimitz and His Admirals*, 456.

10. Springer, *Inferno*, 165.

11. November 8, 1944, Deck Logs, NACP.

12. "Captain Leslie E. Gehres, the New Captain," in FMA, *Original Documents*, 304–5.

13. Springer, *Inferno*, 165.

14. Jackson, *Lucky Lady*, 346.

15. November 11, 1944, Deck Logs, NACP.

16. "Plan of the Day, November 12, 1944," in FMA, *Original Documents*, 115.

17. "Plan of the Day, November 13, 1944," in ibid., 116.

18. Bob Walcott related in our July 2005 interview that he had his own close call when the ammunition ship USS *Mount Hood* exploded on November 10 back at Manus, doing terrible damage to other ships and showering the *Piedmont* with bombs and shrapnel.

19. "Plan of the Day, November 19, 1944," in ibid., 117.

20. "Roster of Officers, USS Franklin, March 1, 1945," in FMA, *Original Documents*, 170.

21. "Kincaide," in Nilo and St. Peters, *The Ship That Wouldn't Die*, 96.

22. "Plan of the Day, November 24, 1944," in FMA, *Original Documents*, 123.

23. Gerald B. Rogers, e-mail to author, July 30, 2012.

24. "Tucum" was a common slang for Tucumcari, New Mexico.

25. A receipt from Zale Jewelry Co. in Amarillo dated October 12, 1944, shows that Grace had paid $62.50 for a man's Election Waterproof watch, a remarkable amount for the Rogers family at the time.

26. Bill and Loretta Swanson were a young couple living in Vega.

27. "Plan of the Day, November 27, 1944," in FMA, *Original Documents*, 125; Jackson, *Lucky Lady*, 290; Springer, *Inferno*, 165.

Chapter 18

1. This letter was written on the back of an issue of *Longhorn News*.

2. OCHC, 341.

3. "Taylor, Memorandum Regarding Special Train, December 19, 1944," in FMA, *Original Documents*, 300.

4. "Taylor, Memorandum to All Hands, December 19, 1944," in ibid., 299.

5. Elden did not speak of where he had been, but while home on leave he drew lines on *Hagstrom's Map of the Pacific and the Far East: Showing Progress in the War against Japan* (New York: Hagstrom Company, 1944) indicating his voyages on the USS *Franklin* up to that time.

6. Jackson, *Lucky Lady*, 293.

7. McKendree, *Barbed Wire and Rice*, 183.

8. This letter of Virginia's was addressed to Vega.

9. Hoyt, *Nimitz and His Admirals*, 478.

10. This communication was on a postcard.

11. Jackson, *Lucky Lady*, 283.

12. Ibid., 301.

13. Olson, *Tales from a Tin Can*, 211–12.

14. McKendree, *Barbed Wire and Rice*, 184–85.

15. Hoyt, *Nimitz and His Admirals*, 469.

Chapter 19

1. Springer, *Inferno*, 170.

2. "Casserino," in ibid., 174.

3. "Noyes," in Nilo and St. Peters, *The Ship That Wouldn't Die*, 113.

4. February 2, 1945, Deck Logs, NACP; Jackson, *Lucky Lady*, 303, 321. The USS *Hornet* (CV-12), a sister ship of the *Franklin*, is now docked at this location and serves as a museum.

5. "Noyes," in Nilo and St. Peters, *The Ship That Wouldn't Die*, 113.

6. Jackson, *Lucky Lady*, 321.

7. Springer, *Inferno*, 175, 178.

8. Halsey and Bryan, *Halsey*, 197.

9. Odell Price, in discussion with author, August 11, 2012.

10. Bowman and Warrick, *Big Ben the Flattop*, n.p.

11. Friedman, *U.S. Aircraft Carriers*, 394; Charles Myers e-mail to Jerry Rogers, June 12, 2015.

12. February 7, 1945, Deck Logs, NACP.

13. On January 20, 1945, Army Rangers, Alamo Scouts, and Filipino guerrilla fighters liberated more than five hundred prisoners from the Cabanatuan camp, where Bish McKendree and Jimmy Bales had been held, although Bales was dead by then and McKendree was far away in Japan.

14. Gerald B. Rogers, "Wilburn 'Wig' Price's Last Contact with Elden Rogers," e-mail to author, May 4, 2010; February 22, 1945, Deck Logs, NACP; Jackson, *Lucky Lady*, 323.

15. The Corsairs were not literally new but were newly assigned to carrier use after problems of deck landings had been solved.

16. February 16, 1945, Deck Logs, NACP; Springer, *Inferno*, 182–83.

17. "Man Recounts Ship's Bombing," in *The Noble and Brave Stories of War*, 25, special publication of the *Amarillo Globe News*, November 11, 2010.

18. Taylor, *Dresden*, 475–76; Wilfried Braakhuis, http://www.euronet.nl/users /wilfried/ww2//ww2.htm (accessed June 29, 2016).

19. Hoyt, *Nimitz and His Admirals*, 471.

20. Elden's references to Virginia in his letters of February 7 through March 3, 1945, suggest that he received two or three letters from her during this seemingly critical phase in their relationship, but we do not have them. Might they have contained something that led him not to save them or Grace to destroy them after his death?

21. Myers to Rogers, June 12, 2015.

22. The letters of February 21, 24, and 28 all have "Somewhere in the Pacific"/"Big Ben" written above the dates. Elden had told his family while at home on leave that this would indicate Pearl Harbor.

23. Hoyt, *Nimitz and His Admirals*, 471–73.

24. Ibid., 471–74.

25. February 27, 1945, Deck Logs, NACP.

Chapter 20

1. March 2, 1945, Deck Logs, NACP; "St. Peters," in Nilo and St. Peters, *The Ship That Wouldn't Die*, 133; Satterfield, *Saving Big Ben*, 56.

2. "Ray Larsen," in Springer, *Inferno*, 178.

3. "George Black," in ibid., 181.

4. February 28 and March 3, 1945, Deck Logs, NACP; Nilo and St. Peters, *The Ship That Wouldn't Die*, 16; Jackson, *Lucky Lady*, 327; Springer, *Inferno*, 185.

5. "USS *Franklin*, February 28, 1945," 101, Muster Rolls, NARA; "Obituary, Nelson A. Myers, September 22, 2010," Find a Grave Memorial, http://www.findagrave.com/cgi-bin/fg.cgi?page=gr&GS1n=MY&GSfn=n&GSpartial=1& (accessed May 18, 2012); "USS *Houston* (CL-81)," Wikipedia, https://en.wikipedia.org/wiki/USS_Houston_(CL-81) (accessed May 19, 2012).

6. March 4, 1945, Deck Logs, NACP; Jackson, *Lucky Lady*, 323.

7. March 3, 1945, Deck Logs, NACP.

8. "Roster of Officers, March, 1945," in FMA, *Original Documents*, 168.

9. Odell and Verda Mae Price to Ancell and Grace Rogers, June 2, 1945; Elsie Treadaway to Grace Rogers, June 2, 1945.

10. Jackson, *Lucky Lady*, 323–24.

11. March 9, 1945, Deck Logs, NACP.

12. Taylor, *Dresden*, 88.

13. Jackson, *Lucky Lady*, 311.

14. "Donald Arthur Gary," in Nilo and St. Peters, *The Ship That Wouldn't Die*, 77.

Chapter 21

1. March 13, 1945, Deck Logs, NACP; Springer, *Inferno*, 185.

2. "Gary," in Nilo and St. Peters, *The Ship That Wouldn't Die*, 77.

3. Jackson, *Lucky Lady*, 327.

4. March 14, 1945, Deck Logs, NACP; "Gary," in Nilo and St. Peters, *The Ship That Wouldn't Die*, 77.

5. Springer, *Inferno*, 186.

6. Jackson, *Lucky Lady*, 276.

7. "Bob Blanchard," in Springer, *Inferno*, 187.

8. Jackson, *Lucky Lady*, 328; "Gary," in Nilo and St. Peters, *The Ship That Wouldn't Die*, 77.

9. "Mike Sansone," in Springer, *Inferno*, 187.

10. March 15, 1945, Deck Logs, NACP.

11. On the plains, "Vitamin K" was a joking reference to blowing dust, which was said to contain the nutrient.

12. March 16, 1945, Deck Logs, NACP.

13. Jackson, *Lucky Lady*, 328.

14. "Alphabetical List of Enlisted Personnel of 'E' Division 23 February, 1945," in FMA, *Original Documents*, 154; "Early Mess Pass for Gunnery Department," in FMA, *Original Documents*, 151.

15. Elvin Dean Rogers, "Visit with Roy G. Treadaway," Laguna Park, Bosque County, TX, e-mail to Jerry L. Rogers, February 19, 2012.

16. March 17, 1945, Deck Logs, NACP; "Noyes," in Nilo and St. Peters, *The Ship That Wouldn't Die*, 113.

17. Jackson, *Lucky Lady*, 333; Satterfield, *Saving Big Ben*, 69.

18. Jackson, *Lucky Lady*, 328.

19. Springer, *Inferno*, 189.

20. March 17, 1945, Deck Logs, NACP.

21. "Frank Richard Sepesy," in Nilo and St. Peters, *The Ship That Wouldn't Die*, 126.

22. March 18, 1945, Deck Logs, NACP; Jackson, *Lucky Lady*, 317.

23. Manuscript by Irvin R. Dahlen (Grattinger, Iowa, n.d.), copy in possession of author; Springer, *Inferno*, 189.

24. Jackson, *Lucky Lady*, 328; Springer, *Inferno*, 189.

25. Jackson, *Lucky Lady*, 331; Springer, *Inferno*, 190–95.

26. The USS *Enterprise* (CV-6) was older and smaller than the *Franklin*, but it still carried ninety planes.

27. Satterfield, *Saving Big Ben*, 72.

28. March 18, 1945, Deck Logs, NACP; "Gary," in Nilo and St. Peters, *The Ship That Wouldn't Die*, 77; Jackson, *Lucky Lady*, 317, 331; Springer, *Inferno*, 190–95.

29. Jackson, *Lucky Lady*, 363.

30. "Nick Turcic," in Springer, *Inferno*, 258.

31. Jackson, *Lucky Lady*, 334–35.

32. Musician Deane Kincaide, of the Dowell orchestra, was another whose birthday fell on March 19—his thirty-fourth. "Kincaide," in Nilo and St. Peters, *The Ship That Wouldn't Die*, 96.

33. March 19, 1945, Deck Logs, NACP; "Gary," in Nilo and St. Peters, *The Ship That Wouldn't Die*, 77.

34. Ibid.; Springer, *Inferno*, 209.

35. Rogers, "Visit with Roy G. Treadaway."

36. Jackson, *Lucky Lady*, 336–37.

37. Ibid., 326–27.

38. Springer, *Inferno*, 195.

39. Everett R. Beaver, quoted in "USS Franklin Tragedy: 19 March 1945," http://www.battleshipnc.com/teach_reso/oral_history/battle/franklin.php (accessed December 23, 2004).

40. Springer, *Inferno*, 196.

41. March 19, 1945, Deck Logs, NACP.

42. Springer, *Inferno*, 196; Satterfield, *Saving Big Ben*, 14–16. Satterfield believes the Comet was piloted by Lt. Tominori Kawaguchi.

43. Beaver, in "USS Franklin Tragedy"; Robert L. Palomaris, quoted in "USS Franklin Tragedy: 19 March 1945," http://www.battleshipnc.com/teach_reso/oral

_history/battle/franklin.php and http://www.battleshipnc.com/teach_reso/oral
_history/battle/franklin.php (accessed December 23, 2004); Springer, *Inferno*, 207.

44. Jackson, *Lucky Lady*, 340.

45. "Franklin Albro," in Nilo and St. Peters, *The Ship That Wouldn't Die*, 47.

46. "Donald A. Bye," in Nilo and St. Peters, *The Ship That Wouldn't Die*, 58.

47. "Joseph Pipolo," in Nilo and St. Peters, *The Ship That Wouldn't Die*, 120.
James Pipolo was killed; the book entry was written by his brother.

48. Bureau of Ships, Navy Department, "War Damage Report," in FMA, *Original Documents*, 350; Jackson, *Lucky Lady*, 360; Springer, *Inferno*, 205; Ray Emery, telephone interview with author, January 6, 2012.

Chapter 22

1. Roy Treadaway to Frances "Jackie" Rogers, June 2, 1945; Elsie Treadaway to Grace Rogers, June 13, 1945; "Roy G. Treadaway," in Nilo and St. Peters, *The Ship That Wouldn't Die*, 138; "War Damage Report," in FMA, *Original Documents*, 351.

2. Beaver and Palomaris, in "USS Franklin Tragedy."

3. "Cole," in Springer, *Inferno*, 216.

4. "Blanchard," in Springer, *Inferno*, 220.

5. Ibid., 220.

6. "Bob Mallgraf and Nick Turcic," in Springer, *Inferno*, 210–11; Satterfield, *Saving Big Ben*, 79. Satterfield says the captain's disorientation was brief, understandable due to the shock of what had happened, and associated with smoke inhalation.

7. "Jurika," in Nilo and St. Peters, *The Ship That Wouldn't Die*, 93; Springer, *Inferno*, 209–10.

8. Springer, *Inferno*, 232.

9. Ibid., 224.

10. Ibid., 229.

11. "Grimes Weldon Gatlin," in Nilo and St. Peters, *The Ship That Wouldn't Die*, 79.

12. Marion Leedy, "His Adventure Began after His 'Death,'" *Benton Harbor (MI) News-Palladium*, May 29, 1965, 16.

13. March 19, 1945, Deck Logs, NACP; Jackson, *Lucky Lady*, 374; Satterfield, *Saving Big Ben*, 85, 88.

14. Springer, *Inferno*, 248.

15. Treadaway to Rogers, June 2, 1945; "Treadaway," in Nilo and St. Peters, *The Ship That Wouldn't Die*, 138; "Famed Carrier's Most Heroic Hours Recalled by Local Navy Recruiter," *Sweetwater Reporter*, March 19, 1959; "Gehres," in Nilo and St. Peters, *The Ship That Wouldn't Die*, 81.

16. Treadaway to Rogers, June 2, 1945; Roy Treadaway to Jerry Rogers, December 17, 2004; "Treadaway," in Nilo and St. Peters, *The Ship That Wouldn't Die*, 138; "USS *Franklin*, December 31, 1944," 52, *Muster Rolls*, NARA.

17. Edward B. Brown, "John Franklin Brown," in Nilo and St. Peters, *The Ship That Wouldn't Die*, 56.

18. Treadaway to Rogers, June 2, 1945; Treadaway to Rogers, December 17, 2004; "Treadaway," in Nilo and St. Peters, *The Ship That Wouldn't Die*, 138.

19. March 19 and 20, 1945, Deck Logs, NACP.

Chapter 23

1. Jackson, *Lucky Lady*, 433.
2. Springer, Inferno, 269.
3. "Gary," in Nilo and St. Peters, *The Ship That Wouldn't Die*, 78; Jackson, *Lucky Lady*, 442.
4. Gerald B. Rogers, "Interview with Dave Lawson," e-mail to Jerry Rogers, February 19, 2010; "William Joseph Fowler, Jr.," in Nilo and St. Peters, *The Ship That Wouldn't Die*, 76; Jackson, *Lucky Lady*, 442–45; "Don Conard," in Springer, *Inferno*, 289.
5. Names deleted by author. Grace here is snickering about two women being pregnant at a somewhat more advanced age than she thinks appropriate, but two years later she herself will be pregnant past the age of forty.
6. "Saving Up Coupons" was a popular country song by J. E. Mainer and Jimmie O'Neal, and it referred to the singer's pregnant wife.
7. "Joseph T. O'Callahan," in FMA, *Original Documents*, 320–21.
8. Alvin S. McCoy, "Aboard the USS *Santa Fe* in the Western Pacific," March 19, 1945, release delayed by Associated Press and published widely May 18, 1945.
9. "Gatlin," in Nilo and St. Peters, *The Ship That Wouldn't Die*, 79.
10. Treadaway to Rogers, December 17, 2004.
11. March 4, 1945, Deck Logs, NACP; Springer, *Inferno*, 301–2.
12. Dahlen, unpublished manuscript, n.d.
13. Treadaway to Rogers, June 13, 1945.
14. "Robinson," in Springer, *Inferno*, 303.
15. March 7 and 8, 1945, Deck Logs, NACP.
16. Joe Springer to Jerry Rogers, e-mail, December 23, 2010.

Chapter 24

1. Springer, *Inferno*, 312.
2. Ed Shroba to Grace and Ancell Rogers, June 18, 1945, and July 25, 1945.
3. Thomas Ellis to Grace Rogers, June 2, 1945.

4. Treadaway to Rogers, December 17, 2004; "Treadaway," in Nilo and St. Peters, *The Ship That Wouldn't Die*, 138.

5. Hornfischer, *Last Stand*, 412.

6. McCoy, "Aboard the USS *Santa Fe* in the Western Pacific," March 19, 1945.

7. Treadaway to Rogers, June 13, 1945.

8. "Gabriel Heatter, May 17, 1945," in FMA, *Original Documents*, 70–75; "Walter M. Newland," in Nilo and St. Peters, *The Ship That Wouldn't Die*, 110; "Kincaide," in Nilo and St. Peters, *The Ship That Wouldn't Die*, 96; Jackson, *Lucky Lady*, 446–50, 455; Springer, *Inferno*, 316.

9. Art Gomez, National Park Service historian, "Conversation with Takeshi Maeda, Oahu, Hawaii, December 5, 2006," e-mail to Jerry Rogers, February 5, 2013.

10. The missing in action message was actually received April 13.

11. Gerald Blane Rogers, "They've Found Bish McKendree—He's Alive!," e-mail to author, June 10, 2011.

Epilogue

1. Jackson, *Lucky Lady*, 452.

2. Springer, *Inferno*, 321.

3. Ernest Scott and Frank Turner, in discussions with the author at Franklin Museum Association Reunion, Arlington, VA, October 13, 2005.

4. "Obituary, Nelson A. Myers."

5. That "there are no foxholes on ships" was commonplace in the navy; it appears in Halsey and Bryan, *Halsey*, 145.

6. Many well-informed people disagree about Truman being right to use the atomic bombs. Halsey believed Japan was on the verge of falling, and that the bomb's use, together with Russia's belated declaration of war on Japan, merely provided an excuse to surrender before the inevitable collapse. Dwight D. Eisenhower believed the bomb's use had been unnecessary.

7. From Robert Louis Stevenson, *Requiem*.

BIBLIOGRAPHY

Archival Sources

J. Y. Joyner Library, East Carolina University, Greenville, NC
  East Carolina Manuscript Collection
    Beaver, Everett R. Oral History Interview (OH0024-036). USS *North Carolina* Battleship Collection. http://www.battleshipnc.com/teach_reso/oral_history/battle/franklin.php. Accessed December 23, 2004.
    Palomaris, Robert Leroy. Oral History Interview (OH0024-042), USS *North Carolina* Battleship Collection. http://www.battleshipnc.com/teach_reso/oral_history/battle/franklin.php. Accessed December 23, 2004.
National Archives and Records Administration
  Bamburg, Robert Leon. Registration Card, National Jewish Welfare Board, U.S. WWII Jewish Servicemen Cards, 1942–1947. http://search.ancestry.com/cgi-bin/sse.dll?h=14013&db=AJHSservicemen&indiv=try. Accessed August 6, 2012.
  USS *Franklin* (CV-13). Muster Rolls. http:search.ancestry.com/cqi-bin/sse.dll?h=276540&db=NavyMuster&indiv=try. Accessed May 29 and 30, 2012.
  USS *General John R. Brooke* (AP-132). Muster Rolls. http://search.ancestry.com/content/viewerpf.aspx?h=31223820&db=NavyMuster&iid=3285. Accessed June 6, 2012.
  USS *Hoel* (DD-533). Muster Rolls. http://search.ancestry.com/content/viewerpf.aspx?h=31223820&db=NavyMuster&iid=3285. Accessed June 6, 2012.
  USS *PC 1260*. Muster Rolls. http://search.ancestry.com/content/viewerpf.aspx?h=40679340&db=NavyMuster&iid=328. Accessed June 10, 2012.
  USS *Pensacola* (CA-24). Muster Rolls. http://search.ancestry.com/content/viewerpf.aspx?h=42404801&db=NavyMuster&iid=328. Accessed June 10, 2012.
  USS *Piedmont* (AD-17). Muster Rolls. http://search.ancestry.com/content/viewerpf.aspx?h=39978569&db=NavyMuster&iid=3286. Accessed June 8 and 9, 2012.

U.S. World War II Army Enlistment Records, 1938–1946. http://search.ancestry
.comcgi-bin/sse.dll?rank=1&new=1&MSAV=1&msT=1&gss=angs-c. Accessed
June 6, 2012.

World War II Prisoners of War, 1941–1946. http://search.ancestry.com/cgi-bin
/sse.dll?rank=1&new=1&MSAV=1&msT=1&gss=angs-c. Accessed June 6,
2012.

National Archives at College Park, MD

USS Franklin (CV-13) Action Reports. Record Group 38. Records of the Office
of the Chief of Naval Operations. Boxes 870, 990.

USS Franklin (CV-13) Deck Logs. Record Group 24. Records of the Bureau of
Naval Personnel, January 31, 1944, to September 30, 1944. ARC ID 594258
Entry P 118-A1. Boxes 3469, 3470, 3471.

Price, Asahel Leon. "World War II Correspondence," consisting of letters and related materials by himself and Mamie Price. In possession of Laverna Higgins,
San Antonio, TX.

Rogers, Elden Duane, S 2/c USNR. Personal Information Booklet, USS Franklin,
1944. In author's possession.

———. "World War II Correspondence," consisting of letters and related materials by Elden Duane Rogers, Grace Coin Rogers, and others, 1943–45. In author's
possession.

Rogers, Gerald Blane, with Jerry L. Rogers and Elvin D. Rogers. "A Session for
Memories." Unpublished manuscript of stories about growing up in Vega,
Texas, shared at Santa Fe, NM, June 20–22, 2008. In author's possession.

U.S. Census, 1910, 1920, 1930, 1940. http://search.ancestryinstitution.com/cgi-bin
/sse.dll?rank=1&new=1&MSA. Accessed June 30, 2016.

Interviews with the Author

Dahlen, Irvin Richard. By telephone, February 24, 2005.

Dalton, Paul. USS Franklin Museum Association reunion, Arlington, VA, October 13, 2005.

Emory, Ray. By telephone, January 6 and 7, 2012.

———. Honolulu, HI, March 19, 2012.

Kraft, Karl. USS Franklin Museum Association reunion, Arlington, VA, October 13, 2005.

Richardson, Jack. USS Franklin Museum Association reunion, Arlington, VA, October 13, 2005.

Scott, Ernest. USS Franklin Museum Association reunion, Arlington, VA, October 13, 2005.

Varady, Charles. USS Hornet Museum. Oakland, CA, May 21, 2015.

Walcott, Bobby I. Jemez Springs, NM, July 15, 2005.

Books and Articles

Bowman, Marvin K., and Paul Warrick. *Big Ben, the Flat Top: The Story of the USS Franklin, 1946.* World War Regimental Histories 135. Atlanta: Albert Love Enterprises, 1946. http://digicom.bpl.lib.me.us/ww_reg_his/135.

"The Carrier *Franklin* Refuses to Go Down," *Life,* May 28, 1945.

Chapman, Robert L. *New Dictionary of American Slang.* New York: Harper and Row, 1986.

Fahey, James J. *Pacific War Diary, 1942–1945: The Secret Diary of an American Sailor.* Boston: Mariner, 2003.

Forester, C. S. "Unsinkable: The Story of the Aircraft Carrier *Franklin*." *True: The Man's Magazine,* September 1945.

Friedman, Norman. *U.S. Aircraft Carriers.* Washington, DC: U.S. Naval Institute, 1983.

Hagstrom's Map of the Pacific and the Far East: Showing Progress in the War against Japan. New York: Hagstrom Company, 1944.

Halsey, William F., and Joseph Bryan III. *Admiral Halsey's Story.* New York: McGraw-Hill, 1947.

Hoeling, A. A. *The Franklin Comes Home.* New York: Hawthorne, 1974.

Hornfischer, James D. *The Last Stand of the Tin Can Sailors.* New York: Bantam, 2004.

Hoyt, Edwin P. *Nimitz and His Admirals: How They Won the War in the Pacific.* New York: Lyons, 2000.

"Idaho Was Site of Major Navy Training Base." *Headquarters Heliogram: Newsletter of the Council on America's Military Past,* July/August 2010, 9–10.

Jackson, Steve. *Lucky Lady: The World War II Heroics of the USS* Santa Fe *and* Franklin. New York: Carroll and Graf, 2003.

Karig, Walter, Russell L. Harris, and Frank A. Manson. *Battle Report: The End of an Empire.* New York: Rinehart and Company, 1948.

Manchester, William. *American Caesar: Douglas MacArthur, 1880–1964.* Boston: Little, Brown, 1978.

McKendree, Bishop D. *Barbed Wire and Rice: Poems and Songs from Japanese Prisoner-of-War Camps.* Ithaca, NY: Cornell University East Asia Program, 1995.

McManus, Larry. "Big Ben." *Yank: The Army Weekly,* June 15, 1945.

Mooney, James L. *Dictionary of American Naval Fighting Ships,* vol. 2. Washington, DC: Navy Department, 1963.

National Park Service. "The War Years on Saipan, Transcripts from Interviews with Residents." Micronesian Area Research Center, 1981. http://www.nps.gov/history/online_books/wapa/wapa_interviews.pdf.

Nilo, James R., and Robert St. Peters, eds. *USS* Franklin *(CV-13): The Ship That Wouldn't Die.* 1989. Reprint, Paducah, KY: Turner, 1996.

Oldham County Historical Commission. *Oldham County: 1881–1981.* Lubbock, TX: Taylor, 1981.

Olson, Michael Keith. *Tales from a Tin Can: The USS* Dale *from Pearl Harbor to Tokyo Bay.* St. Paul, MN: Zenith, 2007.

Prato, Peter J. *Saving Big Ben: The Saga of the USS* Franklin *(CV 13), and the Most Decorated Crew in Naval History.* Englewood, CO: Stress Resource, 2001.

Reeves, L. W. "The Ship They Couldn't Sink." *Saga: True Adventures for Men,* Summer 1955.

Reynolds, Quentin. "Chaplain Courageous: How Faith Saved the *Franklin.*" *Colliers,* June 23, 1945.

Satterfield, John R. *Saving Big Ben: The USS* Franklin *and Father Joseph T. O'Callahan.* Annapolis, MD: Naval Institute Press, 2011.

Sol, Martin. "Fighting Chaplain of the US Navy's Kamikazed Hell-Ship." *For Men Only,* November 1963.

"Spectacular Photos Tell Tale of Gallant Carrier, Heroic Men." *Abilene (TX) Reporter-News,* May 21, 1945, 3.

Springer, Joseph A. *Inferno: The Epic Life and Death Struggle of the USS* Franklin *in World War II.* St. Paul, MN: Zenith, 2007.

Taylor, Frederick. *Dresden: Tuesday 13 February 1945.* London: Bloomsbury, 2004.

Treadaway, Roy G. "Famed Carrier's Most Heroic Hours Recalled by Local Navy Recruiter." *Sweetwater (TX) Reporter,* March 19, 1959.

"U.S. Aircraft Carrier Defies Bombs and Fire." *Wichita (KS) Beacon,* May 19, 1945.

U.S. Navy. Bureau of Yards and Docks. *Building the Navy's Bases in World War II,* vol. 2. Washington, DC: U.S. Government Printing Office, 1947.

USS *Franklin* Museum Association. *USS* Franklin *(CV-13): Original Documents, 1943–1946.* Paducah, KY: Turner, 1994.

Utley, Robert M. *Lone Star Lawmen: The Second Century of the Texas Rangers.* Oxford: Oxford University Press, 2007.

Walton, Colonel. Frank E. "The Agony of the Franklin." *Military,* March 1988.

"We Can Take It, Too!: The Story of the USS *Franklin.*" *Air Ace.* December–January, 1946.

Video and Film

"Odell Price Talks about His Military Service." Video with Greg Conn and David Medlin. Milburn-Price Culture Museum, Vega, TX, May 26, 2015. https://www.youtube.com/watch?v=SYS-Os_SSWc&feature=youtu.be. Accessed August 29, 2015.

Oldham County Historical Commission. Video of WWII veterans Robert Fulton, Lloyd Glass, and William Russell. February 9, 2001.

U.S. Navy. *The Fighting Lady.* Motion picture documentary, 1944. http://www.youtube.com/watch?v=6dVq7lB0G6k. Accessed June 30, 2016.

ACKNOWLEDGMENTS

THE first acknowledgment must go to our mother, Grace Rogers, who soon after word came that Elden was "missing following action" began to write to others who might help her learn what had happened. She never found the evidence she wanted that he might still be alive somewhere, but she accumulated information that has been valuable in this effort. She bought an elegant cedar chest that became a shrine to Elden's memory, and in it she saved his uniforms and other mementos of his life, most importantly all of the letters and cards that make up the skeleton of this story.

Other family members have done important work. My two brothers, Gerald and Elvin, contributed immeasurably in recovering Vega, Texas, events and stories and in presenting them as accurately as possible. Their participation in our June 2008 "Session for Memories" and the 118 single-spaced pages of vignettes spanning almost four decades of experiences growing up in Vega were very important and may remain important in other ways in the future. Both of them interviewed surviving veterans of the USS *Franklin* to collect information, and Elvin has participated in five of their reunions. Our cousin Frances Rogers Dauner provided letters she had received from Elden's buddies during the war and sent other pertinent information over the years. Unfortunately neither Frances nor Gerald lived to see this book in print. Gerald's funeral occurred on March 19, 2013, sixty-eight years to the day after Elden's death. Gerald's sons, Steven Blane Rogers and Mark Alan Rogers, helped with research;

my son, Jeffrey Martin Rogers, and his daughter, Lauren Hunter Rogers, assisted me at the 2005 *Franklin* reunion; and my daughter, Tiana Rogers Conklin, helped me research Ancestry.com and joined me in gleaning details from the *Franklin's* deck logs, war diaries, and action reports at the National Archives in College Park, Maryland.

Several friends from Vega are owed thanks, above all the late Bishop D. McKendree, whose foresight in recognizing the importance of poems and songs written by fellow prisoners of war and whose courage in collecting and preserving them at the risk of his life stands out in this story. The closeness of the McKendree family to ours and Elden's frequent use of Bish as a reference point made him inescapably part of this story. His book, *Barbed Wire and Rice: Poems and Songs from Japanese Prisoner-of-War Camps,* published by Cornell University in 1995 as part of its East Asia Series, has been vital to me in many ways, and I am grateful to Bish's children, Alan D. McKendree, Dr. Jean McKendree, and Edith M. Shipley, for permission to quote selections from it and to use photographs. Bobby I. Walcott of Albuquerque, New Mexico, provided deep personal insights and vital information about his own experiences and about his brothers as well as about his close friend Elden. Laverna Price Higgins kindly shared letters and other documents of her late brother Asahel Leon Price, and her brother Odell Price and her cousin Wilburn Price provided vital information about Elden's mood in days shortly before his death. Greg Conn, of the Oldham County Historical Commission, captured Odell's recollections in a videotaped interview and provided earlier video interviews of veterans William Russell, Lloyd Glass, and Robert Fulton. Quincy Taylor, editor and publisher of the *Vega Enterprise,* informed people of my quest for photographs, and I am obliged to her and to those who responded, including Carolyn Richardson of the Oldham County Library, Karen Hobbs Wagner, David T. Whatley, and Sharon Mongomery Worsham. Gray's Studio kindly permitted use of Elden's portrait. William Henry Russ provided information about the Steward family, the late Harlow Sprouse shared insights into Vega nicknames, and I am especially fortunate to have been told by the late Merle Denny his recollection of the poignant moment when news came that Bish McKendree had survived.

I am most deeply indebted to the scholars, scribes, and collectors who ensured that the history of the USS *Franklin* was captured for posterity. The *USS* Franklin *(CV-13): Original Documents, 1943–1946*, made easily accessible by the USS *Franklin* Museum Association, and the personal recollections compiled and published by James R. Nilo and Robert St. Peters in USS Franklin *(CV-13): The Ship That Wouldn't Die* have provided an amazing array of detail. I am especially indebted to Steve Jackson for his book *Lucky Lady: The World War II Heroics of the USS* Santa Fe *and* Franklin, and to Joseph A. Springer for *Inferno: The Epic Life and Death Struggle of the USS* Franklin *in World War II*. These two outstanding works capture the histories of the ships in their subtitles and include numerous important documents and more than four hundred personal recollections of *Franklin* survivors; I have relied heavily on them in extracting the story of one sailor who did not live to be interviewed, and I gratefully commend both of them to anyone wanting to learn more. The online research service Ancestry.com has also been very helpful.

Several *Franklin* veterans contributed directly. Plane Captain Irvin R. Dahlen went out of his way to make sure I knew certain things. Also helpful were Paul Dalton, Karl Kraft, Jack Richardson, Ernest Scott, and especially Elden's best buddy, Roy Treadaway.

For advice and assistance in research, writing, and manuscript preparation I am indebted to David Brown, Chuck Myers, and Charles Varady of the USS *Hornet* Museum; Texas Tech University Professor Emeritus Paul Carlson; Valor in the Pacific National Historical Park historian Amanda Carona; retired National Park Service historian and superintendent Gary Cummins; Pearl Harbor survivor and outstanding volunteer researcher Ray Emory; retired National Park Service historians Harry Butowsky and Jerome Greene; retired National Park Service interpreter and Nimitz Naval Museum director Douglass Hubbard; Veterans Administration historian Sara Amy Leach; the USS *North Carolina* Museum; the USS *Yorktown* Museum; Tai Kreidler of the Southwest Collection, Texas Tech University; Warren Stricker and Millie Vanover of the Panhandle-Plains Historical Museum Research Center; Melvena Heisch of the Oklahoma Historical Society; Ian Thompson and Dora Wickison of the Choctaw Nation of Oklahoma; and the outstanding staff of the National Archives at College Park, Maryland.

David Colamaria and Tiffany Gwynn of the Naval History and Heritage Command provided prompt and courteous assistance with archival photographs. John Gilkes of John Gilkes Maps provided maps quickly and correctly. Gary Capshaw's assistance with family photographs was vital.

Retired National Park Service historians Richard West Sellars, Art Gomez, and David Clary read the entire manuscript and offered important suggestions, and retired National Park ranger Charles McCurdy read and contributed to the sections dealing with Saipan. Diane Albert advised me about special problems.

Distinguished historian of the American West Robert M. Utley has provided an inspiration and an example, and probably more upward boosts to my career than I know. His generosity in contributing a foreword is deeply appreciated.

I also thank the University of Oklahoma Press: editor-in-chief Charles E. Rankin, acquisitions editor J. Kent Calder, and manuscript editor Sarah C. Smith, as well as copy editor Robert Fullilove, all of whose encouragement and assistance have been exceptionally valuable.

My wife, Nancy Mydosh Burgas, assisted me at the 2005 *Franklin* reunion, contributed her considerable skills as an editor, helped me work through numerous dilemmas, and provided consolation on the countless occasions when my own words required me to push back from the keyboard for a moment and brush away tears.

INDEX

Page references in *italics* indicate illustrations.

commendation for, 246–47; used as decoy, 137–38; us-them separations on, 125–26; V Divisions on, 104–6; working conditions on, 126–27. *See also* Dowell, Saxie; Gehres, Leslie; 704 Club

USS *Franklin* Association, 366
USS *Gambier Bay*, 227
USS *General Hugh L. Scott*, 345
USS *General J. R. Brooke*, 63
USS *Gridley*, 228
USS *Guam*, 280
USS *Hancock*, 141, 148, 304, 316, 324
USS *Hickox*, 327
USS *Hoel*, 140, 163, 222, 227, 235, 369
USS *Hornet*, 31, 32, 122, 131, 137, *175*, 283, 389n4 (ch. 19)
USS *Houston*, 207, 279, 367
USS *Hunt*, 322, 327
USS *Indiana*, 385n24
USS *Intrepid*, 313
USS *Irwin*, 226
USS *Johnston*, 227
USS *Langley*, 31, 32
USS *Leary*, 96, 121
USS *Lexington*, 31
USS *Marshall*, 327
USS *Maury*, 228
USS *Miller*, 325, 327, 345, 350
USS *Monterey*, 122, 144
USS *Montpelier*, 378n12
USS *Mount Hood*, 388n18
USS *New Orleans*, 193
USS *North Carolina*, 304, 316, 321
USS *Owen*, 306
USS *Patterson*, 191
USS *PC-1260*, 167
USS *Pensacola*, 110, 299
USS *Phelps*, 144
USS *Piedmont*, 162, 194, 299, 369, 383n19, 388n18

USS *Pittsburgh*, 304, 326
USS *Princeton*, 226, 323
USS *Roberts*, 227
USS *Rowe*, 121
USS *Samuel B. Roberts*, 227
USS *San Diego*, 122
USS *San Jacinto*, 183, 193, 209, 304
USS *San Juan*, 122
USS *Santa Fe*, 304, 316, 323–25
USS *St. Lo*, 228
USS *The Sullivans*, 123, 141, 147–48
USS *Ticonderoga*, 32
USS *Tingey*, 148, 327
USS *Twiggs*, 96, 121
USS *Vincennes*, 123
USS *Washington*, 304
USS *Wasp*, 31, 98, 144, 154, 233, 327
USS *Wasp II*, 122
USS *West Virginia*, 4, 360
USS *Yorktown*, 31
USS *Yorktown II*, 122, 131, *175*, 178, 273, 283, 313, 316

Valentine, Billy, 249, 250
Valentine, R. C., Jr., 161, 162
Van Meter, John, 7
Vásquez de Coronado, Francisco, 12
V-E Day, 361
Vega, Tex., 16–17, 69–70, 83, 115, *171*, *181*, 284, 335, 361; barbershop in, 20–21; childhood in, 22–23; culture of, 18–23; demographics of, 15; fire truck in, 288–89; growth of, 14–15; postwar, 363; Red Cross chapter in, 117–18; Rogerses buying city blocks in, 46; Rogers's family move to, 12–14; school plays in, 8–9, 317–18; scrap drive in, 117; telephone company in, 19–20; town drunks in, 21–22; victory gardens in, 113; war's effect on, 24–25, 27–28
Vega Drug Store, 13, 14, 20, 116
venereal disease, 243